Volume Two

Trends in the Judiciary

Interviews with Judges Across the Globe

Interviews with Global Leaders in Policing, Courts, and Prisons Series

International Police Executive Symposium Co-Publications

Dilip K. Das, *Founding President-IPES*

PUBLISHED

Trends in the Judiciary: Interviews with Judges Across the Globe, Volume One
By Dilip K. Das and Cliff Roberson with Michael Berlin, ISBN: 978-1-4200-9978-2

Trends in Policing: Interviews with Police Leaders Across the Globe, Volume Four
By Bruce F. Baker and Dilip K. Das, ISBN: 978-1-4398-8073-9

Trends in Policing: Interviews with Police Leaders Across the Globe, Volume Three
By Otwin Marenin and Dilip K. Das, ISBN: 978-1-4398-1924-1

Trends in Policing: Interviews with Police Leaders Across the Globe
By Dilip K. Das and Otwin Marenin, ISBN: 978-1-4200-7520-5

Trends in Corrections: Interviews with Corrections Leaders Around the World
By Jennie K. Singer, Dilip K. Das, and Eileen Ahlin, ISBN: 978-1-4398-3578-4

Trends in Corrections: Interviews with Corrections Leaders Around the World, Volume Two
By Martha Henderson Hurley and Dilip K. Das, ISBN: 978-1-4665-9156-1

Trends in the Judiciary: Interviews with Judges Across the Globe, Volume Two
by David Lowe and Dilip K. Das, ISBN: 978-1-4822-1916-6

FORTHCOMING

Trends in Policing: Interviews with Police Leaders Across the Globe, Volume Five
By Bruce K. Baker and Dilip K. Das, ISBN: 978-1-4822-2449-8

Volume Two

Trends in the
Juapgend Judiciary

Interviews with Judges Across the Globe

David Lowe, Ph.D.
Liverpool John Moores University School of Law, UK

Dilip K. Das, Ph.D.
Founding President, International Police Executive Symposium, IPES
Founding Editor-in-Chief,
Police Practice and Research: An International Journal, PPR

With Assistance from
Michael M. Berlin, J.D., Ph.D.
Coppin State University, Baltimore, Maryland, USA

International Police Executive Symposium
Co-Publication

CRC Press
Taylor & Francis Group
Boca Raton London New York

CRC Press is an imprint of the
Taylor & Francis Group, an **informa** business

CRC Press
Taylor & Francis Group
6000 Broken Sound Parkway NW, Suite 300
Boca Raton, FL 33487-2742

© 2015 by Taylor & Francis Group, LLC
CRC Press is an imprint of Taylor & Francis Group, an Informa business

No claim to original U.S. Government works

Printed on acid-free paper
Version Date: 20140728

International Standard Book Number-13: 978-1-4822-1916-6 (Hardback)

Visit the Taylor & Francis Web site at
http://www.taylorandfrancis.com

and the CRC Press Web site at
http://www.crcpress.com

This book is dedicated to the memory of Austin Turk, an excellent scholar, an editor of IPES/CRC Press publications, and an inspiration.

Contents

IPES Preface

The International Police Executive Symposium (IPES) was founded in 1994 to address one major challenge, that is, the two worlds of research and practice remain disconnected, even though cooperation between the two is growing. A major reason is that the two groups speak in different languages. The research is published in hard-to-access journals and presented in a manner that is difficult for some to comprehend. On the other hand, police practitioners tend not to mix with researchers and remain secretive about their work. Consequently, there is little dialogue between the two and almost no attempt to learn from one another. The global dialog among police researchers and practitioners is limited. True, the literature on the police is growing exponentially. But its impact on day-to-day policing is negligible.

The aims and objectives of the IPES are to provide a forum to foster closer relationships among police researchers and practitioners on a global scale; to facilitate cross-cultural, international, and interdisciplinary exchanges for the enrichment of the law enforcement profession; to encourage discussion; and to publish research on challenging and contemporary problems facing the policing profession. One of the most important activities of the IPES is the organization of an annual meeting under the auspices of a police agency or an educational institution. Now in its 17th year, the annual meeting, a 5-day initiative on specific issues relevant to the policing profession, brings together ministers of interior and justice, police commissioners and chiefs, members of academia representing world-renown institutions, and many more criminal justice elite from over 60 countries. It facilitates interaction and the exchange of ideas and opinions on all aspects of policing. The agenda is structured to encourage dialog in both formal and informal settings.

Another important aspect of the meeting is the publication of the best papers presented edited by well-known criminal justice scholars and police professionals who attend the meetings. The best papers are selected, thoroughly revised, fully updated, meticulously edited, and published as books based upon the theme of each meeting. This repository of knowledge under the co-publication imprint of IPES and CRC Press/Taylor & Francis Group chronicles the important contributions of the International Police Executive Symposium over the last two decades. As a result, in 2011 the United Nations awarded IPES a Special Consultative Status for the Economic and Social Council (ECSOC) honoring its importance in the global security community.

In addition to this book series, the IPES also has a research journal, *Police Practices and Research: An International Journal* (PPR). The PPR contains research articles on police issues from practitioners and researchers. It is an international journal in the true sense of the term and is distributed worldwide. For more information on the PPR, visit http://www.tandf.co.uk/journals/GPPR.

It is within the IPES ethos that the second volume of Trends in the Judiciary has been published. Its aim is to bring to scholars, practitioners, and interested parties the personal views from members of the judiciary from around the world. The main medium to ascertain judges' views are case reports. As judges are either interpreting statute or in common law states actually making law, it is difficult to look beneath the surface to find out what judges opinions and values really are. This book goes some way to allowing the reader to do this, thus making it unique in the study of law and criminal justice.

IPES advocates, promotes, and propagates that criminal justice is one of the most basic and essential avenues for improving the quality of life in all nations: rich and poor, modern and traditional, large and small, as well as peaceful and strife-ridden. IPES actively works to drive home to all its office bearers, supporters, and admirers that, in order to reach its full potential as an instrument of service to humanity, criminal justice must be fully and enthusiastically open to collaboration between research and practice, global exchange of information between practitioners and academics, universal dissemination and sharing of best practices, generating thinking leaders and followers, as well as reflecting and writing on the issues challenging to the profession.

Through its annual meetings, hosts, institutional supporters, and publications, IPES reaffirms that criminal justice is a moral profession with unflinching adherence to the rule of law and human rights as the embodiment of humane values.

Dilip K. Das
Founding President, International Police Executive Symposium,
www.ipes.info

Book Series Editor for

Advances in Police Theory and Practice
Interviews with Global Leaders in Policing, Courts, and Prisons
CRC Press/Taylor & Francis Group

PPR Special Issues as Books
Routledge/Taylor & Francis Group

Founding Editor-in-Chief
Police Practice and Research: An International Journal, PPR
http://www.tandfonline.com/GPPR

Foreword

Judges play an important role in society, but society may not always understand the work that judges do or the way in which they do it. Therefore, any endeavor that seeks to bring the crucial work of judging into perspective for the public at large is to be warmly welcomed.

What this book provides is a window into the world of judging—whether in Ghana, Serbia, or the United States. It gives a broad overview of the different ways in which countries have approached the creation of a modern judiciary and a modern judge both from the perspective of the common law and civil law systems.

All judges are required to weigh the interests of the state, corporations, and the citizen in order to do justice or, in the words of the judicial oath in this country, "to do right to all manner of people according to the laws and usages of the Realm without fear or favor affection or ill will." Each country, however, has its own approach. Different judicial systems generate different complaints and, from the perspective of the judges they have interviewed, the researchers have drawn out the idiosyncrasies and tensions inherent in complex systems of modern law.

Too often, academic writing—especially in the law—suffers from being impenetrable to those without legal knowledge. This volume has sought to maximize both readability and fidelity to the views of the judges interviewed and there is substantial reference both to interview transcripts and to wider contextual information. In addition, it provides an insight to anyone interested, whether practitioner, academic, or member of the public, into the way in which judges approach their work. It straddles judicial studies and criminology in a new and interesting way, and I hope it will be of use to all those interested in systems of justice around the world.

As both chancellor of Liverpool John Moores University and the president of the Queen's Bench Division in England and Wales, it was entirely reasonable that Dilip Das and David Lowe thought that I might be well placed to introduce this wide-ranging piece of research. I am delighted to do so.

The Rt Hon Sir Brian Leveson
Royal Courts of Justice
London

Acknowledgments

The editors are most grateful to Michael Berlin, JD, PhD, for the support he gave to this book project, for his reading of the penultimate draft, and for his advice in drawing up the final draft. In brief, his help was most essential in completing the second volume of *Trends in the Judiciary*.

The editors would also like to thank the Right Honourable Sir Brian Leveson, president of the United Kingdom's Queen's Bench Division at the Royal Courts of Justice and one of the United Kingdom's most senior judges, for kindly agreeing to write the foreword for this book.

The editors also want to thank all the judges who agreed to be interviewed along with the interviewers for writing up their contributions. It was their contributions made this book possible.

The editors would especially like to thank CRC Press/Taylor & Francis for their support in the production of this book, in particular; Carolyn Spence, senior acquisitions editor; Richard Tressider, project editor; and Clive Lawson, project manager at Deanta Global; whose patience and advice throughout the production of this book was invaluable.

Editors

David Lowe is a principal lecturer at Liverpool John Moores University's Law School. Prior to becoming an academic, he was a police officer for 27 years with the UK Merseyside Police. Most of his service was as a detective, with most of his detective service being in the United Kingdom's Special Branch Counter-Terrorism Unit. His work in the area of policing, terrorism, and security has been published in books and journals, with his latest work being in 2013, *Examining Political Violence: Studies in Terrorism, Counterterrorism and Internal War.* In addition to his recent publications, he is regularly used by the television, radio, and print media (particularly the BBC) in the United Kingdom and the rest of Europe and the United States for commentary in these areas.

Dilip K. Das is a professor of criminal justice, former police chief, founding editor-in-chief of *Police Practice and Research: An International Journal*, and a human rights consultant to the United Nations. Dilip served in the Indian Police Service for 14 years. In 1994, he founded the International Police Executive Symposium (IPES), which enjoys special consultative status in the United Nations. He has authored, edited, and coedited more than 30 books and numerous articles. He is editor-in-chief of two book series, "Advances in Police Theory and Practice" and "Interviews with Global Leaders in Policing, Courts, and Prisons" (with CRC Press/Taylor & Francis). Dilip has received several faculty excellence awards and is a Distinguished Faculty Lecturer.

Contributors

Brian S. Akrong is a native of Ghana and a lecturer in English and Communication Skills in the University of Professional Studies, Accra, Ghana. Following his secondary education, he trained as a teacher and later graduated in English and theater arts from the University of Ghana with a bachelor of arts (honors) and subsequently obtained a master of arts in teaching English as a second language. He also holds a postgraduate certificate in public administration from the Ghana Institute of Management and Public Administration (GIMPA) and is currently studying law at the GIMPA Law School.

Lauren M. Block is a PhD candidate at Washington State University in the Department of Criminal Justice and Criminology. Her research interests are in the areas of administration of criminal justice, prosecution and adjudication, indigent defense, judicial discretion, racial and ethnic disparity, and inequality.

Remi Boivin is assistant professor at the School of Criminology (University of Montreal) and regular researcher at the International Centre for Comparative Criminology. His research focuses on police interventions, policy-making and crime analysis. His work has appeared in *Police Quarterly, Social Indicators Research, International Journal on Drug Policy, Global Crime,* and *Canadian Journal of Criminology and Criminal Justice.*

Anna Carline and **Clare Gunby** both work at the University of Leicester, in the School of Law and Department of Criminology, respectively. Jointly and individually, they have published extensively on the issues of violence against women and sexual offenses, particularly rape, and the reforms contained in the Sexual Offences Act 2003. As part of their research, they interviewed counsel on the impact of the 2003 rape law reforms. Their most recent project involves evaluating a media campaign, organized by Liverpool City Council, aimed at preventing sexual assault in the night-time economy.

Emma Davies is a senior lecturer in the School of Law at Liverpool John Moores University. Working across the public, not-for-profit, academic, and private sectors, Emma's work has informed research, legislation, policy, and practice in the interests of vulnerable children. She led the establishment of Auckland's multiagency center for child abuse investigations and developed the Court Education for Young Witnesses program in New Zealand. Her research on child witnesses in the criminal justice system includes child victims' experiences of an adversarial system and the language and tactics used in criminal courts to question children.

Oko Elechi is the chair of the Criminal Justice Department at Mississippi Valley State University. He received his PhD from Simon Fraser University, Canada. He also holds two degrees from the University of Oslo, Norway. He was, between 2007 and 2013, an associate professor in the Justice Studies Department Doctoral Program, Prairie View A & M University. His writings on restorative justice, community policing and the African indigenous justice systems have been extensively published in international journals, book chapters and anthologies. He is also the author of the book *Doing Justice Without the State: The Afikpo (Ehugbo) Nigeria Model*, published in 2006 by Routledge, New York.

Michael T. Eskey, Jr. has worked in public education operations and facility management at the University of Georgia for the last 7 years and has also spent time working for the Gwinnett (Georgia) County Government. He was awarded his doctorate of public administration from Valdosta State University (2013). He holds a master's degree in administration from the University of Georgia and a bachelor of arts degree in political science from the University of Georgia. He currently is pursuing a second master's degree in criminal justice from Albany State University.

Michael T. Eskey, Sr. is an associate professor of criminal justice and the program coordinator of the Criminal Justice Administration Department of Park University. The department has over 700 majors, the majority of which are online students. He is currently on half-time release as an online instructor evaluator with Park Distance Learning. Michael earned his PhD in criminology at the Florida State University in 1982. Additionally, he earned a master of science in strategic intelligence from the Joint Military Intelligence College (1994) and a master of science degree from the University of Nebraska at Omaha in 1977. He has taught at the college level since his retirement from the military in 2001 at the rank of colonel. He has developed a number of online courses at the undergraduate and graduate level. Additionally, he has published and presented extensively in the area of criminal justice and online learning.

Jane Goodman-Delahunty is trained in law and psychology and currently is a research professor at Charles Sturt University. She served as editor of

Psychology, Public Policy, and Law, and as president of both the American Psychology–Law Society and the Australia and New Zealand Association of Psychiatry, Psychology and Law. Her research promotes evidence-based policies to enhance justice and is informed by her experience as a litigator, administrative judge, mediator, third-party neutral investigator, and part-time commissioner with the Law Reform Commission of New South Wales.

Tracey Green is associate dean (Policing and International) at Charles Sturt University. She is a former U.K. police officer and since joining the university has developed a history of collaboration with domestic and international police and law enforcement agencies, ensuring that educational and research opportunities are relevant and aligned to policing.

Gerald Dapaah Gyamfi is a PhD candidate at the University of Phoenix; holder of master of science in human resource development, University of Manchester, United Kingdom; and a fellow of the Institute of Chartered Secretaries and Administrators, United Kingdom. He is the dean of management studies and teaches risk management and operations management courses at the University of Professional Studies, Ghana. He is the owner of Geraldo Travel & Tours Ltd. He has authored some refereed books and articles in journals and presented papers at conferences including IPES/UN 2012 at the United Nations.

Pavol Kopinec is a researcher at the Institute of Social Studies and Curative Education at the Comenius University in Bratislava. His main subject of interest is migration and the human rights protection of vulnerable groups. He has worked as a program manager for refugee camps in Slovakia and with the Separated Children in Europe Program as a coordinator of support to unaccompanied children coming to the Slovak Republic. He has participated in international teams monitoring the living and care conditions of children in the asylum process and detention centers in various European countries. From 2011, he worked as a consultant for the International Organisation for Migration in the capacity-building field. He has published two books on working standards and provision of high-quality services to refugees and vulnerable groups.

Peter C. Kratcoski received his doctorate in sociology from Pennsylvania State University in 1969. He accept a position in the Department of Sociology at Kent State University in 1969 and retired from Kent State University in 1996. He currently serves as emeritus adjunct professor of sociology and justice studies. His specialty areas are juvenile delinquency and justice, police studies and corrections. He has written or edited many books, chapters and journal articles, the most recent books being *Juvenile Justice Administration* (2012) *and Financial Crimes: A Threat to Global Security* (2012).

Chloe Leclerc is assistant professor at the School of Criminology, University of Montreal. She teaches penology and sentencing. She is also regular researcher at the International Centre for Comparative Criminology. Her research focuses on decision making in the criminal justice system, with a particular focus on sentencing. She currently studies decisions involving plea bargaining. She is also interested in public opinion on the criminal justice system.

Alison Lui qualified as a solicitor and practiced commercial law before joining Liverpool John Moores University, where she teaches commercial law subjects. In 2011, she was awarded a Winston Churchill Fellowship. The fellowship enabled her to conduct research on corporate governance and regulation of banks in the United States and Canada. In 2012, she was a joint winner of a HEA grant for employability and social media. In 2013, Alison was awarded an Early Career Researcher Fellowship that led to her working at the Rotman School of Management, University of Toronto, on corporate governance projects. Alison has published a number of journal articles in corporate governance and banking regulation.

Ida Nguyen is currently in the final stages of her undergraduate law degree at the University of New South Wales and has been working as a research assistant with Professor Jane Goodman-Delahunty on her research on the relationship between empirical methods and legal practice. She has a passion for social justice and aspires to become an advocate in bringing attention and change to social and procedural justice issues within organizations and the wider community.

Smart E. Otu is the current head of the Political Science/Sociology/Psychology Department at the Federal University Ndufu Alike Ikwo Abakaliki, Ebonyi State, Nigeria. He is a graduate of the University of Port Harcourt (bachelor of science), University of Ibadan (master of science; DLittPhil, criminology), University of South Africa (DPhil, sociology), and the University of the Western Cape, Cape Town. Otu is a fellow of the West African Research Association (WARA) and a former intern of the Drug Policy Research Centre, RAND Corporation, Santa Monica, California. His areas of research interests include illegal drug trafficking and use, armed robbery, corruption, theory deconstruction and reconstruction, and policing, among others.

Gavin Oxburgh is a consultant forensic psychologist, a chartered psychologist and scientist, and chair and founding director of the International Investigative Interviewing Research Group (www.iiirg.org). He works in close collaboration with many police forces and law enforcement agencies around the world (including the International Criminal Court and the United Nations), providing advice, guidance, and training on a variety of topics including communication in legal contexts; investigative interviewing of victims, witnesses, and suspects; historical allegations of child sexual abuse; and online child exploitation.

Cara Rabe-Hemp is an associate professor in the Department of Criminal Justice Sciences at Illinois State University. Her research interests include gender and policing, small and rural policing, citizen perceptions of the police, police deviance, and autonomous learning and student engagement in the online classroom. Her recent publications have appeared in the *Women and Criminal Justice, Police Quarterly, Feminist Criminology, Journal of Criminal Justice,* and *Policing: An International Journal of Police Strategies and Management.* In 2010, Cara was awarded the University Research Initiative Award.

Blake M. Randol is an assistant professor in criminal justice at the University of Wisconsin–Milwaukee. His research interests are in the areas of criminal justice administration, organizational theory, research methods, and statistics.

Branislav Simonović is a full-time professor of criminal investigation (criminalistics) at the Faculty of Law, University of Kragujevac, Serbia. For years, he has taught at the Police Academies in Bosnia and Herzegovina. He has appeared as an expert witness at the International Criminal Tribunal in Hague. Topics of interest and research are community policing, corruption, criminal investigation, interrogation, strategic planning in areas of policing, and so on. He has participated in a number of international conferences. He has written many scientific papers, some of which he has written as a coauthor with his international colleagues.

Introduction

With the judiciary playing one of the most important roles in the criminal justice system, the main method of assessing judges' opinions, values, and ethics is reading case reports. As cases appear before the courts, especially where judges are interpreting statutes, or in common law jurisdictions where they are actually making law, due to the legal rules binding their actions one has to read between the lines to ascertain where each judge stands on issues. Because of this, one can only surmise what factors influence judges in their decision making. As a result, the main reason for embarking on this piece of research was to elicit responses from judges outside the courtroom that reflected their views, opinions, and philosophy that underpin their role. It is believed that this study is an important addition to criminological studies as while there have been plenty of studies conducted on other criminal justice agencies such as the police, very few have been carried out on the judiciary.

Aim of the Interviews and the Instructions to Interviewers

In order to elicit judges' responses that would encourage them to open up and reveal their views on issues affecting their role, a set of instructions that included a questionnaire guide was produced by the editors to assist the interviewers.* The instructions stressed to the interviewers when writing up their interviews that it was important to present verbatim the judges' views along with their interpretations of legal developments and current issues in their particular criminal law and procedural field. The three general themes the interview targeted were

1. What do justices and judges see happening in criminal law and procedure?
2. What are the issues they consider important?
3. What changes do they see as successes or failures? What is the likely lasting future or passing fads?

* A copy of the instructions/questionnaire is in Appendix A.

To facilitate this, in drafting the questionnaire guide's instructions to interviewers, five topic areas were selected by the editors. The first was regarding a judge's career where the intention was to provide the reader with the judges' experiences during their legal careers, the legal developments they had seen, and what they had found as rewarding in their career. To enable the reader to appreciate what underpins the respective judges' decision making, the judges were asked questions related to their personal judicial philosophy. The aim of this topic was for the judges to discuss what they saw as the role of the judiciary in society and how that role conflicted or complemented relations with political groups, other agencies within the criminal justice system, and the community.

This linked into the topic area covering the problems and successes the respective judges experienced where the judges were encouraged to discuss which policies and programs had worked well and those which had not. This section would allow the judges to put forward any changes they would introduce to improve the legal system. To underpin the opinions they had on policies and programs, the fourth topic area was the relationship for the judges between theory and practice. The aim of this section was to draw out views judges had regarding what practitioners could learn from legal/criminological theory. The responses given for this topic area would allow for an assessment to see if this relationship exists and if it does, if it works. This topic area also explores the kind of research judges find the most useful in practice and if they carry supplementary research outside the research required in pending cases.

Increasingly, respective national jurisdictions have to deal with criminal cases emanating from transnational organized crime as well as the international terrorist threat. In addition to this, some jurisdictions, especially those in Europe, have to give consideration to the decision of courts from supranational/quasi-governmental bodies such as the European Union (EU). With bodies such as the EU having a law-making capacity, and with EU law being supreme in its Member States, those states must incorporate that law into their domestic legislative process. A consequence of this is that the decisions of the EU's court, the European Court of Justice's (ECJ), bind those of the national courts in their respective Member States' jurisdictions. Along with the EU, in Europe another supranational body whose jurisprudence is influential is the Council of Europe and its court, the European Court of Human Rights (ECtHR). It has been agreed that the ECtHR decisions are to be applied as guidance by national domestic courts when interpreting the jurisprudence of the European Convention on Human Rights (ECHR) in national domestic courts, and they should be followed. As a result, the fifth topic allowed the judges to discuss transnational relations and give them the opportunity to say how they have been affected by them and if any of these interactions have been beneficial or harmful. The interviewers were also supplied with questions to consider using during the interview relating to the judge's satisfaction with the criminal law and procedure in their respective systems and developments the judges would like to see.

The contributors were instructed to describe how the interview went and their impression of the interview regarding how the views expressed by the respective judges accord with known literature. Where relevant, a glossary of terms is added at the conclusion of each chapter.

Africa

The interviews submitted for this volume are separated into four parts based upon the continent they emanate from. Sections I and II present two interviews from Africa, with judges from Ghana and Nigeria. Gerald Gymfi and Brian Akrong's interview with Justice Anin-Yeboah is the first in this series of interviews. The current judicial service of Ghana can be traced back to the establishment of the Gold Coast Supreme Court of Judicature by the Westminster Imperial Parliament Ordinance in 1876, when Ghana was a colony in the British Empire. Since its independence and following two military coups that resulted in changes to Ghana's court structures, Ghana's legal system is still based on the common law system with the Supreme Court being the superior court in Ghana followed by the Court of Appeal and the High Court. After being called to the Ghanaian Bar in the 1980s, Mr. Justice Anin-Yeboah worked as an advocate for nearly 20 years before being appointed as a judge to Ghana's High Court. After serving for 5 years at the Court of Appeal, Mr. Justice Anin-Yeboah was promoted to his current position as a Supreme Court judge. In his interview, Mr. Justice Anin-Yeboah gives interesting responses on the development of Alternate Dispute Resolution along with the police's role in criminal matters and ensuring the judiciary remains politically independent by avoiding compromises. Mr. Justice Anin-Yeboah's comments on the role chiefs play in land boundary disputes are illuminating.

Elechi and Out's interview with Judge Eze Udu from Ebonbyi's State Court in Nigeria resulted in some very open and frank opinions given by Judge Udu on the judicial process in Nigeria. A federal system with dual jurisdiction, the Nigerian judiciary comprises of two levels of administration: federal appellate courts and the state judiciary that exercises judicial power within that state's jurisdiction. The key themes from Judge Udu's responses was how the Ebonyi state judiciary are experiencing the challenges of federal government interference, corruption, a paucity of funds, and, due to the increase in criminal activity, a pressure to deliver judgments swiftly. Also, the theme of Nigerian judges raising the bar of their transnational relationships emerged, which requires a commitment for judges to attend international conferences and symposia in order to gain from the exchange of ideas

xxx   Introduction

and practices carried out in the judicial sector. Nigerian judges' knowledge of legal developments also needs to be updated, to facilitate quality administration of justice.

Asia and Australasia

Sections III through V contain interviews with judges from Asia and Australasia, and Section III starts with Tracey Green's interview with Duncan Chappell, who was a judge's associate in Tasmania. He has had a varied legal career spanning academia, where he has taught law at a number of universities around the world. He has also had a varied career in legal practice that includes being a commissioner with the Australian Law Reform Commission in 1978; a director of the Australian Institute of Criminology, an Australian government agency; and deputy president of the Australian Federal Administrative Appeals Tribunal. This chapter reveals the inner workings of a number of judicial processes in Australia supported by illuminating responses from Duncan Chappell on judicial life in Australia, covering issues ranging from the loneliness of the role to the decision-making difficulties judges face in balancing the interests of different parties before them equitably. Born from his experience of Mental Health Review Tribunals, unique in this interview are Duncan Chappell's open and forthright views of the links between criminal activity and mental health.

Chapter 4 is Jane Goodman-Delahunty's interview with the Honorable James Wood AO QC. Currently holding the position of chair of the State Parole Authority, after graduating from Sydney University's Law School he became a solicitor, but was a barrister from 1970 to 1984. Following Justice Wood's wide experience as an advocate, he was appointed as a judge to the Common Law Division of the New South Wales (NSW) Supreme Court examining mainly personal injury claims, where he eventually was appointed to the NSW Supreme Court. In addition to serving on the benches of the respective NSW courts, Justice Wood has led a number of high-profile Australian public inquiries including an inquiry into the actions of three members of the Ananda Marga religious sect for their role in potential terrorist acts in 1985, the NSW Police Royal Commission into police corruption in 1994, and an inquiry into child protection services in NSW in 2005. Justice Wood's interview covers a number of key themes including child protection, his concerns about the provision of legal aid, and equitable access to the law and the consistency of sentencing policies.

Section IV contains Alison Lui's interview with the Honorable Mr. Justice Michael Lunn, Justice of Appeal of the High Court in Hong Kong. A former British colony (1841–1997), Hong Kong's judiciary still operates under the English common law framework and retains its judicial independence from the rest of China. In Mr. Justice Lunn's responses, issues regarding the changes introduced since independence are covered, including the current lack of procedural guidance when compared to the protocols and direction that came from England. Giving examples such as bail applications and unmeritorious appeals, Mr. Justice Lunn believes this can only be remedied by a new set of rules. Another significant area of judicial process Mr. Justice Lunn covers is judicial review, where judges review the lawfulness of decisions or actions by public authorities. In what can be a frustrating process, he explains why he believes the boundary of law and politics are often blurred.

Section V contains an interview by Emma Davies with Judge Mick Brown from New Zealand. The main feature in this interview is that Judge Brown was New Zealand's first Maori District Court Judge. He is unique as he not only sat in New Zealand's Criminal Courts, which are based on the British model, he also sat at the Waitangi Tribunals that allow Maoris redress against the New Zealand government for breaches of the 1840 Waitangi Treaty signed between the British government and Maori people. The responses from Judge Brown provide a fascinating insight into the youth justice and court system, where he played an influential role in the development of youth justice in New Zealand. In particular, it shows how his work in this area was influential in the development of New Zealand's legislation on children and young persons.

Europe

Sections VI though VIII contain interviews with judges from Europe. Section VI presents Branislav Simonović's interview with Judge Dragomir Milojević, the president of the Supreme Court of Serbia. Elected to the Municipal Court of Kragujerac in 1982, Judge Milojević became a District Court judge before moving to the Serbian Supreme Court in 1999, where he became president of the Supreme Court in 2013. The interview covers a discussion on how corporate crime cases in Serbia are inefficient because of insufficient training of judges, frequent changes of regulations, and excessively long expert testimony. He also covers how Serbian judges can be intimidated by the possibility of losing their job through political interference, and how the nature of corruption in Serbian courts is a matter of politics and propaganda. Judge Milojević also discusses how Serbia has too many procedural and substantive laws and the impact this has along with the, in his opinion, excessively frequent changes to the law.

Section VII contains Pavol Kopinec's interview with Judge Kamil Ivánek, a judge in Bratislava's Regional Court in Slovakia. Following the Velvet Revolution and the end of the Cold War in 1993, Czechoslovakia was broken up into two republic states, the Czech and Slovakian Republics. Being formed in January 1993, certainly in European terms, Slovakia is a relatively new state. In line with most mainland European states, Slovakia's judicial system is based on the continental law system, which has no common law provision where judges make laws. Being a member of the EU, Slovakia's legal system, along with those of the other 27 Member States, has to implement EU law into its domestic provision and follow the decisions of the ECJ along with taking cognizance of the decisions of the ECtHR on matters related to the ECHR. The primary role of the judges in the Slovakian judicial system is statutory interpretation. Judge Ivánek began his legal career in the late 1980s, when Czechoslovakia was part of the Warsaw Pact countries under the influence of the former Soviet Union. Judge Ivánek reveals an insight into life during this period as following the end of his secondary education he was unable to secure entry into law school and, because under the Communist regime it was a criminal offense to be unemployed, he began work as a laborer. Covering the legal and cultural issues from that point along with his life experiences, the responses given by Judge Ivánek provide a revealing and illuminating account of the transformation the Slovakia judicial system underwent as the state moved from being a Communist regime to one that became a member of the EU engaged in free trade.

Chapters 9 through 11 comprise Section VIII, which includes interviews with three U.K. judges. Tracing the origins of the U.K. legal system is a moot historical point. It has been claimed that it can be traced back to the Anglo-Saxon King Athelstan, who in 932 introduced a legal code that strengthened his royal control over Britain (The Royal Household n.d.). As this was an Anglo-Saxon legal model interrupted by the Norman invasion of 1066, one can understand why there is strong advocacy that the current UK legal system is based on the common law system set up by King Henry II in 1166. As seen in a number of the chapters in this book, the U.K. system has been influential in the origins of a number of legal systems around the world. Underpinning the U.K. legal process is a common law system of judge-made law, but with the increasing number of statutes introduced by the U.K. Parliament from the nineteenth century, one of the main roles of U.K. judges is statutory interpretation. Like Slovakia, the United Kingdom is a Member State of the EU and has signed up to the Council of Europe's ECHR, and it too has to follow EU law (Kaczorowska 2011) and take cognizance of the ECtHR's ruling on human rights issues (Fenwick and Phillipson 2011). Having a legal system established for a 1000 years, rulings from the EU and ECtHR decisions have been a cause of recent political consternation resulting in debates on whether U.K. justice would be better served by leaving the EU and withdrawing from the ECHR.

Chapter 9 is an interview by Emma Davies and David Lowe with the senior circuit judge and honorary recorder Mr. Justice Clement Goldstone QC. Most of his career has been in criminal law as both an advocate and a judge. Mr. Justice Goldstone was appointed as a circuit judge and has been a chairman of the Mental Health Review Tribunal. He is currently the Honorary Recorder of Liverpool, making him a senior circuit judge and since 2009 he has been authorized to sit in the U.K. Court of Appeal (Criminal Division). As with all of the interviews contained in this book, Mr. Justice Goldstone's responses are candid and reveal issues underpinning the judge's role, a role he sees as being to instill confidence in the public by the way they dispense justice. For Mr. Justice Goldstone, that is achieved by trying cases fairly, passing appropriate sentences, and making sure that cases are tried as quickly as possible. With this ethos in mind, Mr. Justice Goldstone's erudite views on the United Kingdom's cuts to legal aid reveal his passion for the law and the equitable deliverance of justice. Likewise, his passion for the law is reflected in his comments on youth justice.

Chapter 10 is Anna Carline and Clare Gunby's interview with His Honor Justice David Harris QC. Although recently retired (2012), Mr. Justice Harris is unique, as not only did he sit in criminal and family courts in the United Kingdom, he is also an academic lawyer. After graduating from Oxford University with a PhD, he researched tort law and has been a coeditor of one of the leading textbooks in tort, *Winfield and Jolowicz on Tort*.* As seen in his responses, jurisprudence has been influential in how he performed in his role as a judge. Examples of this are seen in his candid responses regarding his views on case management and the increasing lengthy sentencing guidelines that have, in Mr. Justice Harris' opinion, resulted in complexity in their application. He also discusses his concerns regarding the gradual reduction in judicial discretion in the areas of both criminal and family law that in Mr. Justice Harris' view is a result of a misconceived distrust of the judicial decision making in the respective courts. Also interesting are the positives Mr. Justice Harris has witnessed such as the development in the quality of judicial training at the U.K. Judicial College.

Chapter 11 is an interview with Recorder Leslie Cuthbert, whose main judicial role is sitting in tribunal hearings. After qualifying as a solicitor in 1996, he became a solicitor advocate, a role that allowed him audience at criminal trials and U.K. appeal courts. In 2002, he sat at the International Criminal Court hearing cases relating to genocide offenses that occurred in the former Yugoslavia. What is interesting in this interview is the focus on tribunal hearings. Although he is a part item judge in Crown Court hearing criminal trials, Recorder Cuthbert's main role is sitting in tribunals, mainly Mental Health Tribunals. Providing an insight into the role of adjudicating in tribunals, one can see from Recorder Cuthbert's responses that there is little difference in what judges face in the role, be it in tribunals or more formal court settings. Being a recorder, he is in a position to evaluate the role as

---

* Published by Sweet & Maxwell.

a judge in both legal settings. This is seen regarding his views on codification, where Recorder Cuthbert sees a need for simple clear guidance in the legal provision.

North America

Section X contains Chapters 12 through 15, which are interviews with judges from the United States. Chapter 12 is Peter Kratcoski's interview with Justice Kennedy, who is a judge in the state of Ohio's Supreme Court. Consisting of seven judges, the Ohio Supreme Court has discretion to hear appeals from the Ohio's Court of Appeal and can hear cases involving state constitutional questions, the Board of Tax Appeals, the Public Utilities Commission, and death penalty cases. For many jurisdictions around the world, especially in Europe, where the death penalty no longer exists, this is an interesting aspect of the judges' role. While studying law, Justice Kennedy was a civilian assistant to Hamilton's chief of police (as being a police officer was her original chosen career). After leaving that position, she clerked for a judge in Ohio's Court of Common Pleas. After graduating, she went into legal practice before entering the judiciary. Justice Kennedy provides an insight into the changes in the law and policing practice related to domestic violence, and she reveals a candid account of the workings of a State Supreme Court judge.

Chapter 13 is Blake Randol and Lauren Block's interview with Honorable Chief Justice de Muniz of the Oregon State Supreme Court. After serving as a judge in Oregon's Court of Appeal, Chief de Muniz was the first Hispanic to serve as a chief justice in Oregon state history. Prior to entering the judiciary, he was an Oregon state deputy public defender who later became a special prosecutor for Douglas County in Oregon. As a result, in Chief de Muniz we have a judge with experience of both prosecuting and defending in criminal courts, which, based on the interviews with the U.S. judges, is more an exception than a rule. Based on his vast experience, Chief de Muniz's responses reveal his long-term concern about the effects mandatory sentencing policy will have, not just on those sentenced, but on U.S. society. In line with a number of the interviews in this book, Chief de Muniz discusses his concern about the cuts to the legal system and the subsequent effects this may have such as the impact high caseloads carried by public defenders will have on representing defendants in criminal trials.

Chapter 14 is Michael Eskey Sr. and Michael Eskey Jr.'s interview with Judge Anthony "Rex" Gabbert, an appellate judge in the Western District of Missouri. As in a number of the jurisdictions covered in the series of interviews in this book, the U.S. legal system is also based on the common law model, and in Missouri the judiciary consists of three levels: trial courts, the intermediate appellate court, and the Supreme Court of Missouri; Judge

Gabbert sits in the appellate court. A member of the Missouri Bar and the American Bar Association, his career commenced as an associate circuit judge in Missouri dealing with a variety of crimes from murder to an array of felony cases as well as civil trials such as medical malpractice. As seen with a number of judges in this book, Judge Gabbert also has an academic background, having taught law at higher education establishments. In his candid responses, Judge Gabbert discusses issues surrounding the increase in litigation, which has had a knock-on effect of increasing the caseload going before the court. He discusses how in his opinion the consequence of a lack of state financial resources is a backlog in cases being heard in the courts. Also in this interview, Judge Gabbert expresses his views on "prior persistent offender status," a sentencing process that is similar to the three strikes policy.

Chapter 15 is Cara Rabe-Hemp's interview with Illinois Circuit Court judge, Judge Elizabeth Robb. After graduating in law, Judge Robb entered the legal profession as public defender in Illinois before entering the judiciary. When she entered the judiciary, Judge Robb was the first female associate judge and went on to become the first female chief judge in Illinois in 2004. In her responses, once more we see the U.S. judiciary's concern about the mandatory sentencing policy, as Judge Robb sees the policy as not giving any judicial discretion and insufficient resources toward community-based supervision. As she develops this discussion, Judge Robb is an advocate of the courts moving from a punitive to a more integrative community model, especially as criminal law's focus has moved, resulting in judges in effect becoming social workers. Once more, as revealed in her responses, Judge Robb discusses the impact the lack of resources is currently having on the role of the judiciary.

Remaining in the North American continent, Appendix B contains an interview by Romi Boivin and Chloe Leclerc with a Canadian judge from the Court of Quebec. The judge expressed the wish to remain anonymous as this is in line with the requirements of the Canadian judiciary, where Canadian judges are prevented from talking to the media and only under strict conditions are Canadian judges allowed to provide interviews as part of empirical research. The editors decided to place this interview as an appendix for two reasons. One, it was out of line with the ethos of the other 15 interviews where the judge is identified and demonstrates their willingness not only to participate with the process, but also to emphasize the openness within which the replies were recorded and written up. Secondly, the data obtained by Boivin and Leclerc in their interview produced candid responses highlighting some of the current issues judges in Canada have to face, and it was felt by the editors that this data could add to the study of the judiciary in particular and criminal justice in general. This interview includes comments regarding the legal aid position in Canada, which does not allow Canadian citizens working on the minimum wage access to legal aid; as a result, there are a number of nonrepresented defendants in criminal trials. This judge is also scathing about the impact of Canada's Safe Street and Communities Act that was recently introduced, bringing in greater use of mandatory sentences and limiting the use of conditional sentences. The judge sees this as diluting the discretion of judges and undermining their position as discretionary power has moved from the judge to the prosecutor. The judge sees this Act as simply a hardening of crime policy. Another area the Quebec judge is critical of is how accessibility to justice is more limited because of high legal costs and delays in trials brought about by the Canadian Human Rights and Freedoms Charter and megatrials.

All the key themes and issues raised in the interviews are drawn together in the conclusion, which examines the relationship between theory and practice, funding justice in criminal courts, policies surrounding sentencing guidelines, and youth justice in the various jurisdictions. As seen in the judges' responses in the interviews, there are more similarities in the issues judges face than there are differences. One similarity that emerges in the interviews is how all of the judges see the legal principle of the rule of law being of paramount importance and underpinning their decision making.

Ghana
Legal System

I

GERALD DAPAAH GYAMFI AND BRIAN S. AKRONG

The Ghana Judicial Service (or the judiciary) is one of the three arms of the government of Ghana, vested with constitutional and other legal mandates to administer justice and provide some other related services to the people of Ghana with a high standard of efficiency and without fear or favor. The judiciary is expected to be independent, show commitment to the truth, and interpret the constitution and other laws of Ghana. It is the public institution of Ghana that is in charge of the administration of the court system of Ghana. Thus it is the branch of government with the constitutional right to interpret, apply, and direct the enforcement of the laws of Ghana.

The judicial system of Ghana is faced with most of the same challenges as the global legal profession. Some issues can create problems in the smooth running of the judiciary. The major problems perceived by the majority of Ghanaians include politicization, systemic weaknesses, and bribery and corruption (Bokor, 2010). Many prominent individuals continually criticize the alarming rate at which these problems and criticisms are tarnishing the image of the judiciary. These include the political leaders, the Ghana Bar Association, and even some judges of the Ghanaian judiciary. For instance, in an attempt to curb the problems that the judicial system of Ghana was going through, in 2012, the chief justice (CJ) of Ghana's judiciary dismissed two magistrate court judges for alleged involvement in corruption. At a press conference, the CJ stated that the perception of corruption was posing a huge threat to the legitimacy of the Ghanaian judiciary and that it was severely affecting its capacity to effectively fulfill the constitutional mandate of the judiciary (Amoah, 2012).

Profile of the Judicial Service of Ghana

The Gold Coast colonial administration established the Gold Coast Supreme Court of Judicature under the Westminster Imperial Parliament Ordinance in 1876 (IBA, 2014). This legal system was established based on Anglo-Saxon

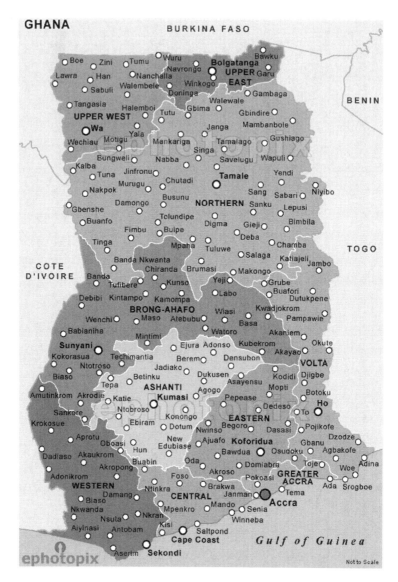

Figure I.1 Political map of Ghana.

common law, religious laws, statutory law, both written and unwritten customary laws, and other indigenous laws (IBA, 2014). In 1966, after the first military coup in Ghana, the ruling National Liberation Council (NLC) abolished the Supreme Court of Judicature and established the Superior Court of Judicature and the inferior courts. Subsequently, the court of appeals and the high courts of justice were created. In 1972, following the second military coup, the National Redemption Council (NRC) that toppled the regime abolished the Supreme Court and suspended the 1969 Constitution of Ghana. Following the 1979 military coup by the Armed Forces Revolutionary Council (AFRC), led by Jerry John Rawlings, the AFRC made provision for the court structure as provided by the 1969 Constitution of Ghana. Ghana is now ruled by the 1992 Constitution that has made provision for the superior courts comprising the Supreme Court, the Court of Appeal, and the High Court of Ghana. Provision was made in the constitution that empowered Ghana's Parliament to establish other courts, including community and circuit tribunals under Ghana's judiciary, headed by the CJ (Ghana Judicial Service, 2014). However, The Courts (Amendment) Act, 2002, Act 620 abolished the community and circuit tribunals and replaced them with circuit and magistrate courts. The 1992 Constitution ensures the independence of the judiciary from the executive.

The Courts (Amendment) Act, 2002, Act 620, parliament established the following lower courts: circuit courts, district courts, juvenile courts, the National Houses of Chiefs, the Regional Houses of Chiefs, and every traditional council to augment the work of the superior courts.

Ghana Judicial Structure

The legal system that Ghana operates is based on the common law system. The system has a hierarchical structure headed by the CJ and other justices of the Supreme Court. The Supreme Court is the final court of appeal that sits on issues related to the enforcement of law and interpretation of Ghana's constitution. Following the Supreme Court is the court of appeal. The appeal court has jurisdiction to hear and determine justice for appeal cases from the high court on judgments made. The last of the superior courts is the high court. Apart from treasonable offenses, the high court hears all civil and criminal cases. Following the superior courts are the lower courts, which include the circuit courts, the magistrate courts, and the district courts (Chapter 11, 1992 Constitution of Ghana; The Courts (Amendment) Act, 2002.

Legal Developments in Ghana

In fulfilling the constitutional mandate to ensure the speedy delivery of justice in Ghana, in 2005, the judicial service of Ghana established a program known as the Alternative Dispute Resolution program (ADR). The aim of the program is to provide an option to easily access justice, which will help to reduce the courts' backlog of cases that are in the process of adjudication. The Judicial Service Annual Report (2012/2013) of Ghana indicated that the ADR program was doing very well in providing alternative resolution of cases and thus a flexible and affordable system of justice in Ghana. Statistics from the report show that as of the end of 2012, 47 commercial courts in Ghana had

Table I.1   Regional Distribution of ADR-Mediated Cases

Region	Cases Mediated	Cases Settled	Percentage
Greater Accra	3363	1423	42
Eastern	594	258	43
Central	169	62	37
Western	241	115	48
Volta	385	272	71
Brong Ahafo	14	10	71
Ashanti	107	71	66
Northern	42	34	81
Upper east	3	3	100
Upper west	—	—	—
Total	4918	2248	46

Source: Data provided by Ghana Judicial Service Annual Report (May 2012–May 2013). www.judicial.gov.gh/index.php/2013-01-28-08-11-41/strategic plan.

been connected to the ADR program and 2248 (46%) out of 4918 cases had been settled through the ADR program with financial support from some benevolent institutions based in Ghana. Table I.1 shows how the mediated cases were handled throughout the 10 regions of Ghana in 2012/2013.

The judicial service embarked on an ADR week celebration in March 2013 and the report indicated that during the weeklong celebration, the service intensified its ADR public education and offered disputants the opportunity to receive affordable means of settling their disputes through the ADR program. During the week, the ADR program received 844 cases and had settled 450 (53%) of the referred cases.

Another area that the judicial service of Ghana uses the ADR program to address is adjudicating land cases. The ADR directorate of the judicial service has instituted the Land Administration Project (LAP) with the aim of providing an alternative dispute resolution mechanism under the ADR directorate. In preparation for the launch of the project, the judicial service had trained 30 surveyors nationwide as of the end of 2013. More magistrates and some staff of the judicial service were also trained in conflict resolution under the facilitation of the Fordham School of Law and St. John's Law School in the United States. The training was to build the capacity of the judicial service in ADR mechanisms.

Ghana Legal Education and Profession

Globally, there is a view in the legal profession that the law schools are graduating more lawyers without much experience in the legal profession. This is happening because most of the schools do not include more internship and clerkship courses in their curricular development. Considering the performance of lawyers, many people have the perception that there is a disjunction between what is learned at law schools and what is practiced by lawyers (Edward, 1992). This has created the perception that most of the law schools concentrate on "abstract theory at the expense of practical scholarship and pedagogy" (Edward, 1992, p. 34).

To overcome the problem of disjunction between what is learned in law schools and what is actually practiced by lawyers, in 1958, following Ghana's independence, the first president, Dr. Kwame Nkrumah, established the Ghana School of Law. In 1960, the Legal Profession Act (1960) established the General Legal Council to regulate the legal profession. To receive the approval of the General Legal Council and enroll as a lawyer, a candidate, after graduation, must demonstrate good moral character. The Ghana Legal Profession Act 32 (Act 1960) mandates the legal counsel, the constitutional right to regulate all legal educational matters in Ghana (IBA, 2014).

To become a lawyer in Ghana, the aspirant is expected to possess a degree from a recognized university as an entry requirement to the Ghana Law School. A student of the Ghana Law School must pass all the professional courses of the school in order to become eligible for a barrister-at-law certificate.

The following interview was conducted with a supreme court justice who, throughout the interview, shared his personal experience of the judicial service of Ghana with the authors. The interview provides a vivid account of the trends in Ghana's judiciary.

Anin-Yeboah, Ghana Supreme Court

1

GERALD DAPAAH GYAMFI AND BRIAN S. AKRONG

Contents

Introduction

For many centuries, the judicial system has played a highly significant role in the administration of law all over the world. For example, in the twelfth century, the leaders of warriors in Japan depended on adjudication in the enforcement of their legal rulings and maintenance of order by their governors. In France, the judicial decision of the council of state has been based on adjudications for many years (Haley, 2013). Even though the judicial system contributes to the justice system of a nation through its interpretation of laws and its adjudication of cases between individuals, most judges and justices have been accused of being bias in their judgments (Mensah, 2009). The functions of the judiciary now call for certain qualities that make these professionals independent and impartial in their adjudication of the law. Over 2000 years, the judicial system has been accused of being made up of people who do not seek the truth (Rhode, 2003). Most lawyers have been described as greedy people who are arrogant, only interested in seeking technicalities to free criminals, and charge huge fees. In a study by the American Bar Association (ABA), only one-fifth of those surveyed considered lawyers as people who are ethical and could be described as honest. In some countries, for example, a lawyer can be described as, "a learned gentleman who rescues your estate from your enemies and keeps it for himself" (Rhode, 2003, p. 3). Notwithstanding the negative perceptions which some people may carry, the legal profession has worked over the years to keep the wheels of justice running in Ghana.

Interpretations of Legal Issues

The work of the judiciary involves applying the statute law and making the interpretation free from doubt in the exercise of judicial discretions through evaluation and assessment of facts that are relevant. In a community, for instance, the jury is expected to be the authentic authority on community standards. One of the most important elements in the practices of the judiciary is the public confidence and trust that the people place in it and the expectation that justice would be administered in the judicial function. Studies by Robert and Hough (2005) revealed that the trust and confidence that the public has in the judicial system are now falling in the system of criminal justice worldwide. The study also revealed that the public now has some misperceptions about the outcome of the courts on their adjudication of criminal cases on grounds of fairness and trustworthiness (Roberts, 2003).

However, the fact that the Ghanaian courts are inundated with numerous cases shows that the citizens still have some trust in the courts.

Challenges Associated with the Judicial System

As a result of the changes and challenges affecting the legal profession, there is the perception that the functions of the judiciary are under scrutiny by many people. The challenges that have a great effect on the judicial system include economic pressures, the effect of technology on the practice of law, the various regulations that affect the legal profession, and the training and equipping of new lawyers with the requisite experience and expertise (Rhode, 2003). During adjudication, judges use legal concepts to engage in dialogue and promote coherence (Leczykiewicz, 2008). It is of interest to note that the Ghanaian Supreme Court seems to be inclined towards the purposive approach to interpretation (Bimpong-Buta, 2007, pp. 183–214). For instance, in the locus classicus decision by the Supreme Court of Ghana in the case of Tuffour v. Attorney-General [1980] GLR 63, Sower JSC stated, inter alia, that a national constitution must be given a benevolent, broad, liberal and purposive construction so as to promote the apparent policy of its framers. In other words, a narrow, strict technical and legalistic approach must be avoided by judges.

The court in this case had to give meaning to Article 127(8) and (9) of the 1979 Constitution of Ghana which provided that:

> "(8) Subject to the provisions of clause (9) of this article, a Justice of the Superior Court of Judicature holding office as such immediately before the coming into force of this Constitution shall be deemed to have been appointed as from the coming into force of this Constitution to hold office as such under this Constitution.
>
> (9) A justice to whom the provisions of clause (8) of this article apply shall, on the coming into force of this Constitution, take and subscribe the oath of allegiance..."

The court held that the incumbent Chief Justice, Mr Justice Apaloo, was a member of the class of persons or justices referred to in article 127(8); therefore, on the coming into force of the 1979 Constitution and by virtue of article 127(8) and (9), Mr Justice Apaloo became the Chief Justice of Ghana.

The court held, inter alia, that the interpretation placed on article 127(8) was in harmony with the use of the phrase "shall be deemed" and was also in conformity with the rationale behind article 127(8) and (9).

The economic pressures on the judicial system emanate from factors such as changes in society and the economic downturn that affect the legal profession as society continues to press for efficiency and responsiveness at a lower cost. The exponential growth in the advancement of technology increases the expectations of clients that force the legal professionals to adapt to the advancement in technology. Most people in the legal profession find it very difficult to understand and keep abreast of new technology. Many educated people today, for instance in Ghana, have basic computer skills and can assess information from the Internet; hence, some clients may be put ahead of their lawyers in the application of technology and this poses a challenge to most legal professionals in the practice of their profession. The combination of sociology and globalization has contributed to a fresh look into the application of traditional ethical rules and mechanisms for regulating the legal profession (Rhode, 2003 ibid).

The interview took place on December 4, 2013, in a cordial and friendly atmosphere. After exchanging initial courtesies and explaining the purpose of the interview, Justice Anin-Yeboah respectfully welcomed the interviewers to his office at the Supreme Court of Ghana building and availed himself for the following conversation.

Career

Q: My lord, could you tell us a little about your career? How you entered legal practice, what motivated you to become a lawyer, and how you rose to this level so far.

A: I completed my bachelor of law degree at the University of Ghana, Legon, in 1981 and then proceeded to the professional law school, the Ghana Law School, to pursue the barrister-at-law (BL) program.

I was called to the Bar in 1981. Thereafter, as expected of me as a Ghanaian, I did 1 year of national service at the attorney general's office. From 1982, after I had completed my national service, I entered private practice in Koforidua and worked for about 20 years. In 2002, the Ghana Bar Association of which I was a member recommended me to the Judicial Council for appointment as a justice of the high court. I was subsequently appointed and the appointment took effect from June 16, 2002, and I was posted to Accra. My career on the bench has all along been in Accra where I served till I was appointed a court of appeal judge in 2003. In 2008, after serving for 5 years at the court of appeal, I was promoted to my current position as a supreme court judge.

It is worth noting that since that time, a considerable number of changes with regard to the training of lawyers have taken place. At that time, two categories of lawyers were trained. First, there were those who went to university to graduate in law and then continued at the Ghana Law School for their professional training for 2 years to become barristers-at-law (BL). Next were those who did not study law in the university but obtained first degrees in other courses and then went to study for the Qualifying Certificate in Law (QCL) at the Ghana Law School, which was later known as the Preliminary Certificate in Law (PCL). The PCL course was for a duration of 2 years after which the graduates could continue to study for the BL program for a further 2 years. Notwithstanding whatever route they took, they could be selected, if qualified, to become judges. The qualification for a judge according to the Constitution of Ghana, 1992, is spelled out in Article 144 of the constitution.

Q: Is it normal procedure that one must be recommended by the Bar Association to be appointed a judge?

A: Yes, it is normal, very normal for the Bar Association to recommend, but one can also apply to the Judicial Council to be considered for appointment. Those in private practice as well as those in the attorney general's office can apply. Normally, it is the Judicial Council that does the recommendations but the Bar Association can recommend any of its members it considers competent enough for appointment. Of late, I think about 3 years ago, they started conducting examinations for appointment even to the High Court except for the Court of Appeal and the Supreme Court. Examinations are conducted for appointments at the magistrate courts as well.

Q: Is it the chief justice who makes the appointments?

A: No, it is the Judicial Council that makes the appointments. It is a constitutional body and it goes through the motions to make the appointments accordingly. The Judicial Council examines the candidates and submits them for consideration.

Regarding the appointment of the judiciary in Ghana, Article 153 of the Constitution of Ghana, 1992, provides that there shall be a Judicial Council which shall comprise, among others, the CJ as the chairman, the Attorney General, a justice of the Supreme Court nominated by the justices of the Supreme Court, a justice of the court of appeal nominated by the justices of the court of appeal, a justice of the high court nominated by the justices of the high court, two representatives of the Ghana Bar Association, a representative of the Chairmen of Regional Tribunals, a representative of the lower courts or tribunals, the judge advocate general of the Ghana Armed Forces, the head of the legal directorate of the Ghana Police Service, the editor of the Ghana Law Reports, as well as a representative of the Judicial Service Staff Association, a chief nominated by the National Houses of Chiefs, and four other persons who are not lawyers appointed by the president.

The current procedure under which examinations are conducted for the selection of prospective judges, falls under the purview of Article 154 of the 1992 Constitution, which provides for the functions of the Judicial Council. Article 154 (1) (a) mandates the Judicial Council to propose judicial reforms to the government for consideration, to improve the level of administration of justice and efficiency in the judiciary.

Q: Since when did you conceive the idea of becoming a judge?

A: A lawyer does not become a judge immediately he joins the Bar; besides, some must be on the other side to keep the wheels of justice running. It was while in the sixth form that I really had the thought of becoming a lawyer.

Q: Sometimes in our system it is parents who push their children to become one thing or the other. Did your parents have any influence in your choice of career?

A: Earlier, my father had wanted me to become a lawyer but I did not give it a serious thought; it was when I got to the sixth form that I had the conviction and decided to become a lawyer.

Q: Have you regretted your decision?

A: No, not at all.

Q: Do you see any difference between what you anticipated before becoming a lawyer and what you experience now?

A: The delays are still there. But we also take into account the number of courts where people can access justice. England and Wales have over 30,000 magistrates and judges. Every village has somebody to see to petty cases, but here if you look at our number, I am sorry to say that we are not that many. As a developing country, we don't have the resources to be opening up courts.

Q: In the course of the development of your career as a judge what has surprised you?

A: Now I understand the delays in the adjudication of cases. One main problem is the inadequate number of judges. Currently, there are 12 judges at the Supreme Court, 25 at the court of appeal, 103 at the high court, 56 at the circuit court, and at the magistrate courts there are 31 professional magistrates and 114 career magistrates. When Professor Kwamena Ahoi was the minister for local government (1992–1996), he made a proposal that a court should be established in every district. I think this should have been supported by statute.

Some district chief executives have been very pragmatic in using innovative ideas to improve their districts, including the courts. One classic example is Mr. Akwasi Oppong-Fosu, the current minister of local government and rural development. During his tenure as district chief executive of Tepa, before becoming a minister, he assisted in building a district court at Tepa in the Brong Ahafo region.

On this theme, the problem has been compounded because there are currently 216 districts. In June 2010, 46 new districts were created to add to the already existing number of 170 districts.

Q: Has your work as a judge proved as interesting or rewarding as you thought it would when you first started?

A: I have found my work as a lawyer and a judge very rewarding and have never regretted joining the legal profession.

Q: Currently, several law schools have been established, so don't you think this will solve part of the problem?

A: Irrespective of the fact that there are many lawyers, the problem will still not be easily solved. The cases suffer adjournment *and this situation will continue until enough facilities are available.** There was a day when the court at Ajabeng in Accra had over 100 fresh criminal cases.

---

* Authors' emphasis.

Personal Judicial Philosophy

Q: What do you think should be the role of the judiciary in society?

A: One of the important areas in which the judiciary has been helping and must continue to help is ADR. Justice Gbadegbe and I had the opportunity of being sponsored on an ADR training program so that we could assist in offering skills and advice in that regard.

The CJ instituted the ADR week and this is observed during every legal year term but we do not have a lot of ADR centers as in the United States. In our jurisdiction, the literacy level is not as high as it is in advanced societies. The legal aid scheme, which was set up by the government, is a vital institution to help the needy but it is not well resourced.

The Bar Council had suggested that every lawyer should do one legal aid case per year. One of the problems of legal aid is accommodation. Currently, it is the Council for Legal Reporting that has given them some space for accommodation. Legal aid could also be giving counseling to litigants.

Q: How do you cooperate with the police and other organizations like nongovernmental organizations (NGOs) who may have some impact on the judiciary?

A: Normally, because of the nature of our work, we have been very careful in looking for assistance from several people. For instance, if you look at the corporate organizations, they have the money but they also access the courts and so looking at it you'll see that it is risky. However, the commercial court was built by the Danish Development Organization (DANIDA). They assisted with the construction and refurbishment of the commercial court to facilitate the adjudication of commercial cases. They furnished the court and provided every machine at the court. Sometimes, the GTZ* also assists us in organizing seminars to train judges. These are very notable institutions I can readily think of that have offered immense assistance to us.

It is worth noting that DANIDA donated two urvan buses [minibuses] to carry workers of the commercial court to and from work. The building, which was funded by DANIDA, was inaugurated in 2005.

Q: What about the police?

A: If it comes to other institutions like the police, they play a major role in criminal matters. The first point of call in lodging a criminal

* Gesellschaft für Technische Zusammenarbeit.

complaint is the police. They take down statements and conduct investigations and process people for the court. Thus, they play a very major role in criminal prosecutions. The judges, and the judiciary as a whole, have received collaboration from the police in dealing with criminal cases.

Q: Are you satisfied with their performance?

A: Their performance is not as it is, for example, in Britain. Sitting on the bench, I have to be very careful; however, I can't say they do not show up at the court at all. The law is that a case can be disposed of for want of prosecution. Some of them have been doing well but some have not been very satisfactory.

Q: Don't you think some of them may use absence in the court as a ploy or strategy for maneuvering justice?

A: It is everywhere; where the law requires the police to play a complementary role, they have to carry out prosecution. But I am more concerned about attitude to work. You have to be punctual for the work of prosecution to be done. Yet, we also have to look at the issue from the other perspective. They also lack logistics. Currently, there is no prison facility in Accra.

There has been cooperation with other criminal justice organizations such as the Economic and Organized Crime Office (EOCO), the Bureau of National Investigation (BNI), and national security in criminal prosecutions.

The Economic and Organised Crime Office (EOCO) was established by an act of parliament.*

It is a specialised independent government organisation or agency which is mandated to investigate and monitor economic and organised crimes. They prosecute these offences and recover or confiscate the proceeds of the economic crimes to the state and provide for related matters.

Under the Act, EOCO has an Executive director who is responsible for the day- to- day administration and operations of of the organization and is answerable to the board of the organization.

The EOCO has 10 regional offices located in the regional capitals of the Republic of Ghana with its head office in Accra.

The United Nations Development program (UNDP) sponsored the publication of a manual on electoral adjudication in 2008. In 2012, a similar manual was published with sponsorship from the Department for International Development (DFID) of the British government.

---

* Economic and Organised Crime Office Act, 2010, 804.

Q: In your view, how should the criminal justice system in Ghana be performed?

A: Some of the challenges facing the judicial system, if dealt with, would enhance the work of judges and the judicial system as a whole. Sometimes suspects are freed because of lack of prosecution. On the part of supporting staff, attitude toward work, particularly punctuality, as well as inadequate logistics has militated against the work of judges. Also, there are not enough prison facilities. In Accra, for example, there are no prison facilities.

Q: Do you have some policy regarding your relationship with the community that is very dangerous?

A: When you want to assert your independence then you don't do the kind of thing which would affect your work. I remember I was sent to contact the chief of Anyinam* to see how we could put up a courthouse. This is one of the very rare occasions when we actually contacted the community for help.

Q: What is the relationship between the judges and the political parties?

A: The court has to be careful in dealing with political parties to avoid compromises, but where the need arises, the court has assisted the political parties. For instance, electoral manuals are prepared during elections for the smooth running of elections and when we are getting close to elections it is the judiciary that is called on to organize workshops and take the political parties through the manual. It was the UK government that funded the 2012 Manual on Election Adjudication in Ghana. In 2008, it was the UNDP that gave sponsorship for the publication of the manual and workshops to educate the political parties.

Q: Other organizations like EOCO, how do you deal with them?

A: When they bring cases to the court, we adjudicate the cases for them.

Q: You have talked about ADR but when people come to court, sometimes by the way they act, you may know that these people are illiterate or are the less privileged in society. How do you help them?

A: If you look at the court structure, you realize that cases must proceed from the lower courts to the higher courts and customary law is part of our laws. If you look at the nature of the case, without anybody coming to prompt you, You can make an order saying, you are referring this case to the chief of the town to settle and come and report to you. This is also done in some cases.

Q: People consider the court as isolated from society. Even the language the courts use is sometimes not easily understood. Can an ordinary man get up and say, "I am interested in this case, is it not difficult"?

---

* A town in the eastern region of Ghana. See Figure I.1.

A: That was why I was talking about literacy. Even if the judge condemns you to death, it is not in the court's premises that you are going to be hanged. If we look at it, it all boils down to illiteracy and low-income earnings because if you have money to hire a lawyer, you have no problem. He can take you through the full trial of the case. Even where two lawyers are on a case, one can tell the other to let them settle the case amicably out of court. Then concerning the criticisms against us that we are not open to the public, which is not right. If you look at the way medicine is practiced, you can't just enter a consulting room unless you are sick or you are carrying your mother or somebody who is sick.

Q: What about your hours of work?

A: The high court sits from 9:00 a.m. to 4:00 p.m. while the Supreme Court sits from 10:00 a.m. to 4:00 p.m.

Q: How do you get interpreters to assist with interpretation at the court?

A: We often get interpreters from the Ghana School of Languages. Before they start working, the Human Resource Department tests them to ascertain their competence.

Q: How are judges trained in Ghana?

A: Prior to taking up of their appointment, incoming judges (selected qualified lawyers) are given a 6-month training in what is done at the court, ethical issues, and how to relate to the public. They are also trained in Information Technology (IT). Sitting judges and administrators are also given refresher courses.

Q: What about the relationship of the court and society?

A: There is the justice for all programs annually at Nsawam. The purpose is to decongest the prison.

Q: My Lord, do you think swearing by the cross, the Bible, the Quran, and so on truly elicits the truth from the parties in a case?

A: They may not tell the truth always but it is better than not swearing at all.

Problems and Successes Experienced

Q: What are some of the problems that hinder the smooth operation of the courts?

A: There are not enough recorders in the courts. Besides, there is no electricity in some places. For example, Amasaman in the Greater Accra has no electricity at the court. The fast-track court is supposed to facilitate the speedy delivery of justice but the fast-track courts are currently overloaded. Another problem has to do with the training of judges. Judges should be trained on a regular basis but this is impeded because of the lack of facilities.

Q: What other difficulties do you see with the courts?

A: Since the courts are not enough, if a judge sits from about 8:30 a.m. to 6 p.m., he or she wouldn't finish what should be covered in the day but if the courts were many, they would share the work. For each case, the judge has to listen to the parties and record. Assuming you are taking 30 cases and you have to go through this rigorous procedure, obviously it would take some time.

Q: What are some of the new developments in legal practice in Ghana?

A: There are several changes. For example, lawyers and judges do not wear the wig in the court any longer.

Q: In what ways do you think steps can be taken to enhance the work of the courts?

A: The labor commission, if well resourced, could take away some of the cases to ease the pressure on the courts. One of the new ways in which the court and the society can collaborate is planning. There must be coordinated efforts because we need more courts which should be well equipped.

Q: There used to be the West African Court of Appeal (WACA) and now there is the ECOWAS court, what is the relationship between the Ghanaian courts and the ECOWAS court?

A: The ECOWAS court does not operate like an appeal court; therefore, cases from the Supreme Court of Ghana cannot go there. The ECOWAS court deals mainly with border disputes. The West African Court of Appeal was an appeal court to which a party to a litigation who was not satisfied with a decision in the then Gold Coast (now Ghana) could appeal.

Q: What role do the chiefs play in the adjudication of cases?

A: The chiefs play a complementary role and have been doing well, but there are times when the chiefs are related to the parties in a case and that poses a challenge. But they have been doing well. For instance, in the case of land disputes, they go to the land to settle boundary disputes, so they play complementary roles. Besides, if it comes to purely chieftancy matters, it is in their domain. Those are not in our jurisdiction they know the customs more than we do. However, the chief is disabled by want of jurisdiction in cases like fraud, stealing, and so on.

Q: How do you see the role of chiefs?

A: We live in small communities where people know one another. There is a problem because the chief does not sit alone; he sits with the linguists and other elders. Some of these people may have some interest in some cases but if you are dissatisfied, you can apply through the CJ for redress.

Q: Is there anything else the judicial service should be doing which is not being done?

A: In as much as the courts are not opened to the public as pharmacy shops, markets, and so on, it is so everywhere. If you travel from east to west, north to south across the world, it is the same. My only worry is the illiteracy level. Ours is not like the advanced countries where people can assert their rights by contacting lawyers. In advanced societies where lawyers do so much for clients, they may even advise clients not to pursue certain matters in the court. But if you are a judge and certain cases are brought before you, it is your constitutional right to delve into the matter according to the law. You can't just throw the matter away. In advanced societies, they have respect for the law but theirs is also a human institution that we cannot say is devoid of problems.

A: Is there any way by which ordinary people who may not have the means financially are assisted to pursue their cases?

A: We have a legal aid scheme which is set up by government but I must be frank; it is not well resourced to the extent that they have a few lawyers. I remember at a point in time, the whole of the eastern region had just one lawyer for the whole scheme. Besides, the lawyer had no vehicle to travel the length and breadth of the region. From Koforidua to Akyem Oda is about 68 miles (109.44 km) close to 70 miles (112.65km) and then up to Akosombo and Akwamufie. So you can imagine the enormity of the work. Therefore, if the legal aid is well resourced, it can take a chunk of cases whereby those who are less endowed could be assisted. It is a very vital institution that can assist the needy. It has offered so much assistance to the legally aided clients in the area of intestacy (PNDC LAW 111), maintenance, and paternity cases.

Q: How are the lawyers who assist on the legal aid scheme remunerated? Is it the government that pays them?

A: Sometime back when I served on the legal aid board, we decided that each lawyer should do at least one legal aid case a year. I did a couple of cases personally. In criminal trials, like murder, if you do not have a lawyer, the judge will not try the case. I never submitted any claims for payment for the legal aid cases I dealt with.

Q: Was it because the amount was not encouraging?

A: Oh no, but sometimes the bureaucratic systems; the delays will just let you ignore it.

Q: Don't you think the government must give the Legal Aid Scheme the necessary boost so that we can have a similar scheme like the NHIS?

A: It is a good institution but you see, if you go there, they have no facilities; it is the Council for Law Reporting that has granted them some office space. And if you have lawyers who have to travel to do the work it is not easy. If a case is in Accra that is fine, but where the case is in a village far away, it may be difficult for the lawyer. But if they have resources and many lawyers, they can even do counseling as it will certainly help the society to grow.

Q: Do you see the possibility that in the future, resources could be channeled into the establishment of more courts?

A: When Professor Kwamena Ahoi was minister for local government, he made it a point that every district should have a court. The current local government minister, the Honorable Fosu, was the District Chief Executive (DCE) for Tepa (Ahafo Annor) at the time. He managed to put up a state-of-the art court facility in his district. With due respect to our DCEs, perhaps some DCEs think it is more important putting up places of convenience and school buildings rather than courts.

The CJ's forum involves chiefs, regional administrative officers, and other stakeholders. The forum has been moving from one region to the other to educate the society on the need to improve justice delivery.

Q: Is it only at the regional level?

A: If you move from Accra to Kumasi there are only two circuit courts. For a distance of about 175 km, that is from Nsawam in the eastern region to Juaso in the Ashanti region.

We also have the ADR week. At times it takes some of the load off the courts. We give training to chiefs in ADR. We had a program on Joy FM* and after, somebody thanked us for the education but such a program comes at a cost. Some of us went to America for training. We later organized a training program to which we invited some selected individuals.

Theory and Practice

Q: Are you able to undertake research?

A: The Association of Judges and Magistrates publishes a news journal annually. There is the need for research clerks, secretaries, and logistic supports for any effective research to be done.

Conclusion

Ghana's judicial system has been in existence since the era of the British colonial administration under the Anglo-Saxon common law. However, there have been many interruptions to the smooth running of the judicial

---

* Joy FM is one of the FM radio stations in Accra.

system due to interventions in the affairs of government through military coups. Ghana now has a judicial system headed by a CJ. The court structure is headed by the Supreme Court, followed by the court of appeal, the high court, and the lower courts. To aid the speedy adjudication of cases, the judiciary has instituted some programs such as the Alternative Dispute Resolution and Land Administration projects.

Even though the court plays very essential roles in the adjudication of criminal and other cases, the judicial service is confronted with many challenges that impede the work of the judiciary. The challenges include lack of logistics, poor financial resources, inadequate prison houses and other court facilities, overloading the courts with cases, and the perception of corruption of the judiciary.

Acknowledgments

We wish to acknowledge the support obtained from Justice Anin-Yeboah, who availed himself, despite his busy schedule at the Supreme Court of Ghana, for our interview. Our heartfelt gratitude goes to Her Lordship Mrs. Theodora Wood, chief justice of Ghana's judiciary for welcoming us and introducing Justice Anin-Yeboah to us. Our profound gratitude also goes to Professor Dilip Das, UN consultant and president of the International Police Executive Symposium for giving us the opportunity to contribute to the production of this book. We also acknowledge Dr. David Lowe, principal lecturer, Liverpool John Moors University, UK, for assisting us with the guidelines for the interview. Our heartfelt gratitude also goes to Ms. Dziedzorm Zanu for the secretarial services rendered. Finally, we wish to thank the management of the University of Professional Studies, Accra, for introducing us to the chief justice of Ghana.

Glossary

ADR: alternative dispute resolution
AFRC: Armed Forces Revolutionary Council
BNI: Bureau of National Investigations
EOCO: Economic and Organized Crime Office
BL: barrister-at-law
CJ: Chief Justice
DCE: District Chief Executive
ECOWAS: Economic Community of West African States
IBA: International Bar Association
LAP: Local Administration Project

NHIS: National Health Insurance Scheme
NLC: National Liberation Council
NRC: National Redemption Council
PCL: Preliminary Certificate in Law
PNDC: Provisional National Defense Council
QCL: Qualifying Certificate in Law
UNDP: United Nations Development Project
WACA: West African Court of Appeal

Nigeria
Legal System of the Ebonyi State

OKO ELECHI AND SMART E. OTU

Nigeria is a federal system with dual judicial arrangement. This is unlike the police and prisons services, which are exclusively federal institutions. The Nigerian judiciary is comprised of two levels of administration: (1) the federal judiciary, comprising of courts that are basically appellate in nature; (2) the state judiciary, which consists of courts that exercise judicial power over matters that occurred within their area of jurisdiction.

The judiciary, and by extension the court system in Ebonyi state, is made up of the High Courts of the State, Magistrate Courts, the Customary Courts of Appeal, and the Customary Courts of the State. While the administration of the judiciary is under the State Ministry of Justice, and headed by a minister who also doubles as the Attorney General of the state, the day-to-day running of the state judiciary (courts) is headed by a chief judge who is also the chairman of the State Judicial Service Commission—a body charged with the appointment, promotion, and discipline of judges and magistrates. Apart from the high courts, which have wide jurisdiction within the state, all other courts in the state have limited jurisdiction and appeals from them go to the High Court or Customary Court of Appeal (see also Babalakin & Co., 2005). Overall, there are 14 High Court judges including the chief judge and 21 magistrates including the chief magistrate, who also doubles as the secretary of the state's Judicial Service Commission (JSC), spread across the 13 local councils of the state (Figure II.1). The state's Customary Court of Appeal has three judges and a president.

As with all other judicial processes, trials in the regular court systems in Ebonyi state are open and are designed to respect due process safeguards, including the presumption of innocence, and the rights to counsel of choice, to be present during the hearing of one's case, and to confront witnesses and present relevant evidence. However, meager compensation for judges, under-staffing, poor equipment, bribery, special settlements, and a host of other

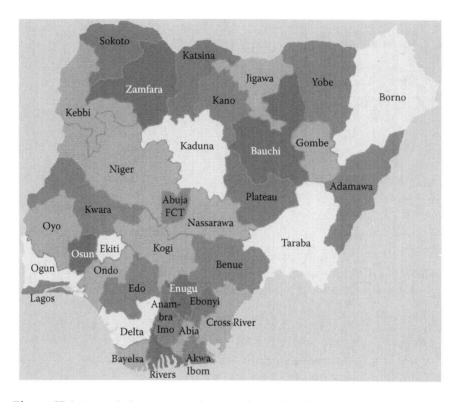

Figure II.1 Map of Ebonyi State showing the 13 local council jurisdictions.

factors such as lack of training and insecurity in the country continue to undermine the independence, reliability, and impartiality of the courts. In addition, the state government's direct control of the judiciary has led to the "over-politicization" of the judiciary. Justice is sometimes miscarried, especially in matters where the government of the day or their allies have vested interest.

Eze Udu, Ebonyi State Court

2

OKO ELECHI AND SMART E. OTU

Contents

Introduction

Interviews were conducted in English, and because of technicalities involved in some of the issues raised, they were interspersed with the use of sentence completion and/or word association, whereby certain statements were made halfway and the interviewee allowed to respond to and/or complete the sentence (see Otu, 2003). We did this mostly when our respondent appeared not to be clear enough about the issue raised before him. In sum, data were collected systematically but in a way that allowed for flexibility on the part of our interviewee such that he was able to address the issues presented to him.

The judge operates a very tight schedule in his office, making it nearly impossible to conduct the interview there. However, the judge was kind enough to grant us interviews in his home on weekends. The interviews took place on two different days, in the judge's home, on weekends. Although our interviewee was already familiar with the study (the purpose and scope were discussed before the interview proper), at the start of the interview, we had to formally introduce ourselves and the topic again. We also made it clear that the research was not in any way meant to discredit the institution of judiciary in Nigeria but to help underscore key issues that will provide support for an understanding of the workings of the judiciary in Nigeria.

The interview during the first day lasted for four and a half hours, while the second interview lasted for two and a half hours. Interviews were conducted in a relaxed and interactive atmosphere. During the interviews, handwritten notes were taken. Sometimes the interviewee requested that the notes be read before him to confirm their authenticity. (For more detail on the methods of research relating to this interview, see Appendix C.)

Career

Our interviewee was born in 1953. He obtained his O level and A level certificates in 1973 and 1975, respectively. In 1977, he received his bachelor of arts in international history and philosophy from the University of Lagos, and in 1981 he bagged his LLB (honors) in law. He was called to the Bar in 1982. Before his call to the bench, he worked as a corporate lawyer in some of Nigeria's major corporations, including the First Bank of Nigeria (FBN) and Golden Guinea Breweries, and also in the Kano State Ministry of Justice (as a National Youth Service Corps [NYSC] member).

He also worked for many years as a private attorney and advocate before joining the government service. As a practicing attorney, he served under retainer for AC, Leventis, Pfizer Products, Abia Hotels, and Ebonyi Hotels. He has also served as a legal adviser to some established institutions such as Eze-in-Council (Assembly of Traditional Rulers) between 1984 and 1991 in Abia state, and the Ivo Local Government council. He has served as member of a judicial panel of inquiry and a member of the Election Tribunal that looked into cases of election complaints in the newly instituted democratic dispensation in Nigeria. He is the third-highest-ranking law officer in the Ebonyi state, Nigeria, judiciary.

This section focuses on the main issues under examination in the current study. It covers areas such as job satisfaction, philosophy of the judges, problems and prospects, theory and practice, and other developments and expectations within the judiciary. Clearly, as our findings show, it seems that judges in Nigeria have encountered mixed experiences during their career trajectory. In the words of our interviewee:

> I observed a continuous delay in criminal justice delivery, particularly the transmission of case files from the police; the system appears to be averse to development. However, a lot of encouraging achievements have been recorded in the system such as improved infrastructure and information and communication technology (ICT) within the judiciary, even though it is still in the pipeline.

As lawyers always brag about the nobility of their profession, it is not surprising that judges including our respondent acknowledged that their careers as judges have been interesting and rewarding though not as expected. He acknowledged that the legal system in Nigeria is besieged by cultural, ethnic, class, and religious challenges that affect the outcome of the process. These challenges continue to hinder the delivery of justice in Nigeria.

Personal Judicial Philosophy

A philosophy of all-time importance to judges, which underlies their role in society, is that of impartiality and objectivity in mediation, arbitration, and settlement of disputes between parties without recourse to extraneous factors. What this implies is that the courts or judges (as it were) should be nonpartisans in the discharge of their constitutional mandates. Notwithstanding the strategic role of judges in resolving disputes, it is generally believed that customary issues should be resolved by nonstate/formal institutions predicated on the principle of "no victor, no vanquish." It is the cornerstone of the restorative justice that in the words of our interviewee is captured thus: "the worst settlement is better than the best judgment."

Judge Edu stated that the structural arrangement of the Nigerian court system follows the British pattern, though there have been emerging structural changes as a result of the growing complexity of the Nigerian social system. In Nigerian court hierarchy there is the Supreme Court, Federal High Court of Appeal, Sharia Court of Appeal, Federal High Courts, State High Courts, Sharia Courts, Magistrate Courts, and Customary Courts. Besides this conventional arrangement, these courts are arranged and occupied in order of seniority: Courts 1, 2, 3, and 4, and so on. In addition, there is the Appeal Office, where records or processes are prepared; the Probate Office, where letters of administration and death benefits are managed; and the Registry, where cases are filed and transmitted to various courts. All these, according to our interviewee, are indications of the serenity in the judicial system, which bodes well for the country.

The key observation made by Judge Edu is a that there is the increasing engagement on policies relations with certain key stakeholders (the community, political groups, and other criminal justice organization work) by the Nigerian judges and likes to promote the administration of justice. For instance, at the community level, the Ezes (Kings) and other community leaders are encouraged to settle issues that parties, in agreement with the courts, refer to Eze-in-Council.

The Nigerian court system encourages party members to take proactive steps to resolve their differences. However, the judiciary (through tribunals) is key in resolving disagreements arising after elections. There is, by and large, a formal relationship between the Nigerian judiciary and other criminal justice organizations like the prisons and police. To the former, policy relations come in the form of jail delivery. For the purpose of decongesting the prisons, judges engage in periodic consultations with correctional officials to determine inmates who deserve clemency based on certain conditions. The judiciary's policy relation with the police is profound. The transmission of case files to the courts or Ministry of Justice is one key policy relation, although this policy is not working well, due to corruption in the system. Another policy relation of the judiciary with the police lies in the issuance of a witness warrant/summons to an Investigating Police Officer (IPO) at any time it is deemed fit by the presiding judge.

Although these policies on relations with the community, political groups, and other criminal justice organizations have a relative degree of success, there are quite a number of factors that hamper cooperation with these agencies. In the view of our interviewee, they include corruption, incompetence, selfish agendas on the part of the stakeholders, and political interference. Findings further show that there is no apparent problem with regards to how judges relate to both the living and social conditions of those from economically deprived backgrounds (the less privileged Nigerians) who appear before them in courts. Sometimes they are referred to legal aid, human rights lawyers, and other agencies for pro bono services. In fact, the principle of equity guides judges as they go about their job and relating to all that comes their way. In the succinct words of our interviewee: "equity is equity."

In line with international best practices, it is obvious that Nigerian judges—even in the face of overwhelming evidence against the accused—endeavor to show empathy by referring them to agencies that can provide them with a defense argument of good quality. The principle of *allocutus*—a situation whereby the defense counsel pleads for leniency for his client—is well observed with the administration of justice in Nigeria.

The performance of the criminal justice system in Nigeria has been an issue of concern to both practitioners and theoreticians. On multiple occasions, the view has been expressed that the criminal justice system as currently being practiced in Nigeria is failing or is not achieving the desired results. "On this Judge Edu said in my view the criminal justice system in Nigeria can perform better, if not excellently, if only the country continues to strengthen the current practice of the advertorial justice system as opposed to the inquisitorial justice system. You see in the Western countries, if you enter an office, you will be asked to sit down because the Western world has a relaxed mind. But here in Nigeria, you will first and foremost identify yourself before taking seat. This is because there is a high level of suspicion in the country."

In addition, it is observed from the findings that criminal law, as it presently stands in Nigeria, is not only costly—in terms of resources and time—but also self-defeating since it only succeeds in throwing culprits into prisons for relatively short periods of time. Thus, the emerging viewpoint, which is shared by our respondent, is that there is a dire need to formalize and enshrine the principle of "plea bargaining" in Nigeria's criminal law, so as to help in recovering some of the billions of naira being siphoned off and stolen by some public office holders in Nigeria. Indeed, imprisonment alone has not done much to deter Nigerians from engaging in rapacious looting and thieving of the nation's treasury. Bearing in mind two prevailing principles of law, the Austanian principle and the Rosco Pan,* due to its universal outlook the respondent's view is that Nigeria's criminal justice system should adopt and apply the Rosco Pan.

Problems and Successes Experienced

There are several policies and programs of the courts designed to help practitioners achieve the aim of the judiciary in general. A few of these policies and programs, such as "case return", have functioned well since their adoption. Case return is about the number of cases a judge is expected and able to deliver within a quarter of a year, and this development has put judges on their toes. There is also the policy or rule of "reclusion," which enables a presiding officer to relieve himself/herself of presiding over a matter on grounds of loss of confidence or faith by a party to the matter. This policy has also functioned very well in Nigeria, as some judges have taken advantage of it to abstain from presiding over some matters, thereby assisting in maintaining judges' integrity while retaining some level of public confidence in the judiciary.

It is important however to note that some of these policies and/or programs have not always been effective in promoting the cause of justice. Some of the policies and programs of the courts that apparently have not functioned well for the judges/magistrates and courts, our respondent in a paradoxical manner referred to case return. Case return has adversely affected the delivery of cases and cast aspersions on the quality of justice delivered. This is because it has tended to put undue pressure on presiding officers to meet certain targets, thereby lowering the quality of judgments. Proof of evidence is another policy that seems not to have fared well in the experience of our interviewee. Proof of evidence denotes a situation whereby information is filed by the

---

* The Austanian principle emphasizes the law as it ought to be, while the Rosco Pan emphasizes the idea of taking cognizance of the social dimension of the law, which is in tandem with the principle of equity.

police while the witness/accused comes to court for a proof. The witness and accused may be cross-examined without limit. The problem with this is that there is always a delay from the Investigating Police Officer (IPO), because of the warrant transfer, the problem of transportation, or general cost.

Apart from these policies, which pose a big challenge to the judges and courts in general in their drive to achieve a fair, just, and quality justice system, there are other challenges facing the judges and court system of Nigeria in their current state. They include delays in the dispensation of cases, police inability to transmit case files on time, incompetence, paucity of funds (insufficient funding), and corruption. However, of all these problems facing the Nigerian courts, corruption, in the view of the respondent, remains the greatest threat to deal with.

Dealing with these problems, which are both internally and externally generated, is certainly an uphill task for the judges and other criminal justice stakeholders. Corruption within the judiciary is described as behavior that mirrors the endemic corruption in Nigerian society, and so it remains a very Hydra-headed issue to deal with. However, in the view of our interviewee, internal problems, such as the police's inability to transmit, delays in transmitting case files, and delays in trials as a result of the antics of counsel, are much easier to deal with than the externally generated problems. It is possible and easy to change internal problems. This is because they are within the control of the court system. Although no problem is easy to change, we can easily institute rules and regulations that could monitor these internal problems.

Theory and Practice

Perhaps the legal profession remains the profession where the law of praxis is best at play. In the legal profession, there is a clear synergy between learning the principles or fundamentals of law and the practice of the law. Clearly, and as affirmed by our interviewee, legal scholarship through research furnishes legal practitioners with information on developments in the law both nationally and globally, while practitioners provide the academics (theorists) with new developments (cases) and other legal realities with which they engage to write their legal texts. Legal practitioners learn the continuously emerging trends in law published by law researchers, while theorists extrapolate and inculcate in their writings the outcomes arising from the interpretations of the law by presiding officers in various courts. This obvious relationship between theory and practice does exist and appears to be working well within the Nigerian judicial milieu, as can be seen in the number of law review publications and texts on all aspects of law in the country. Judges, magistrates, registrars and lawyers (through their powerful platform of the Nigerian Bar Association [NBA]) attend conferences to update their knowledge of the law and its practice, while theorists visit practitioners to observe and update their knowledge of the developments in courtrooms, including the interpretations of the law by presiding officers.

While there is a clear positive relationship between theory and practice in the legal profession in contemporary Nigeria, this relationship, it must be emphasized, is not sufficiently harnessed. Some of the factors identified as holding collaborations or interactions back are the tight schedules of theorists and practitioners, the reclusive nature of the judges' work, and conflicting feelings of supremacy between theorists (scholars and researchers in law) and practitioners. This ego can be seen in the controversy that sometimes in the past trailed the profession on whether or not to include academic lawyers as recipients of the Senior Advocate of Nigeria (SANship) cadre. From the perspective of judges or practitioners, there are current developments in law that should be the focus of Nigerian law researchers and scholars to help improve practice. Case-based and theory-based research has proved very useful to practitioners. These are well documented in practice books such as law of evidence books, civil procedure books, criminal law books, criminal procedure books, and law reports, for example, the Nigerian weekly law reports, monthly law reports, and Supreme Court law reports.

It is clear that it is not only for pending cases that the Nigerian judiciary carry out supplementary research. Indeed, their supplementary research transcends the case at hand as long as such research is perceived as capable of adding value to the overall work of the judiciary. For instance, such research includes what our interviewee described as "society-based problems" like same-sex marriage, which is a vexed issue in Nigeria, and emerging issues such as the current debate on plea bargaining. Such research (as it were) is carried out to ascertain the criminal implications on society, and to determine the impact of such issues on the criminal justice system.

Transnational Relations

It is obvious that transnational relationships between Nigerian judges and their counterparts in other parts of the world are at a distance and hard to come by. Platforms for such rewarding relationships, such as conferences and overseas training, are hardly provided by the authorities, so that judges in Nigeria continue to operate as an island in the comity of judges worldwide.

> I attended my first and last conference in England in 2004. I couldn't even attend all the sessions because it was very expensive for me to do so. I went with only N400,000 while a session of the conference cost over 10 pounds. So I was just in London biding my time before flying back after attending the opening session.

The poor state of transnational relations exists against the backdrop of the fact that Nigerian judges clearly appreciate that developments outside their jurisdiction (country as it were) impact significantly on their work and the way the judiciary generally works in Nigeria. For instance, our interviewee made references to critical issues such as human rights, which he described as a yardstick in the administration of the criminal justice system (trial, sentencing, treatment, and judgment), and codes of ethics, even though sometimes diluted by what he called "cultural differences." There is also increasing acceptance of the development of alternative dispute resolution (ADR) by Nigerian judges. ADR grew out of the British legal system and is known within Nigerian legal parlance as out-of-court settlement (OCS). One merit of OCS is that it leads to quick dispensation of justice in Nigeria. We are now encouraging parties in dispute to settle out of court and come with proof for adoption by the court.

Notwithstanding the external pressure from human rights activists on judges, courts, and the judiciary generally to observe and uphold every aspect of human rights as they affect both the accused and victims alike, it is surprising that our interviewee described this requirement and pressure as the most beneficial to judges in the discharge of their duties, because judges must not only provide justice but must be seen as doing so. Unfortunately, because the justice sector is generally perceived as a closed system, public interaction is highly limited and, consequently, not very beneficial to the judges.

Given that judges in Nigeria have limited opportunities to interact with colleagues beyond the shores of Nigeria, their practical interactions and the consequent impact on their jobs remain minimal or even negligible. Even when these practical interactions do exist, the perceptions and nuances of the Nigerian people, and the widespread corruption in the country, do not allow their influences to be brought to bear on the administration of the justice system by the courts and judiciary in general. However, one significant development in criminal justice beyond the shores of Nigeria that impacts on the work of Nigerian judges is the change in the trend and pattern of crime. The phenomenal upsurge in and sophistication of crimes such as global terrorism, kidnapping, murder, defilement, and rape, among others, have put pressure on Nigerian judges to dispense justice speedily and in a timely manner and, of course, in line with international best practices. According to our interviewee, the threat of terrorism, which cuts across all nations of the world, has brought additional pressure to bear on the judges as there is even more pressure among nations to join hands in the fight against terrorism and also to facilitate the speedy trial of culprits.

With particular reference to terrorism and developments since the terrorist attack on the United States on September 11, 2001, and its effect on the work of judges in Nigeria, it is important to highlight that this study found that several domestic laws on terrorism have been passed. The emergence of the dreaded Boko Haram—a Nigerian al-Qaeda-style terrorist group—has put additional pressure on the government to come up with more legislation against terrorism and related offenses. For one thing, this onerous development has led to an increase in the cost of justice delivery as much as it has increased the workload of the judges by expanding the scope of the criminal justice system in the country. More significant is the impact of this development on the psyche of the judges. From the standpoint of penology (under the theme of aggravating circumstances), and according to our interviewee, judges are under temptation to raise the punishment of an accused person when a new crime suddenly emerges, appearing to have been carefully planned and rationalized, and when its impact involves a large number of the helpless public—all characteristics that terrorism in Nigeria has assumed.

General Assessment

Although the Nigerian criminal justice system is beset with many problems, judges apparently still feel satisfied with developments in criminal law, criminal procedure, and the overall performance of the judicial system. This is because no system is a perfect one; even those of the United States, the United Kingdom, and the rest of the Western world are always improving on what they have.

Given that change is the only constant thing in life, and that innovation is critical to life enhancement, judges in Nigeria are not unappreciative of recent positive developments. They also expect other important developments within the country's criminal law and criminal procedure. For instance, plea bargaining, though highly contentious, is seen as a welcome development in Nigeria's legal system. Since Nigeria's criminal law does not make provisions for the forfeiture of loot saved by recent provisions in laws establishing the Independent Corrupt Practices Committee (ICPC), Economic and Financial Crimes Commission (EFCC), and other extant institutions, it is expected that plea bargaining will provide the opportunity for the recovery of a substantial part of the Nigerian wealth being looted by a few privileged Nigerians. Plea bargaining is a "negotiated justice," which helps among other things to reduce the huge cost of justice delivery, especially in Nigeria, where cases are often unduly delayed and thrown out on mere technical grounds.

One clear development that progressive judges in Nigeria welcome is the birth of institutions such as the EFCC and ICPC. There is a feeling that these institutions have somehow closed the gaps in the conventional court system with provisions that facilitate the recovery of stolen money and property. The emergence of industrial courts that deal specifically with the issue of disputes between labor and employers is also of interest to judges. Recently, the industrial court waded into the dispute between the Ministry of Health (federal government) and the Allied Health Workers Union in the country.

An important development within the Nigerian judiciary and court processes, especially in Ebonyi state (our study state), is the extant directive by the

chief judge of Ebonyi state to the effect that police, as investigators and prosecutors, should henceforth triplicate their case files when charging an accused
in court. Such case files could now be transmitted directly by the court to the
Ministry of Justice, in contrast to the old system whereby it took long periods
for the police to do so. This singular innovation is geared toward fast-tracking
justice delivery and reducing undue and deliberate delay on the part of the
police. Now, special courts to address specific legal matters in the country
are emerging. Chukwuma (2011) noted that some states, led by Lagos, have
introduced alternative dispute resolution mechanisms such as the Multi-Door
Courts and Citizens' Mediation Center (CMC) to create spaces for restorative
justice. He explained that these courts have been limited to civil and commercial matters and not extended to criminal cases, making it difficult for both the
complainants and defenders to reach any restorative agreement once the matter has been brought to court, even if the complainant desires it. Furthermore,
there are "mobile courts" that try motorist offenders on the spot and "sanitation courts" in many states of the federation including Ebonyi state that try
offenders of sanitation offenses—those found loitering during the official state
sanitation exercise from 7 am to 10 pm of every last Saturday of the month.

The developments within the Nigerian judiciary and their positive
impacts notwithstanding, there are other ones judges expect and yearn for
developments that take account of the uniqueness of Nigeria's environment and
are capable of adding value to justice delivery in the country. One of these expectations is the establishment of a special court solely to adjudicate corruption
cases. Unsurprisingly, the call for this special court has gained currency among
many Nigerians in view of the prevalence of corruption in the country.

There is a yearning, or rather there are calls, for the establishment of a
Constitutional Court to deal with constitutional matters. The need for the
establishment of a Constitutional Court has become imperative in the light of
recurring constitutional matters/issues arising among the component units
of the Federated Nigeria. Such issues include the question of local council
autonomy, joint accounts, resource control, and revenue allocations/deriva-
tions. Judges expect that the appointment, promotion, discipline, and financ-
ing of state judges will be transferred to the Federal Judicial Council in place
of its current position of being in the hand of the State Judicial Commission.
The greatest merit of this policy action is that it will free the state judges from
the current stronghold and manipulations of the state governments.

As most issues pertaining to judges are constitution based, the most-
needed action to improve the system and bring about the desired changes
lies in the amendment of the constitution to incorporate new developments
within the judicial sector. The ongoing constitutional amendments notwithstanding, the brouhaha it is generating provides the opportunity for these new
developments to be incorporated. However, critical in all this, as explained
by our interviewee, is the urgent need to make judges and the process ICT

driven and ICT compliant. This is all about generating and accepting electronic-based evidence such as computer-generated video and audio.

Conclusion

According to our respondent, one major problem plaguing the entire Nigerian judiciary and in particular the court system is the congestion of cases in courts. The Ebonyi state judiciary (court) system is not immune to this problem. It is not unusual for cases to drag on at the magistrate's or high courts for several months or years while the defendants languish in prison. The limited resources facing the judicial system in Nigeria and the culture of corruption in the country make it difficult for the poor to receive justice in the court system. As Ebonyi state is reported as being one of the poorest states in Nigeria, it can reasonably be assumed that the majority of poor Ebonyians are in for a hard time in their quest for justice.

As many inhabitants of the state lack confidence in the state's judicial system, it has given room for nonstate forms of conflict resolution to operate, sometimes outside the control of the state. Between 1999 and 2003, vigilante groups sprang up in many parts of the state—for example, to perform the function of providing security and even adjudicating cases—usually meting out jungle justice to ordinary criminal suspects allegedly caught committing minor crimes (see also Human Rights Watch and Centre for Law Enforcement Education, 2002). Such informal justice has been increasingly utilized by Nigerians including Ebonyians who cannot afford the formal justice system because of limited access, high cost, and cultural barriers (Alemika and Chukwuma, 2002; Elechi, 2003).

There is no doubt that Judge Eze Udu was very open and frank in his opinions on the judicial process in Nigeria. What also came across during the interview was his passion for the law and how it should be an instrument of justice applied equitably throughout Nigeria; the rule of law is a principle that must be adhered to as justice is not only done but is seen to be done. Among the key themes that came out of the interview is that the Nigerian judiciary and Ebonyi state judiciary are experiencing quite a number of challenges—the challenges of government interference, corruption, insufficient and inappropriate manpower, paucity of funds, increase in crimes, and pressures to deliver judgments swiftly and in a timely manner. The transformation agenda of the current government and the ongoing constitutional amendments are two major developments in the country that have a direct impact on the administration of criminal justice and the judiciary generally in Nigeria. Already, this transformation is being manifested in some ways, with judges expressing their satisfaction while still expecting far more positive developments in the sector.

As seen in the responses, critical to the effective dispensation of justice in Nigeria is the need for Nigerian judges to raise the bar of their transnational relationships with their counterparts in other parts of the globe. This means a commitment to attending international conferences, symposia, and seminars to profit from cross-fertilization of emerging issues and ideas in the judicial sector. It is being argued in some quarters that many Nigerian presiding officers are "educated illiterates"; that is, they are averse to further research and reading to update their knowledge of new developments in the judicial sector to facilitate their quick and quality administration of justice. A lot more of them are certainly ICT noncompliant. Thus, reading of extant literature on legal matters and direct involvement in research will go a long way to enhance the quality of our judges and the consequent justice delivered. Even more rewarding for the judiciary in Nigeria is the importance of embracing an ICT-based approach to justice delivery. Ultimately, any improvement in the judiciary geared toward effective justice delivery will depend on the political will of the Nigerian government to provide the enabling environment for the Nigerian judiciary. This requires strengthening the independence of the judiciary at both the federal and state levels. It also calls on judges, magistrates, and the like in the judicial sector to be encouraged to continually take part in training programs both locally and internationally.

Australia
Legal System

JANE GOODMAN-DELAHUNTY, TRACEY
GREEN AND IDA NGUYEN

The common law system, as developed in the United Kingdom, forms the basis of Australian jurisprudence. Judges' decisions in pending cases are informed by the precedent of previously resolved cases.

Australia was colonized by English settlers who arrived on the east coast in 1788. In 1901, the Australian Commonwealth was established, allowing the six independent colonies of Australia to self-govern as states, united under a federal system where the Queen of England remains a constitutional monarchy. Each federal and state system incorporates three separate branches of government—legislative, executive, and judicial. Parliaments make the laws, the executive government administers the laws, and the judiciary independently interprets and applies them.

In all, Australia (Figure III.1) has nine legal jurisdictions—eight state and territory systems, and one federal system. The federal system consists of the Family Court of Australia, the Federal Circuit Court of Australia, the Federal Court of Australia, and the High Court of Australia that sits in Canberra, Australian Capital Territory. Each state has local or magistrates courts, district or county courts, and supreme courts. Tribunals have specialist jurisdictions, for example, the children's court looks after cases involving juveniles, or the copyright tribunal. It is the state and territory criminal laws that mainly affect the day-to-day lives of Australians.

Deficits in the common law incorporation of Aboriginal customary laws are a prominent issue considering the overrepresentation of Aboriginal and Torres Strait Islander people in the justice system (Marchetti and Daly, 2004).* The first indigenous court, the Nunga Court, was established 1999 in Port Adelaide, South Australia, and became the model for most indigenous courts in Queensland and Victoria, whereas the New

---

* ALRC report 21 1968.

Figure III.1 Map of Australia showing Australian states.

South Wales (NSW) equivalent, the circle court, is based on the Canadian circle sentencing model (Aboriginal Justice Advisory Committee, 2000).

The State Courts

State courts deal with the bulk of civil and criminal matters. At the bottom of the hierarchy, but integral to the justice system is the magistrates court, also known as the local court. A single magistrate presides; there is no jury. In criminal proceedings, magistrates issue a verdict and decide on the penalty for lesser offenses, including traffic offenses and larceny, by fine or punishment. In addition, they conduct the committal process. If there is a case to be heard, it will then be tried by a judge and jury in the district or supreme court. Some special magistrates courts include the children's court (for offenders or defendants under age 17), the minor debts court, the small claims tribunal, the coroner's court (for unnatural deaths or arson), and the industrial magistrates court (for disputes between employers and employees).

The district court or county court sits above the magistrates court. Indictable offenses committed to the intermediate courts vary from state to state. Judges preside over these intermediate courts; however, in more serious cases a jury (usually of 12 people) determines the guilt of the accused. The supreme courts are superior courts of record for the states, with general juris-diction (Beck, 2013). They have two divisions, the trial or general division, which encompasses criminal and civil matters, and an appellant division. They hear the more serious criminal cases, often empanelling a jury to decide the facts. The court of criminal appeal often includes a panel of two or more judges who preside over sentencing and conviction appeals from judgments issued by inferior courts, including the supreme court.

The Federal Courts

The Family Court of Australia, established in 1975,[*] has registries in all states and territories except western Australia, which has its own family court. Its jurisdiction encompasses the complexities of marriage, the custody of chil-dren, and marital dissolution.[†]

The Federal Circuit Court of Australia deals with "shorter and simpler matters in federal jurisdictions" (Gleeson, 2003). It shares jurisdiction with the Family Court of Australia and the Federal Court of Australia, ranging from bankruptcy to migration.

The Federal Court of Australia is a superior court of law and equity[‡] with a defined jurisdiction conferred by over 150 parliamentary laws, addressing bankruptcy, corporations law, federal administrative law, native title, immi-gration, and federal tax disputes.[§] Its criminal jurisdiction extends only to incidental summary matters. The federal court hears appeals from a final judgment by a single judge of the federal courts, a federal magistrate, judg-ments of the Supreme Court of Norfolk Island, and appeals from a state, the ACT, or Northern Territory court exercising federal jurisdiction.[¶]

Australia's high court, established during federation, consists of a chief justice and six other judges who can preside individually or collectively. As the highest court, it interprets, defines, and applies the law for all jurisdic-tions, binding all Australian courts,[**] and it is also the final court of appeal in Australia. Special leave must be granted to an applicant by the high court for the appeal to be heard.[††]

---

[*] (Cth).
[†] *Family Law Act 1975* (Cth), s 33.
[‡] *1976* (Cth).
[§] *Jurisdiction of Courts (Miscellaneous Amendments) Act 1987* (Cth).
[¶] *Federal Court of Australia Act 1976* (Cth), s 24(1).
[**] Section 76 of the constitution confers to the high court its original jurisdiction to inter-pret constitutional and Commonwealth matters.
[††] *Constitution* (Cth), s 73.

Australian Federal Administrative Appeals Tribunal

Jurisdiction

The tribunal has jurisdiction to review decisions made under more than 400 Commonwealth acts and legislative instruments. The largest part of the tribunal's workload arises from applications about decisions in the areas of family assistance and social security, taxation, veterans' affairs, and workers' compensation. The tribunal also reviews decisions in areas such as bankruptcy, child support, civil aviation, citizenship and immigration, corporations and financial services regulation, customs, freedom of information, industry assistance, mutual recognition of occupations, and passports and security assessments by the Australian Security Intelligence Organization.

Role and Function

The role of the tribunal is to provide independent merits reviews of administrative decisions. The tribunal aims to provide a review mechanism that is fair, just, economical, informal, and quick. The tribunal falls within the portfolio of the attorney general and reviews a wide range of administrative decisions made by Australian government ministers, departments, and agencies, including some other tribunals. In limited circumstances, the tribunal can review administrative decisions made by state government and nongovernment bodies. A merits review of an administrative decision involves considering afresh the facts, law, and policy relating to that decision. The tribunal considers the material before it and decides what is the correct—or, in a discretionary area, the preferable—decision. It will affirm, vary, or set aside the decision under review.

New South Wales Mental Health Review Tribunal

Jurisdiction

In its civil hearings, the tribunal may

- Conduct mental health inquiries and make involuntary patient orders authorizing the continued involuntary detention of a person in a mental health facility
- Review involuntary patients in mental health facilities, usually every 3 or 6 months, and in appropriate cases every 12 months
- Review voluntary patients in mental health facilities, usually every 12 months

- Hear appeals against an authorized medical officer's refusal to discharge an involuntary patient
- Make, vary, and revoke community treatment orders
- Hear appeals against a magistrate's decision to make a community treatment order
- Approve the use of electroconvulsive therapy (ECT) for involuntary patients
- Determine if voluntary patients have consented to ECT
- Approve surgery on a patient detained in a mental health facility
- Approve special medical treatment (sterilization)
- Make and revoke orders under the NSW Trustee and Guardian Act 2009 for a person's financial affairs to be managed by the NSW trustee

The tribunal also reviews the cases of all forensic patients

- Who have been found not guilty by reason of mental illness
- Who have been found unfit to be tried or
- Who have been transferred from prison to hospital because of a mental illness

Role and Function

The Mental Health Review Tribunal (MHRT) is a specialist quasi-judicial body constituted under the Mental Health Act 2007. It has a wide range of powers that enable it to conduct mental health inquiries, make and review orders, and hear some appeals on the treatment and care of people with a mental illness.

The tribunal has a president, two full-time and eight part-time deputy presidents, a registrar, and approximately 100 part-time members. Other than for mental health inquiries, which are generally conducted by a single legal member of the tribunal, each tribunal panel consists of three members: a lawyer who chairs the hearing, a psychiatrist, and another suitably qualified member. All tribunal members have extensive experience in mental health, and some have personal experience with a mental illness or caring for a person with a mental illness. A number of the part-time deputy presidents are former judges.

Duncan Chappell, Federal Administrative Appeals Tribunal

3

TRACEY GREEN

Contents

Introduction

In writing the introduction to this interview, the authors were faced with a daunting task, as Duncan Chappell's judicial roles comprise an extensive and wide-ranging career, which includes writing an authoritative text on the Australian criminal justice system (Chappell and Wilson, 2005). Duncan does not consider himself to have been "judicial" in the regular sense of the word. At most he would say he has held some "quasi-judicial" positions, the details of which will be revealed, but it is Duncan's humility that strikes us most in a man who has achieved so much, intellectually, professionally, and (quasi) judicially. In his words:

> Well I suppose that the purpose of the interview was to talk about my so-called judicial career, but that's been only really a relatively small part of my life. I think it goes for about 15 years, probably, that I was doing judicious ... well I say judicial work. But my background is that of a lawyer and a criminologist, and ... it was fairly unusual at the time, I did a doctorate before I started into academic life and that was in Cambridge back in the 1960s, ... my first job was actually teaching criminal law and criminology at the University of Sydney back in the mid to late 1960s, funnily some 50 years later I have done the full circle, back again teaching law at Sydney as an adjunct professor.

Career

Duncan Chappell is a native of Tasmania, the island state off the southern coast of Australia. Studying political science and then law at the University of Tasmania, Duncan completed his legal articles, a prerequisite to practice law, and then worked as a judge's associate in Tasmania's supreme court before practicing and teaching law. However, his keen intellect had already been recognized and he was accepted into the University of Cambridge where he studied and was awarded a PhD (law and criminology) in 1965. Duncan returned to Australia to teach law at the University of Sydney before taking a position at John Jay College, New York, in 1969, followed by positions at the State University of New York, Battelle Memorial Institute (Washington), the University of Washington, and La Trobe University (Melbourne). Since 1980, Duncan has been a member of the School of Criminology at Simon Fraser University (Vancouver), where he retains an adjunct professorial appointment.

Such was his reputation that in 1978, Duncan was appointed commissioner of the Australian Law Reform Commission (ALRC) in Sydney, Australia. Duncan was the commissioner in charge of reference on sentencing and was responsible for the preparation of the significant ALRC 15 (1980) Sentencing of Federal Offenders (ALRC, 1988). He was also involved in work on Aboriginal custody law and child welfare law references. These postings marked the beginning of Duncan's public life, where he went on to successfully combine his academic prowess with education and a direct, real-world influence in the field to which he has committed his life's work, criminal justice.

For example, from 1987 to 1990, Duncan was the director of the Australian Institute of Criminology (AIC), a government agency, and the national research center on crime and criminal justice. The aim of the AIC is to "promote justice and reduce crime by undertaking and communicating evidence-based research to inform policy and practice" (AIC, 2013). During this period, which followed two mass shootings in Melbourne in 1987, Duncan was appointed by the Australian prime minister to chair the National Committee on Violence. He has been a frequent consultant and advisor to governments and other public and private agencies in both North America and Australia. He is also a prolific researcher and author of academic articles and texts; however, for the purposes of this expose we should direct our attention to his judicial postings.

Duncan Chappell has presided over three tribunals: the Federal Administrative Appeals Tribunal (AAT), the New South Wales State Mental Health Tribunal, and internationally on the Commonwealth Secretariat

Arbitral Tribunal. These are not "courts" in the strict sense, but as tribunals they have the authority to judge, or adjudicate, and determine claims or disputes. As the Commonwealth Secretariat Arbitral Tribunal does not have a criminal justice element, Duncan's work there is not explored but is mentioned as part of his broad background.

Personal Judicial Philosophy

Q: How do you think your social justice background influenced your decision making with this work, do you think it perhaps made you more sensitive to their issues making it harder to make those difficult decisions?

A: I think it did help. I certainly have had quite a lot of exposure to human rights issues while I was… both at the United Nations and also at the Institute of Criminology in some of the earlier work I did, so that assisted, I think, in appreciating how profoundly important these decisions were going to be in the lives of the people.

It was… some very tragic stories were told and it was very hard to make decisions, but you have to make decisions according to the law, and while you had some discretion, in many cases it was always guided by what the rules were.

And I suppose as a… if you're thinking about judicial impact of theory and practice, I suppose I believe strongly in therapeutic justice, and also adopting the humanitarian approach to the law, and laws should not be there as an instrument of oppression but just there to facilitate and help people and so on. I'm not a strict constructionist, but I still have, obviously, as a lawyer, to interpret what the law is, and even though I might have disagreed with some of the legal things I had to administer, that was irrelevant.

And I had to deport people, and/or deny people visas, …and of course there was a strong accountability in a sense because all of your decisions you had to write, in most instances, a decision, or you could give it orally, but I usually gave written decisions, and people could appeal, and did, against decisions they felt (were unfair).

…and I certainly, by the time I left the AAT, I was appealed against a number of times to the federal court, for federal court, I think I was only overturned about once, so I don't think that was too bad a record… that's one of the things that judges obviously fear is being appealed against because obviously you don't want to make an error in judgment or not uphold the law correctly according to the law… being rolled on appeal… it is a huge smack over the wrists isn't it.

Q: Do you think your judgments or decisions were different from those made by your peers?

A: Yes, some of them, certainly. And judicial life is a fairly lonely life, as lots of people have said, you don't really have as many interactions with your colleagues as you would, say, if you were coming from a university background where you'd go and talk about things, and, usually, if you're a decent academic anyway, you should talk about all sorts of things, and pick the brains of your colleagues etcetera… bounce a few ideas around.

I have to admit that some of my colleagues were wonderful; they were quite prepared to shoot the breeze and do things like that, discuss issues, not specific cases of course but likely scenarios or concerns. There were others who you wouldn't want to go and talk to anyway, frankly. But the people you became closest to, really, were your associate and your personal assistant who you had with you the whole time. And I had 5 years full time, so I had, I think, five or four associates, one was with me for 2 years, and they were all extraordinary bright and able young people, and all became good friends, and they were really the people you would talk to the most about things. And so they would help also write decisions and do all sorts of things like that.

But as far as colleagues were concerned, you also had conferences that you would go to which were fellow decision makers from the AAT, so we used to have internal conferences of AAT members, and then we also would go to something called Australia… well I forget what it's called now… Australian Judicial Council, or whatever it is, whatever the national meetings are of judges and things, so that's another avenue of interaction.

But I also did keep up, while I was at the AAT, and then onward when I was at the MHRT, some academic interests…

Q: Do you think the judiciary, generally, can become isolated?

A: Yes, I think that's true, but obviously all the judges are affected by their upbringing and their social background etcetera, and they tend often to come from very similar backgrounds, as we know, and also come from similar gender until recently, so that there was a significant gender imbalance in many of the courts.

I have to say though in the tribunals I was in, I think I came in late in the period, so fortunately that wasn't as much of an issue as it was in the law courts… in fact both presidents of the Mental Health…and the AAT were women and both very effective…

federal court judges, so it was really interesting to work in that environment as well.

But the ability to understand, I suppose, and appreciate the sorts of things that you have to make decisions on is very much influenced by your background, and... as I came to the job later in my career perhaps than most people were, I think I must have been a little over 50 when I first got to the AAT. You've had a fair bit of life experience...

Q: You were making decisions on the fate of refugees, did you find that difficult at a personal level?

A: It is, a very difficult... a very difficult thing. Yeah, I mean I think, too, you've mentioned impact and how much it affects the lives of people, and one of them... and also you asked earlier about some memorable cases, and it brought back that memory of one case that I dealt with when I was at the Administrative Appeals Tribunal where I was dealing with a young man from Vietnam who was facing deportation, he kept... I forget, anyway he had committed a series of quite serious crimes.

And he and his family were having their day in court, basically, and the father was in the witness box, and we were working through an interpreter, and the interpreter said "I do not feel well," and I thought the interpreter was saying to me "I do not feel well," and I said "Oh," you know, "would you like us to pause?." "No," she said, "the witness does not feel well," and the next moment the witness collapsed in the witness box and died. It was this young man's father, and it was just the strain and stress of this had clearly affected his... him to the extent of it... he... just suddenly had... a heart attack there and then. And that was... it really was... it affected everyone who... as you might imagine. I called the counsel for the immigration department who was there, and also the lawyer for the young man, and we had sort of... well we almost need to have... all of us have counseling because it was... a very traumatic experience.

Problems and Successes Experienced

On the period when Judge Chappell was deputy president of the Australian Federal Administrative Appeals Tribunal (AAT), he said:

A: It was at that time when I became director of the Institute of Criminology that I also was appointed to the Administrative Appeals Tribunal, which is the Federal Commonwealth Administrative Appeals Tribunal, as a deputy president. At the time, I think that was about 1990, so that's when I was... my first formal judicial... or quasi-judicial appointment.

...so it was agreed that I would... as a lawyer I would be appointed to the AAT, and when... if and when I finished at the institute I would then become a member of the AAT on a full-time basis, and that's exactly what happened.

When I left the tribunal in 1994, I think it was, I spent a bit over a year with the United Nations working with the United Nations in Rome, and then I went to full-time work here in Sydney with the Administrative Appeals Tribunal, and they asked me to come to Sydney because it's by far the busiest registry and they also have quite a large remit in terms of handling criminal deportations which I spent a lot of my time doing, as well as various other things which have a criminal justice linkage as well.

But also doing the whole range of administrative law, which I'm not an administrative lawyer, and I learned on the job as it were, a crash course...

And I was a full-time member of the Administrative Appeals Tribunal from 1996 through to 2001, and that meant doing all of the things that you do on the AAT.

And I think the main... the main areas of jurisdiction—there are over 300 areas of jurisdiction that the Administrative Appeals Tribunal has.

It reviews all major Commonwealth government orientated... Commonwealth legislation orientated decisions, so the four main areas, I think it was... I remember the worker's compensation, the Commonwealth veteran's matters, social security, and immigration. And of those areas I suppose not by default, but simply because of the volume of business, I tended, because I had a criminal law/criminology background, to do more of the deportation cases, and also some of the refugee matters too I became involved with which were very interesting ones, particularly where crimes against humanity had been involved, and where a person had been denied a visa or entry to the country as a refugee on the basis that they had been associated with various things like that.

Q: What type of cases were you typically dealing with at that time?

A: At that time, the cases that I dealt with mainly as far as crimes against humanity were concerned, and genocide, were people from Sri Lanka, from Chile, and... some from the Balkans ... area.

Now that was a tough, tough gig, really!

Well both the criminal deportation matters and the refugee claims were... you were dealing with people's lives, profoundly affecting them, and... you were always conscious of that and it made it very difficult. And some people I think just probably feel they can't do that sort of work.

On the period when Judge Chappell was president of the Sydney-based New South Wales Mental Health Review Tribunal, he said:

A: I left the AAT in 2001 for another quasi-judicial position as president of the Mental Health Review Tribunal in New South Wales, which is obviously a state tribunal, and that was yet another, and totally different, experience, leading a tribunal of about 110 members and 30 or 40 staff, and doing reviews of people who were to be involuntarily treated for mental illness as well as doing mainly work on… with forensic patients which I can talk about, again, in more detail, which has a criminal justice link to it.

Q: What was your role?

A: Well I was president of the tribunal, and in that capacity I had, as I say, the administrative managerial responsibilities for the tribunal, but the main function of the tribunal is to hear and make decisions about people who are facing involuntary forms of treatment for their mental illness. And there are two groups of them really, there's the civil side of things, so people who may have a severe mental illness and they have to be scheduled… put into an institution for involuntary treatment, or in treatment in the community, and the tribunal hears their case and it sits… the tribunal sits… or it nearly always sits with three people presided over by a lawyer with a psychiatrist member and a third member who is a person who has had some experience of mental health issues, maybe a consultant, maybe a psychologist, social worker, mental health nurse, someone like that.

Q: How does the tribunal operate?

A: The people themselves appear before the tribunal, they have a right to have a lawyer in most instances, and they… also the treating team, and people who are going to give the form of treatment have to appear to justify what they are about to do, and… and if you… you can either decide yes, that they… that this should go ahead, or you can say no it shouldn't. You can also discharge someone into the community on community treatment rather than being in the institution.

But the area that I suppose is of greatest interest to your interview is more the forensic side of things, and the second area of the tribunal I really had a responsibility for was so-called forensic patients, and they are people who've been found not guilty on the grounds of mental illness of a serious crime, usually murder, and instead of sending them into a prison and having them treated as a prisoner or whatever, and given treatment, they are referred to the Mental

Health Review Tribunal for subsequent management and decision making, and eventual release or otherwise back into the community.

And in addition to that function, the tribunal also hears cases where a person's been found unfit to be tried...

...or stand trial. They have to decide whether or not it's a condition that will likely continue, if so, what... what sort of other conditions should be considered. So those are pretty difficult decisions to have to make, if you release someone back into the community who reoffends it's going to be a major political issue if nothing else. Hit the headlines. And also if someone is killed or injured you're obviously... you know, you're going to feel a lot of responsibility for that.

That was a tough, tough job, I did it for 5 years, and I think 5 years is about enough.

Q: So there must be some cases that have had a particular impact on you over that time, what type of cases would you find the most difficult to deal with?

A: Oh, I think the one I remember most probably is a young woman who... who was in... and I have to be careful talking about this... not detail but the information on the public record so the publicly available thing, a young woman who had been found unfit to be tried and was being held in a facility for young offenders, and while there she killed an instructor, and she just personally had an obsession with knives, and was very deeply disturbed, but she was not, at least on the basis of the assessments, mentally ill in the sense of having a defense of mental illness in these situations.

So eventually she continued to be held in different parts of the system, the criminal justice system rather than the mental hospital because she was said not to be mentally ill, and we had to see her and review her on a fairly regular basis, and that was a most difficult case, a very difficult case, and it's one that has... well still hasn't been resolved because a lot of these cases go on for years and years...

...unfortunately some people may spend the rest of their lives in a maximum security facility of some sort, whether it's a mental health one or not.

Q: Do you think that the tribunal is an effective mechanism for dealing with these people, with all of these complicated issues?

A: Well I think the tribunal... the time I was at the tribunal; we only had the power to make recommendations so far as release decisions were concerned. We had some direct powers, but in terms of deciding whether a forensic patient should be released into the community, or should be discharged completely, that was a decision made at the political level by... basically by cabinet, it was a cabinet decision, even though it's closeted in the garbled language of the executive decision making, and it was a governor's pleasure... a person being held by the governor's pleasure.*

A: Of course the irony at that time was... or it still is I suppose, that the governor is indeed a psychiatrist, so... and she took a keen interest in this executive discretion...

...as in addition to the political people involved. But now fortunately the tribunal has been given complete powers to make decisions. That occurred after I left, and my successor in office was able to persuade the political powers that that was a good move, something I'd been unsuccessful in doing. The timing was probably right.

Sometimes it does take quite a lot of time to make changes in these areas. In fact it would have been 150 years or so, I think, to get to this point. Governor's pleasure [existed] from the time of first settlement.

Theory and Practice

Q: I think in your case your whole career has been wrapped up in blending theory with practice, because you've consistently moved between the two and intertwined your career with both theory and practice but, you know, you're in a different situation I think from other members of the judiciary?

A: I am, really, and, yeah, I think that... I'd never say I've ever thought of myself as being a heavy theorist, but as I said earlier I certainly believe in the therapeutic qualities of the law, and if that's the most consistent theory, if there is one, I think I've applied or tried to apply it.

Yes. But my life has also been imbued with the belief in empirical backing for policy and things that you do, and you should, if you can, obtain the best available evidence that things work before you engage in them. And unfortunately I haven't seen that aspect carried out in many of the settings I've been in, it's... where most of my colleagues wouldn't know what research was other than going looking at the case law and deciding what... what the case has said.

---

* "Governor's pleasure," or "Her Majesty's pleasure" in the United Kingdom, is a legal term referring to an indeterminate sentence for some prisoners, particularly those who have raised a successful insanity defense. Typically, the incarceration is reviewed to determine if there has been a significant change in the person's condition and to consider whether the person can be released.

And fortunately the appeal court judges who looked at my decisions obviously must have been persuaded that I had applied the correct interpretations and so on. But the rigidity of the legal system... much of the legal training that does go on doesn't lend itself easily then to trying to bring in much of the social sides and other perspectives of the legal practice... I have seen myself some evidence of that with some of the colleagues I had, and I'm afraid, I have no respect for them whatsoever.

Australia is a federation using a system that was adapted from the United States, whereby each of the states retains sovereignty and the ability to make laws and raise certain taxes. The federal government is responsible for national defense, immigration, health, income tax, and various other matters that are detailed in the Australian Constitution. The system, being a constitutional monarchy, has many parallels with Canadian federalism; however, in Australia there is a direct link, through the state governor to the Australian monarch, the Queen of the British Commonwealth of Nations (Commonwealth). Interestingly, Duncan has served in each realm, state, federal, and the Commonwealth. However, before we reveal his thoughts and experiences in each of these areas, it is important to understand the unique and valuable perspective that Duncan brings to such positions. Early in the interview, Duncan reflected on the value of research in the reform of social policy and in the courts.

I spent a year at La Trobe University in Melbourne as a visiting professor, and then I was asked by the Australian Law Reform Commission to join them as a commissioner in charge of a reference on sentencing... which was I think an important turning point in terms of realizing how one's own research experience could then be applied in a law reform setting. And I was very lucky to have a superb mentor and leader in Michael Kirby who was the chair of the commission at the time, and he was very sympathetic to empirical research informing reform, which is very unusual in the law profession even now.

In fact I remember thinking about the research we did regarding judicial attitudes, we did the first national survey that had ever been done of the judges in Australia as part of the reference group, asking them their views in relation to sentencing and sentencing reform, what they felt was necessary and what would assist. All of the judges in the country, with the noted exception of Victoria, agreed to actually be interviewed for this survey. But the Victorian chief justice, Sir John Young at the time, sent a scathing letter to Justice Kirby saying that "social science research had no place whatever in law," and that the law was there to be interpreted not to be researched. They therefore refused to participate in research designed to assist them, which seemed very strange to me.

And I must say it was an absolute classic. But in fact, since then I think there's been a better understanding of perhaps contributions that could be made by researchers to the judiciary, to changes in the law, and in the legal profession as well.

Duncan's interest and involvement with criminal justice research developed while working in the United States during an era of profound change.

> I became involved in research, I suppose, on policy issues, associated with the criminal law and criminal justice. And it was a very relevant time, of course, in the United States because there was huge ferment and change going on, it was the time of the... post the assassination of both Martin Luther King and Robert Kennedy, and the Attica prison riots, and the Kent state shootings and all those sort of things came in.

Q: What do you see as the greatest issues in this area from both your criminology and judiciary points of view?

A: Well I suppose in the criminal justice area generally, because I've focused so much on mental health issues, I'm really aware that a significant number of the people who come into the criminal justice process do have mental illnesses.

   [Mental illness has a] huge impact and I've done actually quite a bit of work on that, and had a book just published on that topic.

   [Mental illness] affects obviously the prosecution and it affects the judges in terms of sentencing, and it affects corrections even more so because so many of these people wind up in our prisons.

   So I think if there's any area that really lends itself to a major need for reform is to try and manage more adequately the whole process providing access to treatment, and effective treatment, for people with a mental illness and not simply dumping them into the garbage bag... of the correctional system.

Q: How do you see the links of drug abuse with mental illness especially some of the newer synthetic drugs?

A: ... yes, with that, and the linkages between drug abuse and mental illness... the new issues that this brings, there have been a lot of deaths.

   It is. It is, yeah. And especially I think the police see that all too often because people just tend to get recycled in and out, and it takes up an enormous amount of their time, and so...

   [They] come out worse than they went in, I know, it's a very depressing and very challenging job to do. But... so I think of all the areas of criminal law. But the other aspect I suppose is just simply the sheer volume of the business the courts have to deal with, the criminal courts, and the delays that exist in accessing justice, people shouldn't have to wait years for their...

   ...for their trial to come on, they shouldn't have to be detained and without bail in any circumstances. And that's especially the case with young people, I think we incarcerate far, far too many people awaiting trial, and incarcerate far too many people at large, so those are all huge challenges. Sentencing... I suppose sentencing, it was an area that as I mentioned I was involved in significant [unintelligible 19:56] trial and law reform, I've kept a general interest in it all my life, my professional life, and it is the area where also so much of judicial attitudes too impact, so greatly, there is so much power...

Yeah, that's right. Well I suppose I haven't actually directly sentenced in the sense of finding someone guilty and then proposing a sentence, but I have had to nonetheless determine people's fate and lives, in fact their entire life as far as people who've, as I've said, associated with a crime and then mental illness. So it's not so dissimilar to sentencing really...

Transnational Relations

Q: Do you have any thoughts on the different systems in place in the countries you have worked?

A: I think I've found probably the easiest transitions working in Canada to be honest, because it is a federal system, unlike the UK, and I think often that makes a big difference as to how you look at the legal issues and understand there are such major differences between each of the states and territories, and... also a lack of a national approach to things, which I often wish there were a national approach... ... and that's very frustrating.

And it does [have a negative impact] for both policy which I include probably in that funding as well, that the funding mechanisms are not necessarily adequate, are not consistent across different jurisdictions. The amount of money applied, in, say, the mental health area varies from jurisdiction to jurisdiction, and it's not a national responsibility in the main.

But I think I've been very lucky in many ways in being able to work in so many different places, and I suppose again the experiences that you gain in those other places affect how you are, what you are, and how you react. A comparative understanding of things is terribly important, if you know there are other legal approaches... well, for example, the civil law, which is a huge area in itself, and I'm quite impressed with the inquisitorial systems of justice. I think we could probably do a lot more of them here, I think our adversarial approach is often extraordinarily destructive and very damaging to the people involved in it.

Particularly... particularly in the cases we know in sexual assault of children and things like that, and with people with mental illness too.

Q: What impact has 9/11 had on your legal work?

A: Well as far as I'm concerned 9/11 really has had no impact on my legal work, it only has been the extraordinary aggravation of travel which has been utterly ruined by much of this.

[It has added] An hour onto your journey, or 2 h, or whatever. Security has just become appallingly bad, you know, and with what effect...with what effect one has to ask.

Very little. Very little. No. That is not purely true. Some of the people who I dealt with mental illness had new conspiracy theories at least to work with. But that's about the only impact...

Conclusion

Duncan Chappell has a unique perspective on the role of the judiciary or in his words, "quasi-judiciary." Strongly influenced by his academic and practitioner experience, he has a great understanding of the complexity of the criminal justice system and the reality of those people who find themselves impacted by it. It was a privilege to spend time discussing these issues with Duncan who is indeed a judge, a gentleman, and a scholar.

James Woods AO QC, New South Wales Supreme Court

4

JANE GOODMAN-DELAHUNTY

Contents

Introduction

The Honourable James Ronald Tomson Wood AO QC is one of Australia's most senior and accomplished judges. He served for over 20 years as a Supreme Court judge on the highest court in the largest and in the most populous state in the country, New South Wales (NSW), culminating with 8 years as Chief Judge at Common Law. While on the bench, and subsequently, he led a number of special commissions or inquiries, including the renowned Wood Royal Commission into Police Corruption. Since leaving the bench in 2005, Justice Wood has held a series of significant appointments, as NSW Police Integrity Commissioner, Chair of the NSW Law Reform Commission, and Chair of the Sentencing Council of NSW. When I arrived at his Sydney office at the Law Reform Commission to interview him, he and the staff were celebrating his fourth extrajudicial appointment, as Chair of NSW Probation and Parole, a position he assumed in December 2013.

This chapter traces the development of Justice Wood's distinguished legal career and provides examples of his engagement and influence, nationally and internationally, across crucial aspects of the criminal justice system, encompassing not only traditional judicial adjudication of cases in dispute, but also legislation and policy reform, criminal inquiries and investigations, and postadjudicatory sentencing of offenders before their release back into the community. A glossary of legal terms is at the end of the chapter.

Career

Few justices have exerted an impact on as many aspects of the criminal justice system as Justice Wood, in a legal career spanning five decades. The depth and breadth of his influence are apparent in all phases of the criminal justice system in NSW: criminal investigative processes, the adjudication of individual cases, the development of sentencing programs and policy, and legislation and policy making through law reform activities. His career exemplifies how expertise developed in the role of judging can lead to extrajudicial responsibilities and substantial contributions beyond courtroom adjudication.

Justice Wood attended Knox Grammar School in Sydney, NSW. His English grandfather was stationed in Madras, India, as part of the Indian Civil Service, and in his youth James often stayed with him. This formative experience resulted in an abiding interest in comparative legal systems, and enthusiasm for international assignments, especially in Asian and non-Anglo cultures. He graduated from Sydney University in 1964 with the University Medal in Law. After graduation, he worked as a solicitor until 1970, when he became a barrister and then Queen's Counsel. Initially, he had a general practice: mostly civil matters and some minor criminal matters. In 1984, he was appointed a judge in the Common Law Division of the NSW Supreme Court, drawing on his expertise with personal injury compensation claims. His familiarity with criminal law rapidly expanded, as approximately one half of his caseload concerned criminal law matters. For 10 years, he worked on the NSW Supreme Court and, at times, the NSW Court of Criminal Appeal.

In 1985, Justice Wood led an inquiry into the convictions for terrorism charges of three members (Alister, Anderson, and Dunn) of the Ananda Marga religious sect for attempting to kill a politician, after the Hilton bombing in Sydney in 1978 (Anderson, 1992). His findings cast doubt on incriminating affidavits by a police informer, and he recommended pardoning the three men, who were released in 1985 (Molomby, 1986; *R v. Anderson*, 1991). Many details of the wrongful conviction were revealed in an Australian

Broadcasting Corporation documentary that relied on the evidence aggregated by the Wood inquiry (Dellara, 1995).

Following this experience, in 1994 Justice Wood was seconded to chair the NSW Police Royal Commission to lead an inquiry into police corruption, an assignment that lasted over 3 years. His report exposed "noble cause" corruption by police generating false or planted evidence and creating false records of interview to secure convictions of known criminals, as well as traditional corruption by police who ignored obvious crime, took money from offenders, and cooperated with them. Justice Wood had previously observed the presence in police records of interview of "police speak" rather than language you would expect from an accused person and had inferred that these records did not fairly represent what transpired in the interviews and that police were cutting corners. The extent to which the police practice of "verballing" or fabrication of confessions prevailed (Dixon, 2007) was something Justice Wood had not initially appreciated. Because it was hard for defense counsel to prove that the statements were faked, by and large, police records were accepted in court. The Wood Commission noted that verballing was "an art form within certain sections of the NSW Police Service" (Wood, 1996, p. 40). Now cited as an international model for battling entrenched corruption, this "extraordinary investigation that swept through the NSW Police Force like a tsunami"* was the topic of *The Inquisition*, another documentary (Landers and Blowen, 2010). The commission was successful in changing the nature of Australian policing in part because it was proactive in using surveillance techniques, and because one police officer cooperated and exposed systemic organized corruption and cynical, unethical, and unacceptable policing strategies.

In the course of that policing inquiry, Justice Wood learned of institutional failure in that existing laws against pedophilia were not enforced. In 1997, he led a separate inquiry into child sexual abuse, the Paedophile Inquiry, in NSW. It examined the activities of organized pedophile networks in NSW and the adequacy of procedures for protecting at-risk minors and for responding to alleged sex offenses against minors (Wood, 1997, Vols. IV and V). The inquiry exposed corruption in churches and schools and forced the police to take a more proactive role in prosecuting child sexual assault. As a consequence, multidisciplinary Joint Investigation Response Teams were established to more effectively investigate child abuse and achieve better outcomes for the young people involved. Following this inquiry, in 2000, Justice Wood was declared an Officer of the Order of Australia for his distinguished service of a high degree to Australia and to humanity.

---

* http://www.abccommercial.com/librarysales/program/inquisition.

In 1998, Justice Wood was appointed the Chief Judge at Common Law and held this position for 8 years.* In this role, his involvement in criminal law deepened. Because serious criminal cases are tried by a jury of 12, his engagement with juries increased in this period. This experience left him with strong confidence in the jury system in criminal cases, and he would never suggest abolishing jury trials. He observed how juries bring their common sense to bear to discern which are not strong cases, except for a very small and limited number of cases where the accused is unlikely to get a fair trial because of the particular facts or surrounding events. Subsequently, Justice Wood led several reform initiatives to strengthen and support juries, by increasing the participation of more members of the community on juries, and by improving communications between courts and jurors. He expressed concern about juries making independent inquiries on the Internet, or doing their own experiments rather than confining themselves to reach a decision based on evidence before them, so advised judges to constantly remind juries of this obligation. Despite these concerns, he would be sorry to see the jury system weakened or replaced by judge-only trials.

Justice Wood found his work as a judge both interesting and rewarding, and it also opened a number of doors for him to undertake other inquiries. The chronology of his career reveals that it is in the 10 years since The Hon James Wood left the bench that his career has reached its pinnacle, extending his influence on the criminal justice system in the state. In 2005, in acknowledgment of his specialization in criminal law corruption, Justice Wood left the bench for an appointment as Inspector of the NSW Police Integrity Commission (NSW PIC), as an intermediary between the agency and parliament. The oversight of oversight bodies was a rewarding and a responsible position. A year later, in 2006, he was appointed Chair of the NSW Law Reform Commission (NSW LRC), a position he held for 8 years. During that period, the LRC was exceptionally productive, and under his leadership issued 14 review papers on diverse topics, including criminal justice responses to persons with cognitive and mental impairments, bail, privacy, jury directions in criminal cases, penalty notice offenses, and so on.† Concurrently for much of that time, he served as a Member and then Chairman of the NSW Sentencing Council, a position he still holds.

Currently, Justice Wood is a Member of the NSW Customs Reform Board, advising the minister and the Customs Board of Protection Service on how to deal with corruption allegations regarding customs agents who

---

* A photographic portrait of Justice Wood, Chief Justice at Common Law, Supreme Court of New South Wales, in his wig and robes, taken by NSW prosecutor Mark Tedeschi in 1992, is on display in the National Library of Australia. http://nla.gov.au/nla.pic-an21828158.

† http://www.lawreform.lawlink.nsw.gov.au/lrc/lrc_completed_projects.html; for publications, see http://www.lawreform.lawlink.nsw.gov.au/lrc/lrc_publications.html,c=y.

have been aiding and abetting drug dealers. He has also held memberships since 2005 on the Domestic Violence Death Review Panel and the Human Research and Ethics Committee of Sydney Children's Hospital Network (for two hospitals). He is director of Pain Australia and a patron of Pathfinders. Late in 2013, he was appointed chair of NSW Probation and Parole.

Based on his expertise in leading commissions of inquiry, since leaving the bench in 2005, Justice Wood has been appointed to conduct a number of significant inquiries. The first, prompted by community outrage over the deaths of two children in NSW (a 2-year-old boy found folded into a suitcase floating in a lake in southwestern Sydney and a girl starved to death in her home north of Sydney), was the Inquiry into Child Protective Services NSW (Wood, 2008), a follow-up to the Paedophile Inquiry. Justice Wood's report included 111 recommendations and prompted a $750 million overhaul of the state's child protection services. Key recommendations included (a) removal of the business of sheltering abused and neglected children from government to the private sector, so that only the most serious cases, and those involving infants, were handled by government welfare workers; and (b) ending the system of mandatory reporting, so only children at serious risk of harm are reported to the main welfare hotline, and other cases are handled by special units in state hospitals and community health centers.

Justice Wood noted that to protect children, it was critical to establish the Joint Investigation Response Team structure, with collaboration between police, health, and the Department of Community Services to work together when children have been subjected to alleged sexual and physical assault. "The police take on the investigation, the Departments of Community Services and of Family and Community Services (FACS) deal with child-care issues, Health deals with health issues, and nongovernment agencies work better with families, as FACS increases the risk that the child will be removed, and this increases the friction between the parties, which can be an obstacle to a solution. Responses to problems can be shared, not only because of the volume of work, but because problems can be dealt with, can be solved, if the appropriate agency is prepared to work with that family." A mediation process in the Children's Court was implemented as one of the recommendations of this inquiry. This is working well regarding reinstatement of care orders, and promotes cooperation between FACS and families, rather than evoking diametrically opposed positions from which the parties refuse to retreat.

Other recent inquiries that Justice Wood recently led examined integrity issues in sport and resulted in landmark legislation in NSW to criminalize the offense of match-fixing. This has become a cornerstone of the National Policy on Match-Fixing in Sport. He also conducted a national inquiry into the integrity of cycling in Australia in the wake of allegations of drug use against the American former professional road racing cyclist,

Lance Armstrong (*United States Anti-Doping Agency v. Armstrong*, 2012), and the imposition of sanctions upon Armstrong by the US Anti-Doping Agency. Justice Wood's inquiry reviewed Cycling Australia's approach to anti-doping, with a particular focus on how it engaged staff and volunteers, its anti-doping policies and practices to advise on their effectiveness and to develop best-practice policies, and guidelines for adoption across all national sporting codes and organizations. Supported by the Office for Sport and the Australian Sports Commission (ASC) and working with Australian Sports Anti-Doping Authority (ASADA), governance and administrative practices, including its recruitment, employment, and appointment practices. The report provided 16 wide-ranging recommendations to improve anti-doping and the inquiry reviewed governance practices, to identify past or present doping activities, to educate young cyclists, and to ensure high standards of integrity in the sport (Wood, 2013). Some key recommendations included (a) upgrading governance structures; (b) building anti-doping accountability and networks; (c) establishing an ethics and integrity panel; (d) improving anti-doping education; (e) extending the reach of testing; and (f) developing stronger sanction regimes. Following these inquiries, Australia established a National Integrity of Sport Unit.

Most recently, Justice Wood led an inquiry into the release of convicted murderer Terrence Leary, who reoffended similarly while on parole, after serving over 22 years in prison. Justice Wood's track record left him uniquely equipped and well positioned to compare the roles of a judge in an adjudicatory versus an inquisitorial capacity. Justice Wood noted that in the adversarial role of the normal judicial officer, the judge is confined to the facts and the issues placed before him or her, and can't go outside of those parameters, even when aware of ancillary issues that may have impacted a case. In the inquisitorial field, the judge has the latitude to set up the inquiry as he prefers and to use whatever powers available to govern the issues, so determines the ambit of the investigation, constrained only by the terms of reference. If it becomes apparent that there is an issue outside the terms of reference, mechanisms exist to extend the terms. For a judge with a curious bent, the inquisitorial role is satisfying, and he found this work more rewarding and fulfilling than judicial judging.

In reflecting on surprises as his career unfolded, Justice Wood commented that he had sufficient experience at the Bar to realize that there will always be a number of people in the corporate world who will cause harm and wrong to others, both civilly and criminally, but he did not anticipate the extent of corporate malfeasance, malfeasance within business, and, in particular, the extent of the imbalance of power that exists and how that is exploited.

As Inspector of the Police Integrity Commission (PIC) in 2005, Justice Wood observed that oversight agencies established by statute, such as the

Police Integrity Commission (PIC), the Independent Commission Against Corruption (ICAC), and the Prison Correctional Service, may overstep their proper bounds without anyone to police them. The Australian Crime Commission (ACC), for example, has coercive powers, which can be over-zealously applied. The nature of the work makes it difficult for parliamentary committees to be fully informed of the workings of agencies such as the ICAC and the PIC. Appropriate safeguards to avoid abuses of power are needed. In a democratic system, independent inspectors are crucial to police the agency that polices the police.

In thinking about whether the work has been as rewarding or interesting as he thought it would be when he started, Justice Wood commented that it was probably more than he anticipated, in part due to his lifelong inability to say "no."

Personal Judicial Philosophy

The role of the judiciary in society is to ensure that the law is appropriately applied in terms of fairness and complies ethically with the prosecution requirements within the range of sentencing options available to protect society and encourage rehabilitation. "Very importantly, the role does involve ensuring community confidence in the entire justice system, civil or criminal." Thus judges must make sure their decisions are transparent and justifiable. A judge can draw attention to areas of law that are unsatisfactory or unclear for the legislature to take action, but it is outside the role of the judge to advocate for policy change. Justice Wood also emphasized procedural justice elements, recalling advice he had been given early in his judicial career: "The most important person in any case is the person who is going to lose. If that person is not getting the impression that they're listened to and treated fairly, then as far as they are concerned, the system fails."

Organizationally, within the NSW Supreme Court, an arrangement that worked well was the allocation of cases to judges based on the kind of work they could best deal with, that is, a civil law bent to address personal injury cases, or a general common law bent, while others had more interest in the criminal law. As chief judge, he implemented a pretrial management strategy in civil cases. Those innovations need to be extended now to the criminal law field, so defenses are disclosed early. This will reduce delays and encourage people to plead guilty early, conserving the limited resources of legal aid, the public defender, the police, and the Office of the Director of Public Prosecutions (DPP). In addition, expert witnesses should be compelled to agree pretrial on issues and identify common ground. Justice Wood observed that tension between the traditional rights of the accused person to defer and the interests of the court in making sure that court time isn't unnecessarily wasted remains a problem. "We can't afford a justice system that allows parties to work through nondisclosure and trial by ambush as this risks holding the justice system up for disrepute." Members of the legal profession need to be brought on board. A substantial portion of lawyers' fees is only paid to legal practitioners at the trial phase of their case, thus early settlement reduces their fees, giving private legal professionals a financial interest to delay. The fee structure needs review to place more emphasis on resolving cases early, as "justice delayed is justice denied." He added that it was in the interest of crime victims "to bring forward the inevitable."

On the topic of relating to those with economically deprived backgrounds, Justice Wood noted that while some judges are totally unable to relate to the living and social conditions of persons from economically deprived backgrounds, and regard these people with some degree of contempt or mistrust, judges who work in the criminal field, and especially as sentencing judges, hear about these problems day after day. Not all judges come from a privileged background. In his own case, he pointed to experience after school and while at university when he worked on country properties with farm laborers and Aboriginal people. For example, he did a substantial amount of fencing with an Aboriginal man with whom he was friendly. He was embarrassed when he attended an open-air film and was seated in a fairly comfortable chair while the local indigenous people were required to sit behind a rope. In terms of relations with the wider community, Justice Wood acknowledged the need for responsible, fair and balanced media criticism or exposure, and advised courts to use a media officer to spell out critical aspects of a judgment, and provide an executive summary.

Priorities in the Criminal Legal System

In his new position as Chair of the State Parole Authority, Justice Wood is focused on what can be provided to a person while they are incarcerated in prison to rehabilitate them or increase their insight into their criminality. When judges sentence someone to prison, they have a limited basis on which to predict what will happen to that person while incarcerated, and what the person will be like at the end of the sentence, and the concept that the best predictor for the future is past behavior has always worried Justice Wood a bit. The decision at the time of parole entitlement is one of the most important decisions for the effectiveness of the criminal justice system and the safety of the community.

Successes and Problems Experienced

On the topic of law reform, successes were achieved by engaging each of the agencies involved in the criminal justice system to participate and actively consider reforms. First, a background paper is prepared, then submissions are invited, and consultations are held with all the key players, such as NSW Police Force, DPP, Public Defender, Legal Aid, Aboriginal Legal Aid, the Law Society, the Bar Association, Young Lawyers, and so on, to assist the government in discerning the support by key stakeholders for an initiative for change.

On the topic of policies and programs that do not work as well, Justice Wood pointed to challenges with mandatory minimum sentences, which he regards as far too blunt and counterproductive an approach, as it does not allow for the discretion of the judge and application of an individualized sentence, doesn't reduce crime, and fills up the prisons. This approach is premised on unrealistic assumptions of human thinking about general deterrence. In his view, individualized sentencing with a proper exercise of discretion is the only way forward. In NSW, the Judicial Commission is a unique institution that provides support and an information service to judges, exposing them to legislation, Court of Appeals decisions, sentencing statistics, and developments in the law. The commission can provide judges with a summary of sentences in similar cases and objective and subjective facts, to assist them in accessing sentencing trends to maintain proportionality and parity with sentences in similar cases. Justice Wood favors issuance of judgment guidelines even where there is a standard nonparole period.

Justice Wood also pointed to the current criminal appeals system, contained in two separate acts (the Criminal Appeal Act and the Crimes Appeal and Review Act), as unnecessarily complex and confusing, containing many dysfunctional or inconsistent areas. He recommended a single appellate court within the Supreme Court for all criminal activities and sending judicial review to the Court of Criminal Appeal.

Most Difficult Problems Judges Have to Deal With

A real challenge to judges that Justice Wood observed while sitting at the Court of Criminal Appeal was achieving consistency in the application of the principles of sentencing, rather than in the outcome. For example, a landmark decision issued by Justice Wood as a sole judge in *R v. Fernando* (1992) established an enduring framework to take into account the issues of disadvantage such as reduced socio economic circumstances and loss of customary law so often present in the subjective circumstances of individual indigenous offenders. Just last year, in 2013, the High Court, in *Bugmy v. The Queen* (2013), reaffirmed the viability of the Fernando principles, refuting the notion that they lose their force when an Aboriginal person has lived for many years away from his or her community or has repeatedly been engaged in the criminal justice system. Justice Wood commented on the legal difficulty when members of certain racial groups, such as an Aboriginal person, get special consideration at the time of sentencing in light of the Fernando principles, and members of other groups do not, such as a person from a Middle Eastern background with an Islamic tradition. Doctrinally, Justice Wood acknowledged that the Fernando principles that he authored and that the High Court has now made mandatory are a form of positive discrimination in the sentencing process that conflict with principles of individualized sentencing that he endorses, where every person is considered on his or her own merits. The High Court expressed the view that the Fernando principles were not contrary to the notion of individualized justice.

More close collaboration between police and prosecutors is necessary in serious cases to avoid the problem of overcharging following an unlawful and dangerous act that results in death, for example where police and media expectations about punishments are that a murder charge rather than manslaughter will follow. Justice Wood favored a precharge bail process, such as was applied in the United Kingdom in the Rolf Harris case, allowing the police time to investigate the case before charges were determined, so the prosecution can maintain integrity.

Collaboration or interaction between law enforcement agencies is hindered by privacy laws and secrecy laws that impair the ability of organizations and institutions to communicate and exchange information. Strong secrecy provisions in the operations of the Australian Federal Police, the ACC, and the Australian Securities and Investment Commission have affected their efficiency in responding to corporate crime or misconduct. Justice Wood regarded this an area of law where privacy has been overstated. Much information gathered by agencies in law enforcement and other services does not need to be confined to them.

Theory and Practice

On the topic of types of research most useful for practice, Justice Wood emphasized that ongoing and very careful evaluation was necessary of prison rehabilitation programs that work and don't work. A priority in corrections is to implement alternatives to prison for lower-level offenders, that is, replacing short-term imprisonment for run-of-the-mill offenses with something that does have a "bite" but also promotes rehabilitation. He also called for studies on the impact of a new sentencing option on reoffending that will assist judges in how to apply the sentence. In addition, he valued jury research to inform judges as to what affects or assists juries in their work.

Justice Wood endorsed criminal justice theories that had been empirically tested, for example on criminology and penal philosophy, especially with young offenders. With regard to sentencing, for example, he advocated that theory with a sound basis should be put into effect and practiced. He drew on theories about crime prevention that had shown that the fear of arrest was more effective as a deterrent to criminal conduct than other measures, such as mandatory or lengthy prison sentences, and that the deterrent effect of risk of imprisonment was more effective with white-collar than with other types of offenders. He reflected on the fact that in sentencing to imprisonment, the criminal justice system does little to prevent crime, other than through incapacitation. "The reality, for a large proportion of offenders, and particularly for low-level crimes, is that full-time custody doesn't achieve much beyond incapacitation, may well be counterproductive, and often is counterproductive for many offenders. For instance, some offenders make bad associations while in prison which they use afterwards or, alternatively, become angry and bitter with the world." These insights led Justice Wood to place strong emphasis on developing rehabilitation through services and programs within the prison and, most importantly, postrelease support and supervision in the community for offenders on parole before their sentences end. He commented, "There's not much point releasing a person from prison at the end of a sentence when they have no capacity to return to any kind of lawful situation because of what's changed, and the fact that they haven't got housing, haven't got connection to employment, and haven't got any services. They are bound to come back to prison."

Rather than draw on theory about what a particular judge should do in any given case, Justice Wood identified the need for theory about the criminal justice system to provide guidance on the kinds of sentences that should be available. Two priorities emerged: (1) for offenders who are incarcerated, to empirically evaluate individual sentencing options and correctional rehabilitation programs, particularly in relation to recidivism, and whether they actually help offenders by giving them literacy and numeracy skills or preemployment training which will fit them for a job, and dealing with their drug or alcohol addictions and anger management issues, and so on; and (2) to develop appropriate alternatives for lower-level offenders, that is, replacing short-term imprisonment for run-of-the-mill offenses with something that does have a "bite" but also promotes rehabilitation. Alternatives that do not require full-time detention, such as community corrections measures, can entail real restrictions, plus engagement in rehabilitative programs. "If these offenders don't take advantage of the community correction, they can be placed in full-time custody."

Justice Wood was conscious that "It requires a courageous government to place more emphasis on community corrections. In terms of cost-benefits, community corrections programs also require money, but the reality is that the money spent on keeping someone in custody on a full-time basis is likely to exceed costs to supervise and require them to be subject to restrictions in the community." Overall, Justice Wood favored use of theory to guide crime prevention, delivered through appropriate, fair, and justifiable law enforcement, to detect people who are involved in a crime and to provide a measure of deterrence though the consequences.

In response to a question about the potential impact of a bill of rights on the Australian legal system, Justice Wood drew a distinction between the Australian and U.K. contexts. In his view, the English experience with the European Convention on Human Rights has been that they exerted a dramatic legal effect, resulting in changes to or the abandonment of many English laws as a result of their noncompliance with the European Convention. The resulting imposition of civil systems and principles on British common law principles may be resented. Justice Wood did not foresee a similar phenomenon in Australia, as the existing bills of rights tends to be drafted in very broad and general terms, and has not really had much legal impact.

Transnational Relations

Regarding the question of how Justice Wood's work has been affected by influences outside of Australia and personal experiences overseas, he acknowledged that he learned from overseas pioneers of case management at the National Judicial College in Reno, Nevada. He implemented programs to reduce the backlog of civil cases and delays in case processing in the Common Law Division, and later extended these innovations to the criminal justice system.

Justice Wood described his transnational assignments as some of the most rewarding work he started as a judge. For instance, straight after East Timor became independent, the United Nations Transnational Authority established a program that took him and the United Nations Rapporteur for Judicial Independence to New Delhi to train the locals to reestablish a justice system, and administer it and the courts. This was one of the most enjoyable and interesting experiences of his entire life. Later, as a nonresident judge for some years on the Fijian Court of Appeal, sitting with local judges and judges from New Zealand, he observed how it was possible to cut to the gist of a matter without extensive litigation focused on minutiae. Since then, he has spent time in China and Vietnam on programs organized by the Australian Human Rights Commission. He also undertook to assist the justices in Bahrain to develop their evidence laws and enjoyed working in the Middle East. This international work, of immense interest to him, would not have arisen had he not been a judge.

General Assessments

In commenting on whether he was satisfied with criminal law and procedures in NSW, Justice Wood responded that a strength of the Australian system, which is not the case in the civil law countries, is a strong system of legal precedent—the one great virtue of the common law system. An Australian judge cannot simply do what seems fair, as judges may in a civil law country, but must respect a body of law which has been considered and developed at the High Court level, and is capable of adaptation by a higher court after consideration.

In addition, Justice Wood reflected on the need for more community-based custodial options for lower-level offenders, given that full-time custody does not achieve a great deal beyond incapacitation. In his view, for a large proportion of criminality, and especially low-level criminality, incarceration in prison is counterproductive, and the costs of full-time custody exceed the costs of supervision, subject to restrictions, in the community. Short-term imprisonment should be replaced with something that does have a "bite," but also promotes rehabilitation.

A serious issue noted by Justice Wood was the lack of expertise in the forensic field, such as forensic psychiatry or forensic psychology, in part because of a lack of sufficient funds for fees, as private practitioners earn more from private patients than from forensic evaluations and assessments. Their availability was also affected by difficulties of scheduling when cases are in court, the time commitment required, and difficulties in gaining access to the person on remand or the prisoner, who may be held in a location far from the experts. Yet this input at the time of the pretrial or pre-sentencing phase is critical, for example for defenses of substantial impairment or mental illness. The need for impartiality in expertise is very important for the criminal justice system. Certain experts consistently work for the prosecution or defense, and thus lose their value, becoming tainted as "guns for hire" as the judges know that what they offer is a waste of time and money. Allowing experts to testify via video link and increased use of concurrent expert evidence are innovations that can assist in reducing these delays. Finally, Justice Wood noted the need for an independent forensic service to conduct DNA or other forensic scientific tests.

Conclusion

In this interview, the concerns addressed by Justice Wood encompassed investigative and adjudicative phases of the justice system, from police interviews through to the sentencing and parole of offenders. Core issues that were the focus of his thinking included measures to increase access to justice and the fair application of law, but extended beyond the courts to address a gamut of problems that impact justice, such as police corruption, pedophilia, child abuse and neglect, drug use in sports, match-fixing, and offender rehabilitation. Justice Wood reflected thoughtfully on differences between Australian and other legal systems and noted strengths and weaknesses of local systemic and contextual features.

Dominant themes in the interview were his passion to uncover causes of some of the most daunting social issues though an in-depth, systematic fact-finding process to identify vulnerabilities and recommend sound operational procedures, practices and policies to drive reforms. His gracious modesty belies the scope of his many accomplishments in improving law enforcement, crime prevention, and practical agency–community relations to safeguard family welfare and enhance access to justice and in providing innovations in anticorruption practices in policing, customs, border protection, and professional sports.

The legacy of Justice Wood's contributions persist not only in his formal judicial decisions and contributions to the efficient management of the NSW courts, but also through a series of in-depth national fact-finding inquiries and far-ranging law reform initiatives that have reshaped many facets of the local and national Australian justice systems. Now that he is chair of NSW Probation and Parole, with his focus firmly on the efficiency and effectiveness of the probation and parole system, we anticipate that fundamental improvements will soon follow in this arena. Australia remains indebted to Justice Wood's indefatigable enthusiasm and consummate skills in applying his expertise and insights to enhance justice.

Glossary

Australian Crime Commission: An independent statutory body established in January 2003 (replacing the National Crime Authority) to work nationally with federal, state and territory agencies, principally to counter serious and organized crime. It brings together all arms of Australian intelligence gathering and law enforcement to combat major crime.

Australian Customs Board of Protection: Manages the security and integrity of Australia's borders. It works closely with other government and international agencies to detect and deter unlawful movement of goods and people across the border, in particular the Australian Federal Police, the Australian Quarantine and Inspection Service, the Department of Immigration and Citizenship, and the Department of Defence.

Australian Federal Police: Australia's international law enforcement and policing agency, responsible for enforcing criminal laws of the Commonwealth of Australia, and for protecting Commonwealth and national interests from crime in Australia and overseas, such as drug trafficking, illegal immigration, and crimes against national security and the environment.

Australian Securities and Investment Commission: An independent Commonwealth Government body that regulates Australian companies, financial markets, financial services organizations, and professionals who deal and advise in investments, superannuation, insurance, deposit taking, and credit.

Department of Community Services: Promotes the safety and wellbeing of children and young people and works to build stronger families and communities. It provides child protection services, parenting support and early intervention, foster care, and adoption services.

Department of Family and Community Services: Delivers services to over 800,000 vulnerable and disadvantaged individuals, families and communities in NSW through its own services and through non-government agencies (NGOs) that it funds.

Independent Commission Against Corruption: Investigates and exposes corrupt conduct in the NSW public sector agencies, except the NSW Police Force, including government departments, local councils, members of parliament, ministers, the judiciary, and the governor. The ICAC's jurisdiction also extends to those performing public official functions.

Joint Investigation Response Team: Professionals from Community Services, NSW Police, and NSW Health who undertake a combined investigation of child protection matters, linking protective interventions with the criminal investigations.

Law Reform Commission: An independent statutory body constituted under the Law Reform Commission Act 1967 (NSW) to provide expert law reform advice to Government through the Attorney General on matters referred to it by the Attorney General.

Law Society New South Wales: Represents the interests of approximately 23,000 members of the legal profession, and advocates for reform of the law and the legal system.

Legal Aid New South Wales: A statewide organization providing legal services to socially and economically disadvantaged people charged with criminal offenses before the Local Court, Children's Court, District Court, Supreme Court, Court of Criminal Appeal, and the High Court, and advice and representation in specialist jurisdictions including the Parole Authority, Drug Court, and the Youth Drug and Alcohol Court.

Office of the Director of Public Prosecutions: An independent prosecutorial body created in 1987 by the Director of Public Prosecutions Act 1986. It has about 600 staff, comprised of solicitors and administrative officers from the Solicitors Office and Crown Prosecutors. It handles approximately 18,000 matters a year involving offenses under the laws of NSW.

Order of Australia: Appointment to the Order of Australia confers the highest recognition to Australian citizens and other persons for outstanding achievement or meritorious service.

Pain Australia: A national not-for-profit body established in 2011 to improve the treatment and management of pain in Australia.

Pathfinders Ltd.: A not-for-profit company operating across the New England and Northwest Tablelands areas of NSW to provide programs and services promoting youth and family welfare.

Police Integrity Commission: Investigates and prevents police misconduct, especially serious police misconduct by NSW police officers, and by administrative officers of the NSW Police Force and officers of the NSW Crime Commission. It is separate from and completely independent of the NSW Police Force.

Sentencing Council of New South Wales: Advises the NSW Attorney General on sentencing matters and prepares research papers and reports at the request of the NSW Attorney General. The council is dedicated to strengthening public understanding and confidence in the sentencing process.

Hong Kong
Legal System

IV

ALISON LUI

Situated on China's southeastern coast, on the South China Sea, Hong Kong (Figure IV.1) is known as the "Pearl of the Orient." With its low taxes, international financial center, and fusion of the Orient and Occident, Hong Kong is attractive to both tourists and businesspeople. One particular strength of Hong Kong is its robust and independent judicial system (The World Justice Project 2013). Due to the fact that Hong Kong was under British control between the years of 1841 and 1997, the Hong Kong judiciary operates under the English common law framework. Since July 1, 1997, the principle of "one country, two systems" has applied. The Hong Kong Special Administrative Region (HKSAR) was established and is independent from the People's Republic of China (PRC) in that it maintains its own legal system. This is enshrined at both domestic and international levels. Judges in HKSAR still use English common law, unless it infringes the Basic Law, which is the mini-constitution of HKSAR. English common law is also subject to amendments of the legislature of HKSAR. National laws of the PRC are not applied in the HKSAR, except for laws relating to defense and foreign affairs.

The Hong Kong judiciary is separate and independent from the Executive Council and Legislative Council of the Hong Kong government. This is in accordance with the crucial principle of "the rule of law." Under "the rule of law," there is a clear division of powers between the judiciary and executive and legislative bodies. The Chief Justice of the Court of Final Appeal sits at the apex of the judiciary, in both a judicial and an administrative sense. Since July 1, 1997, the constitutional framework for the legal system has been provided at the international level by the Sino-British Joint Declaration and at the domestic level by the Basic Law, enacted by the National People's Congress (NPC) of the PRC under Article 31 of the Chinese Constitution. Both the Joint Declaration and the Hong Kong Basic Law guaranteed the continuance of the existing legal system after China resumed the exercise of sovereignty over Hong Kong on July 1, 1997. The

Figure IV.1 Map of Hong Kong Special Administrative Region.

Hong Kong Basic Law contains the fundamental provisions of the constitutional framework of HKSAR, including the "rule of law." Article 8 states that "the common law, rules of equity, ordinances, subordinate legislation and customary law shall be maintained, except for any that contravene this Law, and subject to any amendment by the legislature of the Hong Kong Special Administrative Region."

The courts in Hong Kong comprise the Court of Final Appeal, the High Court (which includes the Court of Appeal and the Court of First Instance), the District Court, the Lands Tribunal, the Magistrates' Courts (which include the Juvenile Court), the Coroner's Court, the Labour Tribunal, the Small Claims Tribunal, and the Obscene Articles Tribunal. In accordance with the Basic Law, courts in HKSAR can use either Chinese or English. Figure IV.2 shows the hierarchy of the HKSAR court system.

Among a population of 7.17 million in HKSAR (Hong Kong Census and Statistics Department 2012), there were 1155 practicing barristers (Hong Kong Bar Association 2013) and 7152 practicing solicitors (The Law Society

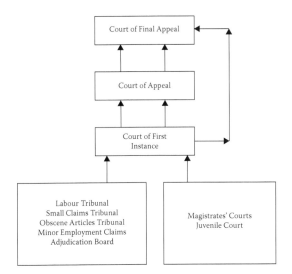

Figure IV.2 Court system in HKSAR. (From Hong Kong Judiciary 2013a. Hong Kong Judiciary Annual Report 2012.)

of Hong Kong 2013) at the end of 2012. In addition, there are a total of 180 judges in the major courts of HKSAR. This includes a panel of 21 judges in the Court of Final Appeal, 11 Justices of Appeal in the Court of Appeal, 26 judges in the Court of First Instance, 47 judges in the District Courts, and 75 magistrates (Hong Kong Judiciary 2013b). Under the Basic Law, judges are appointed by the Chief Executive of the HKSAR on the recommendation of the Judicial Officers Recommendation Commission.

Michael Lunn, Court of Appeal

5

ALISON LUI

Contents

Introduction

Of the 11 Justices of Appeal in the Court of Appeal, I was fortunate to secure an interview with The Honourable Mr. Justice Michael Lunn. The interview was conducted by telephone call on August 8, 2013. It was a very pleasant, interesting, and educational interview in which Mr. Justice Lunn shared some pearls of wisdom. Mr. Justice Lunn's background appeals to a global audience because he has lived, studied, and worked in several jurisdictions. Born in Zimbabwe, Mr. Justice Lunn spent his early childhood years there. In 1968, he won a Richardson Foundation Scholarship to Davidson College, United States. The following year, he embarked on a law degree at Queen's College, Cambridge. He was called to the Bar in 1973 and started his career as a barrister in private practice in 1974. In 1977, he moved to Hong Kong and practiced at the Attorney General's chambers. In 1982, he was called to the Bar in Hong Kong and began private practice. In 1994, he became a Queen's Counsel. In 2000, Mr. Justice Lunn became a Recorder of the Court of First Instance of the High Court. Three years later, he progressed to become a judge in the Court of First Instance of the High Court. Between 2001 and 2003, Mr. Justice Lunn was vice-chairman of the Hong Kong Bar

Association. In 2011, he became Justice of Appeal of the High Court in HKSAR. His areas of expertise are white-collar crime and securities regulation. He was the chairman of the Market Misconduct Tribunal from 2005 to 2012.

Career

Mr. Justice Lunn did not intend to be a judge when he was younger. He was happy to read law as it is an interesting and intellectually challenging subject. He did not want to be a solicitor since he was more interested in the theater of court and advocacy. Joining the bench appeared to be both logical and a nice change from private practice. Mr. Justice Lunn has generally enjoyed being a judge. He has found the work demanding in terms of volume and intellectually challenging. The workload is more onerous than he expected. Some of the work is interesting but a great deal of it is repetitive. One key frustration that Mr. Justice Lunn has encountered in his career is the low standard of advocacy on occasion. This includes a lack of understanding of the basic rules of evidence. He said that, "If you have poor advocates, it can be quite a trying day" (Lunn 2013). Mr. Justice Lunn admits that the low standard of advocacy has been around for so long that it is no longer a surprise as it reoccurs. He was surprised when he first became a judge. This is because when he was a silk he worked on cases where advocacy was good on all sides. The standard of trial was of a higher level.

Funding is the key reason for the low standard of advocacy. In the UK, a defendant in a murder case would be defended by a silk. This has never been the case in HKSAR because the government will not pay for the costs. Mr. Justice Lunn has argued for improvements to the standard of advocacy at the Bar and at the bench. This problem existed more than 30 years ago and the current problem is cost inefficient. Good advocates achieve better results more quickly and, overall, things are done in a cheaper way. Mr. Justice Lunn explained that the root of the problem must go back earlier in the system, that is, in the training stage of barristers. Low standards of advocacy and poor techniques are not always picked up in practice. The best way is to have a good pupillage and then put that into practice in Court.

Mr. Justice Lunn has enjoyed a distinguished career so far. Since becoming a judge, he has presided over many interesting cases. Highlights of his career include being the chairman of the Lamma Island Ferry Inquiry in 2012. On October 1, 2012, two passenger ferries collided off the northwestern coast of Lamma Island. Figure 5.1 shows the position of Lamma Island. Thirty-eight passengers were killed in this accident. Ferry

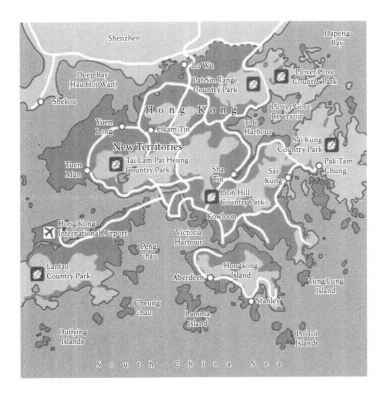

Figure 5.1 Map of Hong Kong and vicinity.

accidents are rare in HKSAR, so this accident prompted an inquiry into the incident. Reflecting on the Lamma Island Ferry Inquiry, Mr. Justice Lunn remarked that the inquiry style is an efficient way of getting the truth, as opposed to the adversarial system. The inquiry style is good for situations where there is a problem that needs to be dealt with quickly. The parties at the Lamma Island inquiry were cooperative and efficient. This was helpful because they were under a time limit of 6 months imposed by the HKSAR Chief Executive. This was achieved. Another highlight is the case of *R v. Law Kin Man.** This case is interesting for three reasons. First, this was the first successful conviction for money-laundering in HKSAR. Secondly, this case was high profile since it involved a sophisticated scheme of laundering money and resulted in proceedings that lasted over a period of 6 years. Finally, the investigation was not limited to HKSAR. Authorities in Singapore, Australia, and the United States were also involved in the trial. The case of *R v. Law Kin Man*† is thus highly important to Mr. Justice Lunn and to the Hong Kong judiciary.

---

* [1994] 2 HKC 118 (HC) 282.
† Ibid.

Personal Judicial Philosophy

According to Mr. Justice Lunn, the judiciary should be a

> [...] transparent and independent arbiter of disputes. Flowing from that are unbiased, ethical judgments. The preferred objective of any criminal system is to achieve the correct result. The guilty should be found guilty. Most of all, the innocent should not be at risk of being found guilty. The HKSAR judiciary is fair and independent. The World Justice Project Rule of Law Index 2012–2013 Report* revealed that HKSAR scored very well in upholding the principle of the "rule of law."

The Rule of Law Index measures how 97 countries have adhered to the "rule of law" in practice. Its methodology consists of quantitative assessments based on nine essential factors. They are as follows:

1. Limited government powers
2. Absence of corruption
3. Order and security
4. Fundamental rights
5. Open government
6. Regulatory enforcement
7. Civil justice
8. Criminal justice
9. Informal justice

Table 5.1 shows the rankings for HKSAR. The highest possible score for each factor is 1.00 and the lowest possible score for each factor is 0.00.

Particular attention should be drawn to factors 2 (absence of corruption), 3 (order and security), 5 (open government), 6 (regulatory enforcement), and 8 (criminal justice). These factors support the fact that judges in HKSAR are able to make fair, transparent, and unbiased decisions. Naturally, the judicial system in HKSAR is not without its problems.

According to Mr. Justice Lunn, delays are common in courts. He added:

> The old adage of "delay is the enemy of justice" applies to the HKSAR judiciary. Unavoidable delays occur from time to time. However, it is unforgiveable to have avoidable delays in courts. Both types of delays take place in HKSAR.

---

* Agrast et al. (2012–2013). The Rule of Law Index uses 400 variables to measure the extent to which countries follow the "rule of law." The aim of this index is to identify strengths and weaknesses in each country and to further implement the "rule of law" through policies.

Table 5. 1   The World Justice Project Rule of Law Index Ratings for HKSAR 2012–2013

WJP Rule of Law Index Factors		Score	Global Ranking	Regional Ranking	Income Group Ranking
Factor 1	Limited government powers	0.73	22/97	5/14	20/29
Factor 2	Absence of corruption	0.89	9/97	4/14	9/29
Factor 3	Order and security	0.93	2/97	2/14	2/29
Factor 4	Fundamental rights	0.71	31/97	6/14	27/29
Factor 5	Open government	0.82	10/97	4/14	10/29
Factor 6	Regulatory enforcement	0.75	14/97	5/14	14/29
Factor 7	Civil justice	0.71	17/97	6/14	16/29
Factor 8	Criminal justice	0.76	8/97	3/14	8/29

According to the Hong Kong Judiciary Annual Report 2012, some targets were not met due to promotions and retirement of judges in the High Court. New judicial appointments were made in late 2012, which will hopefully improve the waiting times and help meet targets (Hong Kong Judiciary 2013a).

In Mr. Justice Lunn's view, judges can list cases to remove delays in courts, adding:

> Too much consideration is given to counsel's private diaries rather than listing cases. Naturally, it is the defendant's right to choose his/her counsel but very often a defendant does not know who their counsel is. Defendants can be given a choice, that is, a defendant is scheduled for trial in February next year but he/she can appear in court in 2 weeks' time if he/she chooses another counsel.

As judges represent clients from a diverse range of background, judges should be able to relate to people from economically deprived backgrounds if they have been in practice, especially if they defend clients. By visiting the scene and having conferences with the defendant as a barrister, judges should have gained a reasonable measure and understanding of the lives of people in many different walks of life.

Problems and Successes Experienced

Over the past 20 years, there has been very little enactment of legislation, policies, programs, or practice direction in crime in HKSAR. This is in contrast to
the large number of changes made to civil law, especially by the Civil Justice
Reform Procedures in 2009. As a result of this lack of guidance, and coupled
with the inability of counsel to focus on the relevant issues, courts have very
limited powers in the Practice Directions to require the parties to focus on the
issues. This is in contrast to the plethora of Protocols and Directions available
to courts in England and Wales with regards to dealing with fraud.

Mr. Justice Lunn thinks that criminal law judges would benefit from the
power to give more directions and guidance, saying

> For example with a bail application for a defendant remanded in custody
> pending trial in the magistracy, if the defendant should not be in custody, it
> can take as much as 10 days to remedy it. This is because it takes time to swear
> and file an affidavit, find an interpreter in some cases and list the case. A new
> set of rules is needed to expedite changes.
>
> As a trial judge, the inability of counsel to focus on the issues is particularly
> frustrating. In the Court of Appeal, a great deal of time is wasted on dealing
> with unmeritorious appeals. The current system has a single judge screening
> for applications of appeals, which is very limited. It only catches those who are
> unrepresented and who are serving less than 5 years' imprisonment. Many
> unmeritorious appeals are listed before a three judge panel. This is inefficient
> since it is wasting the time of three judges.

Nothing is easy to change in the HKSAR judicial system. Maintaining
the status quo seems to be the norm. An example of the jury system was
given as an illustration of his attempts to make changes.

> In HK, there is a jury of seven for serious criminal charges. Jurors are chosen
> by electronic ballot from a list of about 500,000 names. Seventy jurors are
> summoned per day for jury service. In the High Court, a defendant has five
> peremptory challenges in the selection of jurors. Peremptory challenges no
> longer exist in England and Wales. Therefore, a judge in Hong Kong would
> need 12 jurors or, to be safe, perhaps even 14, to empanel for a one-defendant
> trial. This is done via an open ballot in court. Jury empanelment takes place on
> only about 4 or 5 out of 22 sitting days per month. As a result it causes incon-
> venience to jurors as they are notified 6 weeks ahead of the date on which they
> are required to attend court had only "stood down" the evening before. As a
> result, their holiday and work plans are disrupted unnecessarily. I am look-
> ing for ways to cause less inconvenience. One way is that jury empanelment
> would take place on Mondays and Thursdays only. This was met with opposi-
> tion at a criminal practitioners' forum. Another problem in Hong Kong is
> the gross oversupply of jurors. When the 70 jurors are chosen from a ballot

already, it seems unnecessary to have another ballot in court when only about 40–45 jurors will appear in court. My suggestion was met with opposition. It was argued that it is often comforting for the defendant to know that a real choice was made when there are 40 potential jurors in the courtroom.

Two fundamental changes have taken place during my career. First, the Bill of Rights Ordinance of 1991 and the Basic Law introduced a new screening process for legislation. The Bill of Rights Ordinance incorporates the International Covenant on Civil and Political Rights into HKSAR domestic law. Article 11(1) of the Hong Kong Bill of Rights Ordinance recognizes the principle of presumption of innocence: "Everyone charged with a criminal offence shall have the right to be presumed innocent until proved guilty according to law." The right to presumption of innocence is protected in HKSAR under the Bill of Rights Ordinance Article 11(1) and Basic Law Article 87. Under this provision, anyone charged with a criminal offense shall have the right to be presumed innocent until proved guilty according to law. The courts have sought to strike a balance between the concerns of law enforcement on the one hand and the right to presumption of innocence on the other by recognizing that the latter can be limited. The limitation has to be rational and proportional. I welcomed this renewed emphasis on the presumption of innocence in criminal law, since there were too many presumptions in [the Dangerous] Drugs [Ordinance]. Once an inference is properly drawn, it does not require a presumption.

The Court of Appeal case of *R v. Sin Yau Ming** is a good illustration of the presumption of innocence rule and the rationality/proportionality tests. This case was the first Court of Appeal decision on the Bill of Rights Ordinance. It is important since it sets out principles of interpreting the Bill of Rights Ordinance. The Court of Appeal declared certain mandatory presumptions in the Dangerous Drugs Ordinance to be an unjustifiable infringement of the presumption of innocence guaranteed under Article 11(1) Bill of Rights Ordinance. These provisions have been repealed.

There were three presumptions of drugs possession under the Dangerous Drugs Ordinance. First, if someone is found in possession of more than five packets or 0.5 g of morphine, he/she shall be presumed to have been in possession of the drug for the purpose of unlawful trafficking until the contrary is proven. Secondly, if someone owns or controls premises, or the key of any premises, and a dangerous drug is found [there], he/she shall be presumed to have such a drug in his/her possession unless the contrary is proven. Finally, if someone is found to have had a dangerous drug in his/her possession, he/she shall be presumed to have known the nature of such drug unless the contrary is proven.

The Court of Appeal held that for a mandatory presumption to be consistent with the presumption of innocence in Article 11(1) Bill of Rights

---

* (1991) 1 HKPLR 88.

Ordinance, the government would have to show firstly that it was rational. This means that the presumed fact would more likely than not flow from the proven fact. Secondly, the presumption, to be valid, must be rationally capable of achieving an important social objective and be proportional to achieve such an objective.

Drug trafficking was a serious social problem in Hong Kong and the problem must be tackled. With regards to the first presumption mentioned above, the Court of Appeal held that the government failed to demonstrate that the presumed fact (possession of dangerous drugs for the purpose of trafficking) in the Dangerous Drugs Ordinance rationally followed the proved fact (possession of 0.5 g, or six or more packets of morphine). In fact, such a low threshold of drugs would catch a large group of drug addicts. The second provision of drugs is also too wide since it includes the possibility of finding drugs in a house which includes the maid's room. The house owner is presumed to possess drugs even though the drugs are found in the maid's room. Such presumptions were therefore inconsistent with the Bill of Rights Ordinance.

Mr. Justice Lunn said the test is reinforced by the Privy Council in *Attorney General v. Lee Kwong-Kut*,* where Lord Woolf said that it is up to the prosecution to prove that the defendant is guilty to the required standard. He said that exceptions are justifiable in some circumstances, adding:

> Whether they are justifiable will in the end depend upon whether it remains primarily the responsibility of the prosecution to prove the guilt of an accused to the required standard and whether the exception is reasonably exposed, notwithstanding the importance of maintaining the principle which Article 11(1) enshrines. The less significant [the] departure from the normal principle, the simpler it will be to justify an exception.†

Criminal law judges in HKSAR have been busy since the Bill of Rights Ordinance was passed. Supporting Mr. Justice Lunn's point, Johannes Chan's survey revealed that there were around 247 cases involving the Bill of Rights Ordinance between 1991 and 1995 (Chan 1995). Seventy-four percent of these cases were criminal law; 28% of the cases were heard in the High Court. Ghai (1997) expressed the view that: "the courts have therefore had the opportunity to fashion this field, and on the whole the courts have done well". Swede (1995) submits that, "the Hong Kong judiciary has adopted a clear approach to the protection of human rights under the Bill, striving for consistency of interpretation with international norms." The HKSAR judiciary has thus dealt with a large caseload of criminal law cases well while incorporating the Bill of Rights Ordinance and Basic Law.

* [1992] 2 H.K.C.L.R 77.
† *AG v. Lee Kwong-Kut* [1992] 2 H.K.C.L.R. 82.

The other significant change witnessed by Mr. Justice Lunn is judicial review. Judicial review is the process whereby judges review the lawfulness of a decision or action made by a public organization. Mr. Justice Lunn said:

> Issues that are often better resolved politically, that is, by the Legislative Council, often end up in court for airing and not for resolution. The boundary of law and politics is often blurred.
>
> The case of R v. Ng Ka Ling* provides a good illustration. In this case, there was a discrepancy between the Basic Law and the Immigration Ordinance. Article 22 states that, "For entry into the HKSAR, people from other parts of China must apply for approval." The issue in this case was whether Hong Kong residents were included as "people from other parts of China" and therefore needed a permit. The Immigration Ordinance (No. 3) concluded that even those who have residency in Hong Kong must apply for a one-way permit to enter the region. The Court of Final Appeal held that the Immigration Ordinance was unconstitutional and that citizens of Hong Kong did not require a one-way permit.

Although some lawyers in HKSAR welcomed this decision due to its "common-sense approach" and "its defense of human rights and the rule of law" (Davis 1999), many officials from mainland China were dissatisfied with the decision.

Theory and Practice

The "rule of law" is a central tenet of Mr. Justice Lunn's judicial philosophy. He said the judiciary should be "a transparent and independent arbiter of disputes." To achieve judicial independence, he believes that transparency is:

> the "guardian of judicial independence. This can be achieved by making information available to the public so that they can follow more accurately and more fully what the evidence was. Judgments of court decisions are available on the Internet now. This enables the public to analyze if the judgments are logical and reasonable. In the Lamma Island Ferry Inquiry, I adopted some of Lord Leveson's practices [from] when the latter conducted an inquiry into the culture [and] ethics of the press in light of the News International phone-hacking scandal between 2011 and 2012. I asked that a website be created for the inquiry. Transcripts and key documents such as the expert's report were loaded daily onto the inquiry's website. I see technology as achieving transparency for the judicial process. Being the Chairman of the Market Misconduct Tribunal, between 2005 and 2012, I scanned documents onto a big monitor

---

* Ng Ka Ling v. Director of Immigration, Court of Final Appeal, Final Appeal 14 of 1998 (January 29, 1999).

so that the public could see them. One should, however, be cautious [regarding] what information is published. For example in the Lamma Island Ferry Inquiry, they did not show any photos of the deceased in the inquiry."

"Transparency can be further increased by having cameras in courts, but I have reservations. I'm concerned that people may play out for sound bites for the cameras. The purpose of the trial is diverted to the subsidiary purpose of publicity or attention. In England, photography has been banned since 1925 apart from in the Supreme Court. In HKSAR, photography is banned in the precincts of courts. Further, drawing is not permitted in courts. Some legal scholars in Hong Kong criticize that the judiciary is not keeping in pace with modern technology." (Regarding this point Doreen Weisenhaus asks for cameras to be allowed in the Court of Final Appeal, since the cases there are of constitutional importance and public interest (Chiu 2013).) Mr. Justice Lunn said, "The HKSAR government announced in July 2013 that Wi-Fi will gradually be allowed in Courts. However, there are currently no plans to introduce cameras into the Court of Final Appeal (Chiu 2013)."

Judicial education is another area where theory and practice can work together. Integrity, impartiality and competence are skills that are required among judges to conduct trials and appeals fairly and expeditiously. All of this requires ongoing education. The HK Judicial Institute was formed in early 2013. It builds on the previous work of the Judicial Studies Board. Examples of training activities organized by the Judicial Studies Board include lunchtime talks and courses on a variety of topics, ranging from the role of judges to Chinese judgment writing, as well as a visit to the Correctional Services Department. Human resources were lacking at the Judicial Studies Board. A core full-time staff is needed to organize courses and provide bench books for the judges. Full-time support is needed since help has been only ad hoc so far. The Judicial Institute is addressing those issues. This is important since there is a promotional judiciary system in HKSAR. Inexperienced judges should be able to learn and be guided accordingly. Continuous education is also important for judges to keep up-to-date with the latest changes in the law.

Theory comes into play in sentencing defendants as well, especially when sentencing young offenders. Similar to in the UK, the age of criminal responsibility is 10 years old in HKSAR. Under Section 11 of the Juvenile Offenders Ordinance, no young offender aged between 10 and 13 can be sentenced to imprisonment and no young offender aged between 14 and 15 can be sentenced to imprisonment if that offender can be suitably dealt with in any other way. Under Section 109A(1) of the Criminal Procedure Ordinance, no offender aged between 16 and 20 can be sentenced to imprisonment unless no other method of dealing with the person is found to be appropriate. However, there are exceptions to Section 109A(1). These are set out in Schedule 3 of the Criminal Procedure Ordinance and include serious crimes such as manslaughter, robbery, and indecent assault.

There are four main theoretical justifications for punishment: retribution, deterrence, incapacitation, rehabilitation, and reparation (Von Hirsch and Ashworth 1999). According to Chui (2001), there are two main types of punishment for young offenders in HKSAR: community-based sentences and residential care or custody. Rehabilitation is the primary theoretical underpinning of sentencing young offenders in HKSAR (Chui and Lo 2009). The main rationale of criminal penalties in HKSAR is to rehabilitate young offenders rather than punish them. This can be traced back to riots within HKSAR correctional institutions during the 1960s and 1970s. Strict discipline was adopted and the ethos of "custody and care" has been successful (Adorjan and Chui 2011). Even though rehabilitation is not the primary aim in some Western countries, the HKSAR Correctional Services Department adheres strongly to its belief in rehabilitation (Adorjan and Chui 2011). It is still the prevailing rationale of the criminal justice system in HKSAR.

Transnational Relations

HKSAR's common law system has attracted judges from many countries, such as the United Kingdom, Australia, New Zealand, and South Africa, to sit in the HKSAR Court of Final Appeal. The influence of English law on the HKSAR legal system is clear, as seen when I adopted some of Lord Leveson's way of conducting an inquiry in the Lamma Island Ferry Inquiry. Further, the HKSAR Code of Conduct for Expert Witnesses takes its origin from England and Wales.

The key area where transnational relations have had the most impact on my work is human rights law. Cases from the UK Supreme Court and the European Court of Human Rights are all relevant to HKSAR courts. The case of *HKSAR v. Lam Kwong Wai and Another** is an example where both UK and European authorities are cited by a judge in HKSAR. This case concerns the "reverse onus" provision. Sir Anthony Mason delivered the main judgment, mentioning the main cases on presumption of innocence in common law and proof of *mens rea* first, then moved to the European position. The leading European authority on the presumption of innocence is *Salabiaku v France.*† It deals with the presumption in the context of Article 6(2) of the European Convention on Human Rights.

The terrorist attack in the United States on September 11, 2001 had no impact on my work. There was a Libyan man who was claiming for redress for informal rendition through Hong Kong but it hasn't reached the HKSAR

---

* [2006] 3 HKLRD 808.
† (1988) 13 EHRR 379.

Court of Appeal yet. The United Kingdom is involved in this case and has already paid the Libyan some compensation. HKSAR does not have major terrorist funding issues and money-laundering is related to mainland China rather than further afield.

General Assessments

Toward the end of the interview, Mr. Justice Lunn provided some general comments about the HKSAR judicial system. He said that, "there have been very few criminal statutes and legislative developments in HKSAR. Most developments in the criminal justice system have been made by judges." He gave the example that HKSAR does not even have the equivalent of PACE, the United Kingdom's Police and Criminal Evidence Act 1984, codes of practice. PACE aims to provide a balance between the powers of the police and the rights of the public. Maintaining that balance is a central principle of PACE. The PACE codes of practice cover areas such as stop and search, arrests, detention, identification, investigation, and interviewing detainees. Mr. Justice Lunn opined that PACE is overdue in HKSAR saying:

> Judges in HKSAR have always used the Holley test (*Attorney General for Jersey v. Holley**) on the defense of provocation. This is in contrast to English judges where the House of Lords abandoned the objective test of the evaluative limb of Section 3 Homicide Act 1957 and used a subjective test in the case of *R v. Smith* (Morgan).† Adopting a subjective test widened the scope of the defense of provocation. Provocation is a valid defense in the common law system. If provocation is successfully pleaded to a charge of murder, it reduces liability to manslaughter. There are two limbs to the defense:
>
> 1. *The factual limb*: This involves a consideration of whether the defendant was, or may have been, provoked to lose his/her self-control. As far as this limb is concerned, all probative evidence is admissible. This issue is a pure question of fact.
> 2. *The evaluative limb*: Under Section 3 of the Homicide Act 1957, "whether the provocation was enough to make a reasonable man do as he did shall be left to be determined by the jury; and in determining that question the jury shall take into account everything both done and said according to the effect which, in their opinion, it would have on a reasonable man."

The law on the second limb has been through interesting developments in the English courts. Regarding the evaluative limb of Section 3 Homicide Act

* [2005] 3 WLR 29.
† [2000] 1 AC 146.

1957, in the case of *R v. Camplin*,* R v Morhall,† and Luc Thiet Thuan v R‡ the courts held there should not be a distinction between the gravity of provocation and self-control. The judge should direct the jury to consider whether an ordinary person with ordinary powers of self-control would have reacted to the provocation as the defendant did. Characteristics of the defendant affecting the gravity of the provocation will be considered (Ashworth and Horder 2009). In *R v. Smith* (Morgan),§ however, the House of Lords rejected the distinction between the gravity of provocation and self-control. The court held, by a majority, that no distinction should be drawn when attributing characteristics for the purposes of the objective limb of the test imposed by Section 3 of the Homicide Act, between their relevance to the gravity of the provocation to a reasonable man and his reaction to it. Lord Hoffmann delivered the main judgment. In his opinion, aspects of the defendant affecting her ability to exercise control should be considered (Clarkson and Keating 2007). On this legal point, Mr. Justice Lunn said, "I believe that the majority was incorrect to adopt a subjective test and was pleased to see that the objective test was restored in Attorney General for *Jersey v. Holley*."¶

In Attorney General for *Jersey v. Holley*,** the defendant and the deceased were in a violent relationship and both suffered from chronic alcoholism. On April 13, they spent the morning drinking in a pub and arguing. In the afternoon, the defendant went home, chopped some wood and continued drinking. The deceased stayed in the pub and went home in the early evening. The defendant said that the deceased was drunk and told him that she had had sex with another man. The defendant hit the deceased with an axe and she died. The defendant was charged with murder and raised the defense of provocation. He was convicted of murder and appealed on the grounds that the

---

* [1978] AC 705. In this case, the defendant and his wife were both alcoholics. They were originally in a relationship but continued to live together after splitting up. One day, both drank heavily. The defendant was at home chopping wood. The defendant's wife returned home after drinking at the pub. She told the defendant that she had been cheating on him and that he was too scared to do anything. The defendant then used the axe to kill her.

† [1966] AC 90 The appellant was a 15-year-old boy who killed a man. In his defense, he argued that he was provoked because the man raped him and laughed at him. In the House of Lords, the appellant's young age was held to be relevant and the jury could take that into account.

‡ [1997] AC 131 The appellant killed his ex-girlfriend. He claimed she owed him money. The appellant tied her up, took her to a cash machine and forced her to reveal her code at knifepoint. He claimed that she then taunted him about his sexual ability. The appellant lost his control and stabbed her many times. At his trial, medical evidence was given that the defendant suffered from an organic brain problem induced by a head injury. However, the defendant's responsibility was not found to be substantially impaired. At the Privy Council, the original conviction of murder was upheld. The Court said that admitting "purely mental peculiarities" would blur the boundary between provocation and diminished responsibility.

§ n 10.

¶ n 9.

** Ibid.

judge misdirected the jury. His appeal was dismissed at his retrial but was allowed by the Court of Appeal of Jersey. The trial judge should have directed the jury that they were entitled to take into account the disease of alcoholism from which the defendant suffered. The Attorney General appealed to the Privy Council. The Privy Council allowed the prosecutor's appeal. Although the Court of Appeal had applied the approach in *R v. Smith* (Morgan) correctly, the Court (Lords Bingham, Hoffman and Carswell dissenting) advised that the approach was wrong. The jury should not take into account evidence that the defendant was suffering from chronic alcoholism when considering whether a person having ordinary powers of self-control would have done as the defendant did. An objective test for the evaluative limb has thus been restored and I welcome this.

In relation to potential developments in criminal law and procedure in HKSAR, Mr. Justice Lunn said that "it is unlikely that a great deal of legislation will be enacted in the HKSAR." In respect of money laundering, he noted that because there is a general concern of how wide the net is in catching people, change will probably be reached via case law rather than legislation, although legislation is the obvious place to implement changes. "Personally, I do not see many changes in criminal law that can be made by courts, but I would like to see changes in the criminal procedure. Delays should be cut back; trials should address and focus on the essential issues. To achieve the above changes, there needs to be a change of mind-set. That said, I acknowledge that as with all changes of mind-set or culture, it will take time."

Time will tell whether Mr. Justice Lunn's pearls of wisdom will be implemented.

Glossary

affidavit: A written statement of fact voluntarily made under an oath or affirmation, administered by a person authorized to do so by law.
Basic Law: The constitution of HKSAR since July 1, 1997.
Chief Executive: The Chief Executive of Hong Kong is the head and representative of the HKSAR and head of the Government of Hong Kong.
HKSAR: The Hong Kong Special Administrative Region.
ordinance: Law made by the local authority or council.
peremptory challenge: The right to reject a juror without giving a reason.
silk: Senior Counsel, a barrister with at least 10 years' practice.

New Zealand
Legal System

V

EMMA DAVIES

Aotearoa, New Zealand, is a small country with a land area of 268,000 km^2 in the South Pacific (Figure V.1). In 2013, it had a population of just over 4,480,000 people, with the last census in 2006 indicating that 69% of the population identify as European, 14.6% as Maori, 9.2% as Asian, and 6.9% as Pacific Islanders. The Asian population is the fastest-growing minority group.

New Zealand's heritage is largely bicultural—Maori* and Pākehā.[†] Representatives of the British Crown and most Maori chiefs signed New Zealand's founding document, the Treaty of Waitangi, in or just after 1840. The treaty has three broad principles on which the nation state was established, although Maori and the Crown had different understandings of these principles (Kawharu, 1989). That is not to say that there has been an equal place for both cultures. The English soon outnumbered the Maori as Maori numbers plummeted through the effects of war, disease carried in by settlers, and mass English migration. At the 1840 census, 98% of the population was Maori and 2% was European/Pākehā. By the time of the census in 1900, only 5% was Maori and 95% was European/Pākehā.

The Treaty of Waitangi had very little influence on New Zealand's law or administrative structures until the 1970s, some 130 years after it was signed. It is not considered part of New Zealand law, except where its principles are referred to in Acts of Parliament. The legal right to determine the meaning of the treaty lies with the Waitangi Tribunal, which was established through an Act of Parliament in 1975. The Waitangi Tribunal, a commission of inquiry, uses inquisitorial processes to investigate alleged breaches of the treaty by the Crown or its agents and recommends to the government means of redress for

---

* The indigenous peoples of Aotearoa, New Zealand. Literally, the term means "normal," in comparison with immigrants to the country.
[†] A New Zealander of European descent; a non-Māori New Zealander.

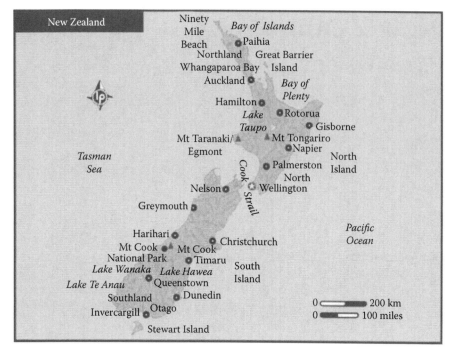

Figure V.1 Map of New Zealand.

the Maori. More than 2000 claims have been lodged with the tribunal and many major settlements have been reached.*

Beyond this, as a former British colony and a member of the Commonwealth, New Zealand's legal system fundamentally follows the British model. The New Zealand Criminal Court structure comprises the supreme court, the court of appeal, the high court, and the district court. The family and youth courts are divisions of the district court with their own principal family and youth court judges, respectively. Family and youth court judges have general warrants as district court judges. They also hold specialist warrants as specialist family or youth court judges. In essence, under the Children, Young Persons, and Their Families (CYPF) Act 1989, the family court deals with care and protection, which are civil proceedings, and the youth court deals with youth justice, which are criminal proceedings.

The youth court largely deals with criminal offending by children and young people between the ages of 12 and 16 that is too serious to be dealt with in other ways. While these courts are closed to the public, media can attend, although they are obliged to check with the judge before publication.

---

* www.waitangi-tribunal.govt.nz. For more information see also New Zealand Ministry for Culture and Heritage (2014) and Orange (2011).

The processes of the youth court acknowledge that children and young people's cognitive and emotional development is such that their offending needs to be dealt with differently than the processes applied to adults who commit similar offenses. Further, its processes established under the CYPF Act acknowledge indigenous processes of conflict resolution, including direct communication between victim and offender and the engagement of the wider family and local community. It also goes some way toward acknowledging the needs and rights of children, consistent with the United Nations Convention on the Rights of the Child 1989, which the New Zealand Parliament ratified 2 years later in 1991.

The CYPF Act 1989 established the role of the principal youth court judge "to ensure the orderly and expeditious discharge of the business of the Court..." [Section 434(7)]. Mick Brown, the interviewee, was the first judge to be appointed to the role.

Mick Brown, District Court

6

EMMA DAVIES

Contents

Introduction

Ehara taku toa, he taki tahi, he toa taki tini: My success should not be bestowed onto me alone, as it was not individual success but success of a collective. (Mick Brown at the start of the interview)

The interview with Judge Brown covered two types of judicial philosophy:

1. The first is how the law can operate.
2. The second is a philosophy of how to bring that about.

For Mick Brown, the two are inseparable.

The philosophies and principles that are being used in the youth justice field in New Zealand are, I believe, inextricably based on a communitarian concept.

We are seeing a greater involvement of families and wider families—a recognition of the strength of attachments that evoke personal obligation to others within a community of concern. (Judge M. J. Brown, quoted in *New Zealand Listener*, 2003)

Career

Judge Michael J. Brown was New Zealand's first Maori district court judge (1980–1995). He contributed notably to reshaping the youth justice system in New Zealand, pioneering the use of communitarian principles of justice with young offenders, first in the Waitakere District Court in the 1980s and then nationally as New Zealand's first principal youth court judge (1989–1995). He nurtured cultural change in youth justice practice, developing the practice of community accountability and responsibility and the philosophy underpinning the CYPF Act 1989. (For a more detailed account of the CYPF Act, see Appendix D.) A decade later, he conducted the ministerial review of care and protection services in the Department of Child, Youth and Family Services (Brown, 2000).

Judge Brown has also had appreciable influence in academia. In the 1990s, he established the Mātāhauariki Research Institute at Waikato University, which explores processes that could help New Zealand's legal system to better accommodate "the best of the values and concepts of indigenous and non-indigenous peoples of New Zealand."

He served on the University of Auckland Council for 15 years and was chancellor of the University of Auckland from 1986 to 1991. In this role, he was instrumental in bringing together universities to challenge the New Zealand government over sweeping changes that would otherwise have eroded universities' autonomy and academic freedom. A decade later, he was pro-vice chancellor Maori at the University of Auckland (2002–2005). The University of Auckland has twice recognized his contribution to law and academia by bestowing on him a Distinguished Alumni Award (2002) and an honorary Doctorate of Laws. He was made a Companion of the New Zealand Order of Merit in 1996 for services to the youth court, education, and the community. In July 2013, he received New Zealand's prestigious Blake Medal for leadership. The citation summed up: "Judge Brown transformed agendas, conversations and systems that endure today."

I have known Judge Brown since 1999. I first met him when he was conducting the ministerial review of the Department of Child, Youth, and Family Services. Having prepared extensive notes of my verbal submission to his review following my doctorate on related matters, I vividly remember going to his home grasping my notes, nervous and hoping that I would be heard by this man whose reputation in New Zealand preceded him. Within 5 minutes, he stopped me, and gently suggested that I left my notes on the bench and that we went for a walk to talk about child protection. I experienced his wit and informality as disarming, and his questions as sharp. During his review, he used me as a sounding board for ideas, although I provided little help with the difficult task of identifying how to significantly improve child protection services. Since then, I have been privileged to have many conversations with this inspiring man who became a mentor and a friend.

I interviewed Judge Mick Brown for this book on August 29, 2013, by telephone from the United Kingdom. I had sent him the questions outlined by the editors and we had discussed the interview by telephone in advance. I found the interview difficult as I missed the nonverbal communication inaccessible in a telephone interview and my questioning felt inadequate to draw out the essence of Mick's judicial philosophy.

In writing this chapter, I have used the interview transcript, fragments of older conversations about key influencers, published articles, and comments from a retired senior public servant, Mike Doolan, the then national director (youth and employment), to reveal the development of Judge Brown's ideas and judicial philosophy. Judge Brown approved the draft manuscript in September 2013.

Personal Judicial Philosophy

In responding to questions about his career and his judicial philosophy, Mick Brown goes back to his roots, the experiences that shaped his identity and his journey through the law:

> I was placed in a foster home when I was about 3 months old because my mother was dying of tuberculosis… My fostering was done by a Pākehā family. I didn't ever feel that I'd been discriminated against as a [Māori] child. I was placed in a loving, loving family with a solo mother and she spoilt me.
>
> I think I've been very lucky. I know I owe it to the lady that brought me up. Otherwise, I could just be coming out of prison myself because it can happen. I am always conscious of that.
>
> Mrs. Dorothy Flood [foster mother] had a daughter, Acushla (about 15 years older than me) who was a teacher of deaf kids. My sister's work brought lots of things home to me—the reality of kids' lives. This also had a big impact on some of my attitudes in later life.
>
> When I was 10, I had a silly accident in the street. Subsequently I was diagnosed with tuberculosis in the knee […] I spent 3 years in the Wilson Home

[a residential facility for children with disabilities] [...] My sister used to bring library books back on her way home from work so I read all the time. I read the entire library... Because I read, I was also spoiled by the teachers at the Wilson Home.

These experiences have fashioned my attitudes, made me conscious of how lucky most of us are in our lives. Most of these children [in the Wilson Home] wouldn't reach middle age and they were brave... My hospital experiences and those things formed me.

Then I went to Mount Albert Grammar [a mainstream secondary school] [...] there were only about five Maori. I didn't feel harshly discriminated against there either... I had this problem with my leg but I got by and disregarded such things as inconvenient. I tend to disregard such things as inconveniences [...] I played cricket and was in the first XI.

I intended to be a teacher [and trained to do so] because of the influence of Acushla but then I decided to do law. I had been to a movie *Witness for the Prosecution*, and my adopted family had a lawyer as a friend of the family. I did law part-time at university, which you could do then—and that was great.

Latterly in my university days, the Maori club at university was my first exposure to Maori values and processes. A large number of them had come from Māori schools in the region, so I became more involved. I enjoyed their company and still do.

Most of us got jobs as clerks in legal firms. We had time off for lectures and law tests on Saturday mornings. The casual New Zealand way of doing things... David Lange, Jim McLay, and Douglas Graham were contemporaries.* David Lange was brilliant, from day one.

When I first left teaching and went into law, I did my first apprenticeship in the State Advancement Corporation (now Housing New Zealand). Most law clerks were on peanuts. [He quips with a smile that comes through the phone] The law profession is better at taking in money than paying it out.

I then went to a legal firm with Peter Williams.† We met through the debating club in the university. Then I got to work for Meredith Connell, the Crown Solicitor's Office—acting for all the legal departments. This was wonderful experience. It differed a lot from private practice as the department sent you the work.

I was also on various committees. At that stage, I was first involved in university administration. Just did it in my own time. I did enjoy it too. Loved it.

Then I did practice on my own. I enjoyed the jury trial. The whole advocate's role—various lies seen again and again—it's a stimulating experience.

---

* In 1984, David Lange (Labor Party) became prime minister of New Zealand and Jim McLay (National Party) became deputy prime minister and leader of the opposition. Douglas Graham (National Party) is most well known in his role as minister in charge of treaty negotiations from 1991, in which he was widely praised by both Pākehā and Maori for his work on treaty settlements.

† Peter Williams, Queen's Counsel since 1987, is president of the Howard League for Penal Reform and has been a constant advocate for change in the penal system so that there is less focus on punishment and incarceration and more on restoration, rehabilitation, and prevention of crime.

But I was too busy, couldn't do it all. I was then approached and asked if I wanted to be a magistrate [changed to the term *district court judge* in 1980 when the jurisdiction also increased]. As a judge, you were just allocated courts. That too was interesting. I'd been daily in the courts—just being on another side—that was all... I'd always been interested in criminal and youth justice.

I enjoyed the criminal law. I admire it as a system that has survived and I think we have been well served by the criminal justice system. And one of the things I have done throughout my career is to have extramural activities, partly to relieve the boredom of the law and partly to meet a cross section of people, and I have found that very interesting. Hearing different attitudes... I have never run into harsh criticism on racial grounds.

Almost inevitably, things outside the law influenced my thinking more than things inside the law. I had a wonderful foster family with love and positive cognitive development. Educating myself about different attitudes around also helped me give better judgments.

The Role of Judge within a Communitarian Philosophy

I made a point of getting to all the youth courts in New Zealand... Going around the circuit was an eye-opener for me. Interesting because coming from Auckland [the largest city in New Zealand] meant you weren't trusted initially in small-town New Zealand, and being a little sun-tanned raised eyebrow in some parts of the South Island. Some assumed we [Maori] were usually bloody liars. [He laughs] some of the courts had expected me to arrive with a haka [a Maori ceremonial war dance] or something.

I saw a lot of people with different attitudes. Because of the background I had, not brought up by a Maori family, it didn't make it feel like I had to compensate for it in another way. I was proud of my background.

I also knew that there were a lot of people, particularly brown people, who valued that there was a brown person giving out sentences. They might not like the sentences, but the fact that I was brown was important.

You get differences in opinion in different areas—a jury in Christchurch [a South Island town] is more conservative than a jury in Whangerei [a northern town]... But in fact, I loved it. It was an adventure... it was tiring though.

I would always make a point of having lunch in a café—it's a people thing; maybe as much unconscious as conscious. It's partly about connectedness with community... I was often rung and asked to join things like the Auckland Cricket Association, or to talk with a community group or at a Marae.* And sailing, that's another world too. I enjoyed meeting New Zealanders... I've

---

* The *Marae* is a communal space that serves social and sometimes religious purposes. Some are pantribal, some are unitribal, some are based within other institutions (e.g., the armed forces, universities), and others are stand-alone, based within urban or rural communities.

always been interested in people with different kinds of intelligence. Many of us are frail and have many human frailties so I admire those from all walks of life who overcome those frailties.

If I had time in the evenings, I would make the time to go out and meet with local clubs—bowls, cricket—very important part of New Zealand. New Zealand is run by amateurs… I felt that engaging with Marae and community groups was part of the job—selling the picture of that word "judge." It's tricky to ensure that you are impartial. I took away piles of books to read at night in motels too. Being a judge is just a role. Trying to be as well prepared as you can be is partly about understanding human nature. The judicial role is to understand human behavior.

Involving Victims

The legislation brought in quite revolutionary changes. One of the attractions was the opportunities it provided to create an environment where the victims and the young people could talk in a safe space; where the child could talk perhaps more about the other things that they did that night and why. I had the hope that it humanized one part of the criminal law.

I am less concerned about processes and more the effect of bringing people together to improve understanding of justice… The ability for offenders and victims to speak to each other can be part of the healing. The family group conferences (FGCs) ordered by the court provided a platform to enable that to happen. The restorative factor is one that I admire greatly.

Early research into FGCs found that victims or their representatives attended approximately half of the conferences; 60% of the victims interviewed described the experience as helpful or rewarding and 25% felt worse after their participation (Maxwell et al., 1993). A total of 6% of victims did not want to meet the offender. But the majority did and appreciated the voice they had in determining appropriate redress. They also valued the opportunity to meet the offender and his or her family so that they understood more about the offending and what could be done to prevent it happening again (Tauri and Morris, 2003). Judge Brown responded to these findings by convening meetings of youth court judges in 1993 to increase participation of victims in FGCs. They focused attention on overcoming practical issues, for example the amount of notice given to victims, ensuring that victims have some control over the date of the FGC when possible, and developing processes to encourage victims to attend, including allaying fears of retribution (McElrea, 1993).

While the outcomes remain imperfect, the active and direct role of victims has arguably helped maintain the nature of the youth justice process to this day. As Mick says:

We look for perfection where it probably won't expose itself.

Problems and Successes Experienced

As a District Court Judge

In the 1980s, years *before* the introduction of the CYPF Act, Mick Brown developed a communitarian approach to justice in his local district court within the parameters of the Children and Young Persons Act 1974. This was at the same time as the national conversation about the role of the state in families' lives including *Puao-te-at-atu* and the emergence of Hoani Waititi [urban] marae in the local community in which Judge Brown lived and worked.

Mick repeatedly said in the interview for this chapter that he was not involved in the development of the CYPF Act. He commented similarly at the time:

> I am neither the architect nor the builder of this legislative edifice. Indeed, I happily subscribe to the constitutional convention that legislators make the law and it is the duty of the court to apply it. By an equally happy coincidence, I am very enthusiastic about the law. (Brown, 1989)

He was quick to acknowledge, then and now, the work of the senior public servant Mike Doolan, for his insight and approach to the development of the new legislation. Mike Doolan reflects on Mick Brown's role prior to the new legislation this way:

> It was well known at the time that at the Waitakere Court, Judge Brown was already using some of the approaches that ultimately became law—he was in advance of his time, without a doubt... The law was not directly modeled on what he had done—much of the bones of the new legal scheme were in place when I heard about his approach, but his work was tremendously validating. His court was living proof that these processes worked—putting matters back to wider family groups (whanau hui*) and minimizing young people's involvement with formal systems, substituting, instead, the empowering of family groups to take back control of the young person offending, seeing that they put the matter right and planning to reduce their involvement in delinquent activities and opportunities. It was useful to have Judge Brown's court as an example of the way things could be when trying to convince politicians that these processes would be a viable alternative to a court-centered system of justice... So while not a formal pilot of the provisions of the new law, Waitakere court was a live example of doing things differently, under the auspices of a person who understood and validated the philosophy of the new Act when it emerged... This was not theory for Judge Brown; it was his way of operating under the old legal scheme. Any other judge could have worked the old law the way he did— but they did not and that is why we ushered in a new legal scheme.†

---

* Hui are gatherings in Maori communities.
† Mike Doolan, personal communication, September 5, 2013.

The Department of Social Welfare developed a pilot to test the viability of aspects of the new proposed legal scheme in 1988/9 in Porirua (near the capital city of Wellington) in association with the local police aid and the presiding judge of the then children and young persons court, Judge David Carruthers. Mick Brown's advice to David Carruthers was characteristically thoughtful and simple (reported in McElrea, 1993):

> There are three questions you must ask: "Who is your community? What are its strengths? And how are those strengths best made use of?"

As Principal Youth Court Judge

The policy-making process inevitably involves many actors. Although the final legislation stipulated that the appointment of principal youth court judge be made by the governor general on the advice of the attorney general, the mere existence of the designation of a principal youth court judge was not initially thought necessary. Mike Doolan comments:

> One of the biggest policy battles that I had was in the creation of the position of the principal youth court judge. There was opposition to this as there was already a chief district court judge and the youth court was to be a division of the district court. However, we were convinced that whoever led the youth court would set the tone and provide the leadership that would ensure the new legal scheme either flourished or floundered. It was a miracle that Judge Brown was appointed (something about which we had absolutely no influence) and I knew from my first meeting with him some months before enactment that the legal scheme was safe in his hands. And so it proved to be.[*]
>
> I cannot emphasize enough what having Judge Brown as the first principal judge meant to my team and me. As we worked with judges, youth advocates, police, social workers, and community organizations to prepare them for the introduction of the new law, we had as the leader of the new system a man who not only understood and advocated the principles and practice approaches we sought, but had done it successfully already in his own court. It's hard to mount an argument against that! On a personal level, I found him affirming and generous with his time (if at times a little overgenerous in public when speaking about me!).[†]

The "miracle" of Mick's appointment may say something about Mick's influence on many New Zealanders, some of whom likely took their experiences of Mick into conversations with politicians and perhaps even into conversations with the governor general at the time, Sir Michael Hardie

[*] Ibid.
[†] Ibid.

Boys, himself an ex-judge. These informal conversations should not be underestimated in the policy-making process.

The mutual respect between Mick Brown, as leading judge, and Mike Doolan, as policy lead on design and implementation of the youth justice provisions within the act from within the state, may also say something about how they succeeded in putting principles into practice. I have no doubt that Mick's oratory also helped embed the process and encourage practitioners to think differently. For example, just prior to the implementation of the act, he endeavored to engage the legal profession in this way in an interview for the professional magazine most read by lawyers:

> Let me suggest one possible way to approach this legislation. It may require what the poets have described as 'a willing suspension of disbelief.' It may require flexibility of mind and a willingness to entertain the unconventional, the innovative. To allow, in Doctor Johnson's words (when referring to second marriages), "optimism to triumph over experience." Hopefully, you as lawyers, a group which by definition is intelligent, educated and powerful, might bring to this statute not only technical skills and knowledge, but also preparedness to enter its spirit. (Brown, 1989)

After outlining the critical aspects of the legislation, he continued:

> The question I anticipate you would raise is: what is the lawyer's role in this legislation? The answer may not be when courts and lawyers are involved, but rather having the deftness of touch to decide when courts and lawyers should keep out. (Brown, 1989)

In 1993, he promoted the legislation in this way to the New Zealand public through the *Listener*, a current affairs magazine:

> All my life experience to date convinces me that there are great strengths within our community. I am positive we can draw on New Zealanders' immense reservoir of concern and sense of group obligation [...] When we talk of communities, we must include victims of offending. The primary objectives of a criminal justice system must include healing the breach of social harmony, of social relationships, putting right the wrong and making reparation rather than concentrating on punishment. The ability of the victim to have input at the family group conference is, or ought to be, one of the most significant virtues of the youth justice procedures. On the basis of our experience to date, we can expect to be amazed at the generosity of spirit of many victims and (to the surprise of many professionals participating) the absence of retributive demands and vindictiveness. Victims' responses are in direct contrast to the hysterical, media-generated responses to which we are so often exposed. (Reported in McElrea, 1994)

Securing Effective Implementation

I'm not sure that you can legislate for everything. When I was given the job and sent the legislation, I was very hopeful. From then on, it is whether you get the cooperation from the people who are most influential in the whole process—probably the police, social workers and the legal profession and the kids. And the other actors the kids are named after—the families.

Understanding Children and Families

Probably my instinct was for the victims at courts but also for some of the others who, when you saw them and got to know them more and often when you got to know their families, you understood why they behaved as they did.

As he said on national television in 1996:

Many times when you sit in court, you say to yourself "I wish I could take this kid home." You know, bring them up, put her in school or him in some sort of business or trade. As a society, which includes me, we continue to be quite naive about what does go on in these households and what adults do to children in the privacy in their own home.

[The young people] had to have a lawyer. But the success of the legislation depended on how well conferences worked. I thought many times that we weren't getting the whole story. Sometimes the young people may have been protecting dad—or themselves—from another hiding if they exposed dad's behavior. But more often, I think kids were in that protective role of their parents. In my idealized view, probably too much is left to the child. That says more about how we bring up children.

Orientating Professionals

Policies are usually, of course, desirable. But how they are utilized may provide a totally different situation. I was pleased at how quickly people adopted it. Generally, this was imposed and picked up around the country. It was good legislation if people understood it and adopted it quickly. [Successful implementation] depends on the social welfare people understanding and embracing the philosophy and letting it work. We probably should have trained lawyers in this first before they were allowed to appear. But most did adopt it and understand the principles that sat behind it. But it is perhaps too easy to fall into old habits of professional knows best and to inadvertently disempower the families that can make the biggest difference.

Nevertheless, it appears that commitment to the principles underpinning the CYPF Act remain important to the key actors to this day, despite political attempts to derail it at the time of writing (with unknown effects because it is too soon) and in 2010 (Lynch, 2012). The CYPF Act was modified in 2010 to reorientate the system to be more punitive by extending and strengthening the sentencing powers of the youth court, by bringing more 12- and 13-year-old children into its jurisdiction and by introducing widely publicized military-style boot camps for young offenders. A recent analysis of changes to the act, two and a half years after their introduction, found that child offender prosecution powers were rarely used by practitioners, transfers to the adult district court had not increased, and the military-style boot camps had been implemented with a less punitive focus than politicians had publicized. The researcher concluded that "practitioners are acting to mitigate the punitive potential of the legislation" (Lynch, 2012).

Conclusion

> Mehemea ka patai mai kow he aha te mean tino nui ka whakahoki ahau, "he tangata, he tangata, he tangata, he tangata": If you were to ask me what is the greatest thing on all the earth, my reply would be, "it is people, it is people, it is people."

This Maori proverb perhaps best sums up Mick Brown's approach to life and his judicial role. His legal scholarship and practice in a commonwealth country alongside his bicultural identity may not have defined his judicial philosophy. They are more accurately seen as tools that helped him use his powers to act according to communitarian values and principles in a multicultural context.

The Personal is the Professional

On an individual level, Mick Brown's insight into his own history and how that formed him are instructive for those who shape this thing we call justice. By understanding where his attitudes come from, and what motivates him, he has perhaps been more able to ask useful questions to help people understand where *their* attitudes come from, what motivates them, and how to change their behavior individually and as part of the collective—be they professionals, volunteers, parents, or offenders.

His positive early life experiences, his role as a brown outsider, his enjoyment of people, his emotional intelligence, and his communication skills have all helped him to use his judicial power carefully in the interests of those he serves. His experiences as a small child brought up by a foster mother who gave him the love and care he needed, helped him to develop a solid core from which he could grow to become an effective leader. Neurobiological research now substantiates the belief that this nurturing in the early years of life is fundamentally important for people to reach their full potential

(OECD, 2009). Mick's life is one illustration that this does not have to come from biological parents; it can come from others of significance, in his case a Pākehā foster parent and an older sister. What matters is not who provides it, but the quality and quantity of nurturing that young children receive (Perry, 1999). His experiences in a residential home for children with disabilities helped him learn how to overcome adversity and understand more about the worldview of others who struggle to survive.

He also understood from his experiences on the bench and his deep connections with many parts of New Zealand society, and research substantiates, that many repeat young offenders are also victims of child abuse and neglect (Perry, 1999; Ryan et al., 2013), so punitive sanctions alone simply cannot work. Moreover, preventing repeated serious juvenile offending is beyond the realms of the criminal justice system; it lies in child protection, health, and education (Becroft, 2009). Therefore, it should be of no surprise that reviews have found limited evidence of the efficacy of FGCs for hardened offenders (Ministerial Taskforce on Youth Offending, 2002; Weatherburn, 2013). Finding more effective ways to break intergenerational cycles of violence and neglect of children remains a critical message that the global community needs to heed if violence in society is to be significantly reduced.

His communitarian approach to dealing with youth offending is one path toward that goal. But this is often too little too late. Mick is the first to acknowledge that more fundamentally it is necessary to deal with adults' abuse and neglect of children earlier in their lifespan too (Brown, 2000). As Bruce Perry phrased it in 1999, "The challenge of our generation is to understand the dynamics and realities of our human living groups in a way that can result in group insight—which, inevitably, will lead to the understanding that we must change our institutionalized ignorance and maltreatment of children."

Systemic Change

Before the CYPF Act and the opportunity to be the inaugural principal youth court judge, Mick Brown did not wait for legislation to share his power with those most affected by the offending. Through independence of thought, mindful of the need for interdependence in action, he took responsibility for what he could do to change the culture and practice in the court over which he had jurisdiction. Looking at this through the lens of Joseph Nye's (2008) analysis of power, he used smart power in the hard sanctions available to him and soft power to persuade people to resolve issues more effectively than he thought the court and professionals could do alone.

One significant outcome of his work, and the principles in the CYPF Act, is the way that the change in professional culture through the family group conference enabled a multicultural framework to thrive within a mono-cultural common law jurisdiction. Figure 6.1 shows that the diversionary

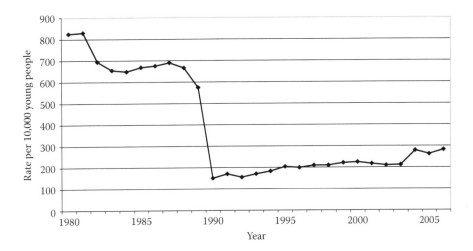

Figure 6.1 Rate per 10,000 population of 14- to 16-year-olds, of cases appearing in the youth court 1980–2006. (From Maxwell, G. (2004). Achieving effective outcomes in youth justice: Implications of new research for principles, police and practice, no. 27, 8 as reported in Becroft, A. (2007), Putting youth justice under the microscope: What is the diagnosis? A quick nip and tuck or radical surgery? Presented at the Conference on Rehabilitation of Youth Offenders, Singapore, p. 22.)

approach of the legislation led to a dramatic reduction in the number of offenses dealt with in the youth court at the time, and Figure 6.2 shows a dramatic reduction in the number of custodial sentences upon implementation of the CYPF Act (Becroft, 2009).

A mark of genius lies in Mick's oratory, which enabled the philosophy to flourish in practice. Influenced by his understanding of human behavior, alongside the emerging theory and practice of cross-cultural communication (e.g., Metge and Kinloch, 1978; Metge, 2001), he was able to connect his communitarian philosophy and the principles of the CYPF legislation with a vast array of New Zealand's peoples—from the legal fraternity to the local maori.

While the FGC is often seen in terms of restorative justice, Mick sees this as one factor. There can also be procedural, retributive, and rehabilitative elements within the process (Daly, 2002). This New Zealand experiment was not *theory driven*—it was a response to a national conversation over years, although the due process aspects of the law arguably reflect international best practice and more recent reviews still maintain the fundamental principles as sound (Ministerial Taskforce on Youth Offending, 2002). The process of development and the resulting philosophy may turn out to be as important as the mechanics. The story shows a complex intertwining of the development of theory and the practice of leadership to put principles into practice.

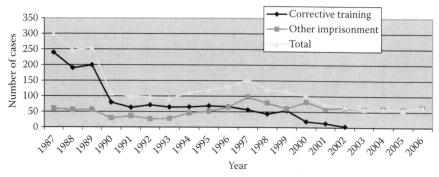

Figure 6.2 Custodial sentences for youth court cases, 1987–2006. (From A. Becroft (2007), Putting youth justice under the microscope: What is the diagnosis? A quick nip and tuck or radical surgery? Presented at the Conference on Rehabilitation of Youth Offenders, Singapore, p. 50.)

The implementation of the youth justice provisions in the CYPF Act has been discussed more fully elsewhere (Daly, 2002; Doolan, 2008; Morris and Maxwell, 2003; Tauri and Morris, 2003; Watt, 2003). There have been no controlled trials of the process. The limited evidence available suggests that satisfactory outcomes partially depend on good practice in preparation for FGCs, support for the offender, and the creation of the offender's feelings of remorse. However, there are still disproportionately high rates of offending among Maori and more can still be done to address mental health issues and drug problems among young offenders (Becroft, 2009).

It appears that active victim participation enhances procedural justice, with many victims who participate feeling some sense of justice in the process (Daly, 2002; Weatherburn, 2013). Victim participation when offenders show remorse may also be one of the factors in reducing recidivism; offenders who apologized to victims were less likely to be reconvicted than those who did not (Morris and Maxwell, 2003).

Similar processes may also be helpful to enhance accountability, safety, and community cultural change through the adult courts in cases of sexual and physical violence against women (e.g., Morris and Gelsthorpe, 2004; Julich, 2009) and business fraud (e.g., Levi, 2003). If ways can be found to balance power in criminal cases involving adults' crimes against children, the same might apply. What matters here is that the processes described in this chapter can improve understandings of justice. Seeking better ways to put right the wrongs, promote safety, enhance participants' sense of justice, and offer reparation and punishment should never be beyond an evolving criminal justice system. The hope remains that more can be done in this way to, as Mick put it, "humanize" the criminal law.

Serbia
Legal System

VI

BRANISLAV SIMONOVIĆ

When certain politicians try to describe Serbia (Figure VI.1) in a few words, they point out that it is a small country (of about 7.5 million people) with big problems. Serbia has simultaneously passed through various stages: disintegration of the country of which it was a federal part, that is, socialist Yugoslavia; wars caused by that disintegration (600,000 refugees came to Serbia as a result); international isolation, sanctions of the international community; transition; economic collapse; emergence of tycoons; growing unemployment; and poverty. When one describes transition in Serbia, one most often uses the metaphor "One step forward, two steps backward." This dynamic is typical of the legal system and the system of justice in Serbia.*

The legal system in Serbia is marked by very frequent changes in legislation, criminal law, substantive law, and procedural law. For example, in the period from 2000 to 2013, the Code of Criminal Procedure was altered more than 10 times in Serbia. In 2006, it was codified but it never came into force (it never entered legal practice). Within the frequent alterations of the Code of Criminal Procedure, deep systematic changes were made and new institutions were introduced, and then altered and amended again (e.g., judicial inquiry was abandoned and prosecutorial investigation was introduced; cross-examination was also introduced, as well as negotiation between the prosecutor and defendant on confessing guilt [plea bargaining]; the legal duty of the court of law to determine the truth was omitted when previously that was the cornerstone of criminal law and practice; the court of law's active role in gathering evidence was removed, that is, it was changed into passive, etc.). Often, alterations in the criminal legislation and the introduction of institutions that were not in the legal system's tradition made the work of judges more difficult, complicating the creation of unique

---

* It is interesting to mention that within Serbian folklore there is a national dance called "Kolo," and its basic moves are one step forward, two steps backwards!

Figure VI.1 Map of Serbian jurisdiction (in dark gray).

court practices and making it impossible to verify (confirm) adopted legal solutions in practice.

Apart from the changes within the legal framework, during the last 10 years or so, changes within the court organization were also frequent. At least two big reforms of court organization were made in the last 10 years in Serbia. Firstly, a great number of judges were removed from the courts in the first reform (their lack of expertise was given as a reason); territorial jurisdiction and subject-matter jurisdiction were also altered. Afterward, when the new government concluded that a mistake had been made, a reorganizational reform of the courts was carried out once again (related to both territorial jurisdiction and subject-matter jurisdiction), and the judges who were fired were brought back into the courtrooms. Although laws and the constitution proclaim judicial independence from political executives, there is a deep-rooted belief among citizens that this is not (fully) achieved.

At the time when this interview was conducted, the media in Serbia were flooded with critical writing at the expense of the Serbian criminal courts. At the same time, the criminal courts produced some verdicts that were considered highly arguable and problematic by the public. There were also gatherings and civil protests, because higher courts had annulled first instance verdicts in several murder cases where the victims were innocent girls. In several other cases, the courts proclaimed expired statute of limitations and brought in acquittal verdicts for defendants charged with serious financial felonies, who were related to ruling political elite. For example, in one of them the statute of limitations expired after 20 years of criminal proceedings, with no judgment on merits being brought in. In another case, which also had a political background and had very serious financial consequences for the whole country, the statute of limitations expired after 15 years. Defendants were released. There were cases with expired statute of limitations against priests charged with pedophilia, and suspects of murder or organized crime or both being released from custody and later fleeing the country. There is a general impression that courts postpone trials until the statute of limitations expires whenever they do not know what to do in certain cases, especially trials with a political background.

Bearing in mind that Serbia is at the starting point of joining the European Union, these and similar affairs came into the focus of public interest and public discussion began (most often in the media) about the need to improve the judicial system, which is considered to be one of the least successful systems in the country. In a public opinion survey, citizens stated that they do not trust the prosecutor's office or the courts, and that they find them slow, inefficient, and corrupt. When judging the work of these institutions, the marks that citizens gave them, on a scale from 1 to 5, were usually between 2 and 3.

Dragomir Milojević, President of the Serbian Supreme Court

7

BRANISLAV SIMONOVIĆ

Contents

Introduction

I had been trying to organize the interview with the president of the Supreme Court of Serbia for 2 months without success. When I lost hope that I would succeed, I was granted an interview, thanks to the persistence of Professor Dilip Das and one prominent Serbian lawyer.

While I was leaving to organize the interview, I was thinking about the public's critique of the courts, which, to some extent, I mentioned at the beginning of this text. Having in mind all that has been mentioned above, I felt uneasy when entering the large building and passing police control. A policewoman led me to the president's office, and from her movements one could see the determination of a police officer with long-term experience. This was especially interesting, because she was a middle-aged woman who was very determined, but also very kind at the same time. When I told her that I was going to interview the president, she said that they (court employees) had finally got a good president and a good man whom everybody respected and appreciated. I was completely surprised by this. From that moment, anxiety and unease disappeared. I thought that this was, after all, a good start and a positive impression before my interview with Dragomir Milojević, the president of the Supreme Court of Serbia.

Career

Q: Tell us a little bit about your career. (Try and include your length of service as a judge, organizations worked in, movements, specializations, etc.)

A: I was elected judge of the Municipal Court of Kragujevac* in 1982. After 10 years of practice in this court, in 1992, I was elected judge of the district court. I started my work as a judge in the supreme court at the end of 1999. I have been the president of the supreme court since February 2013. From the beginning of my career up until now, I have worked as a judge on criminal proceedings. I can say that my specialization within judicial matters is crimes against life and bodily security, war crimes, and organized crime.

Q: As your career as a judge has developed what has surprised you?

A: During my career as a judge, everything wasn't precisely as I expected it to be while I was studying or when I began working in the courts of law, as a probationer judge and judge's associate. The biggest surprise to me was when I realized that in criminal proceedings there is highly expressed inferiority of prosecutors in relation to judges. Prosecutors' passiveness and, one could freely say, disinterest in the outcome of criminal proceedings, was clearly visible. Basically, this was an error in the system. According to the previous legal concept, the court had an active part in the process of gathering evidence. The prosecutor only had the assignment of issuing an indictment and acting in accordance with it. The concept has been changed, prosecutorial investigation has been introduced, and I expect that the prosecutors will be more agile.

Q: Has your work as a judge proved as interesting or rewarding as you thought it would when you first started?

A: My dreams from my student days that the job would be interesting have come true. Judges deal with and solve a whole range of socially disrupted relations. Each case is a different life story. We deal with the noblest human rights: to live and be free. This is why working as a judge was always interesting and represented a great challenge for me.

---

* Kragujevac is a town in central Serbia. Its population is about 200,000 people and it is 120 km from Belgrade, the capital city.

When we talk about the financial aspect of the job, there were periods of discontinuities. Political turmoil, wars, and economic crises all affected the positions of judges, the way they experienced their job, and the height of their salary that was an award for their work. During the last couple of years, the financial situation of judges in Serbia has improved, bearing in mind average income and the standard of living. Therefore, if we observe the country's economic situation, judges have a solid income that enables them to live above the average quality of life.

Personal Judicial Philosophy

Q: What do you think should be the role of the judiciary in society?

A: Being a judge is one of the most honorable vocations. A judge should be a role model in everything. In their private life and at the work-place, they should behave in accordance with their vocation. A judge should give a positive example to people in a courtroom and outside it.

Q: What should be their job, functions, and responsibilities? What should be left to others?

A: It is an assignment of a court and judges to deal with disrupted social relations and to settle them in accordance with the constitution, the law, and international conventions. Only in this way can a country come closer to the ideal of rule of law, respecting human rights and freedoms.

Q: What organizational arrangements work and which do not?

A: One of the big problems of the system is insufficient cooperation between the court and the prosecutor's office. Judges disap-prove of prosecutors' passiveness. This cooperation has to be much better, since many institutes of criminal procedural law cannot be applied properly without promptness and coopera-tion between the courts and the prosecutor's office (e.g., testi-mony, respecting the terms, delay of criminal prosecution, and plea bargaining).

The request for the protection of legality in criminal proceed-ings is not functioning well, because the institute's legal solution is not good. The principle of "equality of arms" between the prosecu-tor and the defender in a proceeding is not respected. The defense has fewer rights than the prosecutors.

There are also other organizational problems, such as the incon-sistency of court practice. There are poor legal solutions; the rights of a defendant are, in my opinion, limited; and so on.

Q: What policies on relations with the community, with political groups, and with other criminal justice organizations work well? What hampers cooperation with other agencies and groups?

A: Cooperation of courts and the community is traditionally not widely established in Serbia. In principle, courts limit their actions to the legal framework and obligations defined by the law.

   However, there are certain types of cooperation between courts and some parts of the community, for example, cooperation between courts and law faculties in the country. Many courts have signed memoranda regarding cooperation with law faculties.

   Judges take part in practical classes in law faculties. Students attend trials and visit courts. In the last several years, cooperation between courts and judges and the judicial academy has started. Judges are teachers at the academy; they present certain cases to students and then they analyze accepted solutions.

Q: How difficult is it for judges to relate to the living and social conditions of those from economically deprived backgrounds who appear before them?

A: Significant problems aren't noticed, bearing in mind that whenever it is necessary courts hire experts (psychiatrists, psychologists, social workers) to assist the defendant or other participants of a trial with visible intellectual, mental, or emotional problems, or problems of social retardation and maladjustment.

Q: How can a judge develop empathy for those from the lower rungs of the social divisions in society from which they can derive a degree of understanding of why the person before them might have done what is alleged?

A: In Serbia, social and cultural differences between layers of society are not expressed to the extent where they would disable communication and understanding. In any case, during their practice, judges gain the ability to act appropriately for socially deprived citizens too, that is, the ones from the lowest level of society.

Q: How should the criminal legal system in your country perform? What should be the preferred priorities and strategies; hard-edged crime control, prevention, services, or ordered work, what mix for which types of problems?

A: The biggest problem for criminal justice in Serbia is tardiness and inefficiency in work with cases. Due to the poor organization of the courts, frequent alterations to procedural laws and alterations in judicial jurisdiction, especially territorial, cases last a long time. Insufficient cooperation between the courts and other state authorities and institutions is clearly visible and it represents a problem. For example, if a court requires a certain report, data, or some information from other state authorities, it often happens that a reply is several months late. Delivery of acts and the system of summoning citizens to court is very inefficient. The problem exists even with the summoning of police officers.

Problems and Successes Experienced

Q: In your experience, what policies or programs have worked well and which have not? Can you speculate for what reasons?

A: Good work goes without saying, which is why, from my position as the president of the supreme court, I do not give much thought to it. Much greater concerns for me are problems we face in the work of courts. There are hundreds of court cases over 10 years old. Court efficiency is low.

Q: Which cases are treated efficiently and which are not?

A: Courts are most efficient with cases of ordinary crimes, in verdicts of murders, robbery, and theft.

The legal norms that regulate combating organized crime can be considered very functional, as well as the organization of that system in general. However, what can be remarked on regarding court procedures related to organized crime is that organized crime prosecution without thoughtful selection chooses certain cases that by their severity do not deserve priority and vice versa. Namely, what I mean is that the prosecution offices do not completely abide by the measures and provisions of the Convention on Transnational Organized Crime.

However, courts are very inefficient in cases related to corporate crime due to insufficient training of the judges, expert testimonies that last too long, and frequent changes of relevant regulations. Something that is defined as a crime in one law is allowed or tolerated by another. Lawyers ably use this, thus leaving courts troubled. Furthermore, when it comes to the economy and economic crime, the problem is that decisions, as a rule, are made by collective authorities in accordance with internal regulations. Criminal proceedings require establishing individual responsibility. This is one of the biggest problems for all courts.

Q: What would you consider to be the greatest problem facing the criminal courts at this time?

A: The greatest problem is that arrests have been announced publicly through the media by politicians. This, as a rule, happens in cases with a political background. In this way, negative public opinion of the defendants is created. The public proclaims them guilty even before the trial starts. This exerts pressure on the courts.

Q: What problems in courts do you find are the most difficult to deal with?

A: The most difficult problem is solving pending cases that have lasted for years. Apart from that, it is necessary to create "powerful judges" with strong moral, personal, and expert characteristics. There are codes of ethics, court administration. Court administration should take action in cases of breaking the ethical codes.

However, in reality, judges are intimidated by the possibility of losing their job. During the previous reform, over a thousand prosecutors and judges have been fired. Executive authorities have won the judiciary. A balance between judicial and executive authorities has been disturbed.*

Q: Would you care to comment on the decisions of the court in Novi Sad regarding the death of innocent girls, which disturbed the public? Do you agree that you should react whenever public trust in the judicial system is shaken?

A: When it comes to an annulment of a decision that stirs great interest in the public, and there are many such cases in Serbia, it is necessary that the court gives an immediate statement and a brief clarification of the reasons and consequences of such a decision, in order to prevent misinformation as happened with the case in Novi Sad. This is not the first or the last annulment of a verdict in a case that has attracted huge public attention.

In the case of the cruel deaths of the girls in Novi Sad, the verdict was annulled due to contradictions...

---

* On April 1, 2012, a fire started at Kontrast nightclub in Novi Sad, Serbia, resulting in six young people who were students in their early twenties being burned to death. During the investigation, 50 people were detained by the Serbian police for questioning, including the owner of the Kontrast nightclub, as at that time the Serbian prosecutors were considering charges of causing general danger. Many mistakes at the different level of the control as the investigation revealed the failure of state institutions regarding the prevention measures and control activities. Since then, families of the victims and Novi Sad citizens have been unsatisfied with the effectiveness of the Serbian courts as they have not been ready to explore the responsibility of the local state and town institutions because of a lack of control. As a result, people organized meetings against the court and judges in that case, and have asked the court to be more effective and to establish the responsibility of all the people responsible. The fire accident in the discotheque Kontrast exemplifies the lack of control and health and safety provisions in society, the corruption of the local town bodies, and the ineffectiveness of the courts. It is within this context that Judge Milojević was asked questions relating to the incident.

The decision of the court of appeal states that the appeal was accepted and the verdict was annulled, while the following stance prolongs the custody for the defendant. Therefore, these were the speculations that he was released. I can freely say that, based on the facts, his guilt does not come into question. This was a mistake in formulating the verdict. The judge probably wanted to reinforce his stand regarding the guilt of the defendant of the severe crime of aggravated murder, so he stated that the murder was carried out in a reckless manner, which is an element of another form of aggravated murder. The court of appeal considers that the judge meant to emphasize the cruelty, but he, carelessly, used this expression that refers to a different form of aggravated murder. I am sure that he did not have ill intentions or a lack of knowledge.

Q: Do you believe that citizens understand that judges should learn from their mistakes in their work?

A: The citizens must understand that. Mistakes are possible in any profession. There is not a single judge in Serbia who does not have one annulled verdict in his or her career. What is important is that the mistake was not intentional or due to recklessness, and that it does not have any kind of criminal background.

In the case of discotheque Kontrast, where seven young people burned in the fire, the trial starts over, because the judge has retired, even though her employment was prolonged for a year, precisely because of this case.

Judge Z. J. was in charge of this case as of October 5, 2012. She should have retired by the beginning of January 2013, but the decision of the supreme court prolonged her employment until January 3, 2014, precisely because she was working on this case. That is why she was not assigned any other trials. She failed to bring this case to an end, whether due to her failure to handle the case or other objective reasons. The new judge, B. P., has already held one preliminary hearing and scheduled the main hearing for six days in March and four days in April. This is why I am assured that this case will be dealt with in a short time. It is an unprecedented tragedy. The efficiency of the proceedings will depend on the expert testimonies too, because the court has to clearly determine the facts and the guilt of several defendants. Still, I believe that the verdict will be reached by the summer.

Q: What would be easy to change—internal problems (culture of the organization, managerial deficiencies, allegations of corruption, gender-related problems, etc.) or externally generated problems (resources, community support, etc.)? Is anything easy?

A: In principle, nothing is simple. Having in mind your question, I would like to point out that we have no problems with gender equality in courts. Over 75% of our judges are women. The problems we have are on the other side.

The matter of corruption in courts is more a matter of politics and propaganda. The level of talk about corruption in courts suggests more corruption than exists in reality. A small number of judges were prosecuted for corruption. Among the ones that have been prosecuted more of them were sentenced than acquitted. A few years ago, a judge of the supreme court was sentenced to several years in prison. When there is indisputable evidence the courts shall certainly do their job. A strategic anti-corruption program is applied in courts. The national strategy for fighting corruption and action plan are applied in practice. Reports are being written about the results, and so on. However, there are problems with cooperation with the Anti-Corruption Agency.

Theory and Practice

Q: What should be the relationship between theory and practice?

A: Theory is the basis. Between theory and practice there must be mutual interaction. General institutes of criminal law and criminal procedural law cannot be applied without the knowledge of theory (e.g., premeditation, negligence, and sentencing). Theory is a general idea and practice is a single norm to which theory is applied. It is important to know the theory to apply standards in individual cases. Problems occur when judges do not have enough theoretical knowledge and when they do not follow scientific trends. Judges are not sufficiently engaged in writing scientific papers; they do not read scientific literature enough. Thus, theory is not sufficiently connected to practice.

Q: What can practitioners learn from theory and what can theory builders learn from practitioners?

A: We are talking about an interconnected relationship that should include cooperation and intertwining. A theoretician who is not in contact with practice can never be a good theoretician. Life gives us many examples that are important to theoreticians. This principle also applies to judges and practitioners, only in the opposite direction.

Q: What is the relationship right now? Does it exist? Does it work?

A: Cooperation between theory and practice is not sufficiently developed. On the whole, there is poor cooperation. Relationships between judges and theoreticians are based more on personal acquaintances and friendships....

Q: What holds collaboration or interactions back?

A: In my opinion, it is the passive attitude of both sides. Generally, the situation in the country destroys the motivation of people to go beyond their basic professional frameworks. People lack motivation to make big steps outside their usual routines.

Q: What kind of research, in what form, on what questions, would you find most useful for practice? If not very useful, what could or should theory builders do to make their products more useful to you?

A: Theoreticians can help significantly in making the law. Fundamental laws are altered too often. There is a lack of research into inefficient existing solutions and suggestions for new solutions together with elaboration on why these new solutions are better. The different perspectives and points of view of theoreticians and practitioners can be very useful. Unfortunately, these resources and existing potentials are not sufficiently applied in practice.

Q: Where do you find theory-based information? Where do you look? What journals, books, publications, or reports do you consult?

A: University books are still a basic source of theoretical information. I still read faculty textbooks, and to a lesser extent comments on the laws. However, good comments on laws are always a very important resource. Apart from that, other important resources of information that you will always find on my desk are bulletins of court practice, as well as scientific magazines such as *Pravni život* and *Pravni informator* (*Legal Life* and *Legal Informer*). These magazines include writings by professors, judges, and ex-judges dealing with current topics, and one can learn a lot from them.

Q: Does the judiciary carry out supplementary research outside the research required for pending cases? If so, what are the areas, issues, or questions of law that are researched?

A: Unfortunately, if truth be told, supplementary research is not carried out. Analyses are focused solely on pending cases. There are several reasons for this. One is the matter of financial resources, as that kind of research is very expensive. Frequent alterations to the laws, even in the basis of the system, disable continual and long-term monitoring of the operation of certain legal institutes in practice. The problem is that the alterations to the law are introduced "with a blindfold" and usually under the influence of international factors.

Transnational Relations

Q: Have you and the work of your organization been affected by developments outside the country (human rights demands, universal codes of ethics, practical interactions with judges or justices from other countries, personal experiences outside the country, new crime threats, etc.), and if so, how?

A: According to our regulations, ratified international conventions take precedence over our national legislation, so they have significant influence on our work. There are no obstacles to immediate implementation of ratified conventions. We maintain contacts with foreign judges and exchange ideas. We have cooperation with international organizations, including the American Embassy. We implement in practice cooperation programs with the United States Agency for International Development (USAID), the Council of Europe, and the European Commission. There is close cooperation with European committees for judicial reform.

Q: Have those interactions been beneficial or harmful? What kind of external international influences are beneficial and which ones less so?

A: There is good cooperation between the supreme court and the international community. Interactions with international subjects and institutions are very useful and positive. They offer us unconditional assistance that is extremely useful and important for us.

Q: How have developments post the terrorist attack on the United States on September 11, 2001, affected your work?

A: This did not have a significant impact, bearing in mind the geographical distance. Security matters or the work of the courts were not disturbed. We do not have such problems.

General Assessments

Q: Are you basically satisfied or dissatisfied with developments in criminal law and criminal procedure in your system?

A: Personally, I am not satisfied. The alterations to the law are too frequent, even in fundamental, procedural, and substantive law. There are many regulations, which happen to be in discordance with each other. This significantly contributes to the confusion of the judges.

Q: What are the most likely developments you see happening and which would you like to see happening?

A: Reorganization of the court network is ahead of us again. We will try to resolve problems in the organization that have been made in the past. We are facing the problem of pending cases. In order to solve this problem, we are working on the development of software and applications for drawing courts' attention to pending cases, so as to avoid the expiration of the statute of limitations, as well as on harmonizing court practice. We cooperate with USAID and the Council of Europe on this program.

Q: You have created a program for solving pending cases. Is it possible to accomplish the goal to deal with all cases more than 5 years old by 2018?

A: At first sight, this does seem too ambitious a plan, but you should always set high demands in order to get good results. In USAID's pilot project, implemented in 10 courts, the number of pending cases has been reduced by 50%. Based on these results, we have seen that it is possible. Judges have to invest additional effort to reduce the number of pending cases since it is truly unacceptable to have first instance cases pending for over 10 years. Now we have better laws that increase procedure discipline of the parties during the proceedings and after the sentencing verdict. However, "the judge holds the knife and the bread" (Serbian proverb). The judge is the one who manages the trial and who should not allow abuse of the proceedings.

Q: What is most needed now to improve the system?

A: It is necessary to perform an analysis of the current situation and create a plan and program for dealing with the situation in cooperation with theoreticians. We need analyses of the situation, regulations and practice; we need to build a stable and functional system of criminal justice.

Thank you very much.

Conclusion

The interview with the president of the Supreme Court of Serbia, a judge and criminal expert, Dragomir Milojević, was conducted in a very pleasant atmosphere. The interviewee has given completely honest and critical opinions about the problems that Serbia's judicial system faces today.

The judicial system of Serbia is in the transition process as well as other systems. A transition means bringing down existing traditional relationships and creating new ones. It brings painful cuts and has winners (usually only a few) and losers (usually many). There is a curse in Serbia: "May you live in turbulent times!" All people and countries that go through the process of transition feel this curse. The same goes for professions. It is hard to be a judge in a period of transition. The collapse of one system (justice, moral, ethical) and the creation of a new one is a big challenge for the average judge. Future generations and their time will show whether the new system being created now is better and more just than the previous one, which was left behind with great sacrifices. The present generation living in this transition period mostly feels like losers. Life is too short for those standing at the beginning of the transition process—anywhere and anytime!

Slovakia
Legal System

PAVOL KOPINEC

The Slovak Republic (also known as Slovakia) is in the geographic center of Europe (Figure VII.1). It has a population of 5.5 million. The Slovak Republic was established on January 1, 1993, following the division of Czechoslovakia into two countries—the Slovak Republic, with Bratislava as its capital, and the Czech Republic. The Slovak Republic is a member of the European Union (EU), the North Atlantic Treaty Organization (NATO), and the eurozone. The Slovak judicial system is based on the so-called continental law, as opposed to the Anglo-American system, which operates on different principles. The Slovak court system is based on a three-level system of general courts, and integrated into this is the specialized criminal court with criminal jurisdiction of a regional court for the prosecution of especially serious crimes and crimes of public officials. The system consists of a supreme court as the highest court of appeal, 8 regional courts based in regional capitals, 54 local courts based in district capitals, and a specialized criminal court, which is at the level of a regional court.[*] District courts are competent courts of first instance. Regional courts hear cases as appeal courts. The Supreme Court of the Slovak Republic based in Bratislava has the function of an appellate review court. Being the supreme judicial body, the Supreme Court of the Slovak Republic never acts as a first instance court. The Constitution of the Slovak Republic stipulates the status of judges, the president, and the vice presidents of the supreme court.[†] Another type of court is the constitutional court based in Kosice, which stands outside this court system and has special jurisdiction to review the legality of legislative acts and decisions by administrative bodies that violate the fundamental rights and freedoms of individuals if no other court can decide on the protection of their rights and freedoms. "The competence of general courts to conduct court review of decisions of administrative authorities arises from Article 142 (1) of the Constitution

---

[*] http://www.juradmin.eu/en/eurtour/i/countries/slovakia/slovakia_en.pdf.
[†] http://wwwold.justice.sk.

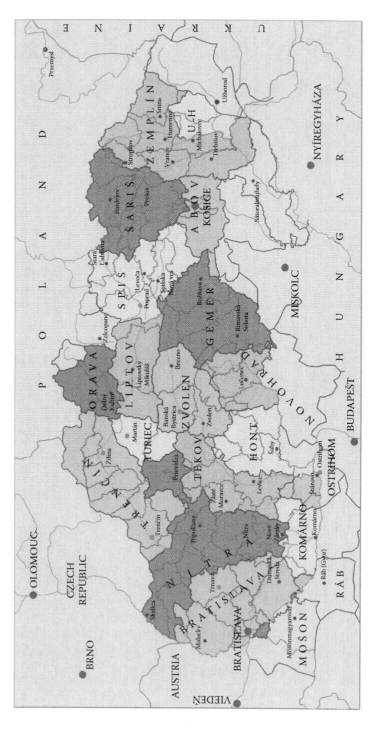

Figure VII.1 Map of Slovakia and its location within Europe.

the Slovak Republic, as well as Part Five of the Code of Civil Procedure (namely §§ 244 to 250 zg). Case-law doctrine, including the principle of court precedent, is not applied in Slovakia. In line with the principle of the rule of law, the Supreme Court of the Slovak Republic is responsible to individuals for the uniform interpretation of legislation (iura novit curia), which is ensured through the publication of fundamental judgments of the court or the court's positions on the uniform interpretation of laws in the event of inconsistent court decisions in cases of the same type (and with the same circumstances)." The president appoints all judges, with the exception of constitutional court judges, from a list proposed by an 18-member council. The president appoints the constitutional court judges from a slate of candidates nominated by parliament. Judges are life appointed and constitutional court judges serve 7-year terms.

Kamil Ivánek, Regional Court Bratislava

8

PAVOL KOPINEC

Contents

Introduction

Judge Kamil Ivánek is a judge of the regional court in Bratislava. His main specialization is criminal law. In 1990, he joined the former municipal court in Bratislava as a judge trainee. In 1993, he was appointed a judge. He worked for 17 years at the first instance court—the District Court Bratislava IV—where he pursued a criminal agenda. He is now in his fourth year at the regional court in Bratislava where he deals exclusively with criminal matters. In 2001, he was selected to work on a pilot project on mediation and probation in criminal law in Slovakia and completed two internships at the court of appeal in 1996 and 2006.

Career

Q: Tell us a little bit about your career.
A: In 1989, Czechoslovakia was in the so-called Velvet Revolution and I did join the judiciary, right after school, which was in 1990. I was very lucky that I attended the first ever tender for the judiciary,

which was held in March 1990. I succeeded and on September 1, 1990, I joined the former municipal court in Bratislava as a judge trainee. Two years I waited in this position to become a judge. This happened on July 2, 1993, so this year it is 20 years since I was appointed to this function.

As a judge trainee, I was already preparing myself for a position in criminal law, and after I was elected to the office of judge (at that time judges were elected through the National Council of the Slovak Republic, now there is a different system) I was able to practice criminal law. I was at the district for 17 years—at the first instance court—the District Court Bratislava IV, where I pursued a criminal agenda and currently I'm in my fourth year at the regional court in Bratislava (a court of second instance), where again I deal exclusively with criminal matters, but only as remedies.

After high school I worked. I studied at grammar school, graduated in 1985 and right after I applied to the Faculty of Law of the Comenius University in Bratislava and … I was not accepted. At that time (it was before the revolution in 1989), you could not stay at home like today, everyone had to be employed. It was classified as a criminal offense   parasitism under Section 203 of the penal code, which was later abrogated. So, I had to be recruited and I worked as a laborer in the Bratislava Automobile Plant, which is today Volkswagen, where I held various positions. I worked for a year as a manual laborer and then I signed up again at the university a second time for entrance exams and I was accepted. I do rate this experience as highly positive, because I gained life experience and views from a different angle. Those experiences are invaluable today. I worked in a factory; I worked with different types of people, from the base to the highest intelligence, so I need to say again, this experience was excellent.

Q: If you look at your career, was there specialized education through which you passed?

A: Yes, but the system is different today. I was lucky enough that I have experienced the justice system, which was very sophisticated in that time. At that time, the expectant judicial function existed. The trainee had tuition in criminal law, civil or trade, and then he or she began to serve as an expectant at the courts of appeal, where again he or she passed through criminal, civil, and trade chambers, and after that could became an operational young judge. At that time, there were statutory regulations for 4 years and every year I had to undergo training of so-called functional young judges. I was undergoing an evaluation system, as well as this I was evaluated by the president of the court, where I worked, and by the courts of appeal.

After that, I went through the approval process within the Judicial Council and the parliament, which appointed me for life in this position, right after the initial 4 years preparation time. Nowadays, the regulation is different, that means that such a system is no longer exists, because there are no more modes for judges for 4 years and functions for life. The current system leaves training and self-study to the judge's discretion. At that time, we were subjected to rigorous evaluation criteria, we had to do the training because it was mandatory, so …

Q: How does self study look?

A: It does not depend really on the system, but I would say on the character, knowledge, and professional level of the judge. We know colleagues in the judiciary who simply float on the surface somewhere and ride on coattails, if I can afford to say so, and are not educating themselves at all. They are happy with that core (information, knowledge etc). We also have categories of judges who improve themselves by studying not only assigned cases, but also literature, law, and the decisive actions of the European Court of Justice and international conventions, which we are bound by.

Q: As your career as a judge has developed what has surprised you?

A: I was surprised that justice in itself is a relatively conservative body, whose thinking is the hardest thing to change. It is not a question of establishing a system, or of system enhancements, or changes in the structure of the system, but it is the Achilles' heel of the Slovak judiciary, to change the way of thinking and of approaches to a big part of Slovak judges' work. Ok, not big, I would say some parts, that I will not exaggerate. The hardest job is working with people and there must be an internal desire of the individual to collaborate, cooperate, because, if there is no internal effort of the individual, the system will not perform (or could only try to) any significant effort, too. It just misses the point in that group of judges we have been talking about.

I was most surprised, if I am honest, that after starting my position I lived under the illusion that all my colleagues were erudite. Then, when I started my first internship (I have completed two internships at the court of appeal in 1996 and the 2006), I was astonished how volatile the professional level is. It was one of my biggest amazements, if not the biggest, that it's not some kind of monolithic (solid) working line, and that the professional level of judges in one circle or in one row, but it is very, very different, I would say. You can also find judges who achieve superior quality and are judges who are deeply graceful.

Q: Has your work as a judge proved as interesting or rewarding as you
thought it would when you first started?

I can definitely say "yes" to that. I did immediately tend to criminal law, as this is what I wanted to do—criminal law. I was also
allowed to do it and realize my ideas, of which I have many. Of
course, in regard to those side issues that I described a moment ago.
So I can definitely say that for me, this work is not only work, but
also a mission. I give my work more time than is required by law
and I try to give the best performance every time, which of course
on the other hand is at the expense of leisure, health, and so on.

Personal Judicial Philosophy

Q: What do you think should be the role of the judiciary in society?
A: According to classical French theorists' division of law it is a third power
in the state and by this is determined its role and position in society, that the interconnecting system of checks and balances should
create a counterweight to the other two powers. Namely, the legislature and the executive team and by this is given the statutory
framework. I would say that this is also the constitutional framework for the functioning of the territory of the Slovak Republic.

When this legal principle changes for the minor, then we assume
that in any type of law that deals with justice, performing the following functions, e.g in criminal, trade law, civil, administrative,
and other kinds of agendas, simply said, should decide the fundamental rights and freedoms of every individual. When we are
talking about the criminal law, and we are considering whether the
offender is guilty or if the offense was committed, we are exploring
the limits of his or her fault, of appropriate sentencing (if it is concluded that there is a fault), and if there are doubts, then he or her
should go free. This question is very broad and we could talk about
it for hours, I tried to condense it to completely bare principles.

Q: What should be their job, functions, and responsibilities?
A: I've tried to answer this question partially in the previous one. When we
are talking about criminal law, the priority is detection, investigation and the subsequent bringing of the perpetrators of the crime
to justice. If the court finds that these crimes were committed by
these offenders, fair and lawful conviction should follow. With this
are then affiliated additional features, such as deciding on protective measures. Today, for example, a well-mentioned question of
criminal liability of legal entities, which we do not have established
in Slovakia yet, could be resolved through protective measures e.g.,

on punishment, ownership punishment of such entities, or even protective treatment. Finally, the decision on compensation of disabled persons in criminal proceedings. This is the basic work.

Q: What should be left to others?

A: All others, except those I mentioned above. This means that criminal justice should not rule on civil matters, it is the so-called and very often used principle of "ultimaracio" and it is the last resort to solve social relations. Today there is a great tendency for individuals or certain groups, whether organized or disorganized, to deal with civil, trade, and legal relations through criminal law, even if the conditions are not met. That means that I would allow other institutions to retain the power to decide on all the social relations that correspond to it. The means of criminal law should be used as a last resort, once all previous methods have been used. This should be the main idea of the Slovak criminal law, I think. Such a theory actually paves the constitutional court of the Slovak Republic and the European Court of Human Rights. So my opinion is not uncommon, but it is a constant practice of these bodies, nongovernmental ones.

Q: What organizational arrangements work and which do not?

A: It really depends on who develops the organizational arrangements. It is my personal opinion from having spent the past years in the judiciary, that if arrangements are prepared by a person who either worked in the judiciary and knows its operations and has relevant experience, or it is a decision-making body, which, although it did not work in the judiciary but let's say it has the counselors to replace this deficiency, then such organizational measures could have a big success, develop the work, and positively resolve something. If such conditions are not met, then such organizational measures are counterproductive. Work is blocked and complicated and thus also comes to the procedural delays, due to the application of such counterproductive actions. I do not want to designate a specific, individual organizational measure, which are many. I could for example show you a collection of instructions, but I would rather define it in general. No matter which part of the judicial authority shall issue such organizational arrangements, at which instance, or in which department, it is primarily important that it be shaped in a manner conducive to the advancement of justice, not to hamper or complicate it.

Q: Are individual departments interconnected when preparing these measures?

A: It depends on what instance we are talking about. If we are talking about the first instance, the district court, such measures shall be decided by the state authority of the court, which is the chairman of the district court, vice-chairman of the district court, by extension, director of administration, which is the supreme authority of the court clerks, except judges, so there we may talk about the interconnectedness of individual departments. The same model can be adopted at the county court, where the county court has several district courts under it (in my case it's seven district courts), where connectivity could be concluded. Problems arise, however, in my opinion, at the national level, where it is sometimes difficult to achieve coherence between all, around 54 district courts, 8 regional courts, 1 specialized criminal court, and the supreme court.

For example, the Ministry of Justice SR examines the extent of the burden of the courts in terms of the whole Slovakia and until now a burden index has not been determined, because the courts, even if they are nominally equal under the law, their burden rate is very different. The most burdened court in Slovakia is the Bratislava Regional Court, because Bratislava houses the vast majority of state bodies, public authorities, and the largest number of companies and accumulates the largest population. The measure of burden is disproportionately higher than at the other courts of the same type, as for example at the regional court in Zilina, or even at the Košice Regional Court, which is the second-largest city in Slovakia, still the burden rate is lower than here. Nominally, judges have equal status at all those courts, nominally receive the same salary, but this burden rate is disproportionately the highest across Bratislava, whether it relates to the county court or to the district court.

Q: Are there coordinators who mediate information between departments?
A: By law, a team of coordinators shall be a body of the state administration of courts, in this case, the chairman or vice-chairman of the district court, by extension, the county court, who by operation of the law on state administration of courts are responsible to their supervisor, in this case, the chairman, the vice president of the district court is directly subordinate and accountable to the regional court chairman, by extension, the vice president who is again responsible to the minister of justice. Through these control structures the minister of justice can therefore effectively interfere in the functioning of the judiciary, what is as well as doing. In the case, that the subsidiary body of the state administration is failing, or is not exercising its functions enough, which arise out of the law on administration of justice, where are all competencies are defined, such authority may be revoked, replaced with another person. It sometimes happens that the dismissed chairman of the district or county court is replaced by another person.

Q: You've mentioned the Ministry of Justice that examines the extent of the burden. Do I understand it correctly, that the statistical information is collected, too?

A: It is a legal obligation. Every month statistical reports are transmitted from each department and each court and are sent to the regional court as a superior authority and then to the supreme authority, which is the Ministry of Justice, which then handles the ongoing, quarterly, semiannual, and annual summaries. For us it is a basic reference which is used to determine whether justice is functional (in terms of basic principles), if it's operating well, quickly, and easily, because these statistical reports report not only the numbers of things that are attacked, but also the numbers of issues that were decided, number of resistance things (cases taking a long time), the length of the proceedings, the quality of decisions, how many cases were cancelled, how many have been confirmed, so the statistical report is very detailed and from it you can immediately detect any amount of data and it is also an essential source to see how each government body performed at each stage. For example, when the monthly statistical report is published, the presiding judge immediately sees how many cases the judge ruled, who slacked off, who was more productive, and who remained constant in performance, whose decision-making activities worsened, also in terms of quality. Then, if the appeal body abolished a greater number or lower number of cases, then you can determine the duration of the procedure, and how many cases the judge in the department has in resistance in percentage and in relationship to cases that he or she has overall. And if the presiding judge finds, as the state administration of courts, that the number, percentage number of resistance cases grew, so by law he or she follows the measures to examine the reason, whether they are subjective or objective, which are resulting in delays in decision-making activities.

Q: Are judges decisions later examined?

A: Well, first of all we need to clarify that the power of review has a superior body. In this case, if the decision was made by the court of first instance it must first be appealed on that decision. Then the governing body will decide. The county courthouse is empowered to review these issues, which are challenged in the appeal. So no one else can review the decision, except until this decision enters into force, then it is under extraordinary remedies reviewed by the supreme court. From my perspective and work in justice, I can say that the judgment index is monitored, under which also falls the index of court appeals, which is higher for those courts that are in big cities. Bigger city, bigger judgment and appeal index. Then it logically follows that the largest judgment index is in Bratislava and the most remedies are administered in Bratislava, too.

In regard to the second part of the question, if it's monitored what is happening with the offender, who carried out the sentence and returned from prison, it is not in the power of justice. I know that the Office of Labor, Social Affairs, and Family of the Ministry of Social Affairs has the department, which is in charge of it. For such a former prisoner after returning from serving a financial benefit, and then they try to get him or her a job, accommodation, and in other words, help him or her to integrate into society. This feature is not for justice, and not at all for criminal justice. There is a so-called enforcement proceeding under the criminal procedure code, where after offender is lawfully imposed for crimes, the court oversees if these penalties and also protective measures are taken into account. But as soon as they are executed, the case for the judiciary and the courts is completed and the file is then closed and it can be put into the archive. These societal functions dealing with return and reintegration of offenders then falls under others authorities than judicial.

Q: What policies on relations with the community, with political groups, with other criminal justice organizations work well? What hampers cooperation with other agencies and groups?

A: With regard to the criminal law, the closest body with which criminal justice in Slovakia is working is the prosecution authority, which represents the state as a prosecutor in criminal matters, so we are in constant daily contact with this organization of criminal justice. The cooperation is very intense.

The second is the police force, under which these crimes are investigated, either by the police or the investigation bureau, and then it is the Corps of Prison and Court Guard who are physically carrying and implementing detention and imprisonment on their premises. Then there are security forces and the National Security Agency, the Slovak Intelligence Service (SIS), Customs Office, and so on… with which the criminal justice also comes into very close contact. This cooperation I think is really good. These are all security forces. This is the police, SIS, the Corps of Prison and Court Guard, and so on. There are more offices for example, the Customs Office, military police, even military defense intelligence, and so on, because the regional court has the legal authority to decide on some proposals of these enforcement units, that alone make suggestions to consent to the use of information and technical resources. The vast majority of the proposals to the court are handled by the prosecutor as a party to the dispute, by extension the perpetrator of an offense, who has different names, depending on what procedural stage he or she stands, from accused, defendant, to convict, before it gets to the criminal proceedings, or may even have the status of a suspect, and when he or she is accused and is charged, when he is accused and ultimately convicted if it is legally recognized as guilty and he is sentenced. Apart from these two sources, namely, the prosecutor and accused, many proposals are coming from these power components within the legal options, which are available to them by the law. For example, proposals to use ITP [Interactive Teaching program] resources, information and technical resources, which is popularly called interception. So again, this cooperation with these listed structures is high.

Q: Where is the collaboration less effective?

A: The question is very broad, of course it could be such a type of organization, that has in itself a negative attitude toward the prosecuting authority or toward the authority of law enforcement, yes? For example, there could be different organizations of the trade association or nongovernmental organizations, third sector organizations, which of course by their focus may defend the rights of people who appear in criminal proceedings in the way that may not be concordant or coherent with criminal state policy, which is implemented through the criminal justice system. For example, I use an example of Fathers League (NGO) now very protracted in the media, campaigning mainly for intermittent care and evolving pressure to various ministries and parliament, certainly not favoring the part of Slovak judiciary which deals with the family law. A particular cooperation with these types of organizations can be problematic, because if the judge decides not according to the vision of such organization, in this case it is an association of citizens, civic association, it may also invade the same types of organizations representing the victims. Abused people, women, and so on, and here it depends on the degree of cooperation on whether these organizations are successful in the proceedings in the application of their rights, how many times they were eligible and ineligible. If they are not successful, so obviously the relationship may be affected by this failure.

Q: How difficult is it for judges to relate to the living and social conditions of those from economically deprived backgrounds who appear before them?

A: It is not a question of the structure of the judiciary but it is the question about the empathetic equipment of a judge. That is the bone marrow of the whole response to this question, because empathy can't be poured into a judge or in any particular measure in the form of the law or in to the organization structure of a state administration. It is therefore very important to ensure that, when are adepts taken to justice, to be subjected to scrutiny in this issue, too. Of course they are, because one day during the entrance exams is given over to the psychological analysis of the adept. So it depends entirely on the ability of the judge to what extent he or she is empathetic, and sensitive. As for me personally, I have no problem with that, because as I told you, after the school years I worked in a factory as a laborer, also I come from a rural and poor background.

Q: How can a judge develop empathy for those from the lower rungs of the social division in society from which they can derive a degree of understanding why that person before them did what is alleged?

A: Yes, this is the presumption of innocence. It is a fundamental principle of criminal law that unless someone is finally found guilty, we are looking at him or her as though not convicted, yes? It should be said that the structure of the people that stand in front of the criminal trial as a suspected, accused, defendant or convicted person is very different. We are mostly dealing with people who have either no education or only a primary one. Less often, people will appear with a moderate education and exceptionally do people appear who have a college education or second or even third level of university degree. A similar structure is also true in terms of social status. Usually, we are talking about people who are either homeless or unemployed or their social status is very low. It then becomes an important lesson that for those kind of people, judges must then select an appropriate approach, that the person concerned does understand the meaning of the criminal proceedings and their position in it, and especially understands what his or her rights are, but also what their obligations are, and that all these factors must be explained in such a way that the alleged offender will properly understand. Thus, in other words, the judge needs to handle the accused at his or her level. From this it then follows that the judge (if he or she can do it) should understand the conditions under which the offender was growing up, from what kind of environment they originate, and what led him or her to such or another behavior, because a big part of the crime is conditioning socially or economically. And this then ultimately needs to be taken into account for the degree of culpability (misconduct) when determining the sentence.

Q: Is there specialized training?

A: No, they don't exist. It's up to each judge how they will approach each case. Whether he or she takes it like another number in the statistics, the accused one, quite frankly said, or he or she takes it as a sentient human being who can rightly or wrongly end up in criminal proceedings as a defendant, whichever occurs then as the result.

Q: How should the criminal legal system in your country be performing? What should be the preferred priorities and strategies; hard-edged crime control, prevention, services, what mix for which types of problems, and so on?

A: I think that we are in the twenty-first century, and we should move away from the customary ways of thinking and patterns that worked in the past century and we should punish less and educate more. That is my personal opinion. I was selected in 2001 to work on a pilot project on mediation and probation in criminal law, which had for its main objective to build the so-called diversions in criminal proceedings, which means to decide in cases differently than with using of punishment. For example by using of conditional stop, settlement and other forms, which are criminal proceedings generating a form of decisions that would not be punishment, but some kind of reeducation, or they will incorporate an active educational aspect. If the system will work, ultimately, to the extent that it was designed, it would be the most important move, or project in the Slovak judiciary since the revolution and since 1990.

Q: What happened?

A: At some point in the launching of this project came his depression for various reasons, whether economic or political or other. Now the project survives somewhere on the outskirts of interest and is practiced only in a formal and minimal way, according to the content requirements, it significantly diminished. It is perhaps also the answer to the next question, about the programs that have worked well. I think, that from 1990 the program had a chance through its content to change something. It's the best program since 1990, which, given the economic situation, the attitude of the other state divisions of power in the country, is at a stage, that I described in answer one, in the previous question.

Q: According to you, how would you revive the interest?

A: Well, very simply, as in the Czech Republic they created a separate office for mediation, probation, which is independent and there mediation takes place in all criminal activities to the extent that they are overwhelmed with work, because I see the sense, that mediation should set up, resp. remove some emotional smog between the offender and the victim of a crime, that some settlement occurs between them after the proceedings. For us (Slovakia) it was not prepared in this way. Here, at every court two positions have been set up, the mediator and probator, because for one case the mediation and the probation could not be done by one person, therefore there were two, but gradually these people were burdened with other types of agenda and now it is already declining. I cannot judge this, because I was in the pilot project and then I was involved in the upbringing and education of these downstream mediators and probators throughout the territory of the Slovak Republic. The level fluctuated as I said and the level of justice depends on individual judges and even then the matter will depend on the individual staff of this mediation, probation, whether in spite of negative circumstances, named above, they are willing to work on their own deployment and do something more than required. It stands and falls on it now.

Problems and Successes Experienced

Q: In your experience, what policies or programs have worked well and which have not? And can you speculate for what reasons?

A: I think that I have already responded to this, that we are in the twenty-first century and we should go down that route, less punishment and more education. It is my personal opinion that this should be a top priority. Because, if you take that Slovakia, its size and number of inhabitants, has a high number of persons in custody and under arrest. Many cases in our country are solved already under the investigation or in court, before a final decision. Disproportionately a greater number of people are prosecuted binding than in other countries, which I think is not a good trend. For example, offenses related to substance abuse. We are leading a long-time professional dialogue here to regularize or be less severe on soft drugs. I think that the system is set up disproportionately to punish drug consumers. Some work has been done in this regard already, but I still think that consumers of soft drugs in my personal opinion should not be criminal at all, respectively. Consumption of soft drugs should, in my personal opinion, not be punished at all, and if someone is the organizer, or hard drug dealers, then those penalties can be severe, I fully agree with that. So there is still a large scope, where a lot of work could be done. Generally speaking, the best strategy would be if we adapt the trends that have long been proven in justice of Western countries, and this is most generally how this can be said.

Q: What would you consider to be the greatest problem facing the criminal courts at this time?

A: The biggest problem is the politicization of the Slovak judiciary; thereby the judges basically come under pressure, especially from the media, which has a negative effect on them, affecting them mentally and perhaps their decisions, too.

Q: What problems in courts do you find is the most difficult to deal with?

A: The hardest problem is burden, as I have said before, there is a very different level of burden of various and same build courts throughout the Slovak Republic, which is sometimes a huge disparity. Then it is the material equipment and staff of the courts. For example, in the building of the regional court in Bratislava is the seat of the District Court Bratislava 1, and it causes problems for example with hearing rooms, which are lacking. Then it is the administrative retrofitting of courts, the numbers of administrative staff, and then it could come to the streamlining and accelerating of the proceedings by the adoption or modification of the rule of law so, that the process itself will not be an obstacle to prompt dispatch of issues.

Q: What could be done?

A: So in terms of the first requirements, these are questions of a material nature, it is a question of the financial security of workers, judges, premises, or material equipment. With regard to the other, there should be legislative changes made in different types of processes, and if I am well informed the Ministry of Justice SR has it as one of the main goals, especially now in civil trials, to simplify and to speed up the proceedings in civil matters. I know that in this respect the amendment of Criminal Procedure of November 1, 2011, has applied. As mentioned above, some of the changes were incorporated, following the legislative actions.

Q: What would be easy to change? Internal problems (culture of the organization, managerial deficiencies, allegations of corruption, or gender-related problems, etc.) or externally generated problems (resources, community support, etc.)? Is anything easy?

A: Nothing is easy in justice. Because during my era I have experienced several simple and fast solutions and usually they did not turn out well. It is a complexity of several interrelated problems, where one cannot artificially rip apart a problem, whether big or small, and separately deal with it. I think it needs to be addressed comprehensively and in interdependence. Well, for example, as I have repeatedly noted that the rate burden in large cities is higher than those of smaller courts. If they would be strengthened by personell's, whether in terms of judges, or administration, and thus by the number pendency fell and thereby it will accelerate.

Theory and Practice

Q: What should be the relationship between theory and practice? What can practitioners learn from theory, and what theory builders from practitioners?

A: In my view, there should be between these two interdependency relationships, because if theorists write theoretical papers that have no basis in practical matters, it will be a detached academic output, which will help, but many times it is not usable in practice. Conversely, a practitioner who performs the function of a judge and is not familiar with the theory, will result in incompetent decision making, or in not as good quality as required. So one affects the other, One person affects the other one, and it's only true, that all interacts and develops together. If on one side the appropriate pressure is raised, it has an impact on the other group and vice versa. Many matters in criminal law have been developed in practice, which in turn have been adopted as a regulation or law in force, in the order and also in theory.

Q: What is the relationship right now? Does it exist? Does it work?

A: I think it is functional, because in recent years several theoretical publications have begun to emerge, in terms of criminal and procedural and I know all those authors well. To divide them into practitioners and theorists is artificial, because all those writers are practicing, whether judicial, they are judges or attorney, or at least academic teaching on the faculties of law, that is, they come into contact with the practice, in one or another form. Therefore, these publications have a high degree of professionalism and high applicability in practice, despite their theoretical basis. So from this point of view, we can evaluate this relationship as functional, because, I must repeat that I speak from my experience, because I know those people and I am in contact with them and they are with me. And I think there is a good trend. A positive one.

Q: What holds collaboration or interactions back?

A: I don't think that there are any structural or organizational problems, or any regulations or organizational decisions that will undermine cooperation. I do not see such barriers there. The only obstacle there may be between these two communities, thus theorists and practitioners, always communicate only among themselves (group). There I would see the biggest problem: the problem in communication.

Q: What kind of research, in what form, on what questions would you find most useful for practice? If not very useful, what could or should theory builders do to make their products more useful to you?

A: If I have to be honest, I do not know of any research. I do not know if there has been some research done. Now I remember, the Slovak Academy of Sciences produced a project, where the speech in courtrooms was converted into written text. I know about this project, because the Ministry of Justice SR is working on a project to digitalize court files and to relieve judges by that, that the hearing will be recorded and the ultimate final product of this recording will be already written text. I know about this project, which is very welcome, because it (writing) reduces the enormous time of the hearing. And the recording itself is not effective because there needs to be a person who rewrites what was said and this takes the time—and of course there can be the failure of the system, too. If the project is followed through, it would be possible to install such a device, and the spoken word should automatically be in written form and by the end of the trial would have been prepared as printed minutes. This is extremely important and useful for the judicial practice in Slovakia.

Q: Where do you find theory-based information? Where do you look? What journals, books, publications, reports?

A: Everywhere. Now is a period of time when a good judge must study and not underestimate any source of law. Whether for professional news, publications, collection of decisions and opinions of the Supreme Court SR, journals, judicial review, from the case practice, expert articles. In this respect, we have a very good program called JASPI [Unified automated system of legal information] where the court decisions are available via the Internet. The number of publications is inexhaustible and if someone is also specializing, in this case on criminal law, he or she can follow the essentials of criminal law.

Q: Does the judiciary carry supplementary research outside the research required with pending cases? If so, what are the areas, issues, or questions of law researched?

A: Case law primarily performs decision in a particular case and in that moment it is binding for that court in which the case it shall act. This follows directly from the law, the court of first and second instance is bound by the decision of the supreme court in that particular case, but another court is not bound by it. But in the case of the publication of such a decision, which is applicable for the same types of cases, that raises unification practice. In contrast with the continental law, where the Anglo-American law system is a source, for us it is not a source of law, not *de jure*, but *de facto*, yes. We do not have it enacted as a source of law, but *de facto* judges use this related case law. Because the precedent is supposedly closer and then follows the further opinion. In the case—it is a decision of one judge, or one senate, which is let say so important that is published in the collection and is applicable. Then a situation happens, and some courts decide the same question differently. Then it is submitted to the supreme court, the unifying practice will be done and then the supreme court will give an opinion, which is the verdict of the whole Criminal College of the Supreme Court on the issue. So this procedure has an instructive, educational function, and it unifies the practice slowly and expertly educates the judges in Slovakia. This is how I define the basic operations of the binding precedence (or case law).

Transnational Relations

Q: Have you been affected by, and how, in the work of your organization by developments outside the country (human rights demands, universal codes of ethics, practical interactions with judges or justices from other countries, personal experiences outside the country, new crime threats, etc.)?

A: Yes, for sure. It should be noted that I joined the judiciary in 1990, when Slovakia was still part of the federal Czechoslovakia and from January 1, 1993, was established as an independent Slovak Republic, where these countries have indeed different, but very similar legal systems, so I watch the professional publications in the Czech Republic, where applicable, for my decision-making activities. Also, it must be realized that Slovakia is a part of the various structures of the EU and our constitution guarantees the Convention on Human Rights and its primacy in the meaning of greater legal force. I am obliged to apply the convention and consequently, I have to very closely monitor and study the jurisprudence of the European Court of Human Rights and base my decision-making activities on this.

Q: Are you meeting judges from other countries?

A: There are exchanges programs that judges go on in other states, judges again come here to learn about the Slovak judiciary, so that interaction within the European region is given and is used. Recently, some judges were in Hungary, to visit some of the judicial authorities.

Q: Have you been in another country?

A: Not officially. I was not, but when I was in the United States on a private residence, so I was interested in how it works there, so I went to hearings at the court.

Q: Have those interactions been beneficial or harmful? What kind of external international influences are beneficial and which ones less so?

A: I think it is beneficial. Since the union leads to unity and unification, I think that such contacts are more than beneficial.

Q: How have developments post the terrorist attack in the United States on September 11, 2001, affected your work?

A: It didn't.

General Assessments

Q: Are you basically satisfied or dissatisfied with developments in criminal law and criminal procedure in your system?

A: I'm pretty much satisfied with the work, because many foreign visitors when they came here after the revolution, they believed that the Czechoslovak and subsequently Slovak penal system was very bad and they were shocked to find that our system is very well redesigned. Of course we do want to improve, but guarantees provided by our criminal procedure to the person, accused or to defense counsel, are at a high level and they can withstand the highest possible scrutiny by international conventions, which unfortunately cannot be said about many other countries.

Q: What are the most likely developments you see happening and which would you like to see happening?

A: I would especially like to see the number of people who commit crimes decline, but that is a societal issue of course. Subsequently, that there are less people on order to pretrial detention than now, because I consider the number to be relatively high, with reference to the situation in other countries. Also, I would prefer if more serious crime was dealt with by so-called diversions and not repressive but educational. And for this purpose the criminal law has been recast, dividing crimes into misdemeanor and felony. Misdemeanor is up to 5 years imprisonment, where the corrective material is different and the legislator clearly states that when deciding on an offense, where the maximum imprisonment rate is more than 5 years, he or she must impose a custodial sentence. It is therefore clear to me, that where the upper limit is less than 5 years, I do not, or I would not impose a custodial sentence. So if this were applicable and put into practice and into the decision-making activities of the Slovak judiciary, I would be very happy.

Q: What is most needed now to improve the system?

A: I have no idea, I do not know the answer to what will happen. I hope it will go ahead, despite all those things that we discussed previously. I am able to compare the past 23 years that I have been in the judiciary, whether as a judge trainee or as a judge, where I see the improvement as a trend. I see this trend, because I saw the situation in 1990, with the adopted recast of the criminal laws and gradually as we entered into the EU, where it was necessary that we complied with the standards established there, under the convention, and so on. In this regard, the trend positive. Really significantly improved respect for human rights in criminal proceedings as a result of the higher mentioned historical circumstances.

Conclusion

The general prosecutor of the Slovak Republic responded positively to the request of the Institute of Social Studies and Curative Education of Comenius University in Bratislava to authorize an interview with a senior judge of the regional court who specialized in criminal law. The questions were sent in advance and were followed by a face-to-face meeting with the senior judge, which lasted one-and-a-half hours. The atmosphere was welcoming and appreciative. The transcript of the interview was sent to the senior judge for his review. Only minor changes have been made, mostly dealing with specifics of the content. Major themes include the extent of the burden of the courts, people in custody, the need for research, and educational matters.

Glossary

CSR: Constitution of the Slovak Republic
CCP: Code of Civil Procedure
CPCG: Corps of Prison and Court Guard
JASPI: common computerized legal information system
NCSR: National Council of the Slovak Republic

United Kingdom
Legal System

EMMA DAVIES AND DAVID LOWE

In the United Kingdom (Figure VIII.1), there are three legal jurisdictions:

1. England and Wales (which is the court of appeal's jurisdiction)
2. Scotland
3. Northern Ireland

It can be said that the Isle of Man and the Channel Islands (Jersey, Guernsey, and Sark), which are also part of the United Kingdom, have their own jurisdiction. Figure VIII.1 shows the geographical boundaries that form the jurisdiction of the court of appeal in England and Wales.

History of the Jurisdiction in England and Wales

The current justice system in England and Wales can be traced back to the reign of King Henry II. In 1166, King Henry set up the Assizes Court (that remained in existence until 1971), which imposed the national law of the King's Bench in Westminster to replace local custom, and thus began "common law," that is, law common to the whole country. In 1178, King Henry II set up the jury system that then consisted of 12 knights in order to settle disputes of land ownership (Elliott and Thomas, 2011, pp. 233–234). In 1283, magistrates and magistrates' courts were formed under King Edward I, where good and lawful men were commissioned to keep the king's peace. In 1346, we see the foundation of the current judiciary that can be recognized today with those appointed as judges taking an oath that said they would not be bribed, and to give "advice to any man great or small in any action to which the King was party himself" (Elliott and Thomas, 2011, p. 236).

The County Courts Act 1846 created county courts to deal with civil cases and in 1856 the central criminal court was given the right to hear cases

Figure VIII.1 Map of UK court of appeal jurisdiction.

outside its jurisdiction to ensure a fair trial where local prejudice existed or when it could offer an early trial and avoid any delay in waiting for the next Assizes. The Judicature Act 1873 established the high court and the court of appeal for England and Wales, while under the Criminal Appeal Act 1907 the court of appeal was split into two with the establishment of the criminal division of the court of appeal. Crown courts were established in 1956 but only incrementally throughout England and Wales as the first ones were set up in Liverpool and Manchester (Radzinowicz, 1968, pp. 252–255).

How the English Court System Operates

Figure VIII.2 shows how the court system in England and Wales operates. Criminal trials are held in either the magistrates (summary only offenses) or the crown court (indictable offenses, which are usually serious crimes),

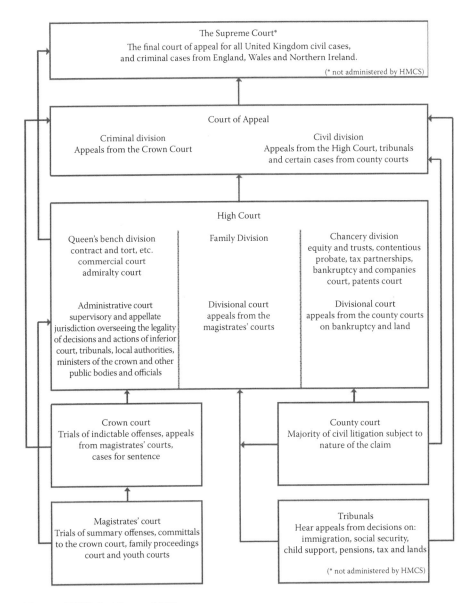

Figure VIII.2 Chart of UK court system.

with the crown court also hearing appeals from the magistrates court. From the crown court, appeals can be made firstly to the court of appeal (criminal division) and then, if granted leave to appeal, to the supreme court. The supreme court replaced the House of Lords appeal court in October 2009 and was established under Part 3 of the Constitutional Reform Act 2005.

Clement Goldstone QC, Senior Court Judge and Honorary Recorder

9

EMMA DAVIES AND DAVID LOWE

Contents

Introduction

The interview process and questions were agreed in advance. The interview was conducted on October 10, 2013, in Judge Goldstone's room in the Queen Elizabeth Crown Court in Liverpool, England. The interview was straightforward and progressed without incident. It was audio-recorded and transcribed. A draft of this chapter was sent to Judge Goldstone for comment prior to submission to the editors. Once the wording of the chapter was agreed, the audiofile and transcript were deleted.

Career

Judge Clement Goldstone was educated at Manchester Grammar School and Churchill College in Cambridge University. Called to the Bar in 1971, he had a mixed practice as a junior barrister for 20 years. He became a Queen's Counsel (QC) in 1993, concentrating on criminal work and licensing, that is, betting, gaming, and liquor. He was appointed as a circuit judge in 2002, and has been a mental health review tribunal chairman in restricted cases. Since 2009, he has been authorized to sit in the court of appeal criminal division. At the time of writing, he is a senior circuit judge and Honorary Recorder of Liverpool (since 2011).

Personal Judicial Philosophy

As a common law country, there is a constitutional convention that legislators make the law and the court applies it. Consistent with convention, Judge Goldstone comments on the role of the judge in relation to the public:

> We are not political animals. We aren't elected… We are not courting popularity… Our role is to instill confidence in the public as a group and individually by the way in which we dispense justice… As a group, we need to try cases fairly, pass appropriate sentences and we have to make sure that the cases are tried as quickly as possible.

He goes on to describe the judge's job in building up rapport with juries:

> I like to think that I establish a good rapport with jurors… I always say to the jury, there may be times when they are not in court when they think they ought to be in court. That they are kept waiting. If there is one thing worse for a juror than being kept waiting it's not knowing why they are being kept waiting. And I always, where the circumstances permit, tell the jury why they are being kept waiting—not in a way that would prejudice the smooth running of the trial—but to make sure that the jury knows that they are part of the process.

He emphasizes the importance of the judge's role in servicing the legal profession:

> As a judge I have an opportunity to give back to the profession by helping to train those who want to get on the judicial ladder. We all have to start

somewhere. We were all privileged to receive very good training… A lot of it from those who were very experienced judges… Giving back is part of our job. We are trained to train… This is an important part of our profession… I enjoy mentoring lawyers.

In this context, and showing concern about keeping experienced full-time judges in the system, he raises some issues about the enforceable retirement age of judges:

Jurors are going to be able to serve until 75. Magistrates can't and judges can't. I think they should be able to. I feel strongly about that—the older I get the stronger I feel! Actually, there is something in it for the government financially because the government gets value for money with my experience and they pay my pension for a shorter period. It's a win/win situation.

Conversely, I firmly believe that when a judge retires, he or she should not be able to sit in a part-time capacity because it clogs up the system and prevents the shoots at the bottom end from developing. The same applies to retired barristers and solicitors—they should not be able to supplement their private pensions with part-time work. When they decide they are going there is a golden opportunity for those who have been trained, at great expense, and who may well have ambitions for a full-time judicial career, to obtain invaluable sitting experience.

Understanding People with Deprived Backgrounds and Working with Other Organizations

Judge Goldstone rejects any notion that it might be difficult for judges to relate to those from economically deprived backgrounds. He described the days of "shoulder-tapping" as over. He believes that the interview processes for judicial appointments ensure that people who cannot relate to all in society are weeded out. He commented

No, we are not aloof. We are not remote. I think the stereotype, the judge being out of touch and being on some sort of pedestal no longer accords with reality.

In responding to questions about liaison with other criminal justice sector organizations, he states

Over the last 10 years or so, judges are working much more closely with others, for example, this afternoon I am going to visit a restorative justice program at Altcourse Prison. There are close links between the judiciary and probation, judiciary and victim support, and so on.

We have court users' meetings quarterly so we meet there with every agency. The judges have an important role to play—liaison judges are appointed to every bench of magistrates, to the probation service, the witness service. So we can liaise with them and much more importantly, they can liaise with us.

Cases That Are Hard to Deal With

Judge Goldstone responds to the question about the problems in courts that he finds hardest to deal with on two levels: first, frustration from poor professional conduct and second, issues on an emotional level.

> I am used to making difficult decisions about the law or sentencing—nobody likes to send someone to jail when they have small children or an elderly relative. That just goes with the job. But when there are avoidable things in the running of the trial—prisoners arriving late from G4S, ill-prepared counsel—that is all deeply frustrating.

He also reiterates the impact of poor preparation of cases on the effective administration of justice:

> There is no excuse for counsels' lack of preparation, higher court advocates or the police—wherever it comes from… Anything that prevents cases from starting on time in the way that they should be presented is most frustrating from the point of view of the administration of justice.

On a personal level, he commented

> I think that on an emotional level, driving cases where death or serious injury has arisen—are hard. Very often I think there but for the grace of God go I… When we are behind the wheel of a car—you often hear victims and defendants who really have no place in the criminal courts—for a moment of madness, a person who has never been in trouble before, might be a friend, has to pay a very heavy price—and those are difficult cases.

Problems and Successes Experienced

A lot of Judge Goldstone's comments focus on the effective and efficient administration of justice. At the time of writing, there have been significant cuts in public expenditure within the criminal justice system. This includes cuts to publically funded legal aid for defendants, the courts, probation, and the police. Some cuts have not yet hit home. For example, a 17.5% cut to legal aid fees will be introduced in two stages—an 8.75% cut in February 2014 and another 8.75% cut in May 2015. Further, in the most serious criminal cases, it is reported that legal aid fees will be cut by 30% (Baksi, 2013). This section records Judge Goldstone's views on some of the causes and consequences of cuts to public expenditure followed by his determination of the building blocks of an efficient and effective criminal justice system.

Cuts to Public Expenditure within the Criminal Justice System

Judge Goldstone perceives some of these cuts to services as inevitable, particularly cuts to publically funded fees for higher court advocates in long cases:

> There had to be significant changes. Long cases in particular cost a fortune. Some people describe them as, well they were, gravy trains. The system was financially bust. The country could not afford it so the money had to be clawed back from all sorts of places... counsel, court staff cut; judges not replaced. Court closures...
>
> Higher court advocates feel undervalued because of the cuts to which publically funded work has been subjected... I have a theory about this... In the 1990s, publically funded fees for personal injury work, family work, criminal work increased exponentially. It was ridiculous. It got totally out of hand and people were paid far too much. I was a beneficiary of it as much as the next person. The problem is that if your fees have increased so quickly, when someone decides to pull the plug, the drop is much harder to take when it is from a very high level than if the fees had gone up more gradually. Indeed, if they had gone up more gradually, there may have not been seen to be the need to cut them at all. As it is, the adjustment was very keenly felt.

He went on to identify ways that the cuts in public expenditure impact on the administration of justice through low professional morale, poor standard of presentation of cases, and judges not replaced.

> Just as the police have had to fight with ever-decreasing resources, so has the CPS [Crown Prosecution Service]. The CPS has been hacked... getting on for a third less than they had. And they have taken on Chester*... Their morale is very low.
>
> The judges... have a lot to be critical about the way that the CPS and the defense teams prepare and present their cases, but it's very difficult to expect a Rolls Royce service when you are not provided with the nuts and bolts to build the car.
>
> Fewer cases coming into the system is being used to justify not replacing judges. But it doesn't take account of the fact that cases are often more complex and last longer than they used to. Nor does it take account of the fact that judges now have far more out-of-court administrative duties and responsibilities than before.
>
> The consequence at the moment of cancelling the recruitment of recorders is I think a disaster. They have to continue to develop a pool from which future judges will be selected. Encouraging retired judges to continue to sit in a part-time capacity is ... not the way forward.

---

* City population approximately 120,000.

Yet, he identifies one silver lining in the public sector cuts:

> The one thing that has happened as a result of enforced belt-tightening is that everyone is pulling together. The effects on legal aid have been to unite the two sides of the profession—solicitors and barristers—like never before. Whether that was design I rather doubt, but it was a consequence... Everyone is in the same boat. Probation, police, witness service, victim support are all under-resourced so we do what we can to support each other.

The Building Blocks of an Effective System

Judge Goldstone named efficient policing, strong counsel, good teamwork, proactive case management, and effective appropriately resourced rehabilitation services as core components of an effective criminal justice system. First, good teamwork:

> I am very lucky here. I have a fantastic staff. And I have a very good team of judges. And I think we are a happy team. And we all go the extra mile for each other. So that's the first thing that makes it work. You need an efficient police force to investigate crime and charge defendants. We have a very strong team of senior officers on Merseyside. That's where it all starts... You also need a strong CPS and defense teams.

On proactive case management he said:

> It's then really up to the judges to case manage proactively, to make sure that the limited resources work—money and time, our most precious resources—aren't wasted either through inefficient management... It can be done without a fuss.
> Most of us are of the newer school here. We are prepared to case manage. We were not born as managers. Our careers were not as managers. Law is a vocation. We have all had to acquire case management skills... This involves preparation, being able to think outside the box, being prepared to engage with counsel proactively—and sometimes even directly with defendants.
> One of our big problems is with defendants who are legally represented at public expense. They very often think that they can chop and change counsel if they don't like the advice they get... Well, the rules explicitly provide that this shall not happen... We spend a lot of time trying to prevent cases from becoming derailed by defendants who want to change counsel.

The emphasis on thinking outside the box to create economies of scale and boost morale is important to Mr. Justice Goldstone. Conversely, he gets frustrated with inefficient decision-making processes. For example, he says:

> We have a situation here in Liverpool. There is a magistrates' court that has been unfit for purpose for many years where the drawing board is littered with plans for new courts...

Civil and family court judges went to a new court [elsewhere in the city]. I question whether this was ever necessary, but that's another point. So the opportunity arose to bring the magistrates here. Brilliant idea. Economies of scale, speed, probation, witness service, CPS all here under one roof. A case which is heard in the morning in the magistrates' court in which a person has gone to jail could have an appeal in the crown court upstairs in the afternoon. That's efficient. And also if it is determined that the sentence was wrong, it saves money because the public aren't paying for someone to be in prison when they shouldn't be there. Everyone thinks it's a great idea. But no one can decide first of all whether the money is available, and if it is, who should pay for it. There isn't a single person concerned with the administration of justice in this city that doesn't support the concept. It's a false economy not to do it. So meanwhile, we still have a magistrate's court that is not fit for purpose and we still have the space here. We have budgets and plans... It has come back that we can do the whole thing for 10 million pounds. Sounds like a lot of money but in the grand scheme of things it is very little. No one has yet been able to make a decision.... This has a profound impact on morale.

Investing in Rehabilitation

At various points in the interview, Judge Goldstone highlighted the importance of well-resourced rehabilitation where he said:

The most effective way of reducing the prison population and the rate of reoffending is to provide proper resources for the rehabilitation of those who are in prison to ensure they don't return to prison and for those who are not in prison to ensure that they don't go to prison in the first place. We have to pay probation officers proper money to rehabilitate offenders. They have got to put in place proper courses to educate people who are not educated... and this does require heavy investment.

I don't believe that the current proposals to privatize part of the probation service are the way forward, because morale is as shot as it is in any of the other agencies.

There is a lot of crime committed to feed drug habits... The answers don't lie in the criminal law; the consequences do.

Role of the Media

Judge Goldstone also shared his frustration about the media's focus on bad news stories; whipping up appetite for harsher sentences and overemphasizing the small number of cases that go wrong, while not reporting on the vast majority of cases that proceed well. On this topic, he said:

The overwhelming majority of cases that no one ever hears or sees anything about are absolutely fine. The problem is that the 1% of cases that go wrong attract 99% of the publicity... Good news, high standard of judicial achievement, and counsel's high standard of presentation of cases doesn't sell papers. So the only cases that tend to get publicized are those in which something has gone seriously wrong... I think we are rather better at doing our job than the press seems to think. But there again, I would say that, wouldn't I?

You know you read certain newspapers, where there are cries for much harsher sentences and judges are pilloried for passing much lower sentences, but if you go to one of these "Meet the Judge" days, organized from within the community, and you ask Joe Public how you would sentence in such a case, using case studies, in the majority of cases Joe Public would impose a lesser sentence than was actually imposed. So the perception that is given comes back to the fact that bad news sells papers.

I think that generally speaking the public is happier with the way that we do things, but where things can be whipped up by the press, this presents a different picture.

Effective and Ineffective Policies

In this section of the interview, Judge Goldstone was invited to identify policies that are working well, policies that are failing, and discussions about changes to the criminal justice system that concern him. They are reported here by theme.

The Jury System Fundamentally Works

Judge Goldstone talked about maintaining the jury system because, at the time of writing, there are government-led discussions about removing the jury system from certain types of cases to save money:

> I don't think that there is a serious argument for changing the jury system. There is an argument but it doesn't prevail. The longer cases are very tough on jurors. Short of introducing a system that any cases lasting longer than X [amount of time] or any case within a particular area of the law be tried by a judge with assessors, the way forward is for judges to manage the cases by either limiting the number of counts or curtailing the type of evidence to ensure that they can be managed within a reasonable length of time.
>
> I think it is very difficult to curtail cross-examination. [You] can't say at the outset you have X time with a given witness because you don't know what is going to happen. However, I don't think there is anything wrong with stopping counsel from repeating questions or asking them inappropriately, but you have to be very sure of your ground if you are going to curtail cross-examination. We can ensure that cases are tried in a way that doesn't change the current system; just need to adapt it a bit.

Special Measures

Special measures for children and victims of violent or sexual offenses such as video-recorded forensic interviews and cross-examination over a live-link or from behind a one-way screen have been available since 1991. Judge Goldstone spontaneously comments:

> I think that some special measures for witnesses have been a very good thing. But I think the type of special measure can be important and I don't know that the police always get that right. The police seem to have as their default position for a victim of a violent or a sexual offense a video-recorded interview and cross-examination over a link in a blank room looking at a screen.
>
> A video-recorded interview is one thing as it gets the account down [nearer to the time of the event(s)], but first of all there has to be more care taken with the way in which those interviews are conducted. You know you get a detailed account from a witness. That should be it. You don't go back to a witness and say well you said X… because every time you go over a topic you are creating room for an inconsistency and interviews take far too long.
>
> I think that the police should encourage adult witnesses to give evidence within a courtroom, wherever possible, from behind a screen. I think that it tends to oversanitize it if it is given over a link. There are cases where, even with adults, it is absolutely necessary but there are many cases where experience has proved after the event that the witness would have preferred to give evidence from within court. Hasn't been given the option—it hasn't been explained to them by the police.

The Youth Justice and Criminal Evidence Act 1999 codified the above special measures and permitted the use of prerecorded cross-examination (Section 28) and the use of intermediaries—independent language specialists—to assist the courts' communication with children under 17 years old (Section 29). The first "intermediaries" to assist the courts' communication with children were piloted in England in 2004 and, after evaluation and gradual rollout, have theoretically been available nationwide since 2008 (Plotnikoff and Woolfson, 2009). Under the Coroners and Justice Act 2009, which came into force on June 27, 2011, access to special measures was extended to 17-year-olds.

From August 1, 2009 to October 8, 2013 (i.e., just over 4 years and 2 months), there have only been 80 registered intermediaries appointed in Merseyside for children under 18 years; 60 of these were used in cases involving alleged sexual offenses.* These data are not broken down by court or by the stage of proceedings at which an intermediary is used, for example, pre-police interview, pretrial stage, at court. These data also exclude

* England, House of Representatives 2013, Child witnesses. *Commons Written Answers* 18.10.13.

intermediaries for defendants, as these intermediaries are not registered and there are no national data available. Judge Goldstone had no trial experience of the use of intermediaries with complainants—only with young defendants. He was unconvinced of their utility with young defendants except in exceptional circumstances.

At the time of writing, prerecorded testimony (Section 28) is not yet implemented in England and Wales. In June 2013, the minister of justice responded to the Home Office Select Committee Inquiry into Child Sexual Exploitation with the statement that Section 28 would be piloted in three courts in 2014; one of which is Liverpool Crown Court where Judge Goldstone presides. There followed an announcement from the lord chief justice that there would be specialist judges involved in implementation. This would build on the existing system of "ticketing" judges who have attended short courses on sexual assault on top of the generic training. On Section 28, Judge Goldstone commented:

What matters most is the delivery of justice. This is not achieved by trying to change things every time *it looks as though* there is a problem… Government is now trying to put on the statute book in a very short period of time that for which provision was made 14 years ago. And it doesn't appear to be thinking it through. I believe that the judicial team who are spearheading it from the judicial angle will put the MoJ [Ministry of Justice] on track but it's going to be counterproductive to try to bring it in too quickly when there is too much of a downside if things don't work out. It's got to be properly thought through.

I would very much like to see how Section 28 works. If it is got right, it will have an impact. I don't think it will be confined to a very few judges as the powers that be tend to think at the moment because it really wouldn't be fair to give only a very few judges the responsibility for trying all those cases.

When asked why, he responded:

You wouldn't want a staple diet for which that type of evidence-gathering exercise is designed. Who would want to try case after case after case of sexual grooming? One of the joys of the job is the variety. Nobody wants to be doing the same thing day in day out. And if you aren't a happy judge, you probably aren't a good judge. (He quips, you may not be a good judge if you are a happy judge, but you have a chance!) And if you are trying the same type of heartbreaking case day in, day out… it is not something that should be the responsibility of one judge all the time. The load has got to be shared.

Any person who is trained as a judge to sit on crime should in due course be able to try any type of case. Some of us will achieve higher levels of recognition than others; some of us will be authorized to try murders whereas others won't. But every single judge ought to be trained to try cases of serious sexual assault… There are training courses already in terms of the management of cases, the management of witnesses in "serious sex" cases. If you are ticketed to try "serious sex," then you should be ticketed to deal with Section 28 matters. And MoJ is going to invest in this. It shouldn't be for the very few... Bearing in mind that we are presumed to know the skills of being a judge, a concentrated 3-day course on "serious sex" is I believe sufficient... children are embraced within the same course... Management of child witnesses is very important.

In responding to the draft of this chapter, Judge Goldstone added:

Since I was interviewed, it has been confirmed that funding is to be made available to ensure that all "sex-ticketed" judges will receive appropriate training in this regard.

Hearsay Legislation

I think that one of the best provisions of the Criminal Justice Act 2003 is the introduction of the Hearsay Legislation [SS 114–121]. I think that has worked very well in particular in relation to hostile witnesses because previously... if a witness was cross-examined as a hostile witness, their testimony had no value. But now, the law has changed and a witness statement, even if it is retracted, is evidence of the truth of its contents. And juries aren't stupid. They know that people withdraw statements, not necessarily because they weren't telling the truth in the first place, but because they are frightened. Mostly in a domestic violence situation or in a situation where there is a fear element, jurors understand. I would have thought there is a fairly high conviction rate when a witness makes a statement, resiles from it and then juries have to make a decision about whether the first account is true or the account they are now given is true. The 2003 legislation has been a great help in that regard.

Sentencing Policies

The Sentencing Council for England and Wales was established in 2010 to promote greater transparency and consistency in sentencing while protecting the independence of the judiciary. Judge Goldstone comments:

I think the Sentencing Council has done a very good job. There were a lot of misgivings about the sentencing guidelines. I think they have helped judges who pass sentences and I think they have reduced the number of sentences going to the court of appeal. That's not to say I agree with all the levels that the guidelines state. I think that they are if anything, too low in relation to some types of acquisitive crime. For example, the punishment levels for benefit fraud are very low. Obviously, there are some people who are convicted for benefit fraud that are desperate. One can understand why in those cases the court should bend over backwards not to imprison, particularly where there are young children and there very often are. But there are also offenses of that kind that are committed for greed. In those cases, sentences are too low. That really goes against the grain and society demands a much higher level of punishment. But by and large, they have done a great job.

Conversely, he is critical of poorly thought through sentencing policies, saying

There have been so many instances in the past of changes being put through to subsequently have been found to be a bad change because it wasn't appropriately thought through. Look at all the changes in the sentencing regime— indeterminate sentences, second strike sentences. All that sort of thing. How much of it has lasted? Very little.

For example, in relation to indeterminate sentences for public protection (IPP), he commented

You can't afford a system whereby people stay in prison far longer than the minimum term that was recommended. Why was this happening? Because the rehabilitation courses were not put in place. Why? Because there wasn't the funding. This is a classic example of a sentencing policy and regime only lasting a short time, because the cost and consequences were not properly thought through. IPP has been replaced by extended sentences of imprisonment for public protection with the power to detain for up to two-thirds of the custodial term and an extended license period thereafter.

He offers another example of poorly thought through sentencing policy in the newly introduced victim surcharge, saying

Knee-jerk reactions to sentencing issues just don't work well. For instance, we have a victim surcharge which I'm supposed to announce in every single case in the crown court in respect of any offense committed after October 1, 2012, whatever the offense, whether or not there was a victim. Now, I am not going to say when I send somebody to prison for life for example, "and you will pay a victim surcharge of £120," I can't bring myself to do it. When it applies, it is administrative and it can be dealt with administratively.

When commenting on this draft chapter, he adds, "This is now to be referred to as a 'statutory surcharge,' [a] far more diplomatic a description." And finally, on breaching prison release licenses, he states

Sanctions for breaches of license conditions following release from prison— in particular the commission of further offenses—are being watered down to the extent where it has become a mockery. What sort of deterrent is it to an offender if you tell him/her that if, following release and before the expiry of the sentence [s]he commits a further offense, [s]he may expect to be recalled to serve the remainder of the sentence, when in reality, the overwhelming likelihood is that there will be a standard recall of 14 or 28 days? This is yet another way of trying to save money to the detriment of the public interest.

General Assessments

Judge Goldstone had no comments to make regarding transnational relations. In the final section of the interview, Judge Goldstone was invited to sum up his overall assessment of the criminal justice system. He came back to the importance of appropriately resourced rehabilitation and the need to avoid change for change's sake, saying

> The greatest problem facing the criminal court at this time is the inability of the government to apply sufficient funding to ensure rehabilitation or at least to ensure that rehabilitation has a better chance of working.
>
> I would like a complete moratorium on any changes in the criminal law for 12 months. There has been a huge increase in the number of laws and changes to the laws. Three thousand new laws were introduced during the last Labor administration [over a 10 year period]. Some of them are minor (like not swimming over the wreck of the Titanic) and some of them are important. Some of them are well thought out and some of them don't fall into any of those categories. But I just think that sometimes the law is changed for change's sake… It is a trite comment but really, if it ain't broke, don't fix it! And it ain't always broke.
>
> What is most needed now in the system is an injection of confidence. I think that despite everything that has been thrown at us and taken from us, we do continue to do a good job. We are not asking for praise. But we are asking for a bit more understanding from the press and the public of the difficulties in which we all have to work.

Conclusion

During the interview, Judge Goldstone did not want to comment on the relationship between theory and practice and transnational relations. He wanted to focus his responses on issues surrounding problems and successes he experienced.

Reflecting on the interview, four key themes stand out. Firstly, Judge Goldstone's sense of teamwork and collegiality. While a judge's job is often described as a lonely one, he emphasized the importance of teamwork. Proud of his judicial team, he spoke of the collegiality that helped the judges of the Liverpool Crown Court to work together in the interests of the community they serve. These comments were consistent with the experiences of the judges of Merseyside; proud of *their* court and giving a clear implicit message to the outsider that they worked as a team. Likewise, Judge Goldstone took pride in the ways that he respected jurors' time and the processes that the judges used to support their colleagues in the wider criminal justice sector (e.g., probation officers, police, victim advisors, and counsel) to make the system work in a time of harsh budget cuts. While this interview cannot of course verify whether other professionals perceived their crown court judges in the same way, what matters here is the intention. For Judge Goldstone, collegiality and teamwork are important dimensions of an efficient and effective justice system.

Second, and related to this, is the extent to which he embraced case management as a core component of the judicial role. Trained as a legal professional, he nevertheless talked repeatedly about case management as an important aspect of his role.

Third, the interviewers do not share Judge Goldstone's view that 3 days training is adequate to understand the various dynamics of adult sexual assault, child sexual exploitation, Internet sexual crime and child abuse, the developmental and linguistic issues for child witnesses, best practice in use of special measures including the use of ground rules hearings, disclosure and case management, as is currently the essence of the curriculum. It is encouraging for children that there are refresher courses for judges. However, it is particularly difficult to build up knowledge and skills when judges and advocates do not confront many cases involving children in any given year. Concern about judicial and advocate training on issues for vulnerable witnesses was the driving force behind the website The Advocates Gateway.* Established in 2012, it offers case law and practical and evidence-informed guidance on working with vulnerable witnesses and young defendants. It is now used in judicial training courses. From the interviewer's perspective, judges and advocates can learn and do more to render a fundamentally adult system of justice more appropriate for the child witnesses who do a community service by giving evidence in criminal proceedings (Davies et al., 2010).

Finally, Judge Goldstone's lack of fear of speaking his mind about the consequences of inadequate resources in the system was striking. He is not alone. There has been an unprecedented backlash about legal aid cuts with the Judicial Executive Board (including the Master of the Rolls, Lord Dyson and the heads of the divisions of the high court) and other senior judges in England raising concerns *publicly* about the potential for more miscarriages of justice (Bowcott, 2013). Such public comment is unusual in

---

* www.theadvocatesgateway.org (accessed January 10, 2014).

a common law jurisdiction because of the separation of court and government powers.

A just system requires professionals that are fairly resourced to do their jobs, including appropriately funded and well-researched prevention and rehabilitation programs. It is shortsighted for politicians to use dog-whistle politics to "get tough on crime" while simultaneously slashing the system and the morale of those who work in it. Reducing crime and reducing budgets to prevent crime and rehabilitate offenders require more thought.

Glossary

Bar Council: The body that governs barristers.

barrister: A lawyer who is an advocate that took the Bar Professional Training Course after completing his or her law degree. Members of the public have no direct access to barristers; this is done via a solicitor. Barristers are recognizable by the horsehair wigs and gowns that they wear in open court.

barrister pupilage: A 12 month period when barristers undergo practical training under the tutelage of a senior barrister.

Crown Prosecution Service: Formed in 1986, the service is responsible for organizing the prosecution case on behalf of the Crown and act in a similar manner to a district attorney in the United States or an examining magistrate in many European jurisdictions.

European Convention on Human Rights: A treaty written in 1953 signed by the member states of the Council of Europe (please note that this is not the European Union), containing the minimum human rights a state must recognize its citizens have. Following the atrocities of World War II, the council was created to ensure that no state should abuse the minimum rights a citizen should expect.

European Court of Human Rights: Located in Strasbourg (France), this is the court that applicants may take their case to when they feel the state has violated their rights contained in the European Convention on Human Rights.

European Court of Justice: Located in Luxembourg, this is the main court of the European Union that hears matters on European Union Law.

Inns of Court: There are four Inns of Court in England and Wales: The Honorable Society of the Inner Temple, Middle Temple, Lincoln's Inn, and Gray's Inn. All barristers have to join an Inns of Court and it is at their Inns of Court that they are called to the Bar after completing their Bar Practice Training Course (formerly the Bar Vocational Course) that follows the completion of a law degree.

Magistrate's court: In the hierarchy of the court system in England and Wales, this is the lowest court.

Queen's Counsel (QC): A title conferred by the Crown in recognition of the ability and work performed by junior advocates. Since 2005/2006, recommendations for the award of Queen's Counsel are made by the Queen's Counsel Selection Board that is independent of the Bar Council, the Law Society, and the government. QCs can wear silk gowns in court, hence the term *taking silk* if an advocate is about to become a QC. This is why QCs are also referred to as "silks."

solicitor: A lawyer who is also an advocate in the lower courts, such as a magistrates' court, who took the legal practice course after completing his or her law degree. Members of the public who require legal services have direct access to firms of solicitors.

Solicitors' Regulation Authority: The body that governs solicitors.

David Harris QC, District Court 10

ANNA CARLINE AND CLARE GUNBY

Contents

Introduction

The interview with Judge Harris was conducted in August 2013 by Dr. Anna Carline and Dr. Clare Gunby in the law school at Liverpool John Moores University. The interview lasted one-and-a-half hours and was digitally recorded and transcribed. It took the form of a detailed exploration with Judge Harris of a number of topics relating to his judicial experience and philosophy. The interview was relaxed and friendly, and due to the established professional relationships between the interviewers and interviewee, it proceeded with ease. Judge Harris was given the opportunity to amend the first draft of this chapter, adding relevant considerations that had occurred to him since the interview. The chapter consequently sets out Judge Harris's responses in the interview and his subsequent additions under each topic, in the order that questions were asked. Inevitably, there was a degree of inter-connection among the topics, which has resulted in some overlap among the areas of discussion.

Numerous key themes developed during the interview and were revis-ited a number of times: First, the implications of the requirement of fair-ness, which Judge Harris regarded to be of fundamental importance to all aspects of his work. Second, the impact of the implemented and anticipated cuts in public funding of legal representation in criminal cases. Third, much needed improvements in the management of the evidence of children and other vulnerable witnesses, including long overdue reforms of the timing and nature of cross-examination. Fourth, the sufficiency of the informa-tion given to the jury in a case of alleged sexual offending to assist them in understanding the psychological, emotional, and behavioral consequences that may result from sexual abuse. Although David Harris has recently retired from the circuit bench, we shall refer to him in this chapter as Judge Harris.

Career

Judge Harris gained an MA in law at Oxford and a PhD on issues in tort law at Cambridge. He was a coeditor of the 9th edition of *Winfield and Jolowicz on Tort*. After teaching law for 2 years at Manchester University, Judge Harris was called to the Bar of England and Wales in November 1969. From 1970 until 1989, he practiced as a barrister from chambers in Liverpool, specializing primarily in various forms of civil litigation; in 1988 he was elected head of his chambers. He was appointed an assis-tant recorder in 1983 and promoted to recorder in 1988.* In 1989, he was made a Queen's Counsel (QC). As a QC, he specialized in large personal injury cases (including clinical negligence work) and increasingly in care cases involving allegations of serious, nonaccidental injury to children. He also undertook a number of criminal cases mainly involving murder, manslaughter, or serious sex crime. In 1992, he was authorized to sit as a deputy judge of the Family Division of the High Court of Justice and on a significant number of occasions sat in that capacity in the Royal Courts of Justice in London, dealing almost exclusively with cases involving the alleged abuse of children.

In 2001, Judge Harris was appointed a full-time circuit judge, sitting initially in Manchester, but soon transferring to his home city of Liverpool.

---

* Recorders, including the now discontinued office of assistant recorder, are part-time judges appointed by the Crown on the basis of their assessed suitability to hold that office. A recorder is expected to sit for a minimum of 20 days each year.

Shortly after his appointment, he opted to sit only on family and criminal cases. Following that decision, he was authorized to deal with cases involving allegations of serious sex crime and he continued to undertake some high court family cases. For the 4 years prior to his retirement in February 2012, Judge Harris sat only on criminal cases and during that period his workload increasingly involved cases of alleged serious sex crime, child cruelty, and domestic violence.

Personal Judicial Philosophy

Judge Harris was questioned in greater depth on his views of the role of the judiciary in society. He explained that his cases as a family and criminal judge involved very important outcomes and decisions that were not just fundamental to the individuals involved, but also engaged major aspects of the public interest. Although, as indicated above, Judge Harris felt privileged to undertake that work, he was conscious of the responsibilities placed on him and the gravity of the harm that could ensue if he got things wrong. This therefore required a judge, in his opinion, to be diligent and thorough and to maintain objectivity and an open mind throughout. Judge Harris again emphasized that proper preparation time is important in minimizing the risk of judicial mistakes.

In the context of the judge's role, Judge Harris was asked whether it was difficult for judges to relate to the living/social conditions of those from economically deprived backgrounds who appeared before them in court. Judge Harris recognized that there was a popular perception that judges, who had normally had successful careers as practicing lawyers and lived middle-class lives, were "out of touch," and therefore had little understanding of the realities of economic or other disadvantages. He believes, however, that this perception is wrong, arguing that these days many judges do not come from affluent backgrounds. More importantly, in his view a substantial proportion of the judges who sit on criminal and family work will have devoted portions of their careers to representing people who suffer from various forms of disadvantage and consequently have a good level of understanding/empathy for its consequences. In his view, most judges do understand such matters and do all they can to make allowances in court for persons who are disadvantaged or in crisis. In his case he did not come from a privileged background. His parents were of modest means and sacrificed much to support his university education.

Judge Harris also believes that the primary contribution a judge can make to society is to carry out his or her functions fairly and justly to the very best of his or her ability. This, he argued, was the expectation and entitlement of those appearing before a judge. In addition, Judge Harris believed that if an individual felt that she or he had received a fair trial, he or she was likely to say so to others, which, to a very limited but still valuable degree, may help correct the false stereotype of out-of-touch judges.

Further, in Judge Harris's view, a criminal or family judge can sometimes use the legal process to support professionals in engaging defendants in criminal cases, and parents and carers in family cases or in remedial work. In family cases, the court can have a longer engagement with the parties and be more involved in assessing and guiding that work. Judge Harris reports that while major change in difficult family cases cannot be described as frequent, it is certainly not infrequent. In his view, however, the potential for such constructive work in the family court is now much reduced by the misconceived removal of legal aid for lay parties in private law cases, except in certain limited situations, and the presumptive rule that a public law case should be completed in 6 months.

Judge Harris proceeded to make a number of specific observations relating to the requirement that a criminal trial should be fair:

1. Conviction rates for various offenses are regularly the subject of critical comment by government, relevant academics, and media. As a result, judges and senior managers of the Crown Prosecution Service (CPS) may come to feel under pressure to "improve" such rates. While Judge Harris recognized that this critical focus could positively impact practice, in his view, those critical of conviction rates were sometimes unable to appreciate that a prosecution correctly fails because despite all reasonable care on the part of the prosecution, the evidence as heard in court is insufficient for a jury to be sure of the guilt of the defendant. Moreover, in Judge Harris's view, in English adversarial criminal proceedings it is not part of the judge's role to assist the prosecution to secure a conviction by a biased management of the case, such as questions to a witness designed to repair damage to the prosecution case in cross-examination, or a summing-up distorted in favor of the prosecution.

2. Judge Harris stated that he strove hard to maintain a calm and informal atmosphere in court, whatever the emotional intensity of the proceedings, and to treat all witnesses, including the defendant, with courtesy, consideration, and respect. He was very aware that a probing cross-examination, although properly conducted, could still be an attritional experience for a lay witness. He believed a hearing should be conducted so as to reduce the stress inherent in giving oral evidence, to avoid unnecessary distress to witnesses, and ensure, so far as possible, a fair result.

3. Another core element of Judge Harris's judicial philosophy is that the summing-up must be fair and balanced. If it was necessary and

appropriate for him to comment on an aspect of the evidence, his objective in doing so was not to influence the jury against that evidence, but to assist them by identifying potential approaches they may take to the evidence. In doing so, he would always remind the jury of the defense submissions on the evidence and emphasize that it was for them to decide what weight, if any, to place on that piece of evidence.

In the interview, Judge Harris gave an example of the application of this approach in relation to cases of alleged child abuse. The defense will often argue that the complainant must be lying as had the allegations been true, the child would have behaved differently than he or she did, for example, by not revisiting the defendant's home and by complaining immediately of the abuse. In accordance with the guidance and specimen directions published by the Judicial College, Judge Harris would remind the jury of the defense case but advise them to avoid making stereotypical assumptions as to how a child might behave because, "in the experience of the courts," children who have been abused react in a variety of different ways. The jury must therefore assess the credibility of the particular child's account on the basis of the evidence and not on the basis of stereotype. There is, however, no reference in this standard form of direction to any expert opinion that may have made a contribution to the experience of the courts. Judge Harris's thoughts on the sufficiency of this direction, particularly today, are summarized below in the section on future developments.

Problems and Successes Experienced

Areas of Surprise and Concern

When asked to reflect on "what had surprised" him in his judicial career, Judge Harris identified the following matters in particular: first, the ever-increasing complexity of his work as a criminal judge. This was due to various factors, including the seemingly unending stream of lengthy and detailed legislation, at times ill-conceived or poorly drafted or both, which often fundamentally changed the criminal law in its various dimensions (substantive, evidential, procedural, sentencing); the increasingly lengthy sentencing guidelines issued by the Sentencing Council, which now require the judge operating on a relevant guideline to apply and set out a structured approach to the determination of sentence; the considerable volume of case law, in part necessitated by the difficulties in applying legislation, sentencing guidelines, and numerous codes to varying factual situations; and finally, the growing complexity of some common forms of criminal behavior, including serious sexual offending involving multiple offenses and/or victims and/or offenders, gang- or group-related offending, major drug importation and supply, and other forms of serious and organized crime.

Second, Judge Harris commented on the inadequate time made available to a criminal or family judge for the advance preparation of cases and for the drafting, or at least detailed formulation, of often lengthy summings-up, rulings, and judgments. He identified the following as illustrative of the problems created by insufficient preparation time:

1. *Greater emphasis now being placed on rigorous and proactive case management at each case management hearing*: Effective case management of this type requires the advance reading of critical material to identify/review the relevant issues and the evidence necessary for an informed determination. The judge must undertake this analysis independently of, and before, discussion with the advocates. This can be a time-consuming exercise in a complex and/or difficult case. In Judge Harris's experience, it was common for a judge to be given a criminal case management list of around 8–10 voluminous files at about 4:30 p.m. the afternoon before the hearing. Based on his experience, Judge Harris strongly believes that insufficient time allocated to the preparation (by judges and advocates alike) of case management hearings results in trials being delayed or disrupted, as attempts are made to rectify problems that would have been addressed in advance had the case management procedure been more rigorous initially. This was considered particularly so in serious sex crime, where the transcripts of the witnesses' visually recorded interviews can be extensive. There may also be a large volume of third-party documentation to be considered, for example, social work and educational records. This category of case delay and disruption at trial can be particularly stressful for children and other vulnerable witnesses.

2. *Criminal sentencing*: Judge Harris's files would frequently include a number of sentences, many not previously known to him, and some involving factual complications. Sentencing is, in his view, a technical subject involving a complex maze of restrictions, requirements, and case law dealing with the principles of, and approach to, the sentencing for each offense (even when the sentencing for the offense is covered by a sentencing guideline). Even when the relevant principles are clear, the exercise of calculating a proper sentence while reflecting the various relevant sentencing objectives and the nuances of the individual case can be challenging. This is made more difficult by important information, for example, presentence reports being

lodged only on the morning of the hearing. Moreover, the judge's sentencing remarks are required to be far fuller than was previously the case, with the structured approach required by any applicable sentencing guideline being properly set out. Ideally, this should be prepared in advance of the hearing.

A third area of surprise and concern for Judge Harris during his period as a full-time judge was the gradual reduction in judicial discretion, both in criminal and family law, by the perceived imposition of unduly limiting guidelines and protocols. While he recognized that there has been a compelling need for increased procedural efficiency, the avoidance of unnecessary delay, and for some standardization of decision making, he strongly feels that the limitation of judicial discretion has gone too far. In his view, this development was driven by a "misinformed" and misconceived distrust on the part of government about the ability and reliability of decision making by the criminal and family judiciary.

When questioned whether his judicial career had been as rewarding and interesting as he assumed it would, Judge Harris stated that notwithstanding the areas of concern mentioned, combined with inadequate funding for the Court Service, he had experienced "tremendous satisfaction" in carrying out his work. In general, he considered that it was a very fulfilling experience, and also a privilege, to be able to make a contribution to the administration of criminal and family justice in the communities he served. In addition, the work he undertook was varied, always interesting, and sometimes involved challenging and stimulating issues of law and/or factual disputes, all of which he enjoyed. Furthermore, he greatly valued the support and companionship of his colleagues, the good relationships he had enjoyed with the advocates and professionals who regularly appeared before him, and the support and friendship he had received from his ushers and other members of court staff with whom he had regularly worked. He emphasized his gratitude and admiration for the staff in all the court centers in which he had sat, but particularly those in the criminal and family courts in Liverpool, who, despite inadequate remuneration and conditions of work, did all they could to give the best service. He strongly believed that the pivotal role of the court staff in the administration of justice was not properly recognized and rewarded by the Ministry of Justice.

Judge Harris mentioned having very much enjoyed working with lay magistrates, sitting with him on appeal from decisions of the magistrate's court, and, particularly, working with juries in Crown Court trials. He greatly valued the involvement of juries in the criminal justice system and respected their commitment to the cases that they tried. It was only vary rarely that Judge Harris found a jury verdict to be perverse. Instead, he believed that decisions were based on the evidence and the applicable law and not least the very high standard of proof required for a guilty verdict. He strongly believes, on the basis of his experience, that trial by judge and jury is the fairest system for determining the guilt or otherwise of fellow citizens.

More specifically, Judge Harris identified the following matters as fundamental to the work of a judge and/or to the fulfillment he experienced from his own judicial career:

1. His first priority had been to strive to be fair and just, not only in the decisions he made, but also in the way he conducted his court. He emphasized that he would treat those appearing before him with fairness and respect, recognizing that any dysfunctional behavior that had likely resulted in the legal proceedings would typically be the result of adverse life experiences or other serious disadvantage or both, which entitled them to compassion (even though it could not and did not affect the ultimate decision in the case). Judge Harris felt that, by and large, he had been, and is regarded as having been, a fair judge and this was at the core of the fulfillment he has derived from his judicial career.

2. A further feature of his judicial career was the benefit of sitting in both the criminal and family jurisdictions. As a result of his own judicial experience, he was strongly of the view that a detailed knowledge and understanding of family law and practice was of great benefit to a judge hearing or managing criminal cases. For example, being exposed, as he was in the family jurisdiction, to matters such as alleged intrafamilial child abuse and sexual or physical offending or both within adult relationships, and witnessing the potential for the successful reintegration of children who had been the victims of abuse or neglect or both with the culpable parent or other carer, provided an important foundational context for subsequently hearing/managing criminal cases. Judge Harris also considers that a knowledge of criminal law and practice is potentially of some, albeit lesser, benefit to a family judge hearing or managing a case with associated criminal proceedings, as commonly occurs in the context of child abuse or neglect and domestic violence allegations.

During the interview, Judge Harris gave further examples of situations where experience of family law can be of particular benefit to a criminal judge. First, in relation to cases involving complex/disputed medical evidence around the interpretation, causation, and timing of injuries to a child. A family judge will have much experience of expert evidence of this nature, whereas a purely criminal circuit judge may well encounter such material far less. Second, when managing and controlling age-inappropriate and confusing cross-examination of a child witness, a judge with family law experience is likely to be (i) more conversant than a judge sitting only on crime about child development and the limitations of a child's cognitive ability; (ii) more sensitive to subtler signs of confusion, tiredness, and distress on the child's part; (iii) better able, in part as a result of experience of interviewing children in family cases, to phrase questions to a child while taking into account the child's age; and (iv) more sensitive generally in the management of the child as a witness. Third, with regard to sentencing, a criminal judge with family court experience will be particularly suited to assessing the proper weight to be given to the plan for rehabilitation, and determining the form of sentence so that the child is not caused further unnecessary harm by the disruption of the authority's care plan. For these and other reasons, Judge Harris strongly believes that every medium or large criminal court center should have among its judges some with family law experience.

Judge Harris found family cases relating to the welfare and protection of children particularly fulfilling. He believes that the potential for the constructive use of the court process to achieve understanding, change, and compromise between parties is greater than in any other field. When this occurs, as it may if the case is properly managed, the outcome can be hugely beneficial to the child, his or her parents, and the wider families, and can avoid the risk there would otherwise have been of future costly social work input, and calls on the health service and litigation.

Administration of Criminal Justice System in Liverpool Generally

As noted, Judge Harris spoke very positively about the administration of criminal justice in Liverpool, including the judiciary, court staff, probation, and mental health liaison services. He was "profoundly impressed by the commitment, integrity and decency of almost everybody who took part in the administration of justice." In general, he also considered that the advocates appearing before him had done their work at least competently, with some performing to a very high standard and few being substandard. There had been an "unacceptably high incidence" of failure to comply with court orders within the time specified, particularly by the CPS, but also, albeit to a lesser extent, by private solicitors. However, Judge Harris felt that, by and large, this was due to public funding constraints, leading to insufficient staff for the workload, rather than due to lack of respect for court orders or "avoidable inefficiency."

Specific Criminal Justice Policies

Judge Harris perceived some of the criminal justice policies implemented during his time to have worked well. He mentioned in particular the provisions in the Criminal Justice Act 2003, providing comprehensive codes for the far greater use in criminal proceedings of relevant and reliable hearsay evidence and relevant evidence relating to the bad character (including criminal convictions) of both defendants and nondefendants. These provisions, which had given rise to a great deal of jurisprudence, had enabled juries to reach their verdicts on the basis of a significantly greater range of relevant evidence.

Judicial Training in Criminal Law

A further major success noted by Judge Harris was the quality of the judicial training delivered by the Judicial College, which he described as "very well managed" and to "a high standard." He considered the monthly electronic newsletter, summarizing or referring judges to recent important decisions of the appellate courts, new legislation, and other relevant developments, to be very valuable in assisting hard-pressed judges to keep up-to-date with the changing criminal law. The availability of a criminal e-library containing publications by the college, practitioners, judges, and academics was also regarded as a valuable resource as was the judicial intranet, which allowed judges to electronically access a range of materials including law reports and practitioner textbooks.

Judge Harris also made the point that judges commonly have to deal with complex disputes involving evidence from other disciplines, such as medicine. He consequently felt that the Judicial College could support judges further by negotiating online access to a medical library and/or commission online reports from medical experts summarizing important developments, such as in relation to the causation of injury patterns, which may be indicative of child abuse.

Developments in Proactive Case Management

Judge Harris recalls that in 2001 when he was appointed to the circuit bench, systematic, rigorous case management was generally in its infancy in the criminal jurisdiction. This contrasted with the strong emphasis on active case management in the family and civil jurisdictions. As a result, some criminal cases did reach trial ineffectively prepared and had to be adjourned or delayed to allow for essential preparation. There was, however, a developing momentum for change, which eventually culminated in the Criminal Procedure Rules. In the meantime, a number of local case management initiatives occurred, one of the most developed of which was in the Liverpool Crown Court under the leadership of its then recorder, Judge Henry Globe QC. The experience of Liverpool, and other case management initiatives, was incorporated and developed in the Criminal Procedure Rules with an emphasis on the early identification of issues and strong judicial control over the preparation of the case. The modern case management system can, and should, be very effective in ensuring that a case is efficiently managed and fully ready for trial.

As previously noted, in Judge Harris's view, "for the case management hearing to operate as effectively as possible, it requires the judge to have sufficient time to have read and considered the case management implications of the court papers... to take control of the case, and, unless impracticable, for the trial advocates to attend the hearing with time to discuss and, if possible agree, case management needs and directions." In Judge Harris's view, this in turn means that the advocates must be properly paid for the work involved, which in a potentially lengthy or problematic case may be extensive. During his period as a full-time criminal judge, fee levels for criminal work were insufficient, which had led to barristers understandably taking on several case management hearings in different courts on a given day in order to maximize their income, with a resulting decline in the quality of their work in an individual case.

Evidence of Children in Criminal Proceedings

Judge Harris was particularly concerned about what in his view are serious deficiencies in the management of children's evidence in criminal cases. He made three main criticisms:

1. In his experience, there is a concerning level of poor practice in the visually recorded interviewing of children who are complainants or witnesses in investigations of alleged child abuse. The recorded interview, which is normally now conducted by a trained police officer, is important because it constitutes the child's evidence in chief in any subsequent criminal proceedings against the alleged perpetrator. Official guidance on the interviewing of children is contained in the document "Achieving Best Evidence in Criminal Proceedings: Guidance on Interviewing Victims and Witnesses, and Using Special Measures" (ABE). Interviewers are expected to follow the guidance

in ABE unless there is very good reason for not doing so. In Judge Harris's experience (which mirrors that of a small number of judges whom he has discussed this issue with), interviews are regularly marred by poor interviewing technique and often include multiple breaches of ABE. Poor interviewing has the potential to undermine the quality and credibility of the child's account and can create unnecessary problems for the child in cross-examination. The interview is also used as the basis for assessments and normally stands as the child's evidence in related public or private law family proceedings. Accordingly, a deficient interview can also create problems in that forum.

2. As stated above, under English law, when a child's visually recorded interview is played in criminal proceedings, the child is typically required to be at court for oral cross-examination and is questioned from the court via a closed-circuit television link. Generally, the trial takes place many months after the child's video-recorded interview, with the child suffering considerable stress during the intervening period and the delays also inevitably impacting on his or her memory of events. In Judge Harris's view, the serious consequences resulting from such extensive delay can be substantially reduced by an early hearing to prerecord the child's evidence under cross-examination and in reexamination. The use of prerecorded cross-examination and reexamination of child witnesses as evidence at trial has been successfully implemented in other comparable common law jurisdictions. In 1989, it was strongly recommended to the then government in a report by The Advisory Group on Video Evidence established by the home secretary. The advisory Group substantially based its recommendations on expert evidence. Since the report, children no longer give evidence in the actual courtroom. However, Section 28 of the Youth Justice and Criminal Evidence Act 1999, which provides for the playing of a child's prerecorded visual cross-examination and reexamination of his or her evidence at the subsequent trial, has not yet been brought into force.

Since 1999, further evidence has accumulated as to the harm and impairment to memory likely to be suffered by a child forced to wait many months between the visually recorded interview and cross-examination at trial.* At a seminar in 2012, organized by the Ministry of Justice, Professor Spencer reported ongoing constructive discussions on the implementation of Section 28, but considered that the main obstacle to its implementation was a concern about

* See in particular Spencer and Lamb (2012).

the costs entailed. Judge Harris strongly argues that cost is a poor excuse for the continuation of a procedure for cross-examination of child witnesses that is acknowledged to be harmful and potentially damaging to the quality of evidence. In addition, he felt certain that the financial and wider consequences of damaged lives and impaired evidence, which potentially leads to wrong acquittals, "simply had not been costed."

Judge Harris said in the interview that the delay in bringing Section 28 into force, "passes any rational understanding." At long last, however, the Ministry of Justice has established a pilot scheme for the trial of prerecording cross-examination and reexamination of children commencing in three court centers, including Liverpool, in early 2014. It can only be hoped that the use of such evidence will be rolled out nationally without further delay.

3. Children still tend to be cross-examined by advocates using modified forms of the techniques that are used for the cross-examination of adults. In Judge Harris's experience, such cross-examinations are not normally in a forceful adversarial style, but nevertheless are frequently confusing and frightening for children. Plotnikoff and Woolfson identify from their research several types of questions put to young witnesses (some of whom must have suffered from speech or communication difficulties), which the witnesses did not understand or caused confusion and distress or both, creating the very clear risk that in response the child might give false answers (Plotnikoff and Woolfson, 2012). In Judge Harris's experience, such confusing questions were common in the cases over which he presided. It was a consequence of lack of knowledge and proper training, as opposed to inappropriate tactics, on the part of the advocates. Indeed, Judge Harris acknowledges that at times he probably inadvertently put inappropriately expressed and confusing questions to child witnesses in his cases. The training bodies of the professions are, however, now beginning to provide the necessary, much needed, education.

Relevant essays in *Children and Cross-Examination* (Spencer and Lamb, 2012) highlight how judges can control inappropriate cross-examination by establishing ground rules for cross-examination prior to trial, enforcing those ground rules rigorously, intervening promptly to stop inappropriate cross-examination, and making comments if necessary in summing-up to negate any unfair questions. Certainly, the Criminal Procedure Rules, supported by increasing pronouncements from the court of appeal, provide the basis for proper, future judicial control of the cross-examination of children.

Legal Aid Changes and Their Probable Consequences

Judge Harris is highly critical of the fundamental changes being made by the government to the public funding of defense costs in criminal cases. He expressed concern that the new legal aid scheme will likely result in:

1. An eligibility criterion for legal aid, which is sufficiently low that a very significant number of defendants will fail to qualify for legal aid, whatever the complexity, sensitivity, or likely length of the proceedings against them. Such litigants will have to act in person, whether or not they have the ability to do so.
2. New arrangements for legal aid procurement that will inevitably cause the replacement of the current large number of established high-street firms, which provide a committed, able, personal, and responsible service for their clients, with a far smaller number of very large, commercially operated, and profit-orientated firms.
3. Significantly lower rates of remuneration for solicitors with the inevitable result that new firms will use insufficiently qualified, skilled, experienced, and accordingly cheaper staff, thus depressing further the quality of the service that they provide for their clients.
4. Severely limited client choice and substantially reduced client confidence in the quality, efficiency, and acceptability to the court of the service provided. These factors are likely to persuade many defendants who qualify for legal aid to opt instead to represent themselves.
5. The substantial reduction of litigation fees in defense Crown Court work, which will inevitably dramatically accelerate the flight of talented barristers from the practice of criminal law.
    Judge Harris is "profoundly dismayed and disturbed" by what he regards as the inevitable collapse of the criminal Bar, which he says "…has in general provided a high standard of advice and advocacy, at the very heart of the success achieved by the English criminal justice system." He felt that the reforms would result in "… the sacrifice of what in general is a network of effective and client-orientated criminal solicitors' firms in favor of a far inferior system of criminal legal aid provision." He argued that this system would be "[Based] on erroneous and simplistic financial calculations by, and approved by, those who have little understanding, and little interest in acquiring an understanding of, the irreplaceable qualities of the present arrangements and how financial savings can be achieved cooperatively with the profession without destroying all that is good and indeed essential in our present publicly funded defense service."

Above all, Judge Harris is, "appalled by the hugely detrimental and costly impact the forthcoming changes will have on the operation of the criminal courts." He instances the following by way of example:

Due to the greatly increased incidence of litigants in person in criminal cases there will be far more full trials. A litigant in person will not have the benefit of an experienced legal representative who can give appropriate advice, if necessary negotiating with the prosecution, which may result in the client pleading guilty at the earliest reasonable point. She or he will typically not be able to carry out the preparation and provide the input needed for effective case management, resulting in unanticipated issues arising during the trial, which have not been prepared for. In the interests of justice, such issues cannot be ignored with consequential delays occurring while investigations commence. Furthermore, the judge presiding over a trial with an unrepresented defendant will have to undertake an additional role, which is always time-consuming and sometimes inappropriate in adversarial proceedings. For example, taking instructions from the unrepresented defendant, translating them into questions for the witness, ascertaining from the defendant his or her response to the answer, and converting that into further questions. Moreover, the judge will lack the important benefit of the defense advocate's legal submissions and will be compelled to research and initiate legal arguments. If the trial contains a represented defendant, he or she may feel that the judge's necessarily interventionist role is unfair and biased. If the trial involves more than one unrepresented defendant, the potential for disruption or delay will be increased significantly.

There is also a high risk of some of the aforementioned problems arising if a defendant is inadequately represented, which is likely to be the case under the new reforms. For example, unless the judge is aware that the advocate is substandard, he or she may incorrectly rely on the advocate to conduct the defense case properly and may be unaware that there is, for example, some important factual or legal issue that the advocate has missed. The potential for miscarriages of justice or unsafe verdicts is therefore greatly increased. Applications for leave to appeal and appeals with leave will almost certainly substantially increase, resulting in a vast outlay of public funds. The court of appeal may have to be more liberal in its approach to appeals in which an important issue that should have been advanced was ignored or overlooked at trial, or a matter was raised inappropriately. There may well be a far greater number of successful appeals, with guilty verdicts overturned and retrials ordered.

In Judge Harris's view, the above examples of failed justice with costly consequences are obvious. There are many others, for example, the cost of imprisonment or community sentences imposed on defendants wrongly convicted due to their defenses being inadequately conducted. In addition, cases in which the defendant's representation is so incompetent, and the defendant's confidence in his or her lawyer so undermined, that it will be necessary in the interests of a fair trial that the representation is transferred to other solicitors, with costly duplication of work.

Systematic Reform of Procedures in Child Abuse Criminal Investigations and Trials

As already indicated, Judge Harris emphasized in the interview that there were "serious deficiencies in the management of children's evidence in English criminal proceedings arising out of allegations of child abuse, principally sexual abuse." Some of these deficiencies were of "principle, that is, the procedure itself, while others related to the ways in which the procedure was operated." In his view, taken together, these deficiencies rendered the procedure in general "unfit for purpose." He appreciated that parts of his criticism extended to other types of criminal case, but felt that they are at their most damaging and unfair in child abuse cases. Thus, he restricted his discussion to that context. He felt that the concerns expressed in this area by many professionals are being more clearly heard and therefore, "considers the time is now ripe for a systematic review of the procedures devised and practiced for taking and managing children's evidence in such cases." He is hopeful that this will take place, as he feels that "piecemeal change" in such a complex area is the lesser option. He expressed serious concern, however, that the anticipated reduction in standards of defense advocates resulting from the government's legal aid changes was likely to impair the implementation of some of the necessary procedural changes, particularly in relation to the difficult exercise of appropriate cross-examination of children, especially very young children.

Judge Harris identified and summarized three "contextual" factors, which he feels must inform decisions on procedural change, as they help define the purposes for which the procedure must be fit:

1. As a consequence of Section 53 of the Youth Justice and Criminal Evidence Act 1999, a child, of whatever age, is competent to give evidence at every stage in criminal proceedings, unless the court concludes that he or she is not able to understand the questions put to him or her as a witness and give answers that can be understood. The judge has to decide on the evidence specific to the particular child and whether that child satisfies the test for witness competence. In England and Wales, it is not uncommon for prosecutions for child abuse to be based solely or substantially on the evidence of a very young child. The procedure must therefore, in his view, be sufficiently informed and flexible to maximize the ability of young children to give their account without unfair pressure that may cause

them to diverge from what they wish to say, while at the same time permitting defense counsel (within clearly defined limits) to test the account under cross-examination.

2. The procedure must be equally carefully managed and responsive if the child witness suffers from any functional limitations over and above those resulting from age alone. In Judge Harris's view, the incidence of children with such problems is likely to be greater among victims of abuse appearing in criminal proceedings because such children are often selected for abuse precisely because they suffer from delayed development or other problems that render them vulnerable. Self-evidently, children with such problems may experience particular difficulties giving evidence. Judge Harris believes that before any child is video-interviewed the police or social services must carry out a careful investigation, including with the child's school and doctor, to identify any cognitive, language, or communication difficulties that the child may have which could adversely affect his or her ability to cope with questioning. Appropriate arrangements can then be made to facilitate the child's interview and evidence in court, including the appointment of an intermediary, if necessary. The assessment must then be provided to the court on the commencement of a prosecution. In Judge Harris's experience, the Crown Court is only rarely given sufficient information, even at the case management hearing, about limitations that a child victim may have in his or her intellectual or psychological functioning.

3. In criminal cases in England and Wales, certain issues are deemed to be within the general knowledge of the jury, who do not therefore typically hear expert evidence on that issue. These issues include (i) the interpretation of the reliability of the answers given by a child in response to leading, suggestive, repetitive, or contaminating questions; (ii) alternative reasons, based on the child's psychological functioning, for features in his or her behavior/responses that might suggest that the child's account is untrue. In these instances, the judge will give the jury a direction tailored to the facts of the individual case, to avoid false stereotypical assumptions. In contrast, in child abuse cases in the family courts, the experienced judge may receive expert evidence on such issues if that evidence is necessary to assist the court to resolve the proceeding.* In Judge Harris's experience, in the past, when the test for the calling of such expert evidence was less stringent, psychological evidence on these issues

---

* Practice Direction 25, para 5.1; *Re TG (A Child)* [2013] EWCA Civ 5.

was incorporated and such evidence became common knowledge among practitioners and judges. A family judge, sitting on crime, therefore can have the bizarre experience of giving the stereotypical assumptions direction, reminding the jury of what is assumed to be within their common knowledge, when the judge had only acquired that knowledge through reading and hearing expert evidence on the subject. In Judge Harris's view, the criminal law approach to such matters involves a "legal fiction."

In Judge Harris's opinion, whatever may have been the merits of this last comment (which he recognizes will be contentious), the picture is fast changing, and in his view, the assumptions as to the general knowledge on the part of the jury (and the sufficiency of the stereotypical assumptions direction) are now seriously open to question, at least in a number of contexts. He relies on the following example in support of this assertion:

1. In the United Kingdom, he argues that we live in a disturbingly sexualized society. It is now known that teenagers and young people are regularly exposed to pornography via the Internet. Pornographic images very often portray women as depersonalized objects, accepting or being the unwilling recipients of violent male sexual activity. Sexting (the sending of sexually graphic text/picture messages) by young people, peer group behavior/pressures, and the (sometimes unwilling) consumption of heavy pornography have caused in certain young people what Judge Harris describes as a dangerous corruption of sexual beliefs and boundaries. This includes beliefs around sexual entitlement and the futility of resistance among females. Judge Harris argues that this has left many young people sexually confused, sometimes emotionally and behaviorally disturbed, and vulnerable to further abuse by adults. Worryingly for the criminal justice system, some are or will themselves become abusers, while others will come to sit as jurors.

2. In his view, during the last decade there has been a marked increase in the United Kingdom in the organized sexual exploitation of vulnerable children, through internal and international trafficking; the so-called street grooming by groups of men who prey on sexually vulnerable children, render them dependent/unable to escape, and pass them around for sexual gratification; and through sexual violence as part of gang-related actions. Many older children who have been abused in this way may feel that they have no option but to submit to the abuse as an inescapable fact of life. Such passivity may give the appearance of promiscuity, but in reality it does not involve true consent.

Judge Harris stated that the developments summarized in the last two paragraphs have presented difficult challenges for the police, child protection agencies, and the CPS. In the last 15 months, a number of published reports have examined the failures of multiple agencies to understand and take effective action to stop organized, serious sexual abuse of young girls by groups operating in different parts of the country.* Judge Harris cites two common and relevant themes in these reports. First, "the worrying perspective held by a number of professionals that children are complicit in, and hence responsible for, their own abuse." Second, there is a lack of awareness of the impact on children of living in dangerous environments and of the consequences of saying "no." In relation to the first theme, there is a tendency for police officers and other professionals to disbelieve the complainant child and categorize him or her as an unreliable witness, as a consequence of his or her sexual experience and chaotic lifestyle. The reports call for more effective and systematic training of professionals in dealing with complaints of the type in question. In October 2013, the then director of public prosecutions (DPP) published final guidance to prosecutors in England and Wales on the prosecution of cases involving child sexual abuse, requiring a radical change of attitude and approach by prosecutors to child complainants (Director of Public Prosecutions, 2013). The new approach focuses on the credibility of the allegation rather than whether the complainant will make a good witness and involves a better understanding of the nature and damaging impact of sexual abuse. The change in approach is correctly described as a move toward, "more sophisticated knowledge of psychology" (BBC News, 2013).

Judge Harris observes that if trained social workers, police officers, and prosecutors have consistently misunderstood the realities and psychological effects of child sexual abuse, and wrongly concluded that particular children could not be telling the truth, it must follow that the task will be far more difficult for lay jurors. He considers that "understanding," which depends on a more sophisticated knowledge of psychology, is unlikely to be within the knowledge and life experience of most jurors, and will be counterintuitive for them. The type of judicial direction that is used to avoid stereotypical assumptions may therefore be insufficient to offset the instinctive, but wrong, response of a jury that lacks a "sophisticated knowledge of psychology," that the complainant is not telling the truth.

Judge Harris feels therefore that juries would be assisted by an understanding that the judicial direction given is consistent with the consensus of expert opinion. In general, the law currently prohibits the use of such expert evidence. At the heart of that exclusionary rule is the need to avoid the time and cost of potentially disputed expert evidence. There may, however, be a

---

* See, for example, Berelowitz et al. (2012, 2013).

viable alternative course that would assist the jury in the majority of cases. In an important decision on the principles to be applied in deciding a contact dispute involving relevant allegations of domestic violence,* the court of appeal approved and annexed to its judgment a report from two distinguished child and adolescent psychiatrists. This report, among other matters, explored the range of harmful consequences of domestic violence on a child and a child's primary carer. The report eventually became received wisdom in family cases, in the main obviating the need for expert evidence of that nature in subsequent cases. A similar form of authoritative and uncontentious psychological report in support of the avoidance of stereotypical assumptions direction, which would constitute evidence in the case, may be helpful in giving the jury a better understanding of the validity of the basic direction. There may, however, be cases where the psychological effects and potential behavioral consequences of the alleged abuse can only be covered by tailored expert evidence in the individual case. The court of appeal should be more willing to uphold the use of such evidence where appropriate.

Otherwise, Judge Harris reemphasizes (i) the need for significantly better standards of visually recorded interviews, to be achieved by more effective training of interviewing officers; (ii) the imperative need for early visually recorded cross-examination and reexamination of children; and (iii) the need for substantial improvements in the cross-examination of children so that questions are age appropriate and fair, with rigorous judicial control of questioning by the setting of ground rules in advance of the child's evidence. Again, this involves in-depth training for advocates and judges authorized to do cases involving evidence by children of child abuse. Judge Harris understands that progress is already being made in the selection of judges to undertake this work. Much remains to be done, however, if the procedure in such difficult cases is to become fit for purpose.

Relationship between Theory and Practice

When asked to what extent there should be a relationship between legal theory and practice, Judge Harris recalled Lord Denning's aphorism that, "... judges find a solution to each difficulty, while academics find a difficulty to each solution." Although ironic, in Judge Harris's opinion it illustrates the divide in England and Wales between legal academics and practitioners. Broadly speaking, in his experience there is little direct deployment of academic learning or legal theory in trials or hearings in criminal cases, either by practitioners in legal argument or by judges in their reasons for rulings. In the court of appeal and the supreme court, however, within the arguments

* Re L, V, M, H (Children) (Contact: Domestic Violence) [2001] Fam 260.

developed, there would be substantial deployment of analyses of the law as understood by academics. Such academic learning/opinion might then be adopted by appellate judges in support of their judgments. Furthermore, the argument may include (and the appellate courts may be influenced by) the approach in other jurisdictions to the issues under consideration. The appellate judgments would then be used in legal arguments and rulings in subsequent trials or hearings, but the practitioners and judges in those cases would tend to confine themselves to the legal principles set out in the judgments, rather than the supporting academic reasoning.

Influenced by his early career as an academic lawyer, Judge Harris regrets the depth of the current divide between academic law and practice, and feels it is unhealthy, saying "there really should be greater involvement and interrelationship between the two." In his view, when a first instance or trial judge has to consider the application of legal principles to a new factual situation it can be important for the judge to have a good academic understanding of how and why these principles evolved. That understanding, for example, may assist in determining how the present law should be adapted and applied to the new, and perhaps unforeseen, situation. Similarly, knowledge of the law and practice in other jurisdictions can be of considerable assistance in developing our own law and practice in appropriate areas. Judge Harris believes, for example, that had the judiciary received lectures on the lessons from other jurisdictions as to the dangers and unfairness of conventional cross-examination practice in England and Wales in relation to children, the changes that are now being introduced would have been recognized and implemented far more quickly.

Transnational Relations

Judge Harris was not authorized to sit on terrorism cases. As a circuit judge, his personal caseload in both the criminal and family jurisdictions rarely, if at all, involved consideration of transnational arrangements, except for the provisions of, and jurisprudence relating to, the European Convention on Human Rights. Judge Harris noted that in general the principles and ethos of English criminal and family law/practice have been consistent with the Strasbourg Courts' jurisprudence.

Conclusion

Judge Harris provided an insightful interview, drawing and reflecting on his experience within both the family and criminal courts. Of particular interest for the interviewers were his perspectives on the reform required in the treatment of child witnesses in the criminal courts, in particular where they give evidence in cases of alleged child abuse. As Judge Harris indicates, this is a key concern in England and Wales at the moment, and as noted, has recently involved the development of guidelines on prosecuting cases of child sexual abuse by the former DPP. Detailed training guidance has also been published by practitioners' training organizations, notably The Advocacy Training Council. Judge Harris's concerns regarding the impact of the cuts to legal aid on the administration of justice are also worthy of repetition. This is a major worry for all of those who are involved in the legal system, from complainants and defendants through to the judiciary, due to the very real potential for such "reforms" to undo the progress that has been made in relation to criminal case building and management over the last 10 years.

From the considered responses that Judge Harris gave it was clear during the interview that he was portraying an honest picture of the current issues facing the UK judiciary along with suggestions for how the judicial process could ensure it applies an effective approach to enable an equitable conclusion to proceedings. It is the feeling that he was open throughout the whole of the interview and this was also evident in his enthusiasm to assist in the write-up of the interview along with proofreading this chapter to ensure that his views remained open and transparent for those reading his interview.

Leslie Cuthbert, South Eastern Circuit Recorder

11

GAVIN OXBURGH

Contents

Introduction

Although he has sat as a judge in crown courts that hear criminal cases, for most of Recorder Cuthbert's judicial career he has sat on tribunals. This reflects the administration of the justice system in the United Kingdom, as a great deal of judicial work is now undertaken by tribunals, which are designed to be a less formal, quicker, and cheaper method of resolving issues surrounding, for example, welfare benefits, immigration, detention due to mental health problems, and so on. There are a number of these first-tier tribunals and from them appeal leads to what is known as the Upper Tribunal, which reduces the burden on the high court from having to deal with judicial review applications. The introduction of tribunals followed the Leggatt Report* in 2002 and was given further structure by the Tribunals, Courts and Enforcement Act 2007.

Her Majesty's Courts and Tribunals Service (HMCTS) provides an overall administrative and supportive function to all courts and a number of tribunals. The Judicial College similarly provides education, training, and

* http://www.adminlaw.org.uk/docs/Response%20to%20the%20Leggatt%20Report.

support to all judges within the HMCTS structure including in some tribunals appraisals against a competency framework. The competencies are split into distinct categories, namely, knowledge of the relevant law and procedure in the jurisdiction, assessing evidence, decision making, and the conduct of cases including equality, diversity, and communication. Appraisals for judges in courts have just begun to be piloted.

Not all bodies performing judicial work sit within the courts and tribunals structure, however, in that regulators of professionals, for example, doctors, nurses, and so on, have their own quasi-judicial processes, which are not contained within HMCTS. Similarly, a number of bodies where civil sanctions are imposed fall outside of the first-tier tribunal structure such as the Road User Charging Tribunal. Some tribunals have a single, legally qualified adjudicator or judge, and other tribunals are made up of a mixture of lay members and specialist members with experience in law, medicine, nursing, employment matters, and similar.

Career

Recorder Leslie Cuthbert qualified as a solicitor in 1996, becoming a partner in a firm of criminal defense solicitors. In 2000, he became a solicitor advocate, handling cases in the crown court and higher courts before obtaining his first judicial appointment in 2002. While still on the list of counsel for the International Criminal Court, the International Criminal Tribunal for the former Yugoslavia, and the Special Court for Sierra Leone, he now spends more time sitting in a judicial capacity and in training investigators, lawyers, and judges.

Q: Tell us a little bit about your career? (Try and include the length of service as a judge, organizations worked in, movements, specializations, etc.)

A: I qualified as a solicitor in 1996 and specialized in criminal defense work including international criminal defense work. I got my first judicial appointment as a road user charging adjudicator in 2002. After that, I was appointed as a tribunal judge for the Mental Health Tribunal in 2007, an independent adjudicator for Companies House in 2009, a part-time crown court judge (known as a recorder), also in 2009, and finally a panel chair for the Nursing and Midwifery Council's Conduct and Competence Committee in 2012.

Q: As your career as a judge has developed what has surprised you?

A: Essentially, making decisions has become much easier and quicker as I have got more and more experience and grown to believe in my own judgment. Also, the recognition that as a judge you will never have all the facts or evidence that you might wish to have available and that you need to fight against this "need for cognitive closure" in order to make a decision on the available evidence.

Q: Has your work as a judge proved as interesting or rewarding as you thought it would when you first started?

A: Absolutely. I continue to love it, especially the variety of the work as well as the opportunity to share knowledge or experience gained in one area in another jurisdiction.

Personal Judicial Philosophy

Q: What do you think should be the role of the judiciary in society?

A: As an independent, impartial voice upholding the "rule of law." Accordingly, the judiciary must have the highest ethical standards both while performing their judicial role and also in their private life.

Q: What should be their job, functions, and roles? What should be left to others?

A: They should not be setting policy or determining the course of society, but rather should reflect the views and opinions of the population tempered by wisdom and an awareness that "the mob" can often be wrong and that knee-jerk reactions are rarely appropriate. The judiciary need to do all they can to ensure that people live in a just society and that abuses of the rule of law are not allowed to occur.

Q: What organizational arrangements work and which do not?

A: A separation of powers between the judiciary, the executive, and the legislative is important to ensure that the judiciary remain independent and impartial, so there cannot afford to be situations whereby the judiciary are under threat if they do not act in accordance with the wishes of the executive. This applies whether in regard to appraisals of the judiciary, salary negotiations, or appointments of judges.

Q: What policies on relations with the community, with political groups, and with other criminal justice organizations work well? What hampers cooperation with other agencies and groups?

A: The media often hamper relations where they do not accurately or fully report on judgments and decisions made by judges. People need to be able to come to court and see the situation in operation, to speak to judges outside the courtroom so that they can understand that they are just as human as anyone else.

Given the separation of powers, it is also important that judges always reveal any political connections or strong views that they have expressed elsewhere to demonstrate that justice will not only be done but will be seen to be done, so whenever there is the potential for a conflict of interest the judge will do all he or she can to prevent this potential problem from undermining the ultimate determination in the case.

Q: How difficult is it for judges to relate to the living and social conditions of those from economically deprived backgrounds who appear before them?

A: It obviously depends on the judge's own background. I personally come from what I would describe as a working-class background; I didn't attend Oxford or Cambridge Universities, but some judges did. It is impossible for everyone to understand every member of society's frame of reference but just because I have never taken drugs doesn't mean that I can't empathize with someone who has a drug addiction. I also believe that any judge needs to continue to engage with popular culture in a variety of ways.

Q: How can a judge develop empathy for those from the lower rungs of the social divisions in society from which they can derive a degree of understanding of why the person before them might have done what is alleged?

A: By meeting and listening to different people, by reading books, by watching films, by recognizing that there are lots of different life experiences that people may encounter.

Q: How should the criminal legal system in the United Kingdom perform? What should be the preferred priorities and strategies: hard-edged crime control, prevention, services, or ordered work, what mix for which types of problems?

A: There needs to be a degree of codification; there needs to be simple and clear guidance rather than convoluted and never-ending "tinkering" with the system. Instead any changes need to be given time to be implemented and time to be reflected on, before more changes are made and the system becomes fragmented. The preferred priorities and strategies have to be focused around the rule of law, public protection, and as far as possible, the rehabilitation of offenders to reduce offending in the future. Recidivism is a huge issue within England and Wales, where the rate is much higher than, for example, in some Scandinavian countries.

Problems and Successes Experienced

Q: In your experience, what policies or programs have worked well and which have not? Can you speculate for what reasons?

A: It is difficult to say because of the lack of time to allow policies or programs to bed in. One aspect that I consider has worked is the introduction of sentencing guidelines for different offenses, which has
led to a much greater consistency of approach between judges.

Also, the introduction of technology, for example, computers,
iPads, and digital recording, is starting to lead to efficiencies in the
process itself.

Q: What would you consider to be the greatest problem facing the criminal
courts at this time?

A: A lack of funding in the courts and for advocates on both sides. This will
lead to delays, inefficiencies, and potential miscarriages of justice
especially if more and more defendants must represent themselves.
This will inevitably lead to judges becoming more interventionist
and as a result there is the potential that there will be a shift away
from the traditional "adversarial" system to a more "inquisitorial"
approach, as currently exists within coroners' courts.

Q: What problem in courts do you find is the most difficult to deal with?

A: Individuals who lack legal knowledge representing themselves, especially
those who refuse to recognize the legal process. This is because the
judge must then seek to both educate and assist at times to ensure
that a fair trial occurs.

Q: What would be easy to change? Internal problems (culture of the organization, managerial deficiencies, allegations of corruption, gender-
related problems, etc.) or externally generated problems (resources,
community support, etc.)? Is anything easy?

A: Nothing relating to money or investment is easy, but allowing time before
introducing yet more new criminal offenses or more complicated
legislation would immediately give everyone involved the chance
to catch up to the current legal framework.

Theory and Practice

Q: What should be the relationship between theory and practice?

A: Reciprocal, in that theory must be rooted in practice and needs to develop
as practice grows and vice versa. Neither can be looked at in
isolation.

Q: What can practitioners learn from theory and what can theory builders
learn from practitioners?

A: Practitioners can find different ways of approaching problems from seeing the theory, while practitioners may be forced to be creative in
their efforts, which may prompt the theory builders to develop new
models on the basis of a spontaneous practical event.

Q: What is the relationship right now? Does it exist? Does it work?

A: The reciprocal relationship does work, to a degree, but due to the lack of time given, it hasn't had the chance to work as well as it could.

Q: What holds collaboration or interactions back?

A: Time to reflect and opportunities to discuss.

Q: What kind of research, in what form, and on what questions, would you find most useful for practice? If not very useful, what could or should theory builders do to make their products more useful to you?

A: In the United Kingdom, judges don't have enough training in psychological principles—for example, the work by Loftus on memory and the importance of the structure and content of questions asked.

Q: Where do you find theory-based information? Where do you look? What journals, books, publications, or reports do you consult?

A: Various journals, *CrimeLine*, Archibald's *Criminal Procedure*, Judicial College monthly bulletins, *The Times Law Reports*, *The Business of Judging*—book, *Making Your Case*—book, *II-RP* journal.

Q: Does the judiciary carry out supplementary research outside the research required for pending cases? If so, what are the areas, issues, or questions of law that are researched?

A: The Sentencing Council certainly does in its efforts to ensure consistency of sentences for specific offenses, plus there are other initiatives such as The Advocate's Gateway,* a website focused on improving the questioning of vulnerable defendants and witnesses, which the judiciary are very supportive of.

Transnational Relations

Q: Have you and the work of your organization been affected by developments outside the country (human rights demands, universal codes of ethics, practical interactions with judges or justices from other countries, personal experiences outside the country, new crime threats, etc.), and if so, how?

A: I have had judges from different countries attend to observe my work and have had the chance to speak with them and learn about the different ways that they conduct criminal trials, for example, a Japanese judge came to sit with me for a week.

　　While discussing their approaches has been interesting, it has not as yet had any actual impact on my own judge-craft, that is, the approach I take while sitting as a judge.

---

* www.theadvocatesgateway.org.

Q: Have those interactions been beneficial or harmful? What kind of external international influences are beneficial and which ones less so?

A: The interactions I have had have been beneficial in terms of demonstrating the different ways different cultures approach the same issues.

Q: How have developments post the terrorist attack on the United States on September 11, 2001, affected your work?

A: No direct effect, but indirectly through legislation that was introduced following the attacks.

General Assessments

Q: Are you basically satisfied or dissatisfied with developments in criminal law and criminal procedure in your system?

A: Basically, I am satisfied that more is right with the system than is wrong with it. The underlying structure is right; it is how it is sometimes fleshed out that is problematic.

Q: What are the most likely developments you see happening and which would you like to see happening?

A: I fear that due to budgetary constraints there may be a shift toward a more inquisitorial approach as the only means of ensuring a fair trial if the quality of advocacy in the adversarial system deteriorates.

Q: What is most needed now to improve the system?

A: Politicians and the media leaving the system alone for a while to allow those involved in it time to reflect, plus, if it were possible, the input of money to ensure that cases are prosecuted and defended as efficiently as possible.

Reflections on the Interview

What is interesting in this interview is the focus on tribunal hearings. Although he is a part-time crown court judge hearing criminal trials, Recorder Cuthbert's main role is sitting on tribunals, mainly mental health tribunals. Providing an insight into the role of adjudicating in tribunals, one can see from Recorder Cuthbert's responses that there is little difference between what judges' face in their role in tribunals and in more formal court settings. Being a recorder, he is in a position to evaluate the role of a judge in both legal settings. This is seen in his views on codification, where Recorder Cuthbert sees the need for simple, clear guidance on the legal provision.

United States IX
Legal System

PETER C. KRATCOSKI, BLAKE M.
RANDOL AND LAUREN M. BLOCK

Federal Courts

The United States has a federal court system for the entire nation, and each of the 50 states has its own judicial structure. The federal court structure's highest court is the supreme court, consisting of a chief justice and eight associate judges. Within the guidelines established by Congress, and at its own discretion, it hears cases that began in the federal or state courts that usually involve important questions regarding the Constitution or federal law. The US district courts are the trial courts of the federal court system.

These courts hear federal cases involving both civil and criminal matters, including bankruptcy cases. There are 94 federal judicial districts, with each state, the District of Columbia and Puerto Rico having at least one district. Three US territories also have district courts. In addition, the Court of International Trade hears cases related to customs and international matters, and the US Court of Federal Claims hears cases involving monetary matters. At the next level, the 94 judicial districts are organized into 12 regional circuits, and each has a US Court of Appeals, which hears appeals from the district courts and appeals from decisions of federal administrative agencies. The state judiciaries consist of several levels, with the highest being the supreme court.*

---

* Federal courts structure, retrieved from http:www.uscourts.gov/FederalCourts.aspx (accessed November 10, 2013).

Civil and Criminal Law

Federal and state courts handle both civil and criminal cases. Civil law aims to protect the interests of individuals. It deals with disputes between people or organizations involving property, contracts, or personal injuries. Individuals bear the responsibility of bringing a civil action and are known as the plaintiffs. For example, the dissolution of a marriage contract would be a civil matter. A case involving an individual suing a driver who caused a car accident that resulted in injury would also be a civil matter. The standard of proof in civil cases is a preponderance of the evidence, or at least 51% certainty that the defendant was responsible for the harm. This is much lower than the standard of proof for criminal cases because the penalties for civil cases are not as extreme. Most civil matters end in some form of compensation.

In contrast, criminal law aims to protect the interests of society. It addresses individuals who commit wrongs against the state, such as murder, child abuse, fraud, prostitution, and possession of illicit drugs. Because these matters are viewed as crimes against the state, the state bears the responsibility for charging an individual with a crime. The standard of proof in criminal cases is proof beyond a reasonable doubt, a much higher standard compared with civil matters. This is because being found guilty of a crime results in the punishment of an individual and this punishment can range from a minor fine to death depending on the seriousness of the offense.

State Courts

There are 50 states in the United States, each with their own unique court systems and set of laws. Due to the unique nature of each state's laws, it can be very difficult to generalize about state courts because they are different depending on where the court is located. There are some similarities across states that will be discussed.

States will delineate between different types of crime depending on the seriousness of the offense. Misdemeanors are less serious offenses that carry lesser punishments. For example, the possession of small amounts of illicit drugs, prostitution, and theft of inexpensive items are often considered misdemeanors. A typical penalty for misdemeanors will involve a fine, probation, or a short jail sentence. Felonies are more serious offenses that carry more severe punishments. For example, homicide would be a felony and a conviction would carry a long prison sentence or even death. Many states also have a third designation for minor violations or infractions. These are the least serious crimes, such as traffic offenses, and are usually punished by a fine.

Similar to the federal court system, there is a hierarchy of courts within states. States will often have a court of limited jurisdiction (frequently known as municipal courts, county courts, district courts, or metropolitan courts) as their lowest court. The jurisdiction of these courts is typically limited to those less serious criminal cases, including misdemeanors, ordinance violations, and traffic violations. Courts of limited jurisdiction may also handle the arraignments, bail hearings, and preliminary hearings for felonies before they are transferred to courts of general jurisdiction. There are approximately 13,500 courts of limited jurisdiction in the United States and they account for 90% of all state courts (Friedman, 2004). Most of the crime committed in the United States falls within the jurisdiction of these courts, and therefore they handle very high caseloads and focus on moving cases through in a timely and efficient manner.

Courts of general jurisdiction handle more serious crimes, and are frequently known as felony courts, superior courts, or circuit courts. While the arraignments, bail hearings, and preliminary hearings for these cases can happen in the lower court, once an individual has been indicted for an offense that falls within the court of general jurisdiction, the rest of his or her proceedings will take place there. Some states do not have courts of limited jurisdiction and these general jurisdiction courts will handle all the criminal cases for the jurisdiction.

The majority of states have an intermediate court of appeals, which is an appeals court that focuses on reviewing cases from the lower courts that are appealed. This is where defendants can appeal the decisions in their case based on legal reasoning, but similar to federal courts of appeals, these courts do not retry cases. The majority of states give defendants a right to appeal, and therefore must review and give a decision in each appeal they receive. As a result, these appeal courts often have very high caseloads. Each state also has a state supreme court, which is the highest appeals court within the state jurisdiction. The state supreme court will hear appeals from the lower courts.

Judges in state courts become judges in several different ways. They are typically either elected by popular vote or appointed by the state legislature or state governor. There are advantages and disadvantages to both of these methods (American Judicature Society, 2008). While having the public vote on judges ensures a democratic process, most citizens lack the knowledge needed to make an informed vote. In addition, judges are valued by remaining neutral and making decisions on a case-by-case basis. Therefore, having them run on a political platform compromises their neutrality. In contrast, the process of appointing judges can help ensure that quality judges are selected. However, state legislators or governors may also rely on personal relationships and political affiliation to make their decisions. In some states, a nonpartisan commission will give recommendations about qualified judges to the governor, and the governor will then choose from the recommendations.

This judicial selection method is known as merit selection or "the Missouri Plan." Each state will use their own unique variation or combination of these methods for judicial selection.

Editors' Note

As there are slight differences in the administration of justice and the judicial role between the 50 states in the United States, the following chapters of the interviews with US judges contain a brief account of the legal system for each of the states' jurisdictions.

Sharron L. Kennedy, Ohio Supreme Court

12

PETER C. KRATCOSKI

Contents

Introduction

The state of Ohio (Figure 12.1), located in the midwestern United States, ranks as the 34th largest state in area and 7th in population. There are three metropolitan areas in Ohio with populations exceeding 2 million inhabitants. The cities located in these metropolitan areas with a population of more than 2 million include Columbus, the state capital and largest city, Cleveland, and Cincinnati. The largest groups according to ethnic background are Germans, Irish, English, those of Slavic ancestry, and Italians. The largest racial groups are white Americans (83%), African Americans (12%), and Hispanics or Latinos (3%).

Ohio's state university system consists of 13 state universities with 24 branches and regional campuses, 46 private colleges and universities, six medical schools, 15 community colleges, eight technical colleges and 24 independent non-profit colleges. The State University System of Ohio has an annual enrolment of over 400,000 students, making it one of the five largest state university systems in the United States.

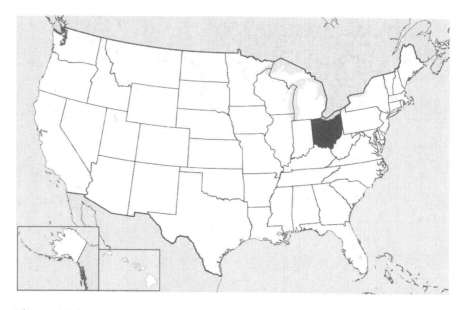

Figure 12.1 Map of Ohio.

Career

Sharon L. Kennedy graduated from Northwest High School in 1980. Thereafter, she enrolled in the University of Cincinnati's School of Social Work and received a bachelor's degree in social work in 1984. In 1985, she achieved her childhood dream of serving as a police officer when she accepted employment with the City of Hamilton Police Department. She resigned as a full-time officer in August 1988 to pursue a law degree at the University of Cincinnati College of Law. During her first year of law school, she remained at the Hamilton Police Department as a civilian assistant to the chief of police and assisted in the drafting of police procedure and policy for the Accreditation Program. Leaving the department in May 1985, she began clerking for the Honorable Matthew J. Crehan, judge of the Court of Common Pleas, General Division, Butler County, Ohio. After graduating from law school, she became licensed to practice law in the state of Ohio in 1991 and began a general private practice in the City of Hamilton in 1992. She remained in private practice until being elected and sworn in as a judge of the Court of Common Pleas, Domestic Relations Division in Butler County, Ohio, in January 1999. She held that position until her election to the Ohio Supreme Court in 2012. She is currently serving her first term of office in that position.

Q: Justice Kennedy, in the interviews of judges we are completing for our books on the role of the judiciary, we are interested in obtaining information about the personal lives of the judges as well as information about the positions they hold. Would you please tell me why you decided to become a member of the legal profession? Be as personal as you want. For example, were there experiences in your childhood, higher education, or in another occupation that had an influence on your decision?

A: I consider myself the least likely person to serve as the 154th Justice of the Ohio Supreme Court. I grew up in a working-class family in the suburbs of Cincinnati, Ohio. My parents were born poor during the Great Depression. Despite growing up poor, my parents rejoiced at the promise of America and taught me to believe that, regardless of circumstances, anyone can achieve the American dream as long as they are willing to do three things. First, they must decide and commit. Second, they must work hard. Third, they must have fortitude, meaning that they can never give up.

As a child, all I ever wanted to do was to serve as a police officer. The first thought of becoming a lawyer was planted by a high school teacher. That teacher challenged me to look beyond the dream of serving as a law enforcement officer and inspired me to believe that I could be a lawyer and even a judge someday.

After obtaining my college degree, I was hired by the Hamilton Police Department to serve as a law enforcement officer. Assigned to a rotating patrol unit, I worked in a number of different areas in the city. Serving as a police officer was a great opportunity. It taught me how to deal with all types of people and situations and challenged me to think on my feet, applying the law in "real time." Serving as a police officer also gave me the opportunity to see the inner workings of the entire justice system and meet other professionals within that system. Until that time, I had never met a lawyer or a judge. I remember the day that I decided to go to law school. I was on the witness stand, being poorly cross-examined by a defense attorney, and thought, if he could graduate from law school, then I could too.

Resigning from the department was bittersweet. Looking back, that was to become one of the greatest defining moments of my life. That decision would foresee my future.

I remained at the City of Hamilton Police Department as a civilian assistant to the chief, working on the Accreditation Program during my first year of law school. In the spring of my first year in law school, I began clerking for the Honorable Matthew J. Crehan, judge of the General Division of the Court of Common Pleas in Butler County, Ohio. Working primarily on civil filings, the clerkship afforded me an opportunity to work

within the noncriminal aspects of the law. As I look back, serving
as a clerk for this judge would become another unforeseen path
in my life's journey, for as my clerkship was coming to an end,
one afternoon, Judge Crehan asked me, "What do you want to
do when you finish law school and get your degree?" I told him I
would like to hang out a shingle and eventually one day I would
like to do what he did, serve as a judge in the court of common
pleas. In response he said, "I can see your dream becoming a reality, you have the ability, motivation, understanding of the law,
and desire to assist people that is needed to be a good judge." He
continued, "Kid, you're so young, you could make it all the way to
the Ohio Supreme Court." I remembering laughing at the notion
that I could make it to serve as a judge, let alone a supreme court
justice.

It was his encouragement that set me on the path to joining the
local Young Republican Club and that became the genesis of my
work in politics. Being a member of the club, then eventually the
president, I met and associated with many young people with a
passion to preserve conservative principles. It also allowed me to
meet elected officials from all levels of government, including my
congressman, now Speaker of the House, John Boehner. Serving in
the Young Republican Club also gave me an opportunity to attend
campaign seminars, volunteer on campaigns, and eventually manage campaigns.

I began practicing law in 1992. As a general practitioner, I handled a variety of cases for a diverse client population. In the back
of my mind, I still had a desire to be a judge and in 1998, when the
opportunity arose to run for a judgeship in the Court of Common
Pleas, Domestic Relations Division in Butler County, I entered the
race. Even though I was considered the underdog, having little
chance of winning, I beat the incumbent.

In 2012, I decided to run for justice of the Ohio Supreme Court.
As Ohio's court of last resort, I believed I could best serve my
community by serving on the court as a justice who would follow
the law, not rewrite it or legislate from the bench. In November
2012, I was elected to an unexpired term on the Ohio Supreme
Court.

I continue to believe and have faith that the future of America
rests with our commitment to adhere to the Constitution and
the balance of governmental power between three separate but
coequal branches of government: the executive, the legislative,
and the judicial. I further believe that one of the key factors in the
economic growth and stability of Ohio rests in our adherence to

the rule of law and its fair and impartial application. Every year, the Heritage Foundation projects which countries will grow economically. Of the factors considered, the existence of the rule of law and its fair and impartial application leading to the stability and predictability of the law is paramount to economic viability and growth. Countries wherein their governments do not have a foundational belief and adherence to the rule of law and its fair and impartial application cannot thrive.

Q: As you progressed through your career, did you ever have doubts about your career choice?

A: No doubts whatsoever. When I discovered the law, I was home.

Q: Did you anticipate becoming a judge someday when you first started your career in the legal profession?

A: No. My professional goal was always to serve as a police officer. I became interested in the other professions of the justice system while in high school, but never dreamed I would become a lawyer, let alone a judge. Achieving my dream of serving as a police officer opened professional pathways I did not appreciate or realize existed for me.

Q: Tracing your career as an attorney, what were some of the major high points of your career?

A: There are no landmark cases, but serving the people of one's community is a rewarding achievement. As a lawyer in private practice, I am proud to say that I protected the lives of children, our seniors, and the mentally ill. I was able to fight on behalf of the taxpayers, defend the Constitution and our right to live free from government intrusion, and give a voice to my clients.

Q: Were there times when you thought the legal profession was the wrong type of work and perhaps working in some other profession would be more satisfying?

A: No. I always believed, even as a child, that the legal profession was where I belonged. My view of serving the legal profession was as a police officer. I could not have imagined all of the pathways that would open as I served as a law enforcement officer.

Personal Judicial Philosophy

Q: What is your personal judicial philosophy on the role of the judiciary in society?

A: Our society is foundationally based on the Constitution of the United States. In 1803, when Ohio became a state, the Ohio Constitution set forth the powers of the executive branch, the legislative branch, and the judicial branch. As outlined in that document, the powers of the judiciary are limited to applying the law as written in a fair and impartial manner. Legislative enactments are presumed constitutional, and it is only when such law is challenged and proven to violate an article of the Constitution that a court may strike it down. As such, I believe my role is limited, and the exercise of judicial power is one of restraint. Regardless of my personal opinion or belief, I am required to uphold the law as written, not rewrite it or legislate from the bench.

Q: Justice Kennedy, as a follow-up to the previous question, can you think of any present day legal matter in which you think the judiciary is obligated to take a more activist role? (For example, the civil rights movement was based on civil disobedience to laws that were perceived as being unjust and the supreme court's activism on civil rights matters stimulated significant changes in society.)

A: No.

Q: In your opinion, are there changes in the administration (philosophy) of the courts (legal system) that you consider a more progressive approach to justice in Ohio than what was followed in the past?

A: Actually, given the historical perspective of the Ohio Supreme Court, I believe that there is a greater exercise of judicial restraint.

Q: Justice Kennedy, would you like to offer an opinion on the method used to select judges in Ohio?

A: When Ohio became a state in 1803, with the exception of the governor, the General Assembly appointed all judges and government officials. With each new General Assembly and change of power came massive turnover in those appointments. The Constitutional Convention of 1850 changed all of that. In a move to create a more democratic state government, in 1851 a new Ohio Constitution was adopted giving the people the right to vote on government officials and judicial posts.

　　While I am open to a conversation about the election of judges, the decision to change their constitutional rights and limit their democratic voice remains with the people of Ohio. I believe the past 20 years have provided significant evidence that there are pros and cons to elections and there are pros and cons to having merit selection and retention elections.

　　Given the methods of judicial selection, I am of the belief that the voice of the people and their right to vote is best. No one can remove politics from any decision-making process established by government. Evidence demonstrates that the retention election system does not yield a better judiciary. When viewed in the light of election outcomes, in 65% of all retention elections judges are retained. This equates to a lifetime appointment. Worse yet, recent trends demonstrate that retention elections have become the battleground on a "single-issue" decision. The historical evidence of Pennsylvania, Illinois, and Iowa demonstrated the largest infusion of money into retention elections and in some cases a complete overturn in the judiciary.

The argument to erode an individual's right to seek an elective judicial office, to stand before their fellow man and ask for their faith and trust through a vote, and the argument to erode the people's right to vote in judicial elections is striking, especially when individuals have the freedom and right to seek to become president and the people have the right to vote for the leader of the free world.

Q: Justice Kennedy, in your opinion, what recent civil law case/s ruled on by the Ohio Supreme Court had a significant impact on the citizens of Ohio?

A: The civil case with the greatest impact was *Westfield v. Galatis*, 100 Ohio St.3d 216, 2003-Ohio-5849. In *Galatis*, the Ohio Supreme Court established three standards on which a court can rely to abandon prior precedence. The court held, "a prior decision of the Supreme Court may be overruled where (1) the decision was wrongly decided at that time or changes in circumstances no longer justify continued adherence to the decision, (2) the decision defies practical workability, and (3) abandoning the precedent would not create an undue hardship for those who have relied upon it."

Q: In your opinion, what recent criminal law case/s ruled on by the Ohio Supreme Court had a significant impact on those charged/convicted of crime?

A: The most recent criminal law case was *State v. Bodyke*, 126 Ohio St.3d 266, 2010-Ohio-2424. In that case, the Ohio Supreme Court held that the reclassification scheme of Ohio's Adam Walsh Act was unconstitutional, as it violated the separation of powers doctrine.

Q: Do you know of any specific piece of legislation by the Ohio legislature that you consider detrimental to the "quality" of justice in Ohio?

A: No.

Problems and Successes Experienced

Q: Justice Kennedy, Would you describe the "typical day" of an Ohio Supreme Court Justice?

A: There is no typical day for a justice of the Ohio Supreme Court. The court is in session year-round and court conference is typically held every other week on Tuesday and Wednesday. Before court conference, each justice will receive a copy of the cases scheduled for that court conference.

Cases fall into two general categories: jurisdictionals and non-jurisdictionals. Jurisdictional cases fall under Article 4 Section 2(B)(2)(e) of the Ohio Constitution. Those cases are discretionary appeals, which must present a matter of "public or great general interest." Nonjurisdictional cases fall under Article 4 Section 2(B) (1) and (2) of the Ohio Constitution. Those cases are matters of original jurisdiction and appeals as a matter of right.

When in session, oral arguments begin at 9:00 a.m. on Tuesdays and Wednesdays. Case conference is held on the conclusion of oral arguments. Case conference begins with a discussion of the cases heard in oral argument. Beginning with the chief justice and then in order of seniority, each justice, without interruption, will state their opinion of the case and assert a cursory vote. When the justice with the least seniority concludes, a general discussion will ensue. During this discussion, points of law and inquiry of others' views may occur. On conclusion of that discussion, a final vote is taken with the newest member of the court voting first. When all the orally argued cases are voted on, a justice is assigned to write the majority opinion. Despite living in the technology age, the author of the majority opinion is selected by what I call the "bingo ball" method. Each member of the court is assigned a number and each number has a corresponding bingo ball. The numbered balls of those justices who voted in the majority are then placed in a leather wrapped bottle. The first ball rolled out of the bottle is read and that justice writes for the majority. After all oral argument cases are assigned, the court will begin voting on the jurisdictional and nonjurisdictional cases.

At the conclusion of conference, each justice manages his or her own schedule and work of the court individually. As a justice, I spend a significant amount of time traveling Ohio and speaking to groups about the court, the law, and my pathway to serving as the 154th justice of the Ohio Supreme Court.

Q: Are there days/times when the work becomes much more stressful than the "typical day"?

A: No. Each justice balances the timely completion of the work of the court with the requests for public appearances. Unlike my service in the trial court, serving as a justice is not a Monday through Friday schedule. As a justice, I have a very flexible schedule and work all hours of the day and night, including weekends. That flexibility is central to maintaining my independent speaking schedule, which often requires driving considerable distances.

Q: Justice Kennedy, reflecting on your judicial career, what are some of the most important changes that have taken place in the law and the justice system in Ohio?

A: While there are many changes in the law that have impacted the administration of justice in Ohio, I believe the two most significant changes that have taken place are the dawning of and implementation of treatment models and means of handling family violence.

I am of the firm belief that the beginning of treatment models commenced in the 1800s when there was recognition that juvenile offenders should be treated differently than adult offenders. In that era came juvenile delinquency prevention and reform school models. The focus was on positive behavior modification with the final goal being that the child became a productive adult in our society.

This shift to prevention and treatment, of curing the underlying condition of the child, was made possible through the creation of juvenile courts and the distinct change in the nature of the case. By the twentieth century, most states across the United States had created juvenile courts. In 1902, Ohio established the first juvenile court in Cuyahoga County. While a juvenile offender was subject to punishment, the case itself was a civil matter.

During that same time came the dawn of probation programs. Juvenile courts, with a focus on intervention and rehabilitation, were a natural fit for probation programs. Through this birth came programs for adult offenders. However, it wasn't until the mid-1990s that courts took a more active role in the intervention and treatment of adult offenders. In 1995, Ohio established the first specialized docket drug court in Hamilton County. Under Chief Justice Thomas Moyer, in 2001 the Ohio Supreme Court created the first specialized docket program. Today, there are drug courts, mental health courts, reentry courts, OVI (operating a vehicle while intoxicated) courts, veteran's courts, sexual offender courts, felony nonsupport courts, and domestic violence courts.

As it relates to family violence, long gone is the opinion that what happened in one's home between a husband and wife was not subject to government intervention. As a law enforcement officer in the 1980s, my ability to arrest for a misdemeanor violation was if I witnessed the crime. All other misdemeanors were subject to the swearing out of a complaint by the victim.

In 1994, with the enactment of H.B. 335, Ohio dramatically changed course. That legislation mandated that law enforcement officers who had probable cause to believe an act of domestic violence had occurred were required to arrest the aggressor. If a law enforcement officer did not make an arrest, then the officer was required to specifically state the reasons for not making an arrest.

Through this legislation also came the right to obtain a domestic violence protection order. In a criminal case, temporary civil protection orders were issued in the court handling the criminal charge. However, proceeding with a criminal offense was not required. In cases in which a family or household member did not make a criminal complaint or call the police, they could make a civil petition in the domestic division of the court of common pleas and nonfamily members could file a petition for a civil stalking protection order in the general division of the court of common pleas.

Q: Justice Kennedy, do you regard the establishment of specialty courts, such as drug courts and honor courts, and other specializations in the municipal and common pleas courts as being a positive development?

A: I do. The justice system is part of a larger governmental system and a member of the community in which it functions. All systems within the governmental unit compete for operational tax dollars and within that context they should have a primary goal of efficient and effective operation. The realization of that goal benefits the community within which the governmental system functions through fiscal and resource conservation.

Typically, as a whole, the criminal justice system is the largest user of fiscal resources. While there are many branches of government within the "criminal justice system," the courts have the power to engage in specific problem solving based on case type that can reduce delays and efficiently process those cases, while closing the door of recidivism by treating the root cause of the criminal behavior instead of the criminal behavior that is merely a symptom of the root cause. While I understand that some judges believe such treatment models are not the role or function of the court, the reality is that the courts are part of a larger community and the courts have an obligation to help improve the welfare of the community. Today, drug courts, mental health courts, reentry courts, OVI courts, veteran's courts, sexual offender courts, felony nonsupport courts, and domestic violence courts are tackling the tough job of treatment and behavior modification so that all of us within our communities live free of criminal behavior.

Q: Do you know of any cases that have challenged the constitutionality of specialty courts?

A: No, there have been no constitutional challenges to specialty courts.

Q: Justice Kennedy, have you noticed any changes in the philosophy of the supreme court since you became a supreme court justice?

A: Since being sworn in on December 7, 2012, I have not noticed any dramatic change.

Q: Have the powers (jurisdiction) of the courts in Ohio changed or remained the same during the time you have been a judge? If there has been change, have you been involved in these changes?

A: Article IV of the Ohio Constitution established the power of the judiciary and the courts. Additional legislative enactments supplement the jurisdictional limitation of the courts.

As a trial judge in the Domestic Relations Division of the Court of Common Pleas, Butler County, I was involved in amending the jurisdiction of the Domestic Relations Division in order to stop multiple forum litigation regarding custody and support of children. Prior to the change, child custody and support cases of married couples who were living separate and apart were filed in the juvenile division. If the married couple then commenced a divorce action, jurisdiction of the custody and support case remained in the juvenile court. As a result, parties were litigating in two forums.

After the jurisdictional modification of the General Assembly, a married couple living separate and apart who seek custody or support order or both files in the Domestic Relations Division. If a complaint for divorce is later filed, then the cases are combined.

Q: Has the use of modern technology led to improvements in the efficiency and effectiveness of legal/justice administration of the supreme court?

A: Yes. The computerization of the courts has dramatically improved the accuracy and efficiency of case management and reporting. Improvements in audio recording technology have also enabled courts to reduce staff needs and efficiently store and manage the record of the court.

As a justice of the Ohio Supreme Court, technology allows me to vote on expedited cases from anywhere and live streaming of oral arguments advances civic education. Looking to the future, the Ohio Supreme Court is in the process of developing e-filing.

Personal Role/Relations in the Community and Larger Society

Q: Justice Kennedy, on a more personal level, do you experience any difficulty in adjusting your professional life to your personal life in the community?

A: No. The advancements in my career have required adjustments in my professional and personal life. The greatest transition occurred when I became a trial court judge. I became very cognizant of what litigants and lawyers who were not my social friends would think if I appeared too friendly with opposing lawyers. The look of impropriety is just as bad as actual impropriety. Because of those concerns, I did not regularly socialize with lawyers, did not engage in personal conversations in the courthouse, and maintained an arm's-length relationship with those lawyers who regularly appeared before me. These concerns have lessened since becoming a justice at the supreme court because I do not preside over trials in my community. The personal adjustment made while serving in the trial court has aided me.

Q: Do you think it is appropriate for a supreme court judge to become involved in community activities, such as fund-raising, school issues, and political issues?

A: Yes, but with some limitations. For example, I believe I can and should volunteer my time and provide personal financial assistance to community service groups and educational institutions, but the Code of Judicial Conduct rightly prohibits me from lending my name to those same fund-raising efforts.

Q: What approach (policy) regarding relations with the community works well and should be continued?

A: The Code of Judicial Conduct is controlling. Beyond that, judges need to use common sense and ask themselves, "Will this compromise my fair and impartial role as a judge or will this have the appearance of impropriety?" I also believe that all judges should regularly speak at civic and community events that provide the opportunity to explain the role of the courts and judiciary.

Q: Can you think of a specific situation in which you had to decline involvement because of a potential conflict of interest?

A: Yes. I have declined opportunities to serve as the figurehead of and as the main speaker for community fund-raising efforts when it would have the appearance of compromising my judicial independence. Additionally, I have recused from cases when the individuals involved were personally known to me or contacted me prior to the hearing.

Q: As a supreme court justice, what policies (guidelines) have been established in regard to relations with other criminal justice professional organizations (police, judiciary, corrections)? Are these policies effective? Should they be continued?

A: Like civic education in my community, I think it is important to speak to law enforcement groups about the role of the judiciary in the criminal justice system and about the rule of law.

Q: In your opinion, what factors hamper positive, effective cooperation of the judiciary (referring to courts at all levels) with other public agencies and private groups in the community?

A: The competition for fiscal resources has created tension between the judiciary and other government entities. Within the community, private groups that try to personally influence judicial outcomes hamper relationships.

Q: Justice Kennedy, specifically comment on the relations of the judiciary with the mass media (newspapers, TV). What, if any, are the major sources of problems?

A: The need of the mass media to quickly broadcast news may result in misinformation being disseminated. Judges are cautioned against and in some cases are prohibited from making public comments. Judges are prohibited from discussing any case or issue that is pending or impending in the courts. Since judges are required to uphold the law as written, their personal opinion of a law is irrelevant. Given these limitations, when a judge responds to the media with "no comment" or is unable to fully discuss a matter, the judge's response is often misunderstood as avoidance or dishonesty.

Q: In general, what types of matters (problems) falling under the jurisdiction of the Ohio Supreme Court are the most difficult to handle (solve)?

A: All the cases that come before the supreme court are important to the citizens of Ohio and as such are difficult. Beyond that, I believe death penalty and professional misconduct cases are the most difficult to handle.

Q: Justice Kennedy, relating back to your entire career in the justice system, did you perceive or personally experience problems relating to gender? (Discrimination in hiring female employees, sexual harassment.)

A: Yes. There were times early in my career that I experienced gender discrimination and sexual harassment. When confronted with those situations I was empowered to directly handle those situations with a supervisor or mentor.

Q: Compared with when you first entered the legal profession, do you believe judges and other personnel in the judiciary are better educated, better trained, and more professional than they were in the past or are they about the same?

A: The same.

Q: Who is responsible for developing policies and operational strategies for the day-to-day administration of the supreme court?

A: The full court. R.C. 2503.05 provides that the supreme court may make appointments to the court, including the administrative director, who handles the day-to-day operation of the court.

Q: As a justice, do you have the power to develop (recommend) administrative policies for the court? If so, explain?

A: Administrative policies and the modification of policies are discussed during administrative conference days. Those discussions are subject to a majority vote of the court.

Q: Do you believe that during the time you have been on the supreme court, the procedures followed in administering the court have led to the court becoming more formal and bureaucratic, less formal and bureaucratic, or it has not changed?

A: No change.

Q: If there have been changes, have these changes resulted in an improved court organization or one that is not as effective as it was in the past?

A: No.

Theory and Practice

Q: Justice Kennedy, are supreme court judges required to attend workshops, training sessions, or conferences in order to keep abreast with recent changes in law, policies, research, or equipment? (Elaborate)

A: Yes, Ohio judges are required to have 40 hours of legal education every 2 years.

Q: Have you been able to integrate the research and the theoretical and factual information you obtained from participation in conferences and workshops into the performance of your duties in your present position?

A: Yes. I attended some great legal education seminars, particularly when I was at the trial court, which helped me to streamline case management functions. Forms from other jurisdictions were adopted and integrated into our jurisdiction.

Q: What type of information from academic or scientific research at training sessions is the most useful?

A: Except for legal research on new laws and prior cases, I do not use research-oriented materials on a daily basis. I have used academic research sources in developing a new program.

Q: Those in the legal professions (judges, prosecutors, defense attorneys) are often reluctant to change once they feel comfortable in an established way of doing things. However, academic research often points out some of the weaknesses in the current system and provides suggestions for change and improvement. Can you give an example of an instance when you changed your procedures as a result of some information that you learned at a conference or from a professional journal?

A: At the trial court we followed the model, "If you think it works well, break it apart and see what you have to make it better." When elected judge of the Domestic Relations Division, I inherited a delinquent caseload. To resolve the problem, I established formal guidelines for the processing of the cases. Discretionary time limits were deemed mandatory for magistrates and compliance with the time limits was a formal aspect of employee evaluations.

General Assessments

Q: Justice Kennedy, please reflect a bit on the future of the judiciary system in Ohio. What do you think are the major concerns (problem areas) that will confront the courts the future?

A: The three major concerns confronting the judiciary are adequate funding, access to the courts, and technology.

As reductions in local government funding continue, courts face unique challenges in maintaining services. Struggles for funding pit the judicial branch against other branches of the government. The independence of the judiciary and the separation of powers permit administrative judges to order reasonable funding, but that often creates ill will. As funding continues to shrink, access to the courts becomes problematic. Across Ohio, a reduction in funding has resulted in courts closing.

Technology advancements and the misuse of technology is an issue that courts will continue to address. Courts have restricted the presence of cell phones and other devices in courtrooms because of streaming capabilities that permit courtroom testimony to be streamed live in hallways for other witnesses to hear and photographic capabilities that permit pictures of jurors to be taken.

Q: To what extent, if any, is the Ohio Supreme Court affected by matters relating to international law and global issues (e.g., immigration, trafficking in drugs and humans, terrorism, human rights, international treaties)?

A: Obviously crimes against persons may come to the Ohio Supreme Court. Within the justice system, specialty dockets are beginning for human trafficking.

Q: What is your opinion on the international movement to develop a common code of ethics for the legal profession?

A: I am not aware of the international movement.

Q: Justice Kennedy, does the establishment of cooperative agreements with other countries, such as police practices, extradition of criminals,

standards for imprisonments, terrorism, and security practices by
the US government have any direct effect on the Ohio courts?

A: The Ohio Supreme Court has made significant initiatives to ensure access
to courts and language interpreters. In criminal cases when the
offender is an illegal immigrant, courts are required to advise the
offender, prior to taking his or her plea, that a conviction may subject him or her to deportation.

Q: Has the movement toward the development of a global justice system
with a standardization of laws been a benefit, detriment, or had no
effect on the Ohio Judicial System?

A: No effect.

Future of the Judiciary in Ohio

Q: In reference to criminal law in Ohio, are you satisfied with the current
criminal code and criminal procedures that are in effect?

A: Yes.

Q: What do you think is most needed to improve the system?

A: Maintaining the quality of language interpreters and having access to
interpreters of nondominant languages.

Q: Being a supreme court justice, are you in a position to recommend and
advocate changes in laws?

A: Yes.

Q: Justice Kennedy, reflecting on your entire career, if you had a chance,
would there be anything you would have done differently?

A: No, not a thing. I have had the greatest professional experience. I have
been truly blessed. How many people can honestly say, "I have
succeeded in achieving everything that I have sought to accomplish in my professional life." I believe I am a living example of the
American dream.

Thank you very much for your informative and candid answers.
It has been a pleasure speaking with you today about the Ohio
Judicial System.

Conclusion

As can be seen in Justice Kennedy's open and candid responses, the above
was an interview where the interviewee was willing to open up and accurately portray what life is like on the judge's bench. What comes through in
Justice Kennedy's responses is how her wide experiences of working in the
criminal justice system—from working in a police department to practicing
law as an advocate—have influenced her approaches to the role of a judge. Of

particular interest is her discussion on specialized docket courts such as the drug court where the court officers are specialists in that particular field, as this can assist in the dispensing of justice at the correct and appropriate level for the offender and ensures the community receives maximum protection. With Justice Kennedy being a judge in Ohio's Supreme Court, her responses on the role that Ohio's Supreme Court judges play in upholding Ohio's Constitution are revealing, regarding how, although presumed to be constitutional, supreme court judges must ensure that Ohio state laws are written in a fair and impartial manner and that they do not violate the Constitution or they will be struck down. Also interesting is Justice Kennedy's coverage of her experiences in the Domestic Relations Division court, in particular regarding child custody and support for the child. What does come through in the interview is that in Justice Kennedy, the Ohio Supreme Court has a judge who has retained a vocational aspect to her work in the judiciary.

Paul J. de Muniz, Chief Justice, Oregon State Criminal Courts

13

BLAKE M. RANDOL AND LAUREN M. BLOCK

Contents

This chapter shares the views, personal developments, and experiences of the Honorable Chief Justice Paul J. de Muniz, who retired in 2013. Justice de Muniz served on the Oregon State Court of Appeals from 1990 to 2000, and served on the Oregon State Supreme Court from 2001 to 2013. Prior to his judicial service, de Muniz had a diverse legal career, serving as an Oregon State deputy public defender and as a special prosecutor for Douglas County in Oregon, and working in private practice. As a defense attorney, Justice de Muniz argued and won several precedent-setting cases. Having prior experience as both a defense and a prosecuting attorney, Justice de Muniz is known for being a fair-minded and impartial judge who understands cases through a multitude of perspectives. De Muniz is a prominent activist for equal justice in Oregon State, and he frequently speaks to the public, attorneys, judges, and court administrators on cultural and racial issues in the justice system.

Prior to discussing Justice de Muniz's views on a variety of legal developments and issues in criminal law and procedure in the United States, this chapter first offers a more detailed description of Justice de Muniz's

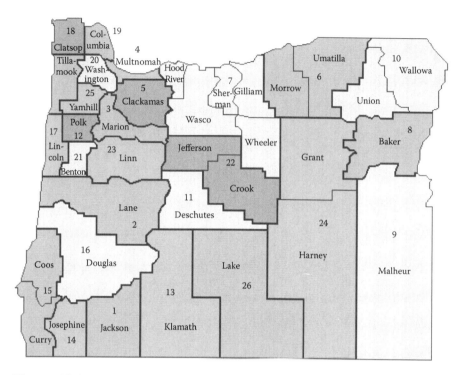

Figure 13.1 Map of Oregon State judicial districts. (From Oregon Judicial Department, *Oregon Judicial Districts*. Retrieved from http://courts.oregon. gov/OJD/aboutus/courtsintro/judicialdistricts. Accessed November 2, 2013.)

jurisdiction, the Oregon State court system. Next, this chapter discusses the development of mandatory sentencing laws in the United States, which have had a substantial impact on sentencing practices and judicial discretion. Then, this chapter gives a short biographic description of Justice de Muniz's legal career, which discusses important details concerning his diverse legal experiences and areas of expertise in criminal law that are not necessarily reflected in the interview.

The latter half of this chapter presents a transcript of the interview with Justice de Muniz. The entire transcript was included rather than mere excerpts because the transcript in its entirety shows the richness and depth of Justice de Muniz's views and experiences that otherwise could not be fully captured. In the interview, Justice de Muniz discusses his legal career, his judicial philosophy, his thoughts on the relationship between theory and practice, his views on the impacts of mandatory sentencing laws on American criminal courts, and an account of what he believes are the greatest challenges facing criminal courts in the United States today.

Career

Justice Paul J. de Muniz retired from the bench and stepped down from his position as the 41st Chief Justice of the Oregon Supreme Court in January 2013. Justice de Muniz was elected as justice to the Oregon State Supreme Court in 2000 and he served two 6-year terms. He was appointed as chief justice of the Oregon Supreme Court in 2006, and he was the first Hispanic to serve as chief justice in Oregon State history. Prior to serving on Oregon's highest court, Justice de Muniz served as a justice in the Oregon Court of Appeals from 1990 to 2000. In over two decades of judicial service, de Muniz reviewed and voted on numerous cases pertaining to Oregon State criminal law.

Prior to his judicial service, de Muniz had a diverse legal career, serving as an Oregon State deputy public defender and as a special prosecutor for Douglas County in Oregon, and working in private practice for the law firm of Garrett, Seideman, Hemann, Robertson & De Muniz. The fact that de Muniz had prior experience as both a defense and prosecuting attorney, and as both a public and private defense attorney, is widely viewed as one of the many strengths he took to the bench, because his diverse experiences allowed him to impartially see cases through a multitude of perspectives.

While in private practice, de Muniz successfully overturned the wrongful conviction of Mexican migrant farmworker Santiago Ventura Morales. Morales was convicted of killing a fellow farmworker in 1986. In the trial leading to his conviction Morales was unable to overcome the language barrier in the courtroom because the court would only provide him with a Spanish interpreter, when Morales spoke limited Spanish as a second language because his native Mexican language and the language spoken by other witnesses was Mixtec. De Muniz, representing Morales in the appeals process, highlighted that the trial had several deficiencies and presented evidence showing that Morales was in fact innocent, which led to the overturning of Morales' conviction and his release from incarceration. The case received national media attention. Since the Morales case, Justice de Muniz has actively worked to reduce language barriers that prevent equal access to justice in Oregon State. De Muniz actively speaks to judges, attorneys, court administrators, and the public on linguistic, cultural, and racial issues in the justice system, and he has served on a variety of committees and task forces aimed at improving access to justice in Oregon State.

Judicial Structure of the State of Oregon

The state of Oregon is located in the Pacific Northwest region of the United States. It shares borders with the states of California, Washington, Idaho, and Nevada and has a Pacific coast. In 2012, the estimated population of Oregon was approximately 3.8 million people (Population Research Center, 2012). Oregon's state laws are set out in the Oregon Revised Statutes. The Oregon Judicial Department is made up of three types of courts: circuit courts, an intermediate appellate court, and a state supreme court. All the judges who serve on the bench of these courts are elected to office by popular vote.

There are 36 counties in Oregon, each with their own circuit court. These circuit courts are courts of general jurisdiction, meaning they handle most, if not all, of the criminal cases in their jurisdictions. Oregon also has municipal, county, and justice courts, which handle minor matters and offenses, but these courts are funded by the local government for the jurisdiction in which they reside instead of by the state. In 2011, the circuit courts in Oregon handled approximately 309,000 criminal cases (Oregon Judicial Department Report, 2011).

The Oregon Court of Appeals is the intermediate appellate court in Oregon. There are 10 judges sitting on the court. The chief justice of the court of appeals is appointed by the chief justice of the Oregon Supreme Court. The court of appeals receives all of the appeals in the state, both civil and criminal. Oregon's court of appeals has consistently ranked as one of the busiest appellate courts in the country, with an average of 3000–4000 filings each year, and 60% of these filings involve criminal cases (Oregon Court of Appeals, 2012).

The highest court in Oregon is the Oregon Supreme Court. The court has seven justices who choose a chief justice to represent the court. The chief justice of the Oregon Supreme Court acts as the administrative head over the entire Oregon Judicial Department. Like all state supreme courts, the only court that has jurisdiction over the Oregon Supreme Court is the US Supreme Court.

Sentencing Guidelines and Mandatory Sentencing Laws

The court systems across the United States have seen many changes during their history, including the implementation and use of presumptive sentencing guidelines and mandatory sentencing laws that started in the 1970s. During this time period, there was a drastic shift in the underlying philosophy of the criminal justice system from a focus on offender rehabilitation and reform to a focus on crime control, just deserts, and incarceration (Tonry, 1996). The rehabilitation of offenders had been one of the main goals of the criminal justice system for decades and this era used indeterminate sentencing. Indeterminate sentencing allowed judges to sentence offenders to a broad range of years of incarceration with the idea that the correctional staff and parole boards would release the offender at an appropriate time based on their rehabilitative progress (Tonry, 1996). However, by the 1970s many perceived rehabilitation as a failure and criticized the broad discretion provided to judges and parole boards by indeterminate sentencing. In addition, studies on sentencing had found vast inequalities across sentences given to similarly situated defendants, meaning that judicial decisions were grossly inconsistent (Frankel, 1972; Tonry, 1996; Von Hirsch, 1976). There was also a strong public perception that courts were far too lenient in their sentencing of offenders. The result was a shift to policies based on determinate sentencing, where judicial discretion is limited and specific sentences are mandated through legislation.

Mandatory minimum sentencing laws were developed in a response to the public perception that the courts were too lenient, and were designed to restrict judicial discretion (Tonry, 2009). Mandatory minimums apply a mandatory sentence to certain types of crimes. For example, a mandatory prison sentence of 2 years may be applied to an offender who commits an offense using a firearm and the judge and prosecutor would be forbidden from mitigating that mandatory sentence. This would ensure that the offender would spend at least 2 years incarcerated for his or her crime. The details of mandatory minimum sentencing laws vary from state to state.

Most mandatory minimum sentencing laws were implemented between 1970 and 1996, and, unlike with sentencing guidelines, all 50 states and the federal government enacted some form of mandatory minimums (Tonry, 2009). For example, in 1994, Oregon voters approved Oregon Ballot Measure 11, Oregon State's mandatory sentencing law. This measure required a mandatory minimum prison sentences for violent crimes such as murder, assault, rape, kidnapping, robbery, and arson. This measure also prevented offenders who were convicted of these crimes from receiving any reduction in their sentence.

The impact of presumptive sentencing guidelines and mandatory sentencing laws has been far-reaching. Firstly, the numbers of offenders being sentenced to prison and the length of prison sentences have drastically increased. This has also resulted in increased costs of building and maintaining prisons. The recent recession and poor economy have forced many states to examine the impact of their "get tough" policies and reconsider their effectiveness.

Secondly, law enforcement, prosecutors, and defense attorneys often went to great lengths to circumvent the laws (Tonry, 2009). In New York, the implementation of the Rockefeller Drug Laws resulted in fewer arrests, indictments, and convictions, but those who were convicted under the laws were more likely to be sentenced to prison and to serve a longer sentence (Joint Committee on New York Drug Law Evaluation, 1978). A report by the US Sentencing Commission showed that federal prosecutors routinely failed to file charges that carried a mandatory minimum sentence (US Sentencing

Commission, 1991). In addition, federal prosecutors often used the mandatory minimum sentences as leverage to coerce defendants into pleading guilty.

In Oregon, an evaluation of Measure 11 also found evidence of circumvention of the law (Merritt et al., 2006). When comparing conviction rates prior with the measure being implemented and after, it was found that offenders were less likely to be convicted of the offenses targeted in the measure and offenders were more likely to be convicted for offenses not included in the measure after it was implemented. However, sentences became harsher for both measure offense and nonmeasure offense convictions. Due to budgetary issues, the Oregon State Legislature is currently debating whether Measure 11 should remain in place (Gaston, 2013). Some Oregon legislators believe that the measure is actually costing the state more money, not less, because of the increased number of offenders who are being held in prison and offenders who are being held there for longer due to the mandates of the measure. These legislators believe the money that is being spent to house these offenders could be better spent on community correction programs.

Thirdly, in some jurisdictions presumptive sentencing guidelines and mandatory sentencing laws were not only circumvented, but they actually created disparity in sentencing. For example, studies examining Pennsylvania's sentencing guidelines showed that female and white defendants were more likely to receive downward departures[*] compared with their male and nonwhite counterparts (Johnson, 2003; Kramer and Ulmer, 1996). A study of the federal sentencing guidelines also found evidence that male defendants and black defendants in federal court were less likely to receive downward departures compared with their female and white counterparts (Mustard, 2001).

Perhaps more than any other mandatory sentencing laws, the federal sentencing guidelines and mandatory minimums have been a subject of great debate and controversy (Tonry, 1996). Surveys of federal judges, prosecutors, and defense attorneys consistently showed widespread disapproval and dislike of the sentencing guidelines and mandatory sentencing laws (Tonry, 2009).

Q: Can you tell us a little bit about your career?
A: I, unlike many lawyers and judges, did not go to college immediately after high school. I enlisted in the US Air Force when I was 18. I served 3 years and 8 months in the US Air Force, including a year of tour duty in Vietnam during the war. After that, I went to Portland State University. I went through college in about two and half years. I was admitted immediately to Willamette Law School, and I graduated

---

[*] In American criminal law, "downward departure" is a term that is used in to refer to judicial decisions that depart downward from the statutory mandatory minimum sentencing guidelines.

from law school in 1975. I would say what sticks out in my mind, and may be of some interest, is that when I went to law school I had absolutely no belief that I would become a courtroom lawyer. It didn't seem to be on the cards for me. I'd never been a public speaker. I had no extracurricular activities in college. I was just a commuter student who had come home from the war and was going to school on the GI Bill. It was surprising to me when I did exceedingly well in the first year of appellate competition, and then got a job in the public defender's office at the end of my second year.

The public defender's office in Salem, Oregon, where I got my first job, was the appellate defender's office. Starting at the end of my second year, I was writing appellate briefs for lawyers to argue in the Oregon Court of Appeals and the Oregon Supreme Court. To my surprise, at the end of the summer, one of the supervising lawyers came to me and said, "You wrote in this homicide case, would you like to argue the case if we could get the court's permission and the client's permission?" Apparently, no one had ever done that before. So, my first day in my third year of law school, I was in the court of appeals arguing my first appellate case. Fortunately, I won that case. So that was sort of the beginning of courtroom work for me. I was fortunate enough to be hired by that office a few days after I passed the bar exam. I really don't want to say that I was unfocused about that. I, unlike the law students of today, didn't have any debts. I had put myself through school. I paid every bit of my tuition myself. I never had a loan. I was taking it one step at a time. I didn't interview for any jobs before I graduated. I just wanted to focus on passing the bar, which I did. A couple of days later, the public defender's office called me and said they had a job. It was three blocks from my house, so I took it.

I started right out of law school arguing cases in the Oregon Court of Appeals. I'm not sure how long it was until I had my first case in the Oregon Supreme Court, but I think about 6 months. About a year after I became a lawyer I argued and won my first case in the Oregon Supreme Court. It was a fascinating case having to do with state criminal jurisdiction on a Native Indian reservation in Oregon. It was a precedent-setting case. The name of the case was *Oregon State v. Austin Louis Smith*. So I spent a total of about 18 months in the public defender's office. Then I decided I wanted to go into private practice and become a corporate or transaction attorney. I joined a small but long-standing law firm in Salem, Oregon. I didn't intend to practice criminal law. About 3 or 4 months after I was in the firm, the son of a wealthy client of the senior partner ran over his wife with their car, and he was charged with murder. I successfully defended him. I had a varied practice.

Most people associate me with high-profile criminal cases, but I was also a civil litigator, represented the city, the county, represented US Bank, First Interstate Bank, and a variety of other businesses in litigation down in that area. I spent 13 years in private practice and I was appointed to the Oregon Court of Appeals in May 1990.

Personal Judicial Philosophy

The phrase *judicial philosophy* is a fairly broad one. I actually had to think about that question in 2000 when I ran for an open seat on the Oregon Supreme Court. I'd been a court of appeals judge for 10 years, and I decided to run for statewide election to the supreme court. In doing so, I thought: people are going to ask me that question. Do I know what my judicial philosophy is and how can I answer it? I would describe it as a restrained judicial philosophy, meaning that I give great deference to legislative enactment. I approach statutes and laws as if they presume to be constitutional. I generally work to find the legislature's intent in enacting the law. I've tried very hard during my 23 years as an appellate judge to sublimate my own views about policy. I would say I have a fairly restrained view.

Q: In the past several decades, we have seen the development of mandatory sentencing guidelines and other restrictions on sentencing. What is your perspective on these developments?

A: First of all—what these mandatory minimum sentences do is they remove judicial discretion from determining a sentence. So, under mandatory minimum sentencing, if you commit the crime, regardless of the nature or the character of the offense, or the character of the offender—you get the same sentence. One size fits all. I happen to believe that there should be individualized sentencing, that you should take into account the character of the offender and the character of the offense in fashioning a sentence. Now, I'm not saying that those laws are unconstitutional. I have voted to uphold them against constitutional challenge. But, I don't agree with the policy, and I think what we should be focused on, as a society, is public safety. Mandatory minimum sentences, while they certainly act as a deterrent for the time that a person is in prison, they're not really focused on safety in the community. These people will come out. I think we should be putting money into reentry services for ex-offenders, reintegrating them into society. Evidence shows that you can reduce the recidivism rate when you fund reentry initiatives. I'm more focused on what's good public safety policy. I'm not convinced that mandatory minimum sentences are serving the public the way the public thinks they are. Certainly, they're punishing the individual, but the question is this: Are they making society safer in the long run? I think the jury is still out on that question.

Q: Do mandatory minimum sentences impact the operation or efficiency of the courts?

A: I think mandatory minimum sentencing removes one branch of government from the process. In other words, the prosecutors hold all the power. They charge, they negotiate, and through their negotiation they end up sentencing the person because the judgment is known. If you're thinking about the three coequal branches of government, and if you remove one branch of government from the process, and you put an inordinate amount of power in the hands of the prosecutors—I think that has a tendency, if you will, to contribute to injustice because the threat of mandatory minimum sentences can impede the ability of people to say, "I want to exercise my right to a trial because I'm not guilty." Particularly when people are telling you, "Listen, you can't take a chance here. The prosecutor's willing to give you a reduced sentence, but if you go to trial and you're convicted of this, there's no judge that can sentence you to anything less." Then, I think it has a stilted effect in the overall process of trying to find a fair system.

Problems and Successes Experienced

Q: What would you consider to be the greatest problems facing criminal courts at this time, or in recent history?

A: 1. First of all—funding is an enormous issue. State courts around the country have had their budgets sliced to the bone. So, that obviously affects dockets, it affects the processing of cases, the docketing of judgments—all of those kinds of things. I think that funding is a serious issue.

2. Another problem facing the criminal courts is high caseloads carried by public defenders and those who represent the indigent. I think we're putting far too great a demand, caseload-wise, on those people. The disparity between what a prosecutor makes and what a public defender with the same level of experience and expertise makes is abysmal and wrong. I think it contributes to injustice. We would be much better off if we recognized how important the Sixth Amendment to the Constitution is, Article I, in our case, Article I, Sections 11 and 12 of the Oregon Constitution on the right to counsel. The right to counsel makes a difference in cases. I think funding

of indigent defense is very difficult. I think Oregon does a better job than most states, but that there is still room for improvement. There are many states that have trouble, such as many states that have the death penalty. The adjudication of death penalty cases is very difficult of course. I gave a speech about this not too long ago, and pointed out five cases that I had voted on to affirm the death sentence; all five cases that I identified had gone into what's called postconviction relief collateral attacks on the judgment, and in all five of them, the penalty phase had been reversed because a very experienced judge found each of their lawyers to be incompetent—not providing adequate assistance of counsel. Our appellate court had no way of judging that and signed off on the death sentence for these people. I think those are troubling and difficult issues.

3. The retention and recruitment of experienced lawyers to the bench is also very difficult. When I was chief justice… every year we had a new crop of trial judges. We would hold, as part of their education, a new judge seminar. Four or five years ago, we had 20 new judges show up for the seminar. I counted 19 of those as having no civil experience whatsoever. They had either been prosecutors or public defenders. Now, I realize maybe that's not such a problem for criminal law, but if you think of the overall system, it is a problem because the low pay for state judges makes it difficult to attract very successful civil lawyers who bring a wealth of experience to the bar. It also makes it difficult, particularly when you have prosecutors who have never had clients. They've never defended cases, and have a hard time understanding the defense side of things.

Q: What are the most likely future developments that you see happening in criminal law?

A: First of all, I think that courts in America are in danger of becoming irrelevant. They're exceedingly expensive. They take way too much time to resolve disputes. We have a new generation that believes that you should be able to navigate the court system with an app on your iPhone. I think courts need to wake up to the needs of the customer. I have spent a good deal of time during my last three years as chief justice attempting to reengineer Oregon courts to make them more accessible to the people electronically. I think there are serious questions about whether we should be using the rules of evidence. These rules make no sense to self-represented defendants, and I think we need to think about adjusting the way in which we adjudicate disputes. Right now, in Oregon family law cases, over 65% of people are not represented by a lawyer. I think it goes as high as 85% of cases where one side is not represented. The phenomenon of the self-represented person is here to stay. In fact,

I think it will increase, and the process is not driven necessarily by poverty. I think it's driven by the social milieu and digital world in which we live, and the ability to navigate institutions and all kinds of issues through the Internet. Courts need to be aware of this trend and take steps to deal with it. I walked by the Multnomah County Courthouse this morning on my way to the federal court, and at about 8:15 a.m. there were lines of people stretching around the block to get in, for whatever reason. We have online programs for the payment of fees and fines and this sort of thing, but we've got to do something else… we have to figure out a better way to make the courts accessible.

Transnational Relations

Q: Have you or has your court been influenced by developments outside this country?

A: I spent almost 5 years involved in what we call the "rule of law" partnership between judges, lawyers, and law professors in Oregon and Russia. I was the chair, I started it, and founded it, and guided it for 5 years. It lasted from around 2001 to 2006. The process advised and guided Russian judges on how to move from an inquisitorial process to an adversarial process. I had the realization that not everybody does it like we do. I realized that there could be other models in the world that are more efficient, that get to the answer quicker—assuming that the answer is to find the truth, so to speak. What it did for me—is that it helped change my outlook on our own system, and my view that this is the only way to do things. Now, I'm not touting the Russian system for anybody, but I'm just saying in terms of how it affected my thinking on case law from other places. We are really the only country in the world that relies on the parties to guide and develop the facts. In other words, to use the parties' own self-interest to support, to develop from the perspective of a neutral fact finder, what the facts are, and that's a pretty tall order.

Theory and Practice

Q: Academics tend to focus heavily on theory, and some of us try as much as possible to use theory to inform practice. Do you as a practitioner have a philosophy or perspective on the relationship between theory and practice?

A: We are not educating lawyers in our law schools today to be ready to prac-
     tice law when they come out of school. Legal education today is
     having... a very difficult time preparing young lawyers to practice
     law. The theory and the practice aren't married very well, at least
     in the majority of law schools in this country. Because of the crisis
     in legal education and in legal employment, law schools are try-
     ing to do a better job of marrying the academic and the practical
     together. I've been teaching a class for 8 years at Willamette College
     of Law and I try to do that. It's a class called "Oregon Criminal
     Procedure and Practice," and I divide the class—half prosecutors,
     half defense lawyers—and they trade off, and they have different
     opponents. Each week, the defense lawyers have to file a motion
     and a two-page legal memorandum supporting their motion in a
     specific fact case that I create for them on a specific criminal pro-
     cedure problem. The prosecutors then have to respond with a two-
     page legal memorandum. I then grade those over the weekend, and
     on the following Monday... students argue their motions. Over the
     last 8 years there's been remarkable feedback about how impor-
     tant it is to understand how to write a motion as a practicality and
     understand how to argue it, as opposed to just understanding that
     defendants have rights such as a right to counsel and a right to
     remain silent. To actually study a factual problem and figure out
     as a lawyer how to deal with it is difficult for some students. There
     are at least two models of legal education in this country. One is the
     Yale model—that it should be all academics. On the other hand,
     there are those who believe that there needs to be a marriage of the
     academic and the practical.
Q: How do you find theory-based knowledge?
A: Well, I tend to follow the famous statement or maxim by the great Justice
     Oliver Wendell Holmes, Jr. In his book titled *The Common Law*, he
     said.... "The life of the law has been experience not logic." What I
     believe that Holmes was saying was that syllogistic logic is really
     not how law gets done by judges; rather the facts contribute to
     the development and the experience of the law from one case to
     another. It is a kind of legal realism that forms in how we develop
     the law. And, that life, that law, is not logic—it's experience. I tend
     to follow that belief.

Discussion and Conclusion

In the interview, Justice de Muniz provided a number of interesting and
insightful statements that illuminate some of the greatest challenges

confronting criminal courts in the United States today. First, it is evident in the interview that Justice de Muniz places a high value on the importance of indigent defense. According to de Muniz, "the right to counsel makes a difference in cases" and one of the biggest problems with the criminal courts is "the high caseloads carried by public defenders and those who represent the indigent." De Muniz thinks that we are placing too high a demand on public defenders and in his opinion "the disparity between what a prosecutor makes and what a public defender with the same level of experience and expertise makes is abysmal and wrong." In his words, "it contributes to injustice." According to de Muniz, we would be much better off if we fully recognized the importance of the right to counsel. Research suggests that Justice de Muniz is not alone in these sentiments. Posner and Yoon (2010) conducted a survey of 272 state trial and appellate judges across the United States. They found that a large proportion of judges also recommended reducing salary disparities and increasing funding for indigent defense. Ironically, despite widespread judicial support for increased funding for indigent defense, judicial perceptions of the quality of public defenders and court-appointed counsel were on average only slightly lower than judicial perceptions of the quality of prosecuting attorneys. Posner and Yoon (2010) also found that contrary to Justice de Muniz's views, many American judges believe that the quality of defense does not have very much impact on case outcomes.

As previously discussed, mandatory minimum sentencing laws have been a subject of great debate and controversy in the United States (Tonry, 1996). Similar to findings from other studies, Justice de Muniz shares a common sentiment of disapproval of sentencing guidelines and mandatory minimum sentencing laws, which is widespread among judges, prosecutors, and defense attorneys in the United States (Tonry, 2009). Justice de Muniz disagrees with the "one size fits all" sentencing approach that mandatory sentences impose on judges. He believes that "there should be individualized sentencing," and "that you should take into account the character of the offender and the character of the offense in fashioning a sentence."

Another important point concerning presumptive sentencing guidelines that de Muniz highlighted is that "mandatory minimum sentencing removes one branch of government from the process." "In other words, the prosecutors hold all the power. They charge, they negotiate, and through their negotiation they end up sentencing the person because the judgment is known. If you're thinking about the three coequal branches of government, and if you remove one branch of government from the process, and you put an inordinate amount of power in the hands of the prosecutors—I think that has a tendency, if you will, to contribute to injustice," and that "it has a stilted effect in the overall process of trying to find a fair system." This perspective is very interesting because it suggests that mandatory sentencing laws have effectively removed checks and balances from criminal courts, which is inconsistent with the design and traditions of American government.

The story of Justice de Muniz's career is interesting, inspiring, and impressive. Justice de Muniz's demographic, socioeconomic, and legal background is atypical for an American judge. De Muniz served in the Vietnam War; he paid his own way through law school; before taking the bench he had a diverse legal career as both a defense and prosecuting attorney; he served for 10 years as an appellate court justice and another 12 years as a supreme court justice; in 2006 he became the first Hispanic American to be appointed chief justice of the Oregon Supreme Court; and throughout his career he has been an outspoken advocate for equal justice for minorities. With these experiences in mind, Justice de Muniz holds a unique perspective on the law that places emphasis on improving the equality of justice. Although Justice de Muniz's views are not mainstream within the American judiciary, there are several benefits to interviewing him for this chapter, which include his diverse background and experience, his dedication to the equality of justice in criminal courts, and the fact that he candidly speaks about problems in criminal courts.

Anthony "Rex" Gabbert, Western District, State of Missouri

14

MICHAEL T. ESKEY, SR., AND MICHAEL T. ESKEY, JR.

Contents

Judicial Structure of the State of Missouri

The Missouri judiciary consists of three levels of courts: the trial courts (also known as the circuit courts), an intermediate appellate court (the Missouri Court of Appeals), which is divided into three regional districts, and the Supreme Court of Missouri.

Figure 14.1 Circuit court districts of the state of Missouri.

State Courts

The Missouri Supreme Court is the highest court in the state and is located in Jefferson City. It has supervisory authority over all Missouri courts and adopts procedural rules that are observed in Missouri courts. The state constitution requires the Supreme Court to review certain categories of cases as a matter of right. The Missouri Supreme Court is composed of seven justices. The court's seven judges generally sit together (*en banc*) to decide the cases, motions, and other matters that come before it. The Missouri Court of Appeals is divided into three regional districts: Eastern, Southern, and Western. Any party who loses at the circuit court may file an appeal, which is then heard, in most cases, by a three-judge panel in the respective district of the Court of Appeals. The Court of Appeals receives all cases appealed from the circuit courts of the counties within the respective regions, except for certain types of cases that are sent directly to the Supreme Court. On average, 92% of all appeals are resolved at the Court of Appeals.

Circuit Courts of Missouri

The circuit courts are the primary trial courts in Missouri, and they have general jurisdiction (authority) over almost all civil and criminal matters. That is, cases usually begin in the circuit court, which is where trials may occur. Each circuit court consists of many divisions, such as circuit, associate circuit, small claims, municipal, criminal, family, probate, and juvenile. The type of case determines the division to which a particular case is assigned. Missouri's counties and the city of St. Louis are organized into 45 judicial circuits. There is a court in every county. The circuit court is typically in the county seat (or the city of St. Louis) and there are often additional locations throughout the county. Most civil and criminal cases in Missouri originate at the circuit court level. The circuit courts are courts of general jurisdiction, handling such matters as domestic relations, major criminal offenses, probate issues, civil cases involving amounts greater than $25,000, and appeals from county courts.

Judicial Requirements

The requirements to become a Missouri judge are depicted in Table 14.1. Selection of judges in the Supreme Court, the Missouri Court of Appeals, and five of the state's urban trial courts is governed by the merit-based nonpartisan court plan. In the remaining 109 counties, voters choose trial judges through partisan elections. The constitution establishes a merit selection

Table 14.1 Judicial Requirements by Court Level

Court Level	Requirements
Supreme Court	• At least 30 years old • Licensed to practice law in Missouri • U.S. citizen for at least 15 years • Qualified voter of the state for 9 years preceding selection
Appellate Court	• At least 30 years old • Licensed to practice law in Missouri • U.S. citizen for at least 15 years • Qualified voter of the state for 9 years preceding selection • Lives in the appellate district in which the judge serves
Circuit Court	• At least 30 years old • Licensed to practice law in Missouri • U.S. citizen for at least 10 years • Qualified voter of the state for 3 years preceding selection • Resident of Circuit Court district for 1 year

process for circuit and associate circuit judges in the city of St. Louis and in Jackson County (Kansas City). The constitution also provides that, in other circuits, merit selection may be adopted with the approval of a majority of circuit voters. The question may not be submitted to voters more often than every 4 years. Merit selection has been adopted in this way in Clay, Platte, St. Louis, and Greene Counties (note: Judge Gabbert was selected by a nominating committee in Clay County, MO).

The State of Missouri pays the salaries of all judges and their secretaries. The state shares most of the remaining expenses with the counties. For example, the judiciary spends more than 70% of its budget in its circuit courts, about 92% of which is allocated for salaries for judges and court personnel. Counties are required to fund the operations of the circuit courts. The facilities for the appellate courts are provided by the state and the counties provide facilities for the trial courts.

Introduction

Anthony "Rex" Gabbert (Judge Gabbert) is an appellate judge working in the Western District of the State of Missouri. He has held this position since being appointed by the governor in April 2013. He was appointed to the appellate court after serving 20 years in a number of circuit judge positions in the State of Missouri. Currently, his primary responsibility is to address appeals from the circuit courts with other appellate judges from his district. Judge Gabbert started his law career as a prosecuting attorney and had his own private practice before he accepted a position as an assistant prosecuting attorney in Polk County, serving in this capacity for nearly 5 years prior to selection as an associate circuit judge. He returned to private practice for 3 years prior to selection as an associate circuit judge. He served as an associate circuit judge for 10 years prior to accepting a position as a circuit judge. In 2004, he was selected as a circuit judge for Clay County, Missouri. He held this position until he was appointed to his current position as appellate court judge of the Western District.

Judge Gabbert was appointed associate circuit judge for the 7th Judicial Circuit in 1994. He received his Bachelor of Arts degree from the University of Missouri at Kansas City and his Juris Doctorate degree from the Mississippi College School of Law. He was appointed a circuit court judge for the 7th Judicial Circuit on June 1, 2004. He has served as an adjunct professor at William Jewell College, Rockhurst University, Park University, and Ottawa University. He has previously served as a member of the board of trustees for the Clay-Platte-Ray Mental Health Tax Levy and the North Kansas City Hospital. He is a member of the Missouri Bar and the American Bar Association. Judge Gabbert was retained by the voters at the election in

November 2006 as an associate circuit judge for the 7th Judicial Circuit in Missouri. He was appointed as an appellate judge on the Missouri Court of Appeals on April 3, 2012.

Career

Personal Background

Q: Could you tell us about your career? We have access to your general background as provided on the Internet; however, can you add to this and provide a synopsis of how you got where you are today?

A: I was born in Kansas City, Missouri, in 1956. I spent my undergraduate years at the University of Missouri–Columbia before receiving my Bachelor of Arts degree from the University of Missouri–Kansas City. I was very lucky that while in college, one of my dad's patients was an attorney and was in active lobbying. He was a lobbyist for the public defender's office in Missouri. My dad suggested that since I was looking forward to law school and had this relationship interest with a particular lobbyist, I should call the public defender's office to see if they would consider having me as an intern.

I was offered a position as an intern. I went and met with the public defender in Jackson County (downtown Kansas City, MO) who said he had an obligation to my lobbyist friend to hire me for the summer on a 90-day financial grant. I had absolutely no experience. I learned a lot in 90 days. Then, the grant money ran out and I ended up going downtown to work for a law firm as a court messenger. I loved every bit of it. It was a highly prestigious law firm (still in existence today). About 60 days after working there, the public defender received more grant money and asked me to come back. I ended up working in the public defender's office for an additional 2 years I later worked in the bankruptcy court in Kansas City as a deputy clerk, before I went to law school. I was going to attend a law school that had a 4-year program (evening program), instead of a traditional 3-year program. This allowed me to work during the day while attending school at night, which made the extra year worthwhile. I applied and was accepted to Mississippi College School of Law in Jackson, Mississippi.

Upon acceptance, I made inquiries into available employment. The school offered me a position as a reference librarian for government documents in the law library. I ended up going both summers and cut the length of law school (at night) to 3 years. After

18 months at law school, a defense firm broke off from an oil–gas firm and was looking for a law clerk to abstract depositions. I worked at the law firm in addition to working at the law library. Soon thereafter, I was offered a position as the law clerk for the firm during my second and third years of law school. After graduate school (May 1985), a good friend and law school classmate serving in the public defender's office in Bartow, Florida (Polk County), contacted me about a position opening in his department. He let me know his office was looking for additional public defenders. Purely on a whim, I applied and was hired. I did this for about 6 months and decided that I still had political ambitions and a desire to get back to Missouri.

I returned to Missouri in January, 1986, took the Missouri bar, was hired by a law firm, and was practicing for about 6 months as an attorney doing general practice. There was an election and a changeover in the prosecutor's office. The incumbent at the time, who later became a future colleague on the bench, was the interim county prosecutor during an unexpired term. There was an individual running against him whom I had met at a political fundraiser. He defeated the incumbent in the November election. I knew this individual and expressed an interested in becoming a "part-time" prosecutor while I worked in private practice (in the event that he had any openings). The next day, the prosecutor-elect called me and said he understood I was looking for a job. I was surprised by the call and of course responded yes to his question. He stated that he did not need me part-time, but rather full time. I joined the prosecutor's office as an assistant Clay County prosecuting attorney. I tried misdemeanors before progressing to felonies. I was with the prosecutor's office for four and a half years from 1987 to 1991. I appeared before many judges, including Judge Pat Bills, a well-respected associate circuit judge with over 30 years on the bench. I accepted a job with a large insurance defense firm again in 1991. I was with this firm for approximately 15 months before deciding to go out on my own, in North Kansas City. I started my own law office. While in private practice, I was appointed in 1993 and later elected as the municipal judge for the City of North Kansas City. During this time, I was also appointed as municipal judge pro tempore for the City of Kansas City. I was coming up on 2 years in private practice (GP—civil and criminal) and Judge Bills called me and asked if I ever had thought about applying to be a state judge. In Missouri, we have a nonpartisan merit selection. There is a standing judicial commission in each of the circuits (45 circuits in Missouri and six of them are nonpartisan) where judges do not run for elections. The process involves an application, a commission nomination of three candidates to the governor, and a governor selection within 60 days from those provided by the commission.

I was one of three selected out of 25 applicants. I was appointed 45 h after I was nominated, and I became an associate circuit judge. I served as an associate circuit judge for 10 years (1994–2004). I was appointed in 1994 and reviewed in 1996 and 2000 (4-year terms, of yes/no ballot from voters). In 2004, I was up for retention as an associate circuit judge. I applied for a circuit judge vacancy. I was nominated to the panel and selected by Governor Bob Holden 2 weeks after my nomination. As circuit judge, I handled everything from murder to an array of felony cases, both with and without jury trials, as well as civil trials (medical malpractice, etc.), with anything over $25,000 to $25 million or more.

Q: What in your career as a judge has developed over time and has actually surprised you?

A: I think what I was pleased about was that I was very lucky throughout my career that doors opened and I took advantage of those opportunities and got the experience to the point where I look back now. I am 56 years old and I have been on the bench 20 years.

It is hard to believe that I was appointed a judge and was so accepted as a judge at the age of 36, which in retrospect is quite young for the position. Now I have spent 20 of my 28 years as an attorney on the bench. I look back. It has been a natural fit. I have enjoyed it immensely. I feel very blessed that these opportunities arose when I didn't seek them and it has been a great fit.

I started teaching (and I'm teaching at five different schools). What happened over the years was that after a year on the bench I was asked to teach a procedural paralegal course at a local community college. Then, through other faculty, all of the other schools started calling me to the point that I have been averaging 4 or 5 classes teaching at a time. From this aspect, it is great, for example, teaching criminal procedure for Park University. It is a continuing education for me to lecture students about legal concepts, statutes, and case decisions that come down. It benefits me on the bench. I am able to relate what happens in court to my students online. It has been a great fit: teaching and being on the bench go hand in hand.

Since 1998, I have taught at William Jewell College, including teaching a business law course for students during my lunch hour. This has led to me teaching a graduate-level course in business litigation and other business courses in employment law (generally following Title VII). Most states have human rights laws and have transferred enforcement to state courts for relief on handling these issues (a massive increase in these cases). Ottawa University asked me to teach employment law in their graduate MBA program and I have done this every other semester, one night a week for over a decade. I learn by teaching the students there and have applied what I learn to my cases. On Saturdays, at Penn Valley Community College, I have been teaching paralegal students every potential subject—criminal procedure, to evidence, to litigation, and so on. It has been an excellent refresher for me every semester. I enjoy the work. Something that I am very proud of is that I have had a number of my student go on to law school and now appear before me in court.

I look back: the teaching has expanded, and I enjoy it as an adjunct. It just keeps me fresh on the law because they are all legal subjects that I am teaching so I can apply them to the court, and my experience in the court has helped me in teaching. It has been a good match all the way around and I have enjoyed it—a continuing education for me every day. Park University has been a very good school to teach at both in the classroom and online. I enjoy working with the students in the military and conversing with them overseas. It's always nice to hear from former students that I have helped along the way.

Concerning Your Work as a Judge

Q: Is it as interesting and rewarding as you thought it would be when you first started working in law in 1978?

A: It is more interesting, although it is repetitious at times. That being said, there are few constants in my position. I have been on the judiciary from the lower-level courts to where I am on the appellate court today (dealing with more complex issues). I am always intrigued by the new situations. It keeps my interest going. For example, I was a municipal judge doing traffic court (which I was at one point—before I went to state court) in North Kansas City for 1 year. I did this part-time at night. I would not want to strictly do a traffic docket full time, because it is the same thing day in and day out, assessing fines with little reward and many *pro se* bench trials.

As a current judge, I had many interesting cases and good lawyers, such that I was never bored by it; and things between and with cases have never become tedious. Often lawyers will argue positions that they know they are going to lose, and I was always somewhat skeptical and suspicious that they might be "running the meter" on their business, especially for summary judgments.

Other than the discovery phases, the trials have been simply fascinating. I always enjoyed hearing the cases and working with the lawyers, and working with the jury, so as I moved up through the higher levels of the court, it became more fascinating all the time.

Personal Judicial Philosophy

Q: What do you think should be the role for the judiciary in "judging someone"?

A: It is obviously not to legislate; that should be left to the legislature. But, to basically apply the law in a fair manner and make sure that everyone's liberties that are guaranteed by the constitution or by statute are protected; that there is not an overreach by the government in the way of criminal cases and there is not an overreach by a party in a civil case. It is to ensure a fair playing field and that the parties get their day in court. That is what the due process clause is all about (no matter whether they win or lose, when people leave the court they can see the law is applied fairly). As a trial judge, I always hoped that it was felt that I applied the law in a fair manner. Now as an appellate judge, I hope that my opinions will mean the same thing and that I have correctly addressed and applied the law.

Problems and Successes Experienced

Q: What organizational arrangements of the judiciary work the best and which just don't seem to be working? (from the court's standpoint and, more specifically, from a judge's standpoint)

A: In moving cases through the court, the backlog has always been a concern. Cases get stalled for different reasons, and what I see as a problem is that we have had an explosion of litigation. I was in a suburban county where the population had grown dramatically, and so had the caseload. The state does not have enough financial resources to add divisions. There are only so many weeks in the year to be in court and try cases. So there is always an increasing backlog. There is a lack of resources to expand the court and address the potential backlog, although we have done the best we can. It is not as bad as it was a few years ago.

Q: What about things that have changed?

A: Things that are really working that have changed are the drug court, such as the one I set up in my circuit in 1999. We see a lot of the same offenders come through. I don't know what the exact statistics were; but my feeling was that we had a large recidivism rate. Eighty percent of the drug offenders came back. It was simply constant, in fact, generational. Several generations went through the court system. The main push for drug courts was in Miami in 1981 and Missouri put the first drug court in effect in 1991. We put ours in Clay County, Missouri, in 1999.

Our success rate has been phenomenal. For people graduating from that program, our recidivism rate is less than 6%. That is statewide, and I think it is even better in Clay County, Missouri. People have gone through that and keep in mind that most of the cases I have dealt with as a prosecutor and a judge were based on substance abuse issues. This was related to all types of crimes: property crime, drug crime, and violent crime such as robbery. For the drug court, our rules were that no violent offenders were allowed into the program. It had to be a nonviolent offense and we had a high success rate. It is an indication of how the court leverages what I call *therapeutic jurisprudence*, which has been developed to resolve these issues and cut back the caseload. It also helps the people in the community.

When I left Clay Country, there were some courts across the states that were offering other types of therapeutic programs, not just drug courts, but there is also a driving while intoxicated court and a mental health court. These courts are be developed to deal with those issues that the system just does not have the resources to address.

Q: Does Missouri have a habitual criminal statute or three strikes type of law?

A: It's not the three strikes law, but it is what we call prior persistent offender status where if someone has two or more felony convictions their sentence is enhanced to the next level. So, for example, a B felony would go to an A felony. You simply have to show the two prior felony convictions. Missouri still has some options. We often see young offenders in court that had nonviolent offenses and I have always believed that with first-time offenders, you try to keep them out of jail or prison and place them on probation and give them a chance to rehabilitate. You also give them a chance to keep the conviction off their record and not "pull the trigger." We also have a statutory, suspended imposition of sentence that if successful gives no permanent conviction. There are some felonies, including driving under the influence (DUI), that statutorily an offender cannot receive an SIS (suspended sentence) for. We do not have a statutory court diversion program; however, prosecutors can establish

an implied prosecutorial diversion within an office. We are trying to find a means to help people stay out of the system. What is
much more frustrating for us is that we have many offenders that
are playing games. They are not prior persistent offenders, but with
the cutbacks in resources I was finding that if I gave someone, for
example, a 5-year sentence, they would probably be out of prison
in 6 months. I would get offenders before me who knew the system
and had been revoked on probation and offered a choice of a year
in the county jail or 2 years in prison. They would take the prison,
because it meant they would be out in 3 months. They know it and
it becomes a joke in that regard. The legislature wants to be tough
on crime, but they have limited financial resources.

Q: What policies or relationships with the community or with political
groups or other criminal justice organizations have you found to
work?

A: Here in Kansas City, there is a great relationship with the local law enforcement. There is good communication between law enforcement and
the schools. Of note are the school resource officers, crime prevention programs, ad hoc committees, and citizen advisory groups.
These are all very helpful and important organizations in relation to the court process. These are especially important with the
ever-increasing diversity of the Kansas City population. The diversity is something that I have literally grown up with and experienced. As such, I have truly noticed no negativity in community
organizations.

Q: What hampers the relationships or organizations of the community?

A: I haven't seen too much of this in the Kansas City area. I do not have
personal experience with this. As a prosecutor, I will note that our
criminal courts have become too much local entertainment. The
media makes it so sensational and there seems to be too much
overproduction. There is not enough focus on real-life cases. The
media seems to overlook other situations and blow things out of
proportion. The disappointment is that people focus on the sensational stories.

Q: How difficult is it for you, for judges, to relate to the living and social conditions of the defendants, especially from economically deprived
backgrounds, who appear in your court?

A: That is a valid question and a valid point, especially when you are doing
these large dockets. We don't understand some of these backgrounds and often don't take that into consideration. It is easy to
overlook those situations. Thank goodness, if we don't take a plea,
there is an opportunity to review the assessment of the individual through a presentence report prepared by the State Office of

Probation and Parole. I can look more into the individual's background, but, with the large dockets that we have, we have many cases. On Fridays, for example, I was sitting before 25 felony cases. You simply cannot get into the individual depth and focus you would like to or should. You try to remind yourself to look at the whole person and listen to them.

Every once in a while, one particular case will stand out; but, it is a probable. Because of the number of cases on the docket, it is not possible for a judge to give the individuals the focus they deserve. It is important to do so and try to take into consideration and listen to people—not only the litigants, but also the witnesses.

I attended the Gerry Spence National Judicial College.* He has a trial college for lawyers up in Wyoming to try to get into what is referred to as *psycho-drama*; to get into the depths of knowing your person and knowing your client. It's a very good course and although criticized by many people, it has many good purposes. They provided the course for about 10 years and started/created a judicial college. I was invited in the first year as a judicial college student (25 judges across the country). The following year I was invited by Gerry Spence to come back as part of the staff (2010). He invited me for the third year. But, a trial came up and I couldn't attend and had to cancel. It's lucky that I did, as the fly-out date was 9/11. At that school, despite the criticism and how they approach it, the positive point for both the lawyers and the judges was that you were taught to "listen" to people better than we have done.

On the topic of my approach to the broad spectrum of offenders, I feel that an attempt should be made to ensure that first-time, nonviolent offenders be given a second chance and not have their records damaged for a mistake. On the other hand (and I have had some direct experience on the other side), violent, heinous criminals committing multiple offenses in the same setting may, should, and have received multiple maximum sentences to ensure that they are punished and will not be released to commit such crimes again.

Q: What priority and sentencing needs to be done that will have an effect on recidivism and crime control?

A: Going back, we try to give special priority to violent crimes (although every crime is a priority). To get cases moving into the court system as soon as possible, we ensure that if someone has a prior record we sentence them fairly. We do not have sentencing guidelines in Missouri, but we do have a range of punishments. Again, you take

---

* http://www.triallawyerscollege.com/.

a look at the individual person. If I have a nonviolent offender who has not been in trouble before and I think it won't happen again, I will likely give them a chance to keep this felony off their record so that it does not destroy their future life and career.

At the same time, on the other end of the spectrum, if I have someone who appears before me who has been a violent offender and has a record and doesn't appear to be going anywhere but down the same path, I will likely impose the maximum sentences, even to run consecutively. Although I don't take pride in that, there is a message. For example, I had an individual who had been out of prison for 2 weeks. He was 25 years old with a long record. He and another offender were looking for money for crack. They went to a trailer where a couple resided. They beat the couple almost to death, violently raped the woman repeatedly despite her truthful plea that she was infected with the AIDS virus. She suffered severe trauma and tearing to her vaginal and anus area, including having firearms inserted into those areas as torture. Both victims had their skulls crushed. I ended up sentencing one of the defendants to over 300 years. What I did in that case was take every crime they committed and sentenced the defendant to the maximum for each separate crime. The message was that each felony committed destroyed the victim's lives; therefore, the defendant should be punished separately for each crime committed.

In 19 years, I have had a number of instances of offenders that were disrespectful of the court. A judge must come down on it. If you don't, you are setting a bad example and it is disrespectful of the system. I have had a few offenders give me the finger in the courtroom and if you don't get control of the courtroom and let their behavior go, it will be harmful.

Q: What do the offenders understand that will prevent them from committing the crime in the future?

A: Many judges will take the person they know they are going to sentence and ask for that person first (after you have reviewed the case beforehand). You call this person first and sentence them in front of the full courtroom. This settles the courtroom. People become more attentive. Those that may not have requested an attorney are more apt to request one. I am surprised at the people that come to court dressed as if it's a tennis match. I never allowed shorts to be worn into the state courtroom. I believe the casual attire was inappropriate and disrespectful to our judicial system. I would make statements such as "This is not a tennis court, it is a criminal court." I would continue hearing the person's cases later that day once he/she was properly attired. If I found that an individual was dressed in a coat, tie, and so on, I would make a point to compliment them in front of the courtroom to send a message that I respected their respect for the judicial process.

Q: How would you relate your tenure as a judge to Packer's Due Process or Crime Control Model?

A: It is important to note that 90% of cases before me plead out (plea bargain) (Packer, 1968). Plea bargaining has been remarkably helpful, albeit necessary, in clearing court dockets and reducing delays. It is important to note that discretion is at the heart of all sentencing in Missouri (MO Sentencing Advisory Commission, 2010). An important factor is that a judge has to be very careful to not practice or try to act like an attorney in court and ensure that both sides of the trial are fair. I will state that a high percentage of judges were prosecutors prior to sitting on the bench. There was a small percentage that had served strictly as defense attorneys on the bench. It does make you a better judge to have worked both sides. Being a judge is a powerful position; but, it can be abused by those who are prosecutors or who aspire to be a judge. Impartiality is crucial in the role of serving as a judge.

Q: What are some of the pressing problems that you face daily?

A: In addressing the organizational arrangement of the judiciary as working or not, I would point out that the inordinately large number of cases is an issue. The influx of cases has created a backlog that will always be a problem. Additionally, we have experienced an "explosion" of litigation, which increases the backlog. Trying to move cases through the court with the resources available is always a problem.

The treatment court diversion has been most effective in reducing recidivism, diverting nonviolent offenders from increasingly serious future crimes, and making overall cost savings for the justice system. The drug court diversion program is projected to save more than $7800 per offender per year when replacing incarceration with drug court diversion statewide in Missouri. In the state of Missouri, drug treatment court graduates have resulted in a 10% recidivism rate compared to a 19% incarceration rate for probationers with drug offenses within 2 years of completing probation and a 39% incarceration rate within 2 years for drug offenders who are sentenced to prison. There are obvious related benefits for successful completion of drug-related diversion programs to the community as a whole (Mendel, 2010).

Q: What percentage of public versus private defense do offenders have that come before you in your court?

A: I estimate that 60%–70% of cases that come before me have public defenders. Most utilize an attorney at the felony levels. Based on the typical incomes of those appearing in court, I feel strongly that bonds should not be used as punishments. Bonds are used to guarantee the individual's appearance in court. Denial of a bond is permissible; however, to avoid a threat or harm to the community or to avoid the risk of flight.

Q: What civic service have you provided to the community?

A: From the civic and community-service standpoint, I served as a member of the board of trustees for the Clay-Platte-Ray Mental Health Levy Board from 1986 to 1989. I was a member of the board of trustees for the North Kansas City Hospital from 1989 to 1993. I also was a US Sixth Congressional District member of the United States Marshal Congressional Selection Committee in 1993. Just as an aside, results from a survey taken by a sample of Missouri attorneys found a strong favorable agreement to a number of questions related to my demonstration of appropriate demeanor on the bench; maintaining and requiring proper order and decorum in the courtroom; treating people equally regardless of race, gender, ethnicity, economic status, and any other factor; showing competence in the law; and showing an understanding of the rules of procedure and evidence. The committee performing the survey also surveyed jurors who had participated in jury trials before me. The responses were overwhelmingly positive. Likewise, in a survey submitted by other judges of the 7th Judicial Circuit, a perfect score was given on all issues presented to my peers.*

Q: Based on your judicial experience, which policies or programs have worked well and which have not?

A: Drug courts have been extremely beneficial and successful. One thing that has not worked is the institutional treatment programs within the prison and jail walls. In Missouri, there is a policy that when someone is to receive, for example, drug and/or alcohol treatment for 120 days (state "jurisdiction over the body"), a type of shock-and-awe treatment is established. This is not, in my opinion, working well. It is important to note that all but three of Missouri's 45 judicial circuits have treatment court divisions, making Missouri a national leader in treatment courts, with more drug courts per capita than any other state in the nation. Treatment court divisions have proven to be a cost-effective method for diverting nonviolent offenders from incarceration in prisons.

* http://www.showmecourts.org/pdfs/2012/lawyers/gabbert.pdf.

Q: What is the most difficult problem that you faced as a circuit judge?
A: Plainly and simply, it is the economy. The employment problems have
    resulted in a lack of employment opportunities, especially for ex-
    convicts. The lack of social skills and employment skills is amplified.
    Individuals get out of prison and they are in a rut. Many lack employ-
    ment skills, education, and training, and there simply are not tax
    dollars to rectify this. The lack of employment opportunities and the
    conviction itself are difficult to overcome. The lack of employment
    opportunities is having a detrimental effect. People are simply unable
    to get out of a negative situation because of these various factors.

Theory and Practice

Q: As a judge, what should the relationship be between theory and practice?
A: As a judge, the court has to uphold the law. We must uphold the law. This
    is more outcome oriented. Judges have to follow the law. We can
    "interpret" the law, but mostly we apply the law as it is. As I will
    relate, judges all receive much the same training to ensure consis-
    tency. And there is an appellate court that addresses complaints to
    the process and court decisions. We are not an advocate. In prac-
    tice, you want to favor one side or the other. As a judge, you must
    be impartial at all times.
Q: On a percentage scale, where are you on what the law states versus your
    interpretation of the law?
A: I have cases that I would like to rule one way. I have many cases where
    I would "like" to interpret one way, but the law is very clear about
    the direction to follow and decision to make.
Q: Related to the above question, does your pretrial experience go somewhat
    by the wayside or is it helpful and useful in making decisions?
A: Experience as a trial judge, on the bench, and as a prosecutor helps greatly
    and this is helpful in my current position on the appellate court.
    Many judges come directly from private practice to the position
    of judge without public defense or public prosecution experience.
    I am fortunate to have the experience to know the difference (this
    is a key point). Another key point is to know and recognize the dif-
    ference between a harmless error and a prejudicial error. It is hard
    to separate experience and the law (sometimes). The experience
    prior to becoming a judge is not always present and not a require-
    ment. For example, of the 11 judges currently on the appellate
    court bench, less than half have 10 years of experience as a judge.
    In fact, a couple of these appellate court judges came right out of
    private practice and never were judges prior to being appointed as

appellate judges. As a trial judge, you may rule a certain way, but your decisions are often based on experience. It is not crucial, but previous trail work is extremely helpful, such as learning the process of handling a jury trial or courtroom.

Q: What kind of research or practice is most useful—journals, reports, and so on?

A: I use and look at everything: case laws, torts, both from state and federal, from all over, for example. I use primary and secondary sources. I consider the primary sources and case law, especially from the jurisdiction of interest, whether a law review article or other source, as most important. I rely on 19 years of bench experience, but still consider many secondary sources very helpful. As a judge, my ability to make decisions is somewhat restricted. In fact, about 90% of cases are somewhat restrictive in decisions and sentence. Ultimately, outcomes are somewhat determined by higher authorities. You always look for that exception to the rule.

General Assessments

Q: How are you affected by sentencing guidelines?

A: It is important to note that the state of Missouri has not adopted sentencing guidelines. This allows discretion for trial judges to go outside of the box. For example, this typically includes probation for first-time offenders, or maximum/maximum/multiple maximum for egregious offenders. I can relate back to the education and excellent training assistance at Gerry Spence's ranch as a tremendous help in this decision-making process. However, even though in the state of Missouri there is a range of punishment for various crimes, this has not been ratified and adopted. For example, for armed criminal actions, there is a mandatory 3-year sentence. For any type of violent crime in Missouri, the offender must serve 85% of the sentence. It is important for judges, as well as prosecutors and defense attorneys, to decide on punishments that are proportionate to the offense and that will tend to avoid recidivism.

On the armed criminal actions, you must serve a minimum of 3 years of the sentence; the point is that for some cases, judges' hands are simply tied. For others, there is some latitude for discretion. In DUI, for example, after a first offense, an offender loses his or her license because of the statute and must attend mandatory programs. Unfortunately, there is limited mass transportation available in Kansas City. There are some cases where your hands are tied, but you still have some discretion. The offenders end up (in many cases) driving without a license and this just piles on their problems. There is nothing in place to let them drive to work on a restricted license. So, there is a need for "therapeutic jurisprudence," which is starting to emerge to allow individuals to drive to work. Community service has been implemented more so in the last 5 years. Many of these offenders actually had good jobs and the DUI simply created a punitive form of offense and subsequent punishment. We try to prevent this. Also, the types of preventive methods, for example, breathalyzers, ankle devices, and so on, are simply skyrocketing in cost. This is unaffordable to many probationers.

I implemented a 40-h community service per week requirement until the individual finds a job and have found this to be very effective. They find jobs very quickly when they have to find a job and get paid versus free community service for the same amount of time. I feel that judges should not just give a sentence of community service, but should offer incentives to get the offender back into the process and working. In the last 5 years or so, I changed the 40-h community serve requirement to 40 h per week. This has been most effective. These individuals tended to find jobs very quickly when they weighed working for free versus working for money. A judge needs to look past simple community service and, if the probation is granted, that people get to work earning a living to support themselves, family, and pay back any restitution to victims and society.

Q: Economist Steven Levitt, author of the widely read book *Freakonomics*, concludes that each person put behind bars results in a decrease of 15 serious crimes per year. Do you agree with a finding like this and does it have any bearing on your sentencing?

A: Concerning the social benefits associated with crime reduction as equal to or exceeding the social and financial costs of incarceration, I feel that incarceration does reduce crime, but not by as much as Levitt proposed. I don't agree that one person is committing all the crimes at the rate that Levitt posits, but crime definitely has an impact on the economy. I understand the reluctance to hire an ex-offender. One thing I have little sympathy for are deadbeat dads (a felony in the state of Missouri if over $5000 in arrears). Clay County, Missouri, was the number one county in the state in collecting child support. I had no problem revoking probation for such parents who intentionally failed to pay support without a justification. I recall that probationers were going through prosecution to pay back payments in child support and found that incentives result in positive outcomes. I had an individual that had not paid child support in 4 months for a total of $1200. I may suspend the individual's probation, set a hearing whether to revoke the probation, and incarcerate the individual. Then I might set the probation violation bond at $1200 cash only. I was never surprised by the high percentage of such defendants who would post the cash bond that same day. The court can then apply the cash bond to the child support arrearage.

Q: What about probation? Can you provide your views on private probation versus public probation?

A: Currently, those on public probation are not paying, but private probationers do have to pay a monthly fee for supervision. Private probation was allowed by state statute to meet the shortfall in probation offices. When I came on in the early 1990s as an associate judge, probation officers were not going to supervise misdemeanants any longer. This was taken over by private probation. What has developed now is that Missouri probationers and parolees funding is getting cut back to a point that probationers are required only to "call in" telephonically. This is of little to almost no value. They supervise felons only. This is a formula for disaster. We would not place them on regular probation for private probation for felons. I began to use "bench probation" for felons and have private probationers do the supervision, which began to cost the probationer. This is a better alternative, with better attendance. I feel that public probation will, in the future, go by the wayside. There is a reluctance to revoke probation, mainly because the jails and prisons are already full. There is a reluctance to revoke any probationers to simply enhance overcrowding. The number of probationers that simply stop reporting is very high. They simply have no goals.

Q: How can this be remedied? What is needed?

A: Financial resources must be provided, manpower must be funded, and an overriding system must be improved to make it more efficient. Ironically, Missouri spends more than $660 million a year to keep 31,130 people behind bars and 73,280 offenders on probation and parole. More than 11,000 employees (one out of every five people on the state government payroll) work for the Department of Corrections (Young, 2012).

Q: What type of training of professional development is there for judges in Missouri?

A: The state of Missouri has an excellent trial education training program for judges. Twice a year there is Trial Education at the Lake of the Ozarks and either St Louis or Kansas City, Missouri, has been very effective with this. It is 20 h of training. The trial education course is not mandatory, but has a high attendance. The course runs Tuesday through Thursday. The training covers the range from civil to criminal. There is a new judge orientation. It is not mandatory, but there is a requirement for 15 h of CEU (which this more than covers). This training provides updates to the laws and instructions on proceedings. Here, they get to talk and interact with judges. There is always something new and beneficial. There is less recreation and three very productive days at each session. Family law is discussed with expertise from judges and commissioners. There is refresher training in all areas of the court. There are choices of electives in the afternoon on criminal and civil law. Other judges, who have been on the bench 20-plus years, are generally instructing the seminars. There is an opportunity to mix with trial judges. There is an opportunity to share perspectives on how the law is integrated across the state. The instructors for these courses have decades of meaningful and beneficial experience.

Q: What are some of the improvements and detriments in the court system?

A: I am most impressed with the quality of improvement in the areas of DNA, forensics, and technology. Some of the negatives are the decrease in resources and the sheer increase in the volume of crime without reciprocal increases in the criminal justice system to enforce the law, try the criminals, and house the offenders. The speed of computers and the Internet have been positives in the progress of the court. Some advice I would have for future judges would be to always continue to educate one's self and not rest on one's laurels. It is important to use your experience in public and private practice and build upon it. Always be attentive. Develop good listening skills. Develop good patience. Listen to both sides. Do your best to be knowledgeable about the case you are hearing from both sides. Do your best to make a fair ruling.

Q: What type of pro bono activities do you engage in?

A: As a trial judge, ethical law does not allow involvement in literally "anything" that may be involved with any cases that involve issues in court (and that is just about everything). Because I am in a nonpartisan selection district, I cannot contribute to any political party's endorsement. Whether a trial judge or appellate judge, you must be very careful. You are carrying the image of the trial court. We have an ethical obligation, we must be mindful of anything that comes before the court, and we cannot be involved as or perceived as advocates, particularly in politics. But, I am able to speak to a number of schools and teach. I just have to be careful concerning particular "causes."

Conclusion

On April 3, 2013, Governor Jay Nixon (Missouri) announced the appointment of the Honorable Anthony "Rex" Gabbert, of Kansas City, to the Missouri Court of Appeals, Western District. At the time, Judge Gabbert was serving as a circuit judge on the 7th Circuit in Clay County and was selected to fill the vacancy on the appellate court created by the retirement of the Honorable James M. Smart. In his current position at the appellate level, he sees the end in sight to his career. He is in his second month as an appellate judge. He will be considered (in 10 months) for a 12-year appointment which will end when he is 70 years old (the age for mandatory retirement). Currently, his main contact is with his clerks, office staff, and other judges on the appellate court. He finds it more trying to stay informed but is absolutely fascinated with the challenges of the position.

Judge Gabbert truly believes in the importance of the court system and in his service as a judge. He emphasized the importance of not being a bully. Individuals in the courtroom are under a great deal of stress. He does not intend for his position to add to their stress, but to ensure that the law is applied in a fair manner. He retains that he favors punishing the serious offender, but providing the important second chance to the nonviolent first offenders. He values his role as a judge and an instructor. He considers teaching at the undergraduate level and graduate level as benefiting both his students and his personal efforts to stay tuned in to the current law and court proceedings. Gabbert strongly favors therapeutic jurisprudence, especially with the proven success of the Missouri drug courts. He points to both the success and cost-saving benefits of therapeutic and diversion programs. He sees the shortage of resources as a major obstacle in the entire criminal justice system, which is exacerbated by the limited opportunities in the current down-turned economy.

Glossary

alternative sentencing: Sentencing that avoids traditional sanctions of the penal system such as rehabilitation programs.

appellate court (Missouri, Western District): Based on the number of counties in its jurisdiction (45), the Western District is the state's largest intermediate appellate court and is located in its own courthouse in downtown Kansas City. The court is composed of 11 judges and handles almost 40% of the appellate caseload in Missouri. Oral arguments are normally conducted in Kansas City, but are also conducted in Jefferson City, Colombia, St. Joseph, Kirksville, and other Western District locations.

bench probation: A probation to be monitored by the judge holding that bench, with no need to check in with a probation officer or to pay for probation monitoring fees. For individuals placed on probation, this is the least restrictive and least expensive form of probation to utilize.

circuit courts in Missouri: The circuit court consists of six divisions: a circuit division, an associate division, a probate division, a municipal division, a juvenile division, and a family court division. The circuit division exercises jurisdiction over all civil and criminal cases and is served by 135 circuit judges. The remaining divisions are served by circuit judges in conjunction with 175 associate circuit judges, 331 municipal judges, and various commissioners. Associate circuit judges are appointed in the same manner as circuit judges and serve 4-year terms. Municipal judges are elected or appointed according to city ordinance or charter and serve terms of at least 2 years. Commissioners are appointed by circuit judges, usually to 4-year terms.

gubernatorial appointment: Appointment by state governor for a position that becomes open such as a judge in the middle of a term without an election.

merit selection: The process for selecting state court judges by nomination to appointing authority for final appointment. This selection process may require legislative confirmation.

recidivism: The relapse to a previous behavior or condition such as the repetition of criminal activity.

Suspended Imposition of Sentence (SIS): Sentence that is placed in a holding pattern, until some event happens (often completion of probation). Once that event happens, the judge can impose the sentence (a number of days of jail usually called the "back-up"), a different sentence, or no additional sentence.

therapeutic jurisprudence: This is a holistic, interdisciplinary approach to studying the effects of law and the legal system on the behavior, emotions, and mental health of people.

victim impact statement: Written or oral statement made as part of the judicial legal process, which allows a victim of crime the opportunity to speak during the sentencing of their attacker or at subsequent parole hearings.

Elizabeth Robb, Chief Judge, 11th Judicial Circuit of Illinois

15

CARA RABE-HEMP

Contents

In this chapter, we will introduce the views and legal interpretations of US criminal courts judge, Elizabeth Robb, who is currently the Chief Judge of the 11th Judicial Circuit of Illinois. Judge Robb's interview will be divided into three general areas: (1) the role of the judiciary and the current state of criminal law and criminal procedure, (2) the important trends and developments of the criminal courts, and (3) the challenges the courts will face in the next decade in responding to modern crime problems.

Judicial Structure of the State of Illinois

The state court structure and name vary according to the state. Generally, it is shaped in a pyramid structure with the trial courts at the lowest rung, the appellate courts in the middle, and the state Supreme Court at the top (Baker, 1999). At the bottom of the state court system, trial courts initially hear legal disputes and conflicts from minor to serious criminal offenses. Their names differ by state, while their functions are the same across the states. The most common names used are as follows: superior court, circuit court, and district court. The trial courts also include specialized jurisdictions such as juvenile courts and surrogate's courts. In these specialized courts, only particular cases that fit into the court's theme can be filed. At the intermediate level, the appellate courts only rehear and review for the lower courts' appeals. The highest court in each state is the State Supreme Court; however, this is not the same agency as the US Supreme Court. Their function is to review cases from the lower courts' appeals as the highest agency in the state court system.

Specific to the state under examination, Illinois has 23 judicial circuits made up of 517 circuit judges and 389 associate judges (see Figure 15.1). The

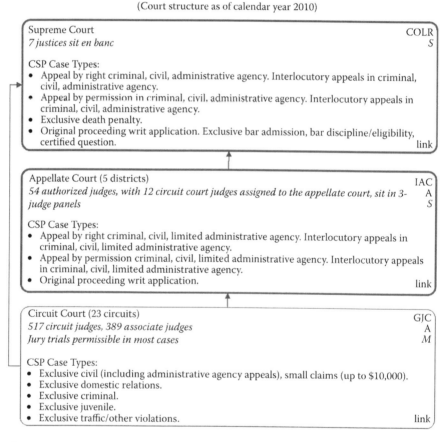

Figure 15.1 An example of state court structure in Illinois. (From National Center for State Courts. (2010). *Courts Statistics Project: Illinois.* Williamsburg, VA: National Center for State Courts. Retrieved from http://www.courtstatistics.org/OtherPages/State_Court_Structure_Charts/Illinois.aspx.)

Circuit Court is the trial court of general jurisdiction in the state of Illinois.* Judges of the Circuit Court are elected in all of the counties of the circuit and each has the same jurisdiction to hear cases. After first being elected in a general election on a partisan ballot, circuit judges must be retained every 6 years by receiving at least 60% yes votes from those who vote on their retention. All circuit judges run for retention in the entire circuit. By comparison, associate judges are elected by the circuit judges, serve 4 year terms and have general jurisdiction to hear all cases other than those criminal cases (felonies) that carry a penalty of incarceration in the Department of Corrections for 1 year or more. Associate judges can and many are certified by the Illinois Supreme Court to hear felony cases as well. Each circuit, of which there are 23 in the state of Illinois, has a chief judge who is elected by the circuit judges and who serves a term of 2 years but can be reelected to that position without limitation. As chief judge, Robb oversees all administrative matters related to trials involving both circuit and county courts in the 11th circuit (National Center for State Courts, 2010).

In criminal cases, judges set bail, rule on pretrial motions to suppress evidence, accept pleas, and, after conviction, set punishment. During these activities, the judge is expected to be a neutral party, umpiring between two adversaries: the state's attorney and the defense attorney. In the case of a trial, the judge gives instructions to the jury regarding how to carry out their duties. The jury system was initially proposed to take the role of a "passive decision maker" in court (Burnham, 2011, p. 81). One of the assigned duties for juries is to determine facts throughout hearing evidence. Usually, citizens serve on jury duty no more than once every 10 years and jurors are randomly selected from registered voters. However, because most criminal defendants plead guilty, negotiating activities and maintaining a timely docket (calendar of cases to be heard) are also common parts of a judge's workday. Based on either a guilty plea or a guilty verdict, the accused faces the judge whenever a decision affecting their future is made (Neubauer and Meinhold, 2010).

During the past 30 years, the United States has relied heavily on sentencing guidelines to bring increased uniformity to the sentences that judges dole out to criminals. The guidelines determine sentences based on two factors: (1) the conduct associated with the offense and (2) the defendant's criminal history. For each pairing of offense level and criminal history category, the sentencing guidelines specify a sentencing range, in months, within which the judge may sentence a defendant. These strategies limit judicial discretion and have been associated with mandatory sentencing and increasing incarceration rates, especially in comparison to other developed countries.

---

* The exception being those for which the Supreme Court has original jurisdiction.

Introduction

Robb earned her bachelor's degree from Illinois Wesleyan University in 1978. After college, she attended Loyola University, Chicago, Illinois, for her juris doctorate. She was admitted to the Bar in 1981. Throughout her career, Judge Robb has broken down gender barriers, being both McLean County's first female associate judge, in 1993, and its first female chief judge, in 2004. She has enjoyed a decorated career. Robb has been recognized in Bloomington-Normal among the WEEK TV 25 Women in Leadership, the United Way Volunteer of the Year, and the YWCA's Women of Distinction. In 2012, she was awarded the Distinguished Alumna Award from her alma mater (Illinois Wesleyan University, 2012). Her career started as a public defender and one of her proudest moments in her career comes from when she was a public defender where she said:

> One of my most memorable experiences was from the work I did as a lawyer. It was when I was the public defender in a juvenile court and representing kids. One day in court, after I became a judge, there was this young woman who came in to the courtroom and told me her name and I remembered it. She said I am now in social work school at Illinois State University. The girl had been abused and in the courts for years. Her mother was substance abuse dependent and this girl had been cared for by her aunt off and on. Her aunt would let her mother have her back when she was sober. But this girl was dedicating her life to social work and she wanted me to know because we had a connection.

Who knows how many other children's lives Robb has touched through her professional career? What is clear is that she has left a legacy of leading by example and by taking on issues that are most critical to her community. It was a privilege to interview Judge Elizabeth Robb on December 19, 2013, at a local coffee shop in Normal, Illinois. She was forthcoming about the challenges and successes of her career, her perceptions of the role of the judiciary in dealing with modern social problems, and the future direction of the US criminal courts.

Personal Judicial Philosophy

Regarding the role of the judiciary, Robb discussed the importance of the three branches of American government (i.e., executive, judicial, and legislative) to the balance of powers and the rule of law saying

> I kind of like that three-branch system. I was a history and American studies major. So I still read a lot of Jefferson and Madison. I try to go back to that to appreciate that. When you are down in the trenches you don't have the

opportunity to think about that as often as you might in an appellate court situation or policy situation. There was supposed to be a balance, a true balance among the three branches of government. In the concept of the rule of the law that is our culture and our citizens ultimately allowed that balance to happen.

However, Robb suggested that more discussion between the three branches of government, particularly at the state level, may provide for a better outcome. One example she gave was regarding an improvement in the communication between the state judiciary and legislature, which may clarify the implications of laws that the legislatures enact, in advance of implementation. She said,

> There is this tension always between the legislature and the judiciary and the executive branch. Laws are drafted by legislators, and judges are required to make certain laws are implemented and applied. I think that a lot of times judges are not asked enough before laws are written about their use and how these laws might affect the individuals who come before them and on their families and economics and the community. There is less of an opportunity for judges to share the wisdom that they have gained with the legislature on the laws. And I think this is pretty frustrating for most judges.

Problems and Successes Experienced

When asked about the current state of the criminal courts, Judge Robb identified a trend toward a more rehabilitative, community focus in the American criminal justice system, moving away from the retributive system rife with mandatory sentencing and incarceration. During the last 30 years, the United States has enacted some of the harshest sentencing practices in the Western world, resulting in an incarceration rate that far exceeds those in other developed countries. Through the use of mandatory sentencing and sentencing guidelines, judges' discretion has been severely limited. Robb's comments suggest progress away from these practices adding,

> The greatest problems are mandatory sentences, no judicial discretion, and insufficient resources to work toward community-based supervision as opposed to incarceration. It is changing, but not fast enough. Also, the proliferation of new crimes being created by the legislature. And every state, every agency, no matter who or what they are, requests a law in order to impose a fee or fine as way of funding their programs. You can't do that. People cannot afford that.
>
> I think in the last 5 years particularly, things are happening to improve the administration of justice. For example, I do see a recognition that we need to use incarceration less and community-based supervision more, and I see a real push to change the funding mechanism so that can happen. I would

like to see that happen. Two things have precipitated it frankly: (1) how much
it costs and (2) the recognition of the total loss of opportunity for so many
people who get caught up in the system.

Important Trends and Developments of the Criminal Courts

When discussing the trends and developments of the modern court, much of
the discussion revolved around the shift that Robb discussed to move away
from a punitive model to a more integrative community model. The trends
discussed were problem-solving courts, the accessibility to the courts, and
the impact of the international and research communities on everyday court
practices.

One criminal justice trend that Judge Robb identified is the growth of
problem-solving courts. With the recognition that the traditional criminal
justice response is inappropriate for the mentally ill and addicted offenders,
problem-solving courts were created to divert qualified offenders from the
criminal justice and correctional systems to the appropriate health systems
with the ultimate goal of providing immediate alternatives to incarceration.
Mental health courts encompass the principles of therapeutic jurisprudence,
which advocate using the criminal justice system to address the underlying
factors that may lead a person to come into contact with the law. As chief
judge, Robb has worked collaboratively with both criminal justice and community organizations to establish both a drug court and mental health court
in her county. To this end, she has pioneered efforts to obtain a $1.2 million
dollar federal grant to enhance the services provided by these therapeutic
courts. As seen in her response below, according to Robb, viewing the courts
this way requires a shift in how judges see their role in the system. On this
shift she says,

> In criminal law, the focus has shifted to recognize that, in reality, judges are
> social workers, so we ought to have the tools that we need in order to do the
> social work. Now some judges are going to say that I'm not a social worker,
> but I think if you look at the criminal law arena, we are. We are dealing with
> families in crisis and people in crisis who have substance abuse disorders,
> mental health disorders, learning behaviors. They lack jobs, they lack skills,
> they lack support, and we have to understand how all of those things impact
> the decision-making or lack of decision-making that defendants exhibit when
> they come before us. One of the biggest problems in the criminal law setting is
> the seriously mentally ill with co-occurring disorders who have no appropri-
> ate treatment opportunities or so few that it might as well be none.

Another trend that Judge Robb identified is an effort by the courts system to be more accessible to a culturally diverse citizenry. The courts are

addressing this in a variety of ways, including the provision of translation services to citizens who speak English as a second language or who are limited in English proficiency. Such a provision would increase the ability of citizens to physically navigate the courts system through signs and maps that display the layout of the building and relevant courtrooms and cultural sensitivity training for courtroom workers. Regarding the advantages of this provision, she said,

> Concerning language accessibility, our Administrative Office of Illinois Courts has hired a language access specialist. And every single court in Illinois will have a plan developed to provide an interpreter to persons who speak English as a second language or who are limited in English proficiency.
>
> There is an effort to make the bench more diverse. In fact, I just read that the law schools are attempting to bring in students from very diverse backgrounds, and eventually that will impact that the bench. It takes decades. Currently, I think that law schools are much more diverse than they used to be, but the bench does not reflect that diversity in all areas of the state. There is more diversity in urban areas than in rural areas in the state. At education conferences, we now teach cultural sensitivity and bias.

Relationship between Theory and Practice

Judge Robb also discussed the impact of legal developments internationally and how they impact everyday court practices. She provided an example of how laws and perceptions of juveniles involved in sexual crimes have been altered by the work of the Human Rights Council, saying,

> Sometimes it takes a world push to change policy in a country. For example, with regard to requiring juvenile sex offenders to register. The Human Rights Council has issued this report on the effect of that and suggesting that might be a human rights violation. That's a pretty new concept. With sex trafficking, there are changes in the perception of women who are prostitutes who are now regarded as victims, and not criminals. And I think that has been initiated by an international focus on this issue. And there were some laws that were changed recently in Illinois. You can no longer charge a minor with prostitution and you can't put them in the delinquency system for that conduct. They can only go into the child abuse system, where they are treated as a neglected minor.

Finally, the importance of social science research and the applicability of theory were mentioned by Robb as becoming increasingly influential in judicial decision making. This influence is seen none more so than in the availability of evidence-based practices that succinctly provide judges with information about "what works." On this theme she said,

In reality, we are social workers, so we ought to have the tools that we need in order to do the social work that needs to be done. We need the support of the social sciences and behavioral health sciences in order for us to be successful. If done correctly, the meta-analysis and statistical analysis can really teach us a lot. As long as it is applicable to what we do, we read it and use it. If we implement a theory, we have to be confident that it is right.

Judges want research. We do not have time to read a 400-page book, we just don't. So make it simple, make it straightforward. Give me the answers and the tools that I need to implement and to appreciate and adopt new policy. For practitioners and judges in the trenches in trial courts, it has to be brief, concise, and persuasive.

General Assessments

In discussing the future challenges of the criminal courts and the role of the judiciary in the next decade, two challenges became apparent: lack of resources and lack of understanding by citizens of the role of the judiciary. On this point she said

It would be helpful if the legislature and the executive branch gave us sufficient resources to carry out our job. In the state of Illinois, the judicial branch gets less than 1% of all appropriations every year. Less than 1% and we are the third branch of the government in Illinois. Our job is to decide the disputes. I think we ought to have sufficient resources to be able to do that. The lack of resources is changing how we operate courts. We are talking more and more about using teleconferences, video conferences, and maybe regionalizing offices to provide court services. We don't have resources in every single county. There aren't even lawyers in some counties anymore.

I really believe that the citizens need to understand the system in order to respect it and we don't ask them or involve them enough.

On the road ahead, two themes emerged as solutions on how to do more with less in the criminal courts system: collaboration among criminal justice and community leaders and long-term planning before executing a change. Collaboration was an important theme that was a thread in Judge Robb's interview. Throughout her career, she has successfully brought agency and community stakeholders together to create programs uniquely tailored to the criminal justice problems facing her local state. In fact, Judge Robb spoke recently in a statewide panel on collaboration in the form of a Criminal Justice Coordinating Council. Her collaborative efforts do not stop there. She is also a member of the Illinois Judicial Conference, Executive Committee of the Court Reporting Services Agency, and Supreme Court Advisory Committee for Justice and Mental Health Planning; and serves on the Study Committee on Juvenile Justice of the Judicial Conference and the Judicial

Mentor Committee. She currently serves as the chair of the McLean County Criminal Justice Coordinating Council (Illinois Criminal Justice Authority, 2010). When asking about the secret to collaboration, she had this to say:

> I think that having the judiciary work with community organizations is sort of a new thing. Although, for the past 20 years it's been percolating with the drug courts, with the mental health courts, and criminal justice coordinating councils. For many years, judges viewed themselves as needing to be isolated and I think we realized we can't do it our own. So, the collaborations are extraordinarily important. Again, because of the fiscal situation in our state, when you bring together different disciplines, you start talking to each other and working together. You know, when you just listen to judges, you are very isolated. You have one view of the world, and when you bring other views and other disciplines and theories together, just that interplay creates new ideas and innovations. So I think that is really important. What are the barriers to cooperation? Turf issues—for some judges you need to break down the belief that talking to others will impede your ability to be impartial and fair. You have to be clear when working with outside agencies and individuals that you do have to maintain your independence and impartiality. But, I think that people recognize and appreciate the limits that a judge has.

Given her vast experience as a lightning rod for change and effective collaboration, Judge Robb discussed how important planning was to a successful outcome and how difficult it was as a judge to leaving a lasting imprint on the system, saying,

> When it comes to change, I don't think anything is easy, because if it was easy it would have happened. You have to do a lot of groundwork before you implement new programs. You have to bring in all of the stakeholders. You have to do research and you have to gather support for a different approach. Because if it is top-down imposed, it is not going to be successful. It can be the best program ever, but if you don't have support, it won't go anywhere. Next, efforts to improve the administration of justice must include education and training. Cross-training and multidisciplinary training might be necessary.
> I suppose every judge, most trial judges, perhaps with the exception of the Supreme Court Justices, come to the realization that you have less impact over lives and processes when you rule than you hoped or expected. The times you do have an impact are probably few and far between and memorable for that reason.

Conclusion

In conclusion, we began this chapter by introducing Elizabeth Robb, Chief Judge of the 11th Judicial Circuit of Illinois. Through her comments on the

US criminal courts, we see an example of how modern US judges are increasingly taking on a policy-making role, collaborating with community and criminal justice leaders to bring about a positive change for the communities they serve. It is clear that the criminal courts are at a pivotal moment in history, with scarce resources and rising incarceration rates, to make a significant policy change that will rely on problem-solving courts, greater discretion in the judiciary, and a greater emphasis on social justice.

Glossary

administrative law: The branch of public law that deals with the various organs of the sovereign power considered as in motion and prescribes in detail the manner of their activity. It is concerned with topics such as the collection of revenue, the regulation of military and naval forces, citizenship and naturalization, sanitary measures, poor laws, coinage, police, public safety, and morals.

ballot: In the law of elections, a slip of paper bearing the names of the offices to be filled at the particular election and the names of the candidates for whom the elector desires to vote.

certiorari: An order issued by the US Supreme Court directing the lower court to transfer records for a case that it will hear on appeal.

docket: An official court record book that lists all the cases before the court and may also note the status or action required for each case log containing brief entries of court proceedings.

due process: The powers of the government as the settled maxims of law permit and sanction, and under such safeguards for the protection of individual rights as those maxims prescribe for the class of cases to which the one in mission belongs.

evidence-based practice: Practice based on the best documented scientific evidence currently available.

federalism: A system of government in which power is divided between a national (federal) government and various state governments. In the United States, the US Constitution gives certain powers to the federal government, other powers to the state governments, and yet other powers to both.

human rights council: An intergovernmental body within the United Nations system made up of 47 states responsible for the promotion and protection of all human rights around the globe.

jurisdiction: The authority of a court to hear and decide legal disputes and to enforce its rulings.

mandatory sentencing laws: Statutes that require automatic punishment for a crime.

probable cause: Facts and evidence that lead many to believe that the accused actually committed the crime.

problem-solving Courts: Courts that seek to promote outcomes that will benefit not only the offender, but the victim and society as well. Although most problem-solving court models are relatively new, early results from studies show that these types of courts are having a positive impact on the lives of offenders and victims and in some instances are saving jail and prison costs.

retributive justice: A system emphasizing that pain to be inflicted on the offender by way of punishment to outweigh the pleasure derived from his/her criminal act.

self-incrimination: A declaration or an act that occurs during an investigation where a person or witness incriminates themselves either explicitly or implicitly.

state attorney: The prosecuting officer of the US government in each of the federal judicial districts. Also, under the state governments, the prosecuting officer who represents the state in each of its judicial districts. Analogous terms are district and country attorney.

therapeutic jurisprudence: The study of the effects of law and the legal system on the behavior, emotions, and mental health of people.

trial courts: The court that will determine the facts and the laws in a certain case.

warrant: Issued after a complaint, filed by one person against another, has been presented and reviewed by a magistrate who has found probable cause for the arrest.

Conclusion

What emerges from these interviews with judges from ten countries covering four continents in the different jurisdictions is the passion and truly vocational attitude judges have toward their role. The interviews allow the reader an opportunity to cut through long-held concerns and perceptions of the judiciary being drawn from a narrow, but privileged social background and confirm the observation that judicial appointments are slowly being drawn from a broader social background (Newburn, 2013). There is evidence of this in this book including interviews with the first female chief judge in Illinois, United States (Elizabeth Robb), the first Hispanic chief justice in the United States (Paul de Muniz), and in New Zealand the first Maori district court judge (Mick Brown). One factor used in a negative sense regarding judicial appointments is that they are well educated. However, to practice law one has to graduate with a law degree or its equivalent and proceed to postgraduate study, be it in the form of a professional qualification, such as Bar qualifications, or further academic study. Yet most of the judges interviewed for this book emanate from humble social backgrounds.

Relationship between Theory and Practice

From the responses, it was difficult to draw out one concise and clear coherent view regarding how theory influences practice. In Nigeria, Judge Udu claims there is a clear synergy between the theoretical principles and fundamentals of law and the practicing of law. He says that legal practitioners learn the continuous emerging trends in law that are published by law researchers. However, he does add a caveat that while the relationship between theory and practice does exist and is working well, it is not sufficiently harmonized. If one is to find a common theme regarding the relationship between theory and practice, it is the last point Judge Udu makes that appears to be present in all of the interviewees' jurisdictions: that it is not harmonized. For example, Judge Chappell in Australia, who, having taught at various universities is also an academic and who was involved in criminal justice research that fed into policies affecting law, states that in general most Australian judges would not know what research was other than legal research that involved looking solely at case law. The US judges echo a similar sentiment. Judge

Gabbert said that the main research used by the judiciary is case law, while secondary research such as academic work, if used at all, could be seen only as occasionally helpful. Chief Judge de Muniz adds to this point regarding the US jurisdictions where he finds that theory and practice are not married very well in the majority of law schools. It appears that Chief Judge de Muniz is dismissive of the possible use of legal theory in legal practice. He says there should be two models of law school, a "Yale model" that should be solely for all academic lawyers and a second model—the practice module that equips young lawyers for the workplace.

Similar sentiments to those espoused by Chief Judge de Muniz are seen in the responses from the UK judges who were interviewed. Mr. Justice Harris claims there is a divide between legal academics and practitioners. From his experience, there is a clear division between legal academics and practitioners, with little direct deployment of academic learning or legal theory in trials or hearings in criminal cases. However, he does add that the UK appellate court judges may adopt theoretical concepts of law. In Mr. Justice Harris' opinion, there should be greater interrelationship between theory and practice, especially in first instance trials, as this could benefit judges in the decision-making process. This view is seen in Mr. Justice Goldstone's interview (also from the UK), where throughout most of his interview he was constantly making links between theory and practice, which was evident in his comments on the proposed changes to youth justice and dealing with child victims. Recorder Cuthbert believes there should be a reciprocal relationship between theory and practice. Acknowledging that legal practitioners are forced to be creative in their efforts to tie legal theory with practicing law, one way forward could be to ensure there is a relationship between the two is for legal theorists to develop new models that account for spontaneous practical events.

Although he finds case commentaries useful, the president of the Serbian Supreme Court, Serbia Judge Milojević, says the cooperation between theory and practice is not sufficiently developed. On this theme, Judge Ivánek says that in Slovakia a problem in applying theory in practice had been with legal theorists writing theoretical papers that had no basis in practical matters, resulting in those papers being unusable in practice. However, in Slovakia's jurisdiction he has seen in increase in the influence theory has in the practical application of law in the courtroom. He says that a judge who is not familiar with theory will result in a judge who is an incompetent decision maker. He adds that in recent years there have been several influential theoretical publications that have contributed to the development of criminal and procedural law in Slovakia.

A tenuous thread of consistency that came out from the interviews regarding the relationship between theory and practice is that at trial level there is little or no application of legal theory by practitioners, be they lawyer advocates or judges. It appears that legal theory only has some impact in the appeal process where appellate court judges consider legal theory, but even then this is only in a limited capacity. This is understandable, especially in common law countries where, as seen with most of the jurisdictions covered in this series of interviews, judicial precedent exists, with lower courts being bound by the decisions of the higher courts. This has the effect of judges in lower courts ensuring their decisions stay within legal boundaries by taking cognizance of the higher courts' rulings as provided in case reports. The impact of this is that at lower court level such as trial courts, both the advocates and the judges will focus more on case reports than legal theory. However, legal principles such as the rule of law and how it has and is currently developing should be the foundation on which other legal theory is built and considered by the judiciary regardless of which level that court lies within the principle of judicial precedent. As seen in Mr. Justice Lunn's responses, this appears to be the practice of the Hong Kong courts.

Funding Justice in Criminal Courts

Another factor that emerges from the judges' responses that has a degree of a commonality is the funding of the criminal court cases. In Australia, Justice Wood states in his interview that funding to the public defender should be increased as, in his view, there is currently inadequate resourcing of the legal aid in Aboriginal legal aid systems. The Quebec judge interviewed by Boivin and Leclerc was scathing in relation to legal aid provision in Canada, saying that in effect only the unemployed can obtain legal aid and due to means testing it does not extend to employed citizens who are on the Canadian minimum wage. The Quebec judge finds that this is exacerbated by the rise in legal costs and delays caused by the Canadian Human Rights and Freedoms Charter, which has adversely affected the accessibility of justice to many Canadian citizens. In the United Kingdom, Recorder Cuthbert has concerns that the lack of funding such as cuts to legal aid will lead to delays and inefficiencies, and of greater concern is the potential for miscarriages of justice should it lead to an increase in defendants having to represent themselves. Still regarding the United Kingdom, Mr. Justice Goldstone states, while acknowledging that in the past the United Kingdom's legal aid system got "out of hand" with some lawyers being paid too much, the current cuts can lead to a skewing in the quality of advocacy defendants have in criminal trials. However, one positive affect he sees the cuts having is how court officers are being forced to pull together. It has united solicitors and barristers "like never before" as well as increasing support between probation officers, police officers, witness services, and court officers.

From their respective jurisdictions, North American judges echo similar sentiments. Regarding the funding of state courts in the United States, Chief Justice de Muniz states that with budgets being "sliced to the bone," it is adversely affecting the processing of cases. One effect of the cuts he sees is the apparent disparity this is having between state prosecutors and public defenders. His concern is that in turn, due to the poorer quality of defense advocacy, the cuts are contributing to injustices. Citing the US Constitution's Sixth Amendment, Chief Justice de Muniz says the right to counsel makes a difference and the funding of indigent defense is very difficult, especially regarding the adjudication of death penalty cases, where he found experienced judges reversing the penalty phase because of the incompetence of some defense lawyers who, as a result of their incompetence, were not providing adequate counsel. Judge Elizabeth Robb echoes similar concerns regarding the fall in funding, saying that the courts should have sufficient resources as the current lack is changing how courts are operating. With more reliance on teleconferences and video conferences, there aren't the same resources in every county in the state of Illinois and there are not even lawyers to represent defendants in some of the counties.

These are important points as in both jurisdictions there are similar protections for defendants. In the United States it is the Sixth Amendment that states defendants have the right to a speedy trial, in public (although this is not an absolute right[*]), and that trial is by an impartial jury with the defendant allowed the assistance of counsel. As was confirmed by the US Supreme Court,[†] all defendants in the United States are entitled to the help of a lawyer where judicial proceedings are initiated against them. Regarding rights for defendants in criminal trials in Europe, the governments of those European jurisdictions that are members of the Council of Europe have signed up to the European Convention on Human Rights. In the convention, Article 6 provides for persons to have the right to a fair and public hearing that has to be held within a reasonable time and includes a defendant's right to access to legal advice from arrest and detention at a police station through to their trial. As in the United States, this is not an absolute right.[‡] However, what is virtually absolute is that under Article 6(3) the defense must be given adequate time and facilities to prepare a defense and the defendant has the right to legal advice.[§]

While the focus of this section has mainly been on European and US jurisdictions, Justice Anin-Yeboah discusses the lack of resources in Ghana.

---

[*] *Sheppard v. Maxwell* (1966) 384 US 333, US Supreme Court.

[†] *Brewer v. Williams* (1977) 430 US 387.

[‡] *Brown v. Stott* (2003) 1 AC 682 was concerned with speed cameras where the owner of a vehicle was asked who was driving at the time. The Article 6 issue centered on whether this breached the issue surrounding self-incrimination.

[§] *Avrill v. UK* (2001) 31 EHRR 36.

For him, this is the main cause of delays in cases coming before the courts. It appears this issue will not be remedied in the near future and he states this is because Ghana does not have enough resources to open up more courts. This problem is exacerbated further as the Ghanaian government's legal aid system is not sufficiently resourced, which for Justice Anin-Yeboah has resulted in only a few Ghanaian lawyers being part of the scheme and has left many defendants unrepresented in criminal trials. In neighboring Nigeria, there are similar issues regarding lack of funding. Judge Udu says that alongside a culture of corruption present in Nigeria, this lack of funding makes it difficult for the poor to receive justice in the court system.

Sentencing Guidelines

There were varied views in the responses of government policies regarding judges' sentencing guidelines. In the United Kingdom, Mr. Justice Goldstone thought that overall the UK Sentencing Council had done a very good job in ensuring consistency in sentencing throughout the country. In discussing how the guidelines have clearly helped judges in first instance trials, one measure of this success can be seen in the reduction of appeals against sentence going to the UK Court of Appeal. However, he is critical of the Indeterminate Sentences for Public Protection, where due to the lack of funding to rehabilitation courses, some convicted defendants were remaining in prison longer than the recommended minimum period of sentence.

From the interviews with the US judges we see similar responses regarding sentencing guidelines, where in the 1970s the United States saw the introduction of sentencing guidelines and mandatory sentencing. In their chapter, Randol and Block comment how this change was a shift of focus on offender rehabilitation to a focus on crime control, incarceration, and just deserts. The interview with Chief Justice de Muniz, Oregon, covers how Oregon voters approved of the 1994 Oregon Ballot Measure 11, which requires a mandatory prison sentence for violent crimes such as murder, assault, rape, kidnapping, robbery, and arson. Under Measure 11, those convicted for these categories of crime are prevented from receiving a reduction in their sentence. In Oregon, the state legislator is currently debating whether Measure 11 should remain in place. This is due to the numbers of offenders in prison increasing along with the respective increase in the length of the sentence the offenders are receiving. The legislators are examining the cost of this, as they believe the money should be spent on more effective measures such as community correction programs. Chief Justice de Muniz sees sentencing guidelines and mandatory sentencing as removing judicial discretion in determining a sentence. This is not his only concern: he believes there should be individualized sentencing that takes into account the character of the offender and the nature of the offense. He says that while mandatory sentencing is punishing the individual, it is questionable whether it is making society safer in the long run. Chief Justice de Muniz adds that mandatory sentencing/sentencing guidelines have handed US prosecutors all the power in criminal trials, certainly when in negotiation resulting in the court process stilted in trying to find a fair system. This is not the same across the United States: as Judge Gabbert points out in his interview, the state of Missouri has not adopted sentencing guidelines, and as a result Missouri trial judges do have discretion in the decisions regarding sentencing. Yet in the Nigerian system, Judge Udu comments on how the Nigerian policy is concerned with decongesting the prisons and as a result judges engage in consultations with correctional officials to determine, with certain conditions required to be in place, which inmates deserve clemency.

In Canada, the Quebec judge interviewed by Boivin and Leclerc was highly critical of the Canadian Safe Streets and Communities Act, which introduced mandatory sentences and limited the use of conditional sentences. For him, two issues have emerged from this Act. One is it has diluted a judge's discretion when sentencing and as a result undermines a judge's position as the discretionary power in court has in effect shifted from the judge to the prosecuting advocates. The second is he sees the Act as nothing more than a hardening of crime policy. It is not just in Canada that this is a problem: Justice Wood says there should be more community-based custodial options available for judges to grant in their sentencing for low-level offenders as he sees incarceration as counterproductive in reducing crime.

Youth Justice and Protecting Young Victims

A starting point on this issue is with Judge Brown from New Zealand. As can be seen in his interview, he was an influential figure in the development of policy and legislation (The Children, Young Persons and their Families Act 1989) surrounding youth justice in New Zealand as he adopted a communitarian approach to dealing with youth offending. Likewise in Australia, Justice Wood's leading of the Inquiry into Child Protection Services New South Wales has resulted in an overhaul of child protection services resulting in a joint investigative team structure consisting of a multiagency approach to investigations along with a mediation process in Children's Courts being introduced to improve the protection of children. Mr. Justice Goldstone welcomes the moves made in the United Kingdom since 1991 toward the special measures taken to protect child and vulnerable witnesses in criminal trials that includes the use of intermediaries for children under 18 years of age and prerecorded cross-examination. (These were being piloted in Liverpool at the time of the interview with a view to being rolled out across the United

Kingdom in 2014.) If prerecorded interviews work well, Mr. Justice Goldstone sees this move as having a positive impact in criminal trials where children and vulnerable witnesses have to give evidence. Mr. Justice Harris (also from the United Kingdom) endorses this view where for him prerecorded cross-examination of child witnesses can only be a good thing and should already be rolled out across the United Kingdom. As seen in his interview, Mr. Justice Harris' views are influenced by his judicial work in both criminal and family courts, where he says the family court experience could benefit criminal judges as the judge is likely to be more conversant with a child's development and the limitations of a child's cognitive ability and more sensitive to a child's confusion, tiredness, and distress.

Challenges Facing the Judiciary

Although, and only to be expected, differences exist between the respective jurisdictions the judges interviewed operate in, what these interviews have revealed is that there are more similarities than differences in the challenges they face and the conditions the judges operate under. Many of those interviewed have seen dramatic changes within the legal systems they operate, none more so than Judge Ivánek from Slovakia. He went to Law School in Bratislava in the 1980s during the regime of the Communist government and after graduating, which was at the time of the Velvet Revolution, Judge Ivánek joined the judiciary. This was during the fledging days of what is now the current Slovakian republic, and as the political government changed he witnessed dramatic changes in the legislative process along with the judicial process. Mr. Justice Lunn from Hong Kong also witnessed changes to the legal system, in Hong Kong following Hong Kong's independence from the United Kingdom in 1997. However, one significant point relating to Hong Kong is that the legal and judicial system did not fall in with that in the People's Republic of China, as the principle of one country, two systems applies following the establishment of the Hong Kong Special Administration Region in July 1997. While maintaining its own system independent of China and no longer under the control of the United Kingdom, only in the areas relating to defense and foreign affairs do the national laws of the People's Republic of China apply in Hong Kong. This is contrast with the more established Western states such as Australia, the United Kingdom, and the United States, where there has been a degree of consistency in the respective jurisdictions with the introduction of change being a more gradual process.

Despite this, law and order and therefore the criminal courts have the potential to fall victim of politicization as respective governments attempt to portray to an electorate they take a hard line with criminality in their attempt to prevent their citizens from becoming victims of crime. This has been perceived by the judges interviewed for this book as political interference, and tinkering has taken place, the only difference being the level of political interference. Judge Milojević sees Serbian judges being intimidated by the possibility of losing their jobs as in his words the political executive authorities "have won the judiciary" and he says a balance is required between judicial and executive authorities. While acknowledging there has been a degree of success in cooperation between the criminal justice organizations in Nigeria, Judge Udu sees corruption and political interference with the judiciary as hampering further cooperation and thereby preventing any further enhancement of the benefits the judicial and legal system can provide to its citizens. As already mentioned, in the United Kingdom, Mr. Justice Goldstone expressed concerned over political interference with the legal aid budgeting and support for sentencing guidelines with one other political interference being statutory changes to criminal law introduced by the UK Parliament. In the last 10 years, he has witnessed over 3000 laws introduced, a number of which he believes were ill thought out, and in his opinion this legislative change is nothing more than an exercise in changing the law for the sake of change. Similar issues to those experienced in the United Kingdom are seen in the responses from the US judges, which are summed up by Judge Robb. Her two challenges facing the judiciary are the lack of resources and the lack of understanding of the role of the judiciary. In her opinion, to maintain an effective judiciary and legal system, politicians in both the executive and the legislature should provide sufficient funding based on collaboration.

What comes through strongly in all of the interviews is how the judges see the legal principle of the rule of law as being of paramount important along with equitable distribution of justice for all. One concern in all of the interviews is the importance of the most deprived, dispossessed, poorest, and weakest in society having adequate and professional representation in criminal trials and therefore a voice in the court system. From the responses, it is evident that all of the judges see the law as applying to all and not simply a tool or resource available only to the powerful or wealthy in society. This could also explain why the judiciary are concerned about increasing political interference; their role as the judiciary is and should be an independent arm within a state as the legal principle of the rule of law applies to the state just as much as it does to its citizens. Under the rule of law, there should be an absence of arbitrariness, where a government governs by known law, not a whim. There should be equality before the law, with no separate system applying to the government and the public sector, and civil liberties are best protected by an independent judiciary (Tomkins, 2003).

Appendix A
Questionnaire Used
by the Interviewers

Instructions to Interviewers for the Book *Trends in the Judiciary*: *Interviews with Judges Across the Globe*

Thank you for agreeing to help with this book project and agreeing to interview a judge. The following are guidelines to help you know what it is that we are looking for and to keep a degree of consistency across the chapters. If you have any questions, please contact one of the editors: David Lowe (D.Lowe@ljmu.ac.uk) or Dilip Das (dilipkd@aol.com).

Main Aim of the Interviews (and the Book): Suggested Guidelines for Interviewers

We have listed a number of topics that should be covered in the interview. Please try to cover the topics mentioned below, acknowledging that the conduct and flow of the interview will dictate this. Also, feel free to add, elaborate, and follow up as you see fit and necessary to clarify points, expand on ideas, or pursue an insight offered.

All the topical areas should be asked, but the specific questions listed below for each topic area are suggestions. Interviews have their own dynamics. Follow them down their most fruitful avenues, using questions that cover the topic and fit the interview. Since each of you will be interviewing justices or judges from different world legal systems, the list and sequence of questions may be adjusted in any case.

The wording of questions is of course your own. In follow-up questions, try to get specific examples or details of generalizations made. (Examples are *probably* among the most useful pieces of information to readers.)

General Themes to Be Covered in the Interview

The main goal of the interviews is to present the views and interpretations of legal developments and current issues in the criminal law and procedural field

by experienced justices and judges. What do they see happening in the criminal courts and legal profession in their countries and internationally, and how
do they evaluate or interpret developments? There are many interpretations of
legal issues by scholars and policy makers who are not justices or judges or who
are from outside the organization. What we would like to have are interpretations from within the organization and by the individuals making the judicial
decisions. We are looking to obtain responses on the general themes of:

1. What do justices and judges see happening in criminal law and
   procedure?
2. What are the issues that they consider important?
3. What changes do they see as successes or failures, what is the likely
   lasting future or passing fads?

The reason for the interviews is that justices and judges do not get time
to write and reflect on their experiences, views, opinions, and perspectives.
We are requesting researchers like you to record their views and make them
meaningful contributions to our understanding of the criminal law and procedural problems of today. This may involve the interviewer going beyond
simple questions and answers to allow the interviewer to analyze and reflect
on the issues discussed.

Role of the Interviewer

The basic goal of the interviews is to capture the views of the justices or judges,
not those of the interviewers. Your role is not to be too critical or interpret
what they meant to say, but to write as accurately as possible what they told
you. When we said above "reflect," we hope you reflect on what the official
said, not on what your views are of the issues discussed. It is the judges views,
based on their experience and thinking, that we are interested in. We know
what scholars think about legal issues, but we know less what the people who
do the judging think about and how they evaluate trends, developments, and
issues in criminal justice. That is the important goal.

Having said that, by not being too critical, we do not mean to suggest
that you should not challenge and draw out what it is that the justices or
judges tell you. We do not want the official rhetoric that high-level people
sometimes fall back on during interviews; we want their personal views and
thinking. If you have the sense that you are getting the formal language, see
if you can get the justices or judges to go beyond that and push them for their
own views. The basic reason for doing the interviews in the first place is our
firm belief that justices and judges know a lot; it is that knowledge and their
judgments of the legal issues that we are after.

What to Do before the Interview

Get a sense of how much time you are likely to have and what questions you can get to during that time. In no interview will you be able to ask all the questions you want. And, when you write-up the interview, you will have space for about 6000–8000 words. Choose your priorities. The top priorities for us are the reflections by the judges or justices interviewed on the changes experienced and the interrelations of theory and practice. These are high priorities for the book.

Topic Areas That Should Be Covered in the Interview

Section 1: Career

Q1: Tell us a little bit about your career? (Try and include the length of service as a judge, organizations worked in, movements, specializations, etc.)

Q2: As your career as a judge has developed what has surprised you?

Q3: Has your work as a judge proved as interesting or rewarding as you thought it would when you first started?

Section 2: Personal Judicial Philosophy

Q1: What do you think should be the role of the judiciary in society?

Q2: What should be their job, functions, and roles? What should be left to others?

Q3: What organizational arrangements work and which do not?

Q4: What policies on relations with the community, with political groups, with other criminal justice organizations work well? What hampers cooperation with other agencies and groups?

Q5: How difficult is it for judges to relate to the living and social conditions of those from economically deprived backgrounds who appear before them?

Q6: How can a judge develop empathy for those from the lower rungs of the social division in society from which they can derive a degree of understanding why that person before them did what is alleged?

Q7: How should the criminal legal system in your country perform? What should be the preferred priorities and strategies; hard-edged crime control, prevention, services, order work, what mix for which types of problems, and so on?

Section 3: Problems and Successes Experienced

Q1: In your experience, what policies or programs have worked well and which have not? And can you speculate for what reasons?

Q2: What would you consider to be the greatest problem facing the criminal courts at this time?

Q3: What problems in courts do you find are the most difficult to deal with?

Q4: What would be easy to change? Internal problems (culture of the organization, managerial deficiencies, allegations of corruption, gender-related problems, etc.) or externally generated problems (resources, community support, etc.)? Is anything easy?

Section 4: Theory and Practice

Q1: What should be the relationship between theory and practice?

Q2: What can practitioners learn from theory and theory builders learn from practitioners?

Q3: What is the relationship right now? Does it exist? Does it work?

Q4: What holds collaboration or interactions back?

Q5: What kind of research, in what form, on what questions would you find most useful for practice? If not very useful, what could or should theory builders do to make their products more useful to you?

Q6: Where do you find theory-based information? Where do you look? What journals, books, publications, reports?

Q7: Does the judiciary carry out supplementary research outside the research required with pending cases? If so, what areas, issues, or questions of law are researched?

Section 5: Transnational Relations

Q1: Have you and the work of your organization been affected by developments outside the country (human rights demands, universal codes of ethics, practical interactions with judges or justices from other countries, personal experiences outside the country, new crime threats, etc.), and if so how?

Q2: Have those interactions been beneficial or harmful? What kinds of external international influences are beneficial and which ones less so?

Q3: How have developments post the terrorist attack on the United States on September 11, 2001, affected your work?

General Assessments

Q1: Are you basically satisfied or dissatisfied with developments in criminal
law and criminal procedure in your system?

Q2: What are the most likely developments that you see happening and
which would you like to see happening?

Q3: What is most needed now to improve the system?

After the Interview

1. Please write a short introduction to the actual interview. The introduction should:
   a. Summarize the highlights of the justices or judges' careers, some
      of this information you can get from the interview and other
      parts from published sources or vitae.
   b. Briefly describe the basic structure of the *legal system* in your
      country. You have to be the judge of how much an informed
      reader is likely to know about your country and how much
      should be explained.
   c. Briefly describe the interview itself. Where, when, how pleasant
      or not, and so on.
2. You should, if at all possible, tape-record the interview. For publication, edit the interview to bring out the most important discussion
   and answers. Chances are that you will have much more information
   than we will have space for your interview in the journal or proposed
   book.
3. Write a short conclusion on your impression of the interview. What
   the major themes were, how well the views expressed accord with
   known literature, but do not be overly critical on this point, please.
   Again, keep it brief.
4. Write a glossary of terms or events mentioned in the interview that
   a reader might not be familiar with, for example, if the interview is
   with a German judge and the *Rechtstaat* is mentioned, describe very
   briefly what that is, or, if interviewing an American judge and the
   Miranda warning is mentioned, describe what the warning is. Just
   select the most likely terms that nonexperienced readers might not
   know.
5. We have had two basic styles in writing up interviews. Both are
   acceptable, but we prefer the second style. One style is to simply tran-
   scribe the interviews—questions asked, answers given. The second
   style, which requires more work, is to write short statements about

the topic of a question and then insert long excerpts from the interviews. The main point is to have the voice and views of the judge being interviewed, not your own.

6. Send the completed interviews to the editors.

Including the introduction, conclusion, and glossary of terms, the total word length of the interview should be about 6000–8000 words.

Finally, each interview will be a book chapter, which should be usable to teach students in a university class or, as a book, it should be a source of knowledge and information to readers interested in legal systems including judges, lawyers, prosecutors, and related professionals.

Appendix B
Canada: Interview with
Quebec Court Judge

REMI BOIVIN AND CHLOE LECLERC

The Canadian Justice System

The Canadian Legal system is based mainly on the British adversarial system. The criminal code, which includes infractions that could be subject to criminal prosecution, is a competence of the Parliament of Canada who alone can legislate. Law enforcement is under provincial jurisdiction, each of the 10 provinces has its own legal system. The Canadian system also follows the principles of common law.

One of the fundamental principles of the Canadian system is the presumption of innocence. The accused is always presumed innocent until proven guilty and the burden of proof lies with the Crown prosecutor who must prove beyond all reasonable doubt that the accused has committed the crime (*actus reus*) and had criminal intent (*mens rea*). A lawyer may choose to present a defense, but he or she can also seek to raise a reasonable doubt about the evidence. In most trials it is the judge who decides whether the accused is guilty, but anyone accused of an offense punishable by a prison term of 5 years or more (e.g., murder or robbery) can exercise his or her right to be tried by a jury of 12 people. In this case, the jurors assess the evidence and the judge acts as legal advisor and explains the rules of law.

In all cases, the sentencing is up to the judge who is guided by a number of principles (proportionality, harmonization, and individualization of sentences, and also moderation). The criminal code provides maximal penalties for each offense but they are rarely, if ever, imposed (Canadian Sentencing Commission, 1987). The criminal code also provides mandatory minimum sentences for a number of offenses. For offenses for which there is no mandatory sentence, judges are free to choose the type of sentence that they wish to impose (imprisonment, conditional sentence, probation, fines, etc.), provided they do not exceed the maximum allowed.

In reality, most criminal cases are settled by a guilty plea from the defendant. It is estimated that in nearly 90% of cases there is no trial

Figure A1. Map of Canada showing location of the province of Quebec.

because the accused pleads guilty (Verdun-Jones and Tijerino, 2002). In most of these cases, the two parties present a single penalty recommendation to the judge. The judge's role is then to determine if the accused is uncoerced to plead guilty and if the proposed recommendation is reasonable. Judges are guided in their decision by judgments from the appeal court: they can only reject an agreement if it is "unreasonable," "against the public interest," or if it "would bring the administration of justice into disrepute." In the vast majority of cases, judges endorse the recommendation of the lawyers.

Introduction

The judge insisted on remaining anonymous, stating that judges in the province of Quebec have to remain neutral and not provide public opinions about the justice system. Consequently, we are not allowed to give the name of the judge. We sent the text to the judge before we submitted it, and he agreed that the write-up was a true record of what was said during the interview. It is a policy that judges in Quebec do not give interviews to journalists, and they rarely participate in research projects if they feel that there is a possibility that they will be identified. The judge we interviewed was willing to be open and honest in his responses; however, in doing so, he had concerns regarding his anonymity and only agreed to be interviewed on the provision that in the write-up we kept his identity anonymous. Following negotiations with the judge whom we interviewed, we appreciated his concerns regarding any potential retribution from the Canadian legal system as a result of the responses we obtained from him, some of which are highly critical of the current position, which adds value to the international study and knowledge of the judiciary.

Career

The judge whom we interviewed for this project has been on the bench for 20 years. Before being appointed a judge, he worked for 10 years in criminal law as a Crown prosecutor at both the provincial and federal level (where he specialized in cases of drug offenses and money laundering). He also regularly acts as a visiting lecturer in two law schools where he teaches criminal law and also civil, corporate, and tax law. He began his career in private practice where he practiced tax and commercial law.

Problems and Successes Experienced

The judge cited three factors that have changed the work of judges in Canada in recent years: (1) an increase in the number of self-represented or unrepresented defendants, (2) the complexity of certain trials, and (3) the limitation of judicial discretion given to judges. For each of these, we will endeavor to describe the phenomenon, identify its consequences, and also possible solutions or adaptations.

The Increase of Self-Represented or Unrepresented Defendants

The first problem identified by the judge is the increased number of defendants who self-represent or are unrepresented. The Canadian Charter of Human Rights and Freedoms, as in many countries around the world, ensures that the accused has the right to contact a lawyer, but this is not an obligation. Although he estimated that the number of people who self-represent or are unrepresented has increased over the last 7 or 8 years, he considered that the problem has intensified in the last 2 years such that today, nearly one in three defendants will self-represent without the assistance of a lawyer. According to the judge, the situation is partly explained by the fact that an increasing number of people are not eligible for legal aid and lack the means to pay for a lawyer. In Quebec (where the judge interviewed sits), the legal aid service ensures that low-income people receive the services of lawyers at no charge. However, the threshold for eligibility for legal aid is so low that it does not currently enable someone working full time but on the minimum wage to obtain free legal aid. Furthermore, the fees charged by many lawyers are such that even the middle classes are unable to pay for the services of a lawyer. On this theme, he said:

> Middle-class people do not have the means to pay a lawyer! We read in the newspapers that the office of a large law firm—an institution in Montreal—is closing. You know, lawyers charged six, seven hundred dollars an hour,* of course... the time comes when this has its limits!

The judge also said that, "Another section of these clients are people who do not want a lawyer anyway... and who flood the judicial system."

This phenomenon of defendants unrepresented by a lawyer has several important consequences. First, this issue puts judges in a difficult position where they have a duty to inform the accused of their rights without becoming their legal counsel, as the judge said:

> ... for example if there is a problem related to the charter,† the accused does not know that. The judge, at the constitutional level, has an obligation to intervene to advise that there may be a problem. The judge should not become counsel for the party, but he must also inform them about some of their rights. So it's really... it's a balance that is not easy!

---

* The Canadian dollar could be considered equivalent to the US dollar. In Quebec, the minimum wage is $10.15/h, and the median annual income of individuals is $28,000. For reference, in January 2014, the eligibility threshold for free legal aid was increased to $16,306 for a single person and $26,737 for a family of two adults and two children.

† The judge refers to the Canadian Charter of Human Rights and Freedoms, adopted in 1982. Articles 7–14 of this charter are intended to protect people in criminal matters (e.g., the right to not be subject to search or unreasonable seizure; the right to be tried within a reasonable time, etc.). The judge spoke of the enactment of the charter as one of the major changes that occurred during his professional practice. He explained that the charter has several implications for the work of judges: "It's a lot more work! Cases that previously took a day can now take 3 days because of the arguments about the charter." The charter has significant consequences for the outcome of cases. "When you exclude evidence, knowing very well that the accused is guilty, but because there was a violation of the charter, you acquit him." He concluded by saying: "It is clear that the charter has contributed to the fact that cases are more onerous, they take more time, so time frames are longer. Of that, I have no hesitation in my mind! No hesitation! [...] But in a democratic society, it is a tool that is essential. [...] I think this is a blessing in disguise."

The judge continued:

> This is a major problem because we need to balance between the person who has a lawyer and the one who does not. One should not favor someone who does not have a lawyer while the other person pays for a lawyer. So we are constantly walking a tightrope.

Another major consequence identified by the judge is, "...that the trial takes twice as long," thus contributing to the diminishing access to justice since delays for a hearing are being extended. The accused are not accustomed to the judicial machinery and so procedures are longer and require more explanation.

Finally, the judge explained that there are some associated additional costs, giving the example of when:

> ... in cases of sexual assault... we do not want the accused cross-examining the victim and so we appoint a duty counsel for the cross-examination of the victim: these are additional costs.

The duty counsel, whose salary is paid by the judicial system, must get prepared and conduct the cross-examination.

The judge stressed that this problem is recognized by the entire judiciary and it is the subject of various seminars and training sessions that are designed to equip judges to deal with defendants who self-represent or are unrepresented. For those for whom the decision to self-represent is a choice and who voluntarily flood the justice system with complaints, he said, "The only solution is to forbid them to file private or civil complaints for example," adding that this is something that judges are already doing. For others who are unrepresented, he said, "...the only solution is to increase the threshold for eligibility for legal aid." Some changes in this regard were adopted last December and from June 2015, legal aid will be free for anyone working full time on the minimum wage. Although this increase may help to improve the situation, other measures are necessary for the middle class. The judge cites the example of an organization, the legal clinic Juripop, which provides free or low-cost legal advice to people who are not eligible for legal aid but are nonetheless unable to afford the services of a lawyer.

The Complexity of Some Trials

In recent years, the government has embarked on a number of fairly complex trials, on which the judge said:

> ... it is not at all the same use of judicial resources as it was 20 years ago when the trial lasted a day or two and it was rare that there were several codefendants.

These trials, which today are termed *megatrials*,* are considered to be highly complex, either because of the amount of evidence presented or because of the nature of the evidence. The Canadian Department of Justice and the Barreau du Québec (the professional association of lawyers) have also formed committees and produced reports on issues related to megatrials.

The judge explained that one finds two principal types of highly complex trials. The first type involves several codefendants. They mainly concern charges against members of criminal groups. In the first trial of this kind, referred to as Operation Springtime 2001, several charges were laid against more than 138 individuals associated with a group of criminalized bikers. The judge explained that the expected benefits of these megatrials were primarily financial. The intention was to have a trial for a group of accused in order to avoid getting witnesses to testify several times over. The aim was to avoid not only the costs related to testimonies and disruption for witnesses but also the possible contradictions in the testimonies. In fact, these megatrials present significant challenges for judges, as the judge explained:

> It is more complicated because you have more lawyers and you have more objections and the admissible evidence against one person is not necessarily admissible against another. So when I tell you they are more complex, that's what I mean.

These megatrials have also experienced some setbacks that the judge recognized, saying:

> The megatrial ended up getting nowhere because there were unreasonable delays for people who had been arrested [...] The trial judge had separated the cases. He then ordered a halt to all proceedings in certain cases because the accused couldn't be tried within a reasonable time. Because he said they would not go to trial for 5 or 6 years.

The judge's decision was upheld by a judgment of the court of appeal, which severely criticized the work of prosecutors as the judge explained saying, "...because it was a huge issue and they were not about to send it into the judicial system..." when they filed their charges.

The judge said the other type of highly complex process that has emerged concerns:

> ... financial crimes which have become much more complex: money laundering, [...], stock market manipulations.

---

* The judge explained: "So a megatrial; that's what it takes in judicial resources to be able to deal with the issue."

For the judge we interviewed, the arrival of these new charges is explained as much by the increase in the complexity of the offenses as by a more repressive state response to this type of crime. He said:

> The public was outraged by the *Lacroix* case,* so the government spent more money on financial crimes to protect investors. The AMF began with four lawyers while today I think they are fifteen.

For judges, these trials present a challenge as they call for new skills, "…in accounting, you need to know tax laws, you need to understand international law, securities," and show proof, which is often very cumbersome and complex.

This type of trial has also had its share of problems. One of the first trials of this kind had to dismiss the jury who were unable to reach agreement after several days of deliberations. These jurors, with no specialist knowledge in finance, had heard more than 65 witnesses over a 4-month period; had at their disposal more than 30,000 pages of documents and were required to decide the fate of four codefendants and for a total of 702 charges.

The judge stated that this problem is part of the concerns of the judiciary, which organizes training on the subject to better equip judges. For him, the various actors are slowly readjusting themselves as a consequence of errors committed in some megatrials. Regarding the solutions in the short and long term and the involvement of judges in case management, the judge said:

> I think that one thing that has changed is that judges are now more proactive. We do more case management. Parties are forced to talk. We will seek confessions. We try to shrink it to get to the basics and then really argue what is important to argue. That really is a difference. Honestly, judges are really much, much more proactive. Whereas before we watched the parade and listened to the evidence. But then, if that's three witnesses who say the same thing, the judge will intervene: "do you still need that one or will he come and say the same thing?". Tailing?: "Are you serious? Do you really want a testimony on tailing?" Because they can't just say nothing, they can only read their little paper because it's been 4 years. So we are so much more interventionist in order to achieve a better use of judicial resources.

The Limitation of Judicial Discretion

The judge also noted a trend toward a limitation of judges' judicial discretion. This was felt particularly by two types of legislative changes resulting from

---

* The judge is referring to the *Norbourg* case in which a man, Vincent Lacroix, defrauded more than 9200 investors for a total of $130 million. This case, the biggest financial scandal that Quebec had ever known, has been much discussed in the media and in Quebec homes.

the Safe Streets and Communities Act, which have had a major impact on the work of judges: (1) the introduction of mandatory sentences and (2) conditions limiting the use of conditional sentence.

For the judge:

> A fairly obvious change is the introduction of mandatory sentences. In recent years, there has been an increasing number of mandatory sentences, so that the discretion of judges is gradually being diluted.

Before 2012, the criminal code provided mandatory minimum sentences for 45 offenses. The Safe Streets and Communities Act, in force since 2012, has created new mandatory sentences (ranging from 30 days to 5 years in prison) for 29 offenses and has extended the existing minimum sentences to another 15 offenses.

The other major change that limits the exercise of judicial discretion concerns crimes eligible for conditional sentences (e.g., imprisonment in the community). This sentence was introduced in 1996 to create a credible alternative to incarceration. The judge recalls:

> I remember my first conditional sentences where I gave my conditions, the accused stood up and told me he would prefer to serve time. I told him that it was not he who decides.

Since 2012, as a consequence of the Safe Streets and Communities Act, judges can no longer hand down a conditional sentence for several offenses, which they were accustomed to doing. On this issue, the judge said:

> ... impaired driving causing bodily harm, if there are cases where the conditional sentence could be used beneficially, it was that. But now that's gone. An 18-year-old that I sent to speak in schools to explain what it's all about rather than sending him to prison for 2 years... I think that society is best served if I rehabilitate, but today I can no longer give a conditional sentence.

Many of the offenses covered by the new law are crimes for which the judges most often gave a conditional sentence. The conditional sentence was never a very popular sentence (at most they represent 5% of convictions) and for this judge these new guidelines impose a serious obstacle to the use of this sentence, where he said:

> there is less and less imprisonment in the community. They cut back, they cut back, because they consider that judges have given too many [...].

The conditional sentence was introduced as a credible alternative to incarceration and not to punish defendants who otherwise would not have gone to jail. The judge explains:

as for me the conditional sentence was diverted and it has not always been used as it should have been. The term *net widening* is used to describe the practice of several judges who condemned people, who would not have been incarcerated in a correctional facility, to imprisonment in the community.

Thus, either the new restrictions on conditional sentences for serious crimes will contribute to this net widening that the judge speaks of, or they will contribute to the disappearance of this measure.

According to the judge, prosecutor discretion has also seen circumscribed:

It seems that prosecutors have less discretion than they had before. When I was a Crown prosecutor I had a lot of discretion to make decisions on my cases. Now they are monitored.

This limitation of the discretion in the work of prosecutors may have a direct impact on the decisions and practices of judges as prosecutors have less leeway to "negotiate" their cases and settle cases other than by trial.

This tightening up on discretion may have several important implications. First, it can undermine the confidence of judges and prosecutors who might see their professional skills discredited, as the judge said:

The judges never like it when their discretionary power is removed because discretionary power is related to the exercise of judgment. If you give me discretionary power that is because you think I have judgment and that I'm going to exercise it properly.

In addition, the limitation of discretionary power can have a significant impact on guilty pleas, as the judge explained:

So, before there were guilty pleas and now there are trials. There is no longer an incentive to plead guilty. Unless the accused is likely to get more than the minimum sentence, but otherwise [...] There are people who would have pleaded guilty before but no longer plead guilty. Then, if the witness does not appear, they will be acquitted.

When asked about the possibility that the discretionary power of the judges has simply been transferred to the prosecutors, who may choose to pursue one charge for which there is no mandatory sentence, the judge replied:

It does not happen that much and also there are a lot of crimes, such as sexual assault, to which they cannot plead guilty to a lesser charge [...] the Crown is also pressured to not settle at a discount.

This increase in the number of trials results in increased costs and lengthy procedures, which in turn increase the time before a case can be heard.

Finally, the most direct and most important consequence of this tightening up is clearly, "…a hardening in crime policy. *You cannot call it otherwise!*" In some cases, judges no longer have the option to favor moderation or alternatives to imprisonment. Their job is to enforce the law, even if they would have acted otherwise were it not for the pressure on their discretionary power. The judge is clear on this point, that judges do not have a choice and he does not believe in the Montesquieu effect, according to which judges prefer to acquit an accused rather than impose an unfair sentence. He adds:

> That's an urban legend! I am deeply convinced of it! Then I experienced it myself… No! You cannot because you apply the law. The evidence is there, it's there. It is not true that you will acquit him when you think he's guilty.

In some cases, at the request of defense counsel, mandatory sentences may be declared unconstitutional because they violate the law encapsulated in the charter to protect people against cruel and unusual punishment. But it is an exceptional situation, the norm being that judges impose the mandatory sentence.

General Assessment

For the judge, the current major issue of the justice system is the accessibility to justice. He said:

> In all areas, that's where the problem is. People do not come to court: it's too long, it's too expensive so people solve their own problems. […] There's an 18 months delay! It just does not make sense!

So to ensure better access to justice, it is essential to work on the time and cost of procedures.

The judge explains the problems of delay with several examples, some of which are direct consequences of the changes observed in recent years. The enactment of the Canadian Charter of Human Rights and Freedoms in 1982 and more recently the megatrials have complicated and lengthened the procedures and they, along with the increase in the number of defendants who self-represent or are unrepresented, have contributed to the increases in the length of trials heard by the judges. Also, as already mentioned, the introduction of mandatory sentences impacts, according to the judge, the number of people who choose to go to trial, which in turn increases the time and cost of cases heard by the courts.

On the other hand, what seems to be the most important factor in the inaccessibility to justice is a poor use of judicial resources. He gave a few examples saying:

The detainee:* there are courtrooms that start at 10:30 [with an hour delay] because the detainee has not yet arrived. It does not make sense, lawyers, witnesses are all there, but the detainee is not there, "or," we set a 3-day trial and the person pleads guilty in the morning. It's not good—We lose 3 days of court time [unplanned free time is not filled up with pending cases]. This is not good, because it makes delays longer.

Such time wasters are responsible for many of the delays and they cost the judiciary a lot since many resources are mobilized for nothing.

According to the judge, a better use of judicial resources could certainly contribute to better access to justice. He said:

We must make a trial when we must make trial and plead guilty before so as not to lose our rooms. Here we have 70% of the roll† dropping every day.

The judge pointed out that this use of resources can only be achieved through a greater collaboration between the various stakeholders, saying:

So one of the solutions, too, is that you stop working in silos. Because when detention is late, it costs the judiciary money. When someone comes to give evidence it costs them money. When the judge who's sitting does nothing it costs money.

This change will not be effortless because it is a real change in the practices and attitudes of the various judicial actors. As the judge explained:

You know, in the case of domestic violence, lawyers wait until the morning to plead guilty to see whether or not the victim will come to testify. Attitudes need to be changed. We must get people to understand that it's all the stakeholders in the justice system and that it's the system that pays at the end of the day.

The judge emphasized the fact that although this change in mentality will not be smooth, it has to happen as it constitutes one of the fundamentals for a more efficient and fair system of justice.

For this judge, a more concrete way to improve access to justice is to involve judges in case management. In regard to Ontario, a neighboring province, the judge explained that:

... they set up a system whereby a manager judge manages and that trials are not booked if they have not gone before him. Then 2 months before the trial

---

* The judge is referring to the security officers who are responsible for transporting inmates from the correctional center, where they are held awaiting trial, to the courtroom.
† The roll refers to the list of cases that should be heard in court.

date, he recalls them to find out whether it will proceed or not. He makes them sign documents and then they are locked in...

He concluded by saying that they have 4 months compared with the 18 months where he sits. Although Quebec does not have manager judges as yet, the judge noted that there is a greater involvement of judges so that some cases are settled more quickly and without trial. He took the quite recent example of a facilitation conference in criminal and penal matters, saying:

> It's a bit like mediation, but for a criminal matter. You know, when the Crown wants 4 years and it just does not make sense looking at the record and the weakness of the evidence [...] but the defendant is ready to admit his guilt, but perhaps over 2 years... Well maybe you'll discuss it with others and get the parties to an agreement... In order to avoid going to court.

Otherwise, access to justice also involves a more general philosophy of the justice system, which in his words must:

> identify the real cases where it is necessary to criminalize, to judicialize versus cases where you could, for example, use alternative measures. There is a program of alternative measures, but it is not very developed. So I think we should try, and I think that Quebec is not so bad, to see not only the criminal justice system... punish when you need to punish, but rehabilitate when you can rehabilitate. [...] So the key is to find a balance between punishment, which is clearly needed for certain crimes and restorative and rehabilitative justice, which means that at the end of the day society is better served. Except that getting the balance is not always easy.

Conclusion

The judge expressed concern about tougher crime policies that have been implemented in recent years. The issue of tougher crime policies and practices is far from new in the criminology literature. Over 10 years ago, Garland (2001) suggested that we were witnessing a significant hardening of criminal practices. If the thesis of a punitive shift was hardly challenged in the United States and England, its application in Canada or elsewhere has been greatly nuanced, indeed significantly questioned. In Canada, several arguments have been put forward to refute this argument of a punitive turn. First, it has been argued that the rate of incarceration (one of the most significant symptoms of such a turn) has remained relatively stable in Canada since the 1960s (Doob and Webster, 2006).

Second, authors have observed a clear " bifurcation" in the justice system, consisting of proposing punitive policies for serious crimes or for criminals considered to be dangerous, while in parallel developing policies for less serious crimes (which are much more common) that are more focused on moderation and rehabilitation (see Doob and Webster, 2006; Landreville, 2007 as examples of this dual tendency).

Third, it was suggested that while the tone of penal discourses and policies has considerably hardened, this has not always had major or even any significant impacts on penal practices (Landreville, 2007; Doob and Webster, 2006). First of all because some of the so-called repressive policies merely formalized an already established practice among judges, as was the case with a number of the minimum sentences that were added to the criminal code in the late 1990s. Then, because some policies focused on elements that were highly unlikely to bring changes in practice. For example, the increase in the maximum penalties can serve to reassure the public, but since the maximums are rarely applied by judges, it does not lead to an actual increase in the punitiveness of the judicial system. This, among other things, is what led Doob and Webster (2006) to describe Canadian policies as: "Talk tough, act softly." Lastly, several penal policies toward criminals enabled judges to be more severe while leaving the final decision to their discretion. In fact, judges have never been particularly enthusiastic about repressive measures, which means that there has been few changes in practices (Doob and Webster, 2006; Landreville, 2007).

Doob and Webster (2006) have proposed several possible explanations as to how and why Canada has managed to reduce the impact of repressive penal policies on incarceration rates. Among these reasons, they speak of the fact that "the government and the opposition rarely make crime issues a central part of their political platform" (Doob and Webster, 2006, p. 341) and that they continued to trust the competence of experts and professionals to establish criminal policies. However, this situation has changed considerably since the publication of their paper in 2006, as evidenced by this quote from a Conservative minister in 2011:* "We believe that the best experts in Canada are the electorate who gave us the mandate to do what we said we would do [make Canadian streets safer]." This quote clearly illustrates how expert opinion has become second place in the development of penal policies and how the fight against crime has become a major election issue.

It is reasonable to ask whether this recent penal populism and the proposed legislative reforms of 2011 with the Safe Streets and Communities Act will now have greater impact on penal practices and whether they will result in a punitive turn. Although judges are asked not to comment directly on

---

* The Conservatives were elected in 2006 but with a minority government. New elections in 2011 gave them a majority in parliament and they decided to prioritize the adoption of their draft bills on Safe Streets and Communities.

criminal policies,* several general comments made during the interview allow us to elaborate on the current situation. Based on the judge's comments, two of the recent criminal policies—the introduction of mandatory sentences and the conditions introduced to conditional sentence—may well have a greater impact than measures adopted in the past. First, because the new legal provisions are not always consistent with the practice of the courts. The judge explained that the limitation on conditional sentence has changed their practice because they applied to offenses for which the judges were to grant conditional sentence. Then the judge explained how both of these policies impacted fairly frequent offenses such as impaired driving, drug-related crimes, sexual assault, and so on. In this way, these two legislative changes differ from some previous policies that perhaps had little impact because they related to infrequent offenses (e.g., murder committed by juveniles) or elements that have little effect on practice (maximum penalties). Finally, the judge clearly showed that these two policies had a significant impact in that they prevented judges from exercising their discretion. Unlike policies that give a judge the opportunity to take a more severe decision, these changes in the law require them to follow the new rule.

On the other hand, it is important to highlight important details. Although these two policies are clearly intended to limit the options available to judges, they also offer them a certain freedom. For example, in the case of drug-related offenses the judge said:

> ... there is a section in the new law that allows a judge to avoid the mandatory sentence if the individual has been receiving treatment in a organism recognized by the province.

As to limits on the granting of a conditional sentence, if this penalty is clearly impossible for some offenses it is less so for others since in such cases the impossibility depends not only on the circumstances of the case such as the type of indictment (decided by prosecutors), but also on whether there are aggravating circumstances (identified by the judge). It seems clear that judges will continue to exert significant influence not only on penal practices for these two new legal provisions, but also, and especially, for many of the other provisions of the law that the judge did not discuss.[†]

---

* The Canadian Judicial Council affirmed in 1995 that if a judge wanted to oppose government policies, he could not do this from the platform of a judge.

† The Safe Streets and Communities Act introduces an impressive number of changes to the law. An analysis of these provisions is outside the scope of this appendix. However, it seems that the judge has clearly identified the two provisions that are most likely to impact the practice of the courts. Several of the other provisions have the characteristics of the previous reforms that make their expected impact more limited either because they concern rare crimes (terrorism, mass murder, etc.) or because they provide for new, more repressive options but without making them mandatory.

The Interview

The interview, which lasted an hour and a half, took place in February 2014 in the judge's office. He began by highlighting the main changes that have marked his work in recent years before talking about current issues in the justice system and the best way of coping with these. The interview took place in a pleasant environment without too much outside interference.

It was evident from our discussion with the judge that he was open to alternative measures and less punitive options. This is not without significance because the resistance of the different social actors (e.g., judges, prosecutors) has in the past served to create a large gap between penal discourse and actual practice (O'Malley, 2006; Moore and Hannah-Moffat, 2005; Landreville, 2007). The judge emphasized the importance of judicial independence. The fact that judges' salaries are established by law and that they are appointed for life protect them from public or government pressures (Vanhamme, 2013). On this theme, we leave the final word to the judge we interviewed who said:

> Judicial independence... that's it. I can make a decision that will displease the government without losing my job in the morning as opposed to a judge in some US states where perhaps at the next election, will not be accepted. It is the cornerstone of judicial independence and I think that we have it.

But if we want judges to continue to take their decisions independently, they must be given the necessary flexibility to do so.

Glossary

Autorité des marchés financiers (AMF): A body mandated by the government of Quebec to regulate the province's financial markets (insurance, securities).

Canadian Charter of Human Rights and Freedoms: This charter was adopted in 1982 to protect Canadians against actions, policies, or government legislation. At the judicial level, the charter provides several guarantees relating to unreasonable searches, search and seizure, detention, arrest, and judicial proceedings.

conditional sentence: Allows an accused to serve his or her prison time in the community while respecting certain conditions such as curfew or house arrest. If the conditions are violated, the individual must normally complete his or her sentence in prison.

Court of Appeal of Quebec: The court of appeal has a control function over the lower courts and can modify a decision taken in a provincial court. Its decisions provide guidance for provincial judges. Its decisions can also be sent on appeal (to be revised) to the Supreme Court of Canada, the highest court in the country.

crown prosecutor: A lawyer who acts as a representative of the state and is responsible for the prosecution of criminal offenses.

defense counsel: A lawyer who represents the interests of the accused.

facilitation conference in criminal and penal matters: A conference where the different parties try to find a satisfactory legal solution usually enabling them to avoid a trial. At this conference, the judge facilitates the discussion and promotes exchanges between the lawyers of both parties.

legal aid: A Quebec government program that provides eligible individuals with legal services that are free or contributory ($100–$800). Eligible persons can either use the services of a lawyer who works full-time for legal aid or they can seek the services of a lawyer who works in the private sector but who accepts legal aid clients.

Safe Streets and Communities Act: This act, passed in 2012, amalgamates nine bills. The act provides for mandatory minimum sentences, limits the use of conditional sentences, and makes youth crime subject to more severe penalties.

Appendix C
Research Methods
Used during the
Interview of Judge Udu,
Ebonyi State Court

OKO ELECHI AND SMART E. OTU

This study is based on a nonsurvey, nonsampling method of data collection. Although our interviewee was purposely selected, this was, however, accomplished by the technique of referral (snowballing). Our reason for employing the referral technique was to ensure that we got the right judge who had the intellectual capacity that was needed to understand the depth of the issues under discourse. That is, the interview respondent was purposely selected based on two criteria: the relevance of his official position vis-à -vis issues of legal adjudication, and his reputation among his colleagues for being knowledgeable on legal theory and practice issues in Nigeria. The interviewee was selected after due consultations with judges, magistrates, and solicitors.

The next stage after identifying our respondent was a one-on-one meeting in his office to introduce ourselves and to obtain his consent. His willingness to participate was followed by our making available the questionnaires to enable him to study them before the proper interview. Before the interview proper took place, we were constantly communicating with the respondent to iron out gray areas to facilitate the smooth running of the interview.

The data collection technique was basically non-tape-recorded, in-depth, structured interviews (NTIDI) conducted during July 2013. Using the already mapped out themes as our interview guide, which helped us to remain focused, we were able to confront our respondent with some unlisted questions that arose during the process of the interviews but which nonetheless were considered critical to the issue of legal theory and practice in the Nigerian judicial system. That is, wherever and whenever the interviewee gave relevant information while providing answers to the questions asked, such information was probed further by the interviewer.

Appendix D
New Zealand's Children, Young Persons, and Their Families Act 1989

EMMA DAVIES

The Children, Young Persons, and Their Families Act 1989

This legislation emerged after much consultation throughout the country over 4 years through two government working parties and over 900 submissions (Watt, 2003). The final Children, Young Persons, and Their Families (CYPF) Act enabled young offenders and their families, the community, and the state to take shared responsibility for youth offending, its consequences, and its redress.

It is important to understand the zeitgeist: One take on this is that there was a fairly direct line from the ferment of the 1960s and 1970s to significant antiapartheid protests in 1981 against the Springbok's rugby tour in New Zealand. As a result, Pākehā New Zealanders were challenged by Māori leaders to do more about race problems at home. Three years later, when the Labor Party won the 1984 snap election with a landslide, it uncovered skyrocketing public debt. It promptly implemented economic reforms, which were particularly harsh on the poor; Māori disproportionately lost their jobs. So, in the 1980s there were many challenges to the power of the state.

The values and principles underpinning the CYPF Act were partially motivated by *Puao-te-ata-tu*, the report of the Ministerial Advisory Committee on a Māori perspective for the Department of Social Welfare (1988). The department was challenged to overcome the monocultural practices of state institutions and the disempowerment and removal of responsibility from families by social workers and other agents of the state. Public servants in the department, most notably in this context Mike Doolan, the then national director (youth and employment), rose to this substantive and complex challenge and steered more culturally respectful approaches to youth offending through the policy-making process.

Mike Doolan describes the key elements of the legal proposals for youth justice as follows:

- Greater protections for children and young persons while they are being questioned, and restrictions on the use of arrest.
- Minimizing young people's involvement with the criminal justice system in favor of other means of dealing with their offending.
- Involving more than just professional perspectives in decision making about young people.
- Empowering family groups (extended family collectives) to lead the decision making and take responsibility for the outcomes.
- Providing a role for families in advising courts, where they have to be involved, about outcome.*

The cornerstone of the CYPF Act is the family group conference (FGC), a decision-making forum for offenders, victims, family groups, and professionals to work together to deal with the offending. In essence, the FGC is a process that attempts to empower the wider family and community system of which victims and young offenders are a part.

At its best, the FGC is a process of dialogue, not a one-off event. It is convened by an independent youth justice coordinator employed by the state. The coordinator's independence is important to mitigate the power imbalance between professionals (such as the police) and the families.

The coordinator facilitates discussion among people with a vested interest in the young person and his or her offending to work together in the interests of the participants and the broader community. When operating well, the FGC provides a process through which apologies can be heard, the damage caused by offending can start to be healed, and effective ways of dealing with the offending and preventing recidivism can emerge. In this way, it is hoped that all participants can feel some sense of justice.

The act thus empowers families and communities, including victims, to determine the best ways to respond to child and youth offending. These processes are now recognized as the first example of a legislated restorative justice process within a common law system to determine the primary response to offending, with the sanctions of the court still available if, and only if, agreement cannot be reached. Commentators around the world have seen family group conferencing in New Zealand as "a catalyst for, and beacon of, the restorative justice movement informing both theory" (Crawford and Newburn, 2003). Some form of FGC has been adopted in several jurisdictions, including Australian states, England, Wales, Northern Ireland, Canada, and Belgium (Lynch, 2012).

* Personal communication, September 5, 2013.

Table D.1   Section 208: Youth Justice Principles

(a) Unless the public interest requires otherwise, criminal proceedings should not be instituted against a child or young person if there is an alternative means of dealing with the matter.

(b) Criminal proceedings should not be instituted against a child or young person solely in order to provide any assistance or services needed to advance the welfare of the child or young person, or his or her family, whanau,[a] or family group.

(c) Any measures for dealing with offending by children or young persons should be designed:
  (i) To strengthen the family, whanau, hapu,[b] iwi,[c] and family group of the child or young person concerned.
  (ii) To foster the ability of families, whanau, hapu, iwi, and family groups to develop their own means of dealing with offending by their children and young persons.

(d) A child or young person who commits an offense should be kept in the community so far as that is practicable and consonant with the need to ensure the safety of the public.

(e) A child's or young person's age is a mitigating factor in determining:
  (i) Whether or not to impose sanctions in respect of offending by a child or young person.
  (ii) The nature of any such sanctions.

(f) Any sanctions imposed on a child or young person who commits an offense should:
  (i) Take the form most likely to maintain and promote the development of the child or young person within his or her family, whanau, hapu, and family group.
  (ii) Take the least restrictive form that is appropriate in the circumstances.

(fa) Any measures for dealing with offending by a child or young person should, so far as it is practicable to do so, address the causes underlying the child's or young person's offending.[d]

(g) (i) In the determination of measures for dealing with offending by children or young persons, consideration should be given to the interests and views of any victims of the offending (e.g., by encouraging the victims to participate in the processes under this part for dealing with offending).
  (ii) Any measures should have proper regard for the interests of any victims of the offending and the impact of the offending on them.[e]

(h) The vulnerability of children and young persons entitles a child or young person to special protection during any investigation relating to the commission or possible commission of an offense by that child or young person.[f]

[a] The whanau is an extended family group with common ancestors in any generation.
[b] The hapu is the main unit of Māori society. It is a subtribe or localized group of several hundred people of common descent made up of several interrelated families.
[c] The iwi is a tribe; the largest political unit in Māori society.
[d] Section 208(fa): inserted on October 1, 2010, by Section 6(1) of the Children, Young Persons, and Their Families (Youth Courts Jurisdiction and Orders) Amendment Act 2010 (2010 No. 2).
[e] The term *due regard* was substituted by the term *proper regard* in the amendments of 2010.
[f] Section 208(g): substituted on October 1, 2010, by Section 6(2) of the Children, Young Persons, and Their Families (Youth Courts Jurisdiction and Orders) Amendment Act 2010 (2010 No. 2).

The Principles

Section 208 of the CYPF Act outlines the principles that guide the exercise of power conferred under the youth justice provisions of the act, subject to the general principles outlined in Section 5. Given the significance of these principles, they are reproduced here in full (see Table D.1). By highlighting diversion, victim participation, and family and community engagement, they are consistent with the restorative justice theory with its emphasis on participation, repair, healing, and reintegration into the community (Johnstone and Ness, 2007). However, they were not developed in accordance with this theory (Lynch, 2012), but were instead advanced through a critical national conversation that spanned the broader role of the state in people's lives.

References

Aboriginal Justice Advisory Committee. (2000). Discussion paper: Circle sentencing involving Aboriginal communities in the sentencing process. New South Wales, Australia: Lawlink, Attorney General's Department of NSW.

Adorjan, M., & Chui, W. H. (2011). Making sense of going straight: Personal accounts of male ex-prisoners in Hong Kong. *The British Journal of Criminology, 52*(3), 577–590.

Agrast, M., Botero, J., Martinez, J., Ponce, A., & Pratt, C. (2012). *The Rule of Law Index 2012-2013 Report*. Washington, DC: The World Justice Project.

Alemika, E. E. O., & Chukwuma, I. (2004). The poor and informal policing in Nigeria. A report on poor peoples' perceptions and priorities on safety, security and informal policing in A2J focal states in Nigeria. Lagos: CLEEN.

American Judicature Society. (2008). *Judicial Selection in the States: How It Works and Why It Matters*. Drake University, IA: American Judicature Society.

Amoah, A. K. (2012). When the judiciary is defective. *The Chronicle.* February 17. Retrieved from the chronicle.com.gh/when-the-judiciary-is-defective. Accessed October 8, 2014.

Anderson, T. (1992). *Take Two: The Criminal Justice System Revisited.* Sydney: Bantam.

Ashworth, A., & Horder, J. (2009). *Principles of Criminal Law* (7th ed.). Oxford: Oxford University Press.

Australian Institute of Criminology. (2013). *About the AIC.* Retrieved from http://www.aic.gov.au/about_aic.html. Accessed December 15, 2013.

Australian Law Reform Commission. (1988). Sentencing of Federal Offenders (1978–88). Retrieved from http://www.alrc.gov.au/inquiries/sentencing-federal-offenders-1978-88. Accessed December 16, 2013.

Babalakin and Co. (2005). Resources: The judicial system in Nigeria. Retrieved from http://www.babalakinandco.com/resources/judicialsystem.html. Accessed December 12, 2013.

Bahmueller, C. (1999). Law. In *US Court Cases: Law and Courts* (1st ed., pp. 12–20). Pasadena, CA: Salem Press.

Baker, T. (1999). The US judicial system. In *US Court Cases: Law and Courts* (1st ed., pp. 60–69). Pasadena, CA: Salem Press.

Baksi, C. (2013). Grayling confirms legal aid concessions. *Law Society Gazette.* Accessed September 5, 2013.

Bannon, A. (2013). *Federal Judicial Vacancies: The Trial Courts.* New York University, School of Law, Brennan Center for Justice.

BBC News. (2013). Keir Starmer says new child abuse trial guidelines are "biggest shift for generation", October 17. Retrieved from http://www.bbc.co.uk/news/uk-24555303. Accessed October 19, 2013.

Beck, L. (2013). What is a "Supreme Court"? *Sydney Law Review, 31,* 295.

Becroft, A. (2009). Are there lessons to be learned from the Youth Justice System? Paper presented at the Institute of Policy Studies Forum: Addressing the Underlying Causes of Offending: What is the Evidence? Victoria University of Wellington, 26 February.

Berelowitz, S., Firmin, C., Edwards, G., & Gulyurtlu, S. (2012). "I thought I was the only one. The only one in the world." Office of the Children's Commission inquiry into child sexual exploitation in gangs and groups: Interim report. Children's Commissioner. Retrieved from http://www.nspcc.org.uk/Inform/research/briefings/childrens_commissioners_inquiry_CSE_wda94172.html. Accessed December 12, 2013.

Berelowitz, S., Firmin, C., Gulyurtlu, S., & Edwards, G. (2013). "If only someone had listened" Office of the Children's Commission inquiry into child sexual exploitation in gangs and groups: Final report. Children's Commissioner. Retrieved from http://www.childrenscommissioner.gov.uk/content/publications/content_743. Accessed November 28, 2013.

Bimpong-Buta, S.Y. (2007). *The Role of the Supreme Court in the Development of Constitutional Law in Ghana*. Accra: Advanced Legal Publications.

Black's Law Dictionary. (2001). Retrieved from http://www.thelawdictionary.org.

Bokor, M. J. K. (2010). Confronting Ghana's main problems: Judiciary Part II. GhanaWeb May 7. Retrieved from www.ghanaweb.com-News-2010-05-07. Accessed October 8, 2014.

Bowcott, O. (2013). Legal aid cuts will lead to more miscarriages of justice, top judges warn. *The Guardian*, July 5.

Brewer, D. V. (2012). Oregon Court of Appeals report, 2011–2012. Oregon Court of Appeals.

Brown, M. J. (1989). *The Children's, Young Persons, and Their Families Act: A New Voyage*. Wellington: New Zealand Law Society.

Brown, M. J. (2000). Care and protection is about adult behaviour. The Ministerial Review of the Department of Child, Youth and Family Services (pp. 41–42). Report to the minister of social services and employment Hon. Steve Maharey. Wellington: Department of Social Welfare.

Bureau of Justice Assistance. (2014). Retrieved from http://www.bja.gov. Accessed January 5, 2014.

Burnham, W. (2011). *Introduction to the Law and Legal System of the United States* (5th ed.). St. Paul, MN: Thomson Reuters.

Canadian Sentencing Commission. (1987) Sentencing reform: A Canadian approach: Report of the Canadian Sentencing Commission. Ottawa: Canadian Government Publishing Centre, Supply and Services Canada.

Carp, A. R., Stidham, R., & Manning, L. K. (2011). *Judicial Process in America* (8th ed.). Washington, DC: CQ Press.

Chan, J. (1995). The Hong Kong Bill of Rights, 1991–1995: A statistical overview. In A. Edwards & J. Chan (Eds.), *Hong Kong's Bill of Rights: Two Years before 1997*. Hong Kong: University of Hong Kong.

Chappell, D., & Wilson, P. R. (2005). *The Australian Criminal Justice System* (6th ed.). Sydney: Butterworths/Lexis Nexis.

Chiu, A. (2013). Courts in the dark ages when it comes to communications, say experts. *South China Morning Post*. Available at: http://www.scmp.com/news/hong-kong/article/1295073/courts-dark-ages-when-it-comes-communications-say-experts. Accessed August 24, 2013.

Chui, W. H. (2001). Theoretical underpinnings of community-based sentences and custody for young offenders in Hong Kong. *Hong Kong Law Journal*, 31(2), 266–282.

Chui, W. H., & Lo, T. W. (2009). *Understanding Criminal Justice in Hong Kong*. Devon, UK: Willan Publishing.

Chukwuma, I. (2011). The state of crime, criminal and criminal justice and criminology in a failing state. In C.J. Smith, S.X. Zhang and R. Barberet (eds.) *Routledge Handbook of International Criminology*, New York: Routledge.

Clarkson, C., & Keating, H. (2007). *Clarkson and Keating Criminal Law* (6th ed.). London: Sweet & Maxwell.

Crawford, A., & Newburn, T. (2003). *Youth Offending and Restorative Justice: Implementing Reform in Youth Justice*. Devon, UK: Willan Publishing.

Daly, K. (2002). Restorative justice—The real story. *Punishment and Society*, 4(1), 55–79.

Davies, E., Henderson, E., & Hanna, K. (2010). Facilitating children to give best evidence: Are there better ways to challenge children's evidence? *Criminal Law Journal*, 34, 347–362.

Davis, M. (1999). Constitutionalism under Chinese rule: Hong Kong after the handover. *Denver Journal of International Law and Policy*, 27(2), 275–312.

Dellara, D. (1995). *Conspiracy: True Stories*. Sydney: Australian Broadcasting Commission.

Director of Public Prosecutions. (2013). Interim guidelines on prosecuting cases of child sexual abuse. Retrieved from https://www.cps.gov.uk/consultations/csa_consultation.html. Accessed October 30, 2013.

Ditton, B., & Wilson, D. J. (1999). Truth in sentencing in state prisons. Bureau of Justice Statistics Special Report. Washington, DC: Department of Justice, Office of Justice Programs.

Dixon, D. (2007). *Interrogating Images: Audio-Visually Recorded Police Questioning of Suspects*. Sydney: The Sydney Institute of Criminology.

Doob, A.N., & Webster, C.M. (2006) Countering punitiveness: Understanding stability in Canada's imprisonment rate. *Law Society Review*, 40(2), 325–368.

Doolan, M. (2008). Understanding the purpose of youth justice in New Zealand. *Aotearoa New Zealand Social Work Review*, 20(3), 63–70.

Elliot, M., & Thomas, R. (2011). *Public Law*. Oxford: Oxford University Press.

Edward, H. T. (1992). The growing disjunction between legal education and the legal profession *Michigan Law Review*, 91(1), 34.

Elechi, O. O. (2003). Extra-judicial killings in Nigeria—The case of Afikpo Town. Paper published by the International Society for the Reform of Criminal Law, 17th International Conference, August 24–28. The Hague, Netherlands, Conference Proceedings.

Federal Judiciary Center. (2008). *Federal Court Basics*. http://www.courtstatistics.org/OtherPages/State_Court_Structure_Charts/Illinois.aspx. Accessed January 7, 2014.

Feeley, M., & Kamin, S. (1996). The effect of "three strikes and you're out" on the courts: Looking back to see the future. In D. K. Sechrest (Ed.), *"Three Strikes and You're Out": Vengeance as Public Policy*. Thousand Oaks, CA: Sage Publications.

Fenwick, H., & Phillipson, G. (2011). *Text, Cases and Materials on Public Law and Human Rights* (3rd ed.). London: Routledge.

Frankel, M. E. (1972). Lawlessness in sentencing. *University of Cincinnati Law Review*, *41*, 1–54.

Friedman, M. (2004). *Outline of the US Legal System*. Washington, DC: Department of Justice.

Garland, D. (2001) *The Culture of Control: Crime and Social Order in Contemporary Society* (Vol. 77). Oxford: Oxford University Press.

Gaston, C. (2013). Lawmakers tangle with measure 11 to find $32 million for counties. *The Oregonian*. Retrieved from http://www.oregonlive.com/politics/index.ssf/2013/03/lawmakers_tangle_with_measure.html. Accessed October 28, 2013.

Ghana Judicial Service (2013). Annual report (May 2012–May 2013). http://www.judicial.gov.gh. Accessed October 8, 2014.

Ghana Judicial Service. (2014). *The History of Ghana Judiciary*. Retrieved from www.judicial.gov.gh/indexphp/history/summary.

Ghai, Y. (1997). Sentinels of liberty or sheep in wolf's clothing? Judicial politics and the Hong Kong Bill of Rights. *The Modern Law Review*, *60*(4), 459–480.

Gleeson, M. (2003). *The State of the Judicature, 13th Commonwealth Law Conference* (April 2003, Melbourne, Australia).

Haley, J. O. (2013). The role of courts in making law in Japan: The communitarian conservatism of Japanese judges. *Pacific Rim Law & Policy Journal*, *22*(3), 491–503.

Heumann, M., & Loftin, C. (1979). Mandatory sentencing and the abolition of plea bargaining: The Michigan felony firearm statute. *Law and Society Review*, *13*, 393–430.

Hong Kong Bar Association. (2013). The bar list. Retrieved from http://www.hkba.org/the-bar/bar-list/index-new-eng.html. Accessed August 8, 2013.

Hong Kong Census and Statistics Department. (2012). Hong Kong statistics. Retrieved from http://www.censtatd.gov.hk/hkstat/sub/bbs.jsp. Accessed August 8, 2013.

Hong Kong Judiciary. (2013a). The Hong Kong judiciary annual report 2012. Hong Kong: Hong Kong Judiciary.

Hong Kong Judiciary. (2013b). List of judges and judicial officers. Retrieved from http://www.judiciary.gov.hk/en/organization/judges.htm. Accessed August 9, 2013.

Human Rights Watch. (2002). *Nigeria: The Bakassi Boys: Legitimation of Torture and Murder*. New York: Human Rights Watch and CLEEN Foundation.

Human Rights Watch and Center for Law Enforcement Education (2002) The Bakassi boys: The legitimisation of murder and torture. *Human Rights Watch 14*(5), 2–45.

Illinois Criminal Justice Authority. (2010). *Biographies: Judge Elizabeth Robb*. Retrieved from http://www.icjia.state.il.us/public/strategy2010/bios.cfm. Accessed January 7, 2014.

Illinois Wesleyan University. (2012). Pioneering judge Elizabeth Robb was among the alumni honored at homecoming. *IWU Alumni Magazine*. Retrieved from https://www.iwu.edu/magazine/2012/winter/homecoming12.html. Accessed January 8, 2014.

International Bar Association (IBA). (2014). How to qualify as a lawyer in Ghana. Retrieved from www.ibanet.org/PPID/Constituent/student-Committee/qualify-lawyer-Ghana.aspx. Accessed October 8, 2014.

Jimroglou, K. (2010). Public opinion on sentencing and corrections policy in America, PEW Public Safety Performance Project, March 30, 2012.

Johnson, B. D. (2003). Racial and ethnic disparities in sentencing departures across modes of conviction. *Criminology, 41*, 449–489.

Johnstone, G., & Van Ness, D. W. (2007). Regional reviews: New Zealand. In G. Johnstone & D.W. Van Ness (Eds). *Handbook of Restorative Justice*. Devon: Willan Publishing.

Joint Committee on New York Drug Law Evaluation. (1978). The nation's toughest drug law: Evaluating the New York experience. Project of the Association of the Bar of the City of New York and the Drug Abuse Council, Inc. Washington DC: US Government Printing Office.

Judicial Service of Ghana. (2013). National ADR program report. Retrieved from www.judicial.gov.gh/index.php/2013-01.28-08-11-41/strategic-plan.

Julich, J. (2009). Restorative justice and gendered violence in New Zealand: A glimmer of hope. In J. Ptacek (Ed.), *Restorative Justice and Violence against Women*. Oxford: Oxford University Press.

Kaczorowska, A. (2011). *European Law* (2nd ed.). London: Routledge.

Kawharu, I. H. (1989). *Waitangi: Māori and Pākēha Perspectives of the Treaty of Waitangi*. Auckland, New Zealand: Oxford University Press.

Kosek, J. (2012). The letter of the law and sensus communis in changes of ages. *Pravnik, 5*, 453–469.

Kramer, J. H., & Ulmer, J. T. (1996). Sentencing disparity and departures from guidelines. *Justice Quarterly, 131*, 81–105.

Lagos: Centre for Law Enforcement in Nigeria. (2013). Retrieved from http://www.cleen.org/Poor people and informal policing.1.pdf. Accessed December 11, 2013.

Landreville, P. (2007) Grandeurs et misères de la politique pénale au Canada: du réformisme au populisme. *Criminologie, 40*(2), 19–51.

Landers, R., & Blowen, D. (2010). *The Inquisition*. Sydney: Australian Broadcasting Corporation.

Law Society of Hong Kong (2013). The law list, Retrieved from http://www.hklawsoc.org.hk/pub_e/memberlawlist/mem_withcert.asp. Accessed August 8, 2013.

Leczykiewicz, D. (2008). Why do the European Court of Justice judges need legal concepts. *European Law Journal, 14*(6), 773–786.

Levi, M. (2003). Suite justice or sweet charity? Some explorations of shaming and incapacitating business fraudsters. In E. McLaughlan, R. Fergusson, G. Hughes, & L. Westmarland (Eds.), *Restorative Justice: Critical Issues*. Milton Keynes: Open University Press.

Levine, D., & Ingram, D. (2013, August 12). US moves to curb long, mandatory drug sentences. Reuters. Retrieved from http://www.reuters.com/article/2013/08/12/us-usa-crime-sentencing-idUSBRE97B03320130812. Accessed October 27, 2013.

Lunn, M. (2013). *Interview with The Honorable Mr Justice Michael Lunn*, Hong Kong.

Lynch, N. (2012). Recent reform of New Zealand's youth justice system. *Criminal and Criminal Justice, 12*(5), 507–526.

Marchetti, M., & Daly, K. (2004). Indigenous courts and justice practices in Australia. *Trends and Issues in Crime and Criminal Justice*. Retrieved from http://www.aic.gov.au/publications/currentseries/tandi/261-280/tandi277.html.

Maxwell, G., Robertson, J., & Morris, A. (1993). Giving victims a voice: A New Zealand experiment. *The Howard Journal, 32*, 304–321.

Maxwell, G. (2004). Achieving effective outcomes in youth justice: Implications of new research for principles, police and practice, no. 27, 8 as reported in Becroft, A. (2007), Putting youth justice under the microscope: What is the diagnosis? A quick nip and tuck or radical surgery? Presented at the Conference on Rehabilitation of Youth Offenders, Singapore, p. 22.

McElrea, F. W. M. (1993). A new model of justice. In B. J. Brown & F. W. M. McElrea (Eds.), *The Youth Court in New Zealand: A New Model of Justice.* Auckland: Legal Research Foundation.

Mendel, R. A. (2010). The Missouri model: Reinventing the practices of rehabilitation youthful offenders, The Annie C. Casey Foundation, Baltimore: MD. Retrieved from http://www.aecf.org/~/media/Pubs/Initiatives/Juvenile%20Detention%20 Alternatives%20Initiative/MOModel/MO_Fullreport_webfinal.pdf. Accessed June 30, 2013.

Mensah, K. B. (2009). Legitimacy and interpretation in Ghanaian law: The literal interpretation theory versus the value-based interpretation theory. *Law, Democracy and Development 7*(4), 139–156.

Merritt, N., Fain, T., & Turner, S. (2006). Oregon's get tough sentencing reform: A lesson in justice system adaptation. *Criminology and Public Policy, 5*(1), 5–36.

Metge, J. (2001). *Korero Tam: Talking Together.* Auckland: Auckland University Press with Te Matahauariki Institute.

Metge, J., & Kinloch, P. J. (1978). *Talking Past Each Other: Problems of Cross-Cultural Communication.* Wellington: Victoria University Press.

Ministerial Advisory Committee on a Māori Perspective for the Department of Social Welfare. (1988). *Puao-te-Ata-Tu (Day Break).* Wellington, New Zealand.

Ministerial Taskforce on Youth Offending. (2002). Report of the ministerial taskforce on youth offending. Wellington: Ministry of Justice.

Moore, D., & Hannah-Moffatt, K. (2005). The liberal veil: Revisiting Canadian penality. In J. Pratt, D. Brown, M. Brown, S. Hallsworth, and W. Morrison (eds) *The New Punitiveness: Trends, Theories, Perspectives* (pp. 85–100). Portland, OR: Willan Publishing.

Missouri Sentencing Advisory Commission (2010). Sentencing Advisory Commission makes changes in system of recommended sentences, system assessment report. *Smart Sentencing, 2*(6), 3.

Molomby, T. (1986). *Spies, Bombs and the Path of Bliss.* Sydney: Potoroo Press.

Morris, A., & Gelsthorpe, L. (2004). Re-visioning men's violence against female partners. In E. McLaughlan, R. Fergusson, G. Hughes, & L. Westmarland (Eds.), *Restorative Justice: Critical Issues.* Milton Keynes: Open University Press.

Morris, A., & Maxwell, G. (2003). Restorative justice in New Zealand: family group conferences as a case study. In G. Johnstone (Ed.), *A Restorative Justice Reader: Text, Sources, Context* (pp. 201–211). Devon: Willan Publishing.

Mustard, D. B. (2001). Racial, ethnic, and gender disparities in sentencing: Evidence from the US Federal Courts. *Journal of Law and Economics, 44*(1), 285–314.

National Bureau of Statistics (2012). Retrieved from http://www.nigerianstat.gov. ng/. (see also http://www.thisdaylive.com/articles/issues-in-the-new-poverty-report/137011/). Accessed October 8, 2014.

National Center for State Courts. (2010). Courts Statistics Project: Illinois. Williamsburg, VA: National Center for State Courts. Retrieved from http://www.courtstatistics.org/OtherPages/State_Court_Structure_Charts/Illinois.aspx. Accessed October 8, 2014.

Neubauer, D. W., & Meinhold, S. S. (2010). *Judicial Process: Laws, Courts and Politics in the United States*. Boston, MA: Wadsworth.

Newburn, T. (2013). *Criminology* (2nd ed.). Oxford: Oxford University Press.

Nye, J. S. (2008). *The Powers to Lead*. New York: Oxford University Press.

OECD. (2009). *Doing Better for Children*. Paris: OECD Publishing.

Oregon Court of Appeals (2012). *Oregon Judicial Department: General Information.* Retrieved from http://courts.oregon.gov/COA/Pages/index.aspx. Accessed July 12, 2012.

Oregon Judicial Department. (2013). Oregon judicial districts. Retrieved from http://courts.oregon.gov/OJD/aboutus/courtsintro/judicialdistricts.page.   Accessed November 2, 2013.

Oregon Judicial Department Report. (2011). Statistical report relating to the circuit courts of the State of Oregon, 2011. Office of the State Court Administrator, Supreme Court of Oregon.

Otu, S. E. (2003). Armed robbery in the southeastern states of Nigeria, a criminological analysis. A doctoral thesis (D. Litt & Phil.) submitted to the Department of Criminology, University of South Africa, Pretoria.

O'Malley, P. (2006) "Mondialisation" et justice criminelle: du défaitisme àl'optimisme. *Déviance et société 30*(3), 323–338.

Packer, H. L. (1968). *The Limits of the Criminal Sanction.* Stanford: Stanford University Press.

Perry, B. (1999). Memories of fear. In J. Goodwin & R. Attias (Eds.), *Splintered Reflections*. Washington DC: Basic Books.

Plotnikoff, J., & Woolfson, R. (2009). Measuring up? Evaluating implementation of government commitments to young witnesses in criminal proceedings. Retrieved from http://www.nspcc.org.uk/inform/research/findings/measuring_up_wda66048.html.

Plotnikoff, J., & Woolfson, R. (2012). "Kicking and screaming"—The slow road to best evidence. In J. R. Spencer & M. E. Lamb (Eds.), *Children and Cross-Examination: Time to Change the Rules?* (pp. 21–42). Oxford: Hart Publishing.

Population Research Center. (2012). 2012 Annual population report. Portland State University, College of Urban and Public Affairs, Population Research Center.

Posner, R. A., & Yoon, A. H. (2011). What judges think of the quality of legal representation. *Stanford Law Review, 63*(2), 317–350.

Rhode, D. L. (2003). *In the Interest of Justice: Reforming the Legal Profession.* Oxford: University of Oxford Press.

Rossman, D., Froyd, P., Pierce, G. L., McDevitt, J. F., & Bowers, W. J. (1979). *The Impact of the Mandatory Gun Law in Massachusetts*. Boston, Massachusetts, School of Law, Center for Criminal Justice.

Ryan, J. P., Williams, A. B., & Courtney, M. E. (2013). Adolescent neglect, juvenile delinquency and the risk of recidivism. *Journal of Youth and Adolescence, 42*(3), 454–465.

Spencer, J. R., & Lamb, M. E. (2012). *Children and Cross-Examination: Time to Change the Rules?* Oxford: Hart Publishing.

Swede, R. (1995). One territory: Three systems? The Hong Kong Bill of Rights. *The International and Comparative Law Quarterly, 44*(2), 358–378.

Tauri, J., & Morris, A. (2003). Reforming justice: The potential of Māori processes. In E. McLaughlan, R. Fergusson, G. Hughes, & L. Westmarland (Eds.), *Restorative Justice: Critical Issues*. Milton Keynes: Open University Press.

Tomkins, A. (2003). *Public Law*. Oxford: Oxford University Press.

Tonry, M. (1996). *Sentencing Matters*. New York, NY: Oxford University Press.

Tonry, M. (2009). The mostly unintended consequences of mandatory penalties: Two centuries of consistent findings. *Crime and Justice, 38*, 1–36.

United States Anti-Doping Agency v Armstrong. (2012). Reasoned decision of the united states anti-doping agency on disqualification and ineligibility, Report on proceedings under the world anti-doping code and the USADA protocol. Retrieved from http://usatoday30.usatoday.com/sports/!invesitgations%20and%20enterprise%20 docs/armstrong-reasoned-decision.pdf. Accessed March 12, 2014.

United States Courts. (2008). Federal courts structure. Retrieved from http://www. uscourts.gov/educational-resources/get-informed/federal-court-basics.aspx. Accessed January 7, 2014.

United States Sentencing Commission. (1991). Special report to the Congress: Mandatory minimum penalties in the federal criminal justice system. Washington DC: USSC.

US Legal Definitions. (2014). Retrieved from http://definitions.uslegal.com. Accessed January 9, 2014.

Vanhamme, F. (2013) Le rôle du juge et le pouvoir judiciaire. In E. Jimenez and M. Vacheret (eds) *La pénologie: réflexions juridiques et criminologiques autour de la peine* (pp. 33–47). Montréal: Les Presses de l'Université de Montréal.

Verdun-Jones, S.N., & Tijerino, A. (2002). *Victim Participation in the Plea Negotiation Process in Canada*. Ottawa: Department of Justice Canada.

Vicini, J. (2012, June 21). Supreme Court extends more lenient penalties in crack cocaine case. Reuters. Retrieved from http://www.reuters.com/article/2012/06/21/us-usa-court-cocaine-sentences-idUSBRE85K19S20120621. Accessed October 19, 2013.

Von Hirsch, A. (1976). Doing justice: The choice of punishments: Report of the committee for the study of incarceration. New York, NY: Hill and Wang.

Von Hirsch, A., & Ashworth, A. (1999). *Principled Sentencing: Readings on Theory and Policy* (2nd ed.). Oxford: Hart Publishing.

Walsh, J. E. (2007). *Three Strikes Laws*. Westport, CT: Greenwood Publishing Group.

Watt, E. (2003). *A History of Youth Justice in New Zealand*. Paper commissioned by the Principal Youth Court Judge Andrew Becroft. Wellington: Department for Courts.

Weatherburn, D. (2013). A review of restorative justice responses to offending. *Evidence Base*, 1–20.

Wilson, L. R. (1999). The Bill of Rights. In *US Court Cases: Law and Courts* (1st ed., pp. 50–59). Pasadena, CA: Salem Press.

Wood, J. R. T. (1996). The interim report of the royal commission into the New South Wales police service. Sydney: Royal Commission.

Wood, J. R. T. (1997). Report of the royal commission into the New South Wales police service. Sydney: Royal Commission.

Wood, J. R. T. (2008). Report of the special commission of inquiry into child protection services in New South Wales. Retrieved from http://www.dpc.nsw.gov.au/publications/news/stories/?a=33794. Accessed March 12, 2014.

Wood, J. R. T. (2013). Review of cycling Australia, final report. Canberra: Australian Department of Health. Retrieved from http://www.health.gov.au/internet/main/publishing.nsf/Content/cycling-australia-review-index. Accessed March 14, 2014.

Worrall, J. (2009). *Criminal Procedure: From First Contact to Appeal* (4th ed.). Upper Saddle River, NJ: Pearson, Allyn & Bacon.

Young, V. (2010). Missouri legislature passes sentencing, parole guidelines, *St. Louis Post-Dispatch*, May 3, 2012.

Zimring, F. (1994). Making the punishment fit the crime: A consumer's guide to sentencing reform. In A. Duff & D. Garland (Eds.), *A Reader on Punishment*. Oxford: Oxford University Press.

International Police Executive Symposium (IPES)

The International Police Executive Symposium (www.ipes.info) was founded in 1994. The aims and objectives of the IPES are to provide a forum to foster closer relationships among police researchers and practitioners globally, to facilitate cross-cultural, international and interdisciplinary exchanges for the enrichment of the law enforcement profession, and to encourage discussion and published research on challenging and contemporary topics related to the profession.

One of the most important activities of the IPES is the organization of an annual meeting under the auspices of a police agency or an educational institution. Every year since 1994, annual meetings have been hosted by such agencies and institutions all over the world. Past hosts have included the Canton Police of Geneva, Switzerland; the International Institute of the Sociology of Law, Onati, Spain; Kanagawa University, Yokohama, Japan; the Federal Police, Vienna, Austria; the Dutch Police and Europol, The Hague, The Netherlands; the Andhra Pradesh Police, India; the Center for Public Safety, Northwestern University, USA; the Polish Police Academy, Szczytno, Poland; the Police of Turkey (twice); the Kingdom of Bahrain Police; a group of institutions in Canada (consisting of the University of the Fraser Valley, Abbotsford Police Department, Royal Canadian Mounted Police, the Vancouver Police Department, the Justice Institute of British Columbia, Canadian Police College, and the International Centre for Criminal Law Reform and Criminal Justice Policy); the Czech Police Academy, Prague; the Dubai Police; the Ohio Association of Chiefs of Police and the Cincinnati Police Department, Ohio, USA; the Republic of Macedonia and the Police of Malta. An annual meeting on the theme of "Policing Violence, Crime, Disorder and Discontent: International Perspectives" was hosted in Buenos Aires, Argentina on June 26–30, 2011. The 2012 annual meeting was hosted at United Nations in New York on the theme of "Economic Development, Armed Violence and Public Safety" on August 5–10. The Ministry of the Interior of Hungary and the Hungarian National Police hosted the meeting in 2013 in Budapest on August 4–9 on the theme of "Contemporary Global

Issues in Policing". The 2014 meeting on "Crime Prevention and Community Resilience" will take place in Sofia, Bulgaria on July 27–31.

There have been also occasional special meetings of the IPES. A special meeting was cohosted by the Bavarian Police Academy of Continuing Education in Ainring, Germany, University of Passau, Germany, and State University of New York, Plattsburgh, USA in 2000. The second special meeting was hosted by the police in the Indian state of Kerala. The third special meeting on the theme of "Contemporary Issues in Public Safety and Security" was hosted by the commissioner of police of the Blekinge region of Sweden and the president of the University of Technology on August 10–14, 2011. The most recent special meeting was held in Trivandrum (Kerala, India) on "Policing by Consent" on March 16–20, 2014.

The majority of participants of the annual meetings are usually directly involved in the police profession. In addition, scholars and researchers in the field also participate. The meetings comprise both structured and informal sessions to maximize dialogue and exchange of views and information. The executive summary of each meeting is distributed to participants as well as to a wide range of other interested police professionals and scholars. In addition, a book of selected papers from each annual meeting is published through CRC Press/Taylor & Francis Group, Prentice Hall, Lexington Books and other reputed publishers. A special issue of *Police Practice and Research: An International Journal* is also published with the most thematically relevant papers after the usual blind review process.

IPES Board of Directors

The IPES is directed by a board of directors representing various countries of the world (listed below). The registered business office is located at Norman Vale, 6030 Nott Road, Guilderland, NY 12064 and the registered agent is National Registered Agents, 200 West Adams Street, Chicago, IL 60606.

President

Dilip Das, Norman Vale, 6030 Nott Road, Guilderland, NY 12084. Tel: 802-598-3680. Fax: 410-951-3045. E-mail: dilipkd@aol.com.

Vice President

Etienne Elion, Case J-354-V, OCH Moungali 3, Brazzaville, Republic of Congo. Tel: 242-662-1683. Fax: 242-682-0293. E-mail: ejeej2003@yahoo.fr.

Treasurer/Secretary

Paul Moore, 125 Kenny Lane, West Monroe, LA 21294. Tel: 318-512-1500. Paul@ipes.info .

Directors

Rick Sarre, GPO Box 2471, Adelaide, 5001, South Australia. Tel: 61-8-83020889. Fax: 61-8-83020512. E-mail: rick.sarre@unisa.edu.au.

Tonita Murray, 73 Murphy Street, Carleton Place, Ontario K7C 2B7 Canada. Tel: 613-998-0883. E-mail: Tonita_Murray@hotmail.com.

Snezana (Ana) Mijovic-Das, Norman Vale, 6030 Nott Road, Guilderland, NY 12084. Tel: 518-452-7845. Fax: 518-456-6790. E-mail: anamijovic@yahoo.com.

Andrew Carpenter, The Pier, 1 Harborside Place. Apt 658, Jersey City, NJ 07311. Tel: 917-367-2205. Fax: 917-367-2222. E-mail: carpentera@un.org.

Paulo R. Lino, 111 Das Garcas St., Canoas, RS, 92320-830, Brazil. Tel: 55-51-8111-1357. Fax: 55-51-466-2425. E-mail: paulino2@terra.com.br.

Rune Glomseth, Slemdalsveien 5, Oslo, 0369, Norway. E-mail: Rune.Glomseth@phs.no.

Maximilian Edelbacher, Riemersgasse 16/E/3, A-1190 Vienna, Austria. Tel: 43-1-601 74/5710. Fax: 43-1-601 74/5727. E-mail: edelmax@magnet.at.

A.B. Dambazau, P.O. Box 3733, Kaduna, Kaduna State, Nigeria. Tel: 234-80-35012743. Fax: 234-70-36359118. E-mail: adambazau@yahoo.com.

IPES Institutional Supporters

IPES is guided and helped in all the activities by a group of Institutional Supporters around the world. These supporters are police agencies, universities, research organizers.

African Policing Civilian Oversight Forum (APCOF; Sean Tait), 2nd floor, The Armoury, Buchanan Square, 160 Sir Lowry Road, Woodstock, Cape Town 8000, South Africa. E-mail: sean@apcof.org.za.

Australian Institute of Police Management, Collins Beach Road, Manly, NSW 2095, Australia (Connie Coniglio). E-mail: cconiglio@aipm.gov.au.

Baker College of Jackson, 2800 Springport Road, Jackson, MI 49202 (Blaine Goodrich) Tel: 517-841-4522. E-mail: blaine.goodrich@baker.edu.

Cyber Defense & Research Initiatives, LLC (James Lewis), P.O. Box 86, Leslie, MI 49251. Tel: 517 242 6730. E-mail: lewisja@cyberdefenseresearch. com.

Defendology Center for Security, Sociology and Criminology Research (Valibor Lalic), Srpska Street 63, 78000 Banja Luka, Bosnia and Herzegovina. Tel and Fax: 387-51-308-914. E-mail: lalicv@teol.net.

Fayetteville State University (Dr. David E. Barlow, Professor and Dean), College of Basic and Applied Sciences, 130 Chick Building, 1200 Murchison Road, Fayetteville, North Carolina, 28301 . Tel: 910-672-1659. Fax: 910-672-1083. E-mail: dbarlow@uncfsu.edu .

Kerala Police (Mr. Balasubramanian, Director General of Police), Police Headquarters, Trivandrum, Kerala, India. E-mail: JPunnoose@gmail.com.

Molloy College, The Department of Criminal Justice (contact Dr. John A. Eterno, NYPD Captain-Retired), 1000 Hempstead Avenue, P.O. Box 5002, Rockville Center, NY 11571-5002. Tel: 516 678 5000, Ext. 6135. Fax: 516 256 2289. E-mail: jeterno@molloy.edu.

Mount Saint Vincent University, Department of Psychology (Stephen Perrott), 166 Bedford Highway, Halifax, Nova Scotia, Canada. E-mail: Stephen.perrott@mvsu.ca.

National Institute of Criminology and Forensic Science (Kamalendra Prasad, Inspector General of Police), MHA, Outer Ring Road, Sector 3, Rohini, Delhi 110085, India. Tel: 91-11-275-2-5095. Fax: 91-11-275-1-0586. E-mail: director. nicfs@nic.in.

National Police Academy, Police Policy Research Center (Naoya Oyaizu, Deputy Director), Zip 183-8558: 3- 12- 1 Asahi-cho Fuchu-city, Tokyo, Japan. Tel: 81-42-354-3550. Fax: 81-42-330-1308. E-mail: PPRC@npa.go.jp.

North Carolina Central University, Department of Criminal Justice (Dr. Harvey L. McMurray, Chair), 301 Whiting Criminal Justice Building, Durham, NC 27707. Tel: 919-530-5204/919-530-7909; Fax: 919-530-5195. E-mail: hmcmurray@nccu.edu.

Royal Canadian Mounted Police (Helen Darbyshire, Executive Assistant), 657 West 37th Avenue, Vancouver, BC V5Z 1K6, Canada. Tel: 604-264 2003. Fax: 604-264-3547. E-mail: helen.darbyshire@rcmp-grc.gc.ca.

Edith Cowan University, School of Psychology and Social Science, Social Justice Research Centre (Prof S. Caroline Taylor, Foundation Chair in Social Justice), 270 Joondalup Drive, Joondalup, WA 6027, Australia. E-mail: c.taylor@ecu.edu.au.

South Australia Police, Office of the Commissioner (Commissioner Mal Hyde), 30 Flinders Street, Adelaide, SA 5000, Australia. E-mail: mal.hyde@police.sa.gov.au.

University of the Fraser Valley, Department of Criminology & Criminal Justice (Dr. Irwin Cohen), 33844 King Road, Abbotsford, British Columbia V2 S7 M9, Canada. Tel: 604-853-7441. Fax: 604-853-9990. E-mail: Irwin.Cohen@ufv.ca.

University of Maribor, Faculty of Criminal Justice and Security, (Dr. Gorazd Mesko), Kotnikova 8, 1000 Ljubljana, Slovenia. Tel: 386-1-300-83-39. Fax: 386-1-2302-687. E-mail: gorazd.mesko@fvv.uni-mb.si.

University of Maine at Augusta, College of Natural and Social Sciences (Mary Louis Davitt, Professor of Legal Technology), 46 University Drive, Augusta, ME 04330-9410. E-mail: mldavitt@maine.edu.

University of New Haven, School of Criminal Justice and Forensic Science (Dr. Richard Ward), 300 Boston Post Road, West Haven, CT 06516. Tel: 203-932-7260. E-mail: rward@newhaven.edu.

University of South Africa, College of Law, School of Criminal Justice (Prof. Kris Pillay, Director), Preller Street, Muckleneuk, Pretoria, South Africa. E-mail: cpillay@unisa.ac.za.

University of South Africa, Department of Police Practice, Florida Campus (Setlhomamaru Dintwe), Christiaan De Wet and Pioneer Avenues, Private Bag X6, Florida, 1710 South Africa. Tel: 011-471-2116. Fax: 011-471-2255. E-mail: Dintwsi@unisa.ac.za.

Index

Index

321

I